CHEROKEE INTRUDER CASES
DOCKETS OF HEARINGS
1901–1909
VOLUME II

TRANSCRIBED BY

JEFF BOWEN
NATIVE STUDY
Gallipolis, Ohio
USA

Copyright © 2014
by Jeff Bowen

ALL RIGHTS RESERVED
No part of this publication may be reproduced
or used in any form or manner whatsoever
without previous written permission from the
copyright holder or publisher.

Originally published:
Baltimore, Maryland
2014

Reprinted by:

Native Study LLC
Gallipolis, OH
www.nativestudy.com

Library of Congress Control Number: 2020914991

ISBN: 978-1-64968-025-9

Made in the United States of America.

Other Books and Series by Jeff Bowen

1901-1907 Native American Census Seneca, Eastern Shawnee, Miami, Modoc, Ottawa, Peoria, Quapaw, and Wyandotte Indians (Under Seneca School, Indian Territory)

1932 Census of The Standing Rock Sioux Reservation with Births And Deaths 1924-1932

Census of The Blackfeet, Montana, 1897- 1901 Expanded Edition

Eastern Cherokee by Blood, 1906-1910, Volumes I thru XIII

Choctaw of Mississippi Indian Census 1929-1932 with Births and Deaths 1924-1931 Volume I

Choctaw of Mississippi Indian Census 1933, 1934 & 1937, Supplemental Rolls to 1934 & 1935 with Births and Deaths 1932-1938, and Marriages 1936-1938 Volume II

Eastern Cherokee Census Cherokee, North Carolina 1930-1939 Census 1930-1931 with Births And Deaths 1924-1931 Taken By Agent L. W. Page Volume I

Eastern Cherokee Census Cherokee, North Carolina 1930-1939 Census 1932-1933 with Births And Deaths 1930-1932 Taken By Agent R. L. Spalsbury Volume II

Eastern Cherokee Census Cherokee, North Carolina 1930-1939 Census 1934-1937 with Births and Deaths 1925-1938 and Marriages 1936 & 1938 Taken by Agents R. L. Spalsbury And Harold W. Foght Volume III

Seminole of Florida Indian Census, 1930-1940 with Birth and Death Records, 1930-1938

Texas Cherokees 1820-1839 A Document For Litigation 1921

Choctaw By Blood Enrollment Cards 1898-1914 Volumes I thru XVII

Starr Roll 1894 (Cherokee Payment Rolls) Districts: Canadian, Cooweescoowee, and Delaware Volume One

Starr Roll 1894 (Cherokee Payment Rolls) Districts: Flint, Going Snake, and Illinois Volume Two

Starr Roll 1894 (Cherokee Payment Rolls) Districts: Saline, Sequoyah, and Tahlequah; Including Orphan Roll Volume Three

Other Books and Series by Jeff Bowen

Cherokee Intruder Cases Dockets of Hearings 1901-1909 Volume I

Visit our website at **www.nativestudy.com** to learn more about these and other books and series by Jeff Bowen

This series is dedicated to my big brother,
Jerry Bowen
who taught me how to persevere.

INTRODUCTION

The records in this volume have been transcribed from the National Archival film rolls 7RA53 2-3 Cherokee Hearings on Intruder Cases, Dockets of Hearings on Intruder Cases 1901-1909. For definition purposes there are two parties involved with each case within these pages. One is the "Intruder" and the other is the "Allottee". The term "Intruder" refers to an illegal resident in the Cherokee Nation who is living on land that does not belong to him/her. The term "Allottee" refers to a legal resident of the Cherokee Nation who has been allotted, or given, a parcel of tribal land in the Cherokee Nation through the Dawes Act of 1898-1914.

"In November, 1906 the Senate Select Committee visited Vinita in the Cherokee Nation as part of its tour of Indian Territory to investigate the tribes' situation under the Five Tribes Bill. There it heard testimony from Chester Howe, who claimed to represent 'about one hundred families who were really Indians' but had been rejected by the tribe. One of Howe's clients was William Stevens, whose case became the basis for the Supreme Court's ruling that the 1896 act was constitutional. Howe argued that the Dawes Commission had spent 'less than eight minutes for each application' under that act and that his client therefore had not had a fair hearing. Stevens, who was present, had been born in Ohio and moved into the Cherokee Nation in 1869; he claimed to be one-quarter Cherokee. He had built improvements which were appraised by the three member commission established in 1893, but he refused to accept the $1,117 offered by the tribe because the receipt for the payment contained a waiver of his claim to citizenship. Like many of the people designated as intruders by the tribe, he had stayed on the land and used the 'protection papers' issued by the Indian agent to avoid being removed."

"James Davenport, the attorney who had represented the tribe in this affair, pointed out that Stevens had originally claimed to be a member of another tribe, that his case had twice been appealed unsuccessfully to Congress and the Supreme Court, and that he had refused to comply with an order of the Federal Court at Muskogee to vacate the land even though it had been upheld by the U. S. Court of Appeals for the Eighth Circuit. Howe countered that his client had been 'stripped of his property' and that Congress had refused to grant relief when it was considering the Cherokee Agreement of 1902 because it 'was very loath to open any rolls on account of the contention that there would flow into this country a river of applicants.' The Cherokees denied they had stripped Stevens of anything, but they had sold his property at public auction in 1902 in accordance with a provision in the Curtis act. Howe concluded his plea to the senators by saying that Stevens's 'children have been beggard[sic], his property confiscated' and that he had 'lost the work of a lifetime for the insignificant sum of $382.' Howe filed a written memorial with the committee, but Stevens never was enrolled."[1]

Interestingly, the Stevens' decision before the Supreme Court is referenced five times in Felix S. Cohen's *Handbook of Federal Indian Law, 1982 Edition.* The case actually makes references under the subject of I.R.S. taxation rulings and Indian

---

[1] *The Dawes Commission* by Kent Carter p 121-122, para 3 and 4.

land under trust. "Whether the exemption extends to individual trust property held by an Indian other than an original allottee or her/his heirs was considered in *Stevens v. Commissioner*. In interpreting *Squire v. Capoeman*, the I.R.S. had ruled that trust transfers by gift, devise or inheritance, intrafamily purchases, and purchases by 'needy Indians' out of restricted funds would maintain the income tax exemption. But in *Stevens* the Indian plaintiff had used unrestricted funds to purchase three parcels of trust land, which were placed in trust for him under Section 5 of the Indian Reorganization Act, and the I.R.S. sought to tax the income from these parcels. The court held that the income was exempt under the congressional policy the Supreme Court relied upon in *Capoeman*, particularly because Interior Department policy had consistently treated the different categories of allotted lands alike for tax purposes. The I.R.S. has acquiesed[sic] in *Stevens*, so it is settled that allotted lands acquired by purchase are within the tax exempt status held in *Capoeman*; and there is no restriction on the amount, origin, or intended uses of exempt lands owned by an individual Indian."[2]

The intruders' cases found in these pages are intriguing on a number of counts. There cases refer to hundreds of people because of the assortment of individuals referenced on behalf of both plaintiffs and defendants: allottees, intruders, as well as lawyers. In some cases researchers may have to make their own determination as to whether an intruder qualified as a Cherokee citizen. While an ancient family legend may assert that one's ancestors were *Indians*, the determinations in the Stevens' case leaves much up in the air. On the one hand, the intruder is considered to be a land owner, according to the Supreme Court's reference to how he funded his purchase as an "individual Indian". On the other hand, the intruder does not appear on a roll even though his land is protected under papers issued by the Indian Agent. His land ends up being auctioned off by the Cherokee Nation and in the decision within this series (Case #45, Volume I, page 12-13) his outcome is listed under the heading "Action, No return of service, no answer filed"; under "Remarks, contest pending, Case dismissed for want of prosecution, dismissed." His case as an Indian was important enough to reach the highest court in the land, but he is declared forever null and void--his claim as a Cherokee forgotten except perhaps by his descendants.

There are over 1,300 cases within these two volumes. The last 170 cases were mostly illegible due to poor microfilm quality. This transcriber was able to determine almost every single Allottee's and Intruder's name except in approximately six cases. To give as much information as possible, I have transcribed every entry to the best of my ability even though each Allottee's and Intruder's name of record is the most important part of these documents for genealogical purposes.

Jeff Bowen
Gallipolis, Ohio
NativeStudy.com

---

[2] Felix S. Cohen's *Handbook of Federal Indian Law* p 394-395 para 2

This document titled *Public Auction Indian Land Sale* is likely similar to the auction postings from the Cherokee Intruder cases during 1901 - 1909.

PUBLIC AUCTION INDIAN LAND SALE
UNDER GOVERNMENT SUPERVISION.

The following allotted Indian land will be offered for sale at Public Auction at the office of

E. C. BACKENSTOCE, FIELD CLERK,

MADILL, OKLAHOMA,

AT TWO O'CLOCK, P. M.,

THURSDAY, NOVEMBER 12, '14.

Case No. 109594-Ethel Tonubbee, nee Jack, Miss-Choc. Roll #759. 150 acres. SW4 of SE4 of SE4; SE4 of SW4 of SE4 of Section 13. NE4 of NE4 of NE4; S2 of NE4 of NE4; NW4 of NE4; E2 of SW4 of NE4; SE4 of NE4 of Section 24, Township 5 south, range 3 east in Marshall County. 100 acres tillable, 50 acres in cultivation; 50 acres hilly and gravelly; 60 acres timber land; sandy loam and light gravelly soil; 320 rods wire fencing; 6 miles from Simpson, Oklahoma. Appraisement $1950. Terms: CASH.

Title to be taken in its present condition.

Ten per cent. of the highest bid must be deposited in the hands of the Field Clerk on the day of the sale in the form of a bank draft payable to W. M. Baker, Cashier and Special Disbursing Agent, Union Agency, the remainder of the purchase price to be paid within ten days of call therefor.

Written bids, accompanied by ten per cent. of the amount thereof, if received by the Field Clerk prior to the hour of sale given above, will be opened and considered at the time of sale the same as if the bidder made such offer orally. Such written bids may be presented to the Field Clerk or mailed to him at the above address.

No bids for less than the appraised value will be considered.

The right is reserved to reject any and all bids.

Muskogee, Oklahoma,   DANA H. KELSEY,
Union Agency.   United States Indian Superintendent.

October 12, 1914.

Below is found the Guion Miller application #35320 (pages v-ix) concerning William Stephens/Stevens, which was rejected.

Immediately following the application is an affidavit (8 pages) that Stephens/Stevens used for his Intruder case (Case #45, Volume I, pages 12-13), as well as in his Guion Miller case. This affidavit gives the whole story behind his situation as well as naming the Indian Agent, Jno. B. Jones, who issued Mr. Stevens protection papers during that time and states in his findings that Stevens was in fact a Cherokee. The document also has his name as Stevens but has his signature spelled as "Stephens" as on his Miller application. There are also four letters of correspondence to the commission from his lawyer Philip H. Cass.

No. 30320   Action: Reject

Name: William Stephens   and X children.   Residence: Coppyville, Kansas.

Reasons: Applicant 79 years old but does not appear on the
Sy roll. None of the ancestors through whom applicant
claims appear on either of the rolls. They were not it appears
parties to the treaties of 35-6-46. Information found in application not sufficient upon which to base a right to participate.
Applicant failed to appear when notified to do so.

No. 35320

EASTERN CHEROKEES

APPLICATION OF
OF

William Stephens,

For share of money appropriated for the Eastern Cherokee Indians by the Act of Congress approved June 30, 1906, in accordance with the decrees of the Court of Claims of May 18, 1905, and May 28, 1906.

6—424

COURT OF CLAIMS
EASTERN CHEROKEES
Rec. AUG 21 1907

Special Commissioner of the Court of Claims,
601 Ouray Building, Washington, D. C.

Sir:

I hereby make application for such share as may be due me of the fund appropriated by the Act of Congress, approved June 30, 1906, in accordance with the decrees of the Court of Claims of May 18, 1905, and May 28, 1906, in favor of the Eastern Cherokees. The evidence of identity is herewith subjoined.

NOTE: Answers to all questions should be short, but complete. If you can not answer, so state.

1. State full name—
    English name: William Stephens.
    Indian name: ShoeBoots.
2. Residence and post office: Coffeyville, Kansas.
3. County:
4. State:
5. How old are you? 79   Born December 9, 1827.
6. Where were you born? Ohio
7. Are you married? Yes
8. Name and age of wife or husband: Anna Eliza Stephens, age 64.
9. To what tribe of Indians does he or she belong? none, White
10. Name all your children who were living on May 28, 1906, giving their ages:

NAME	AGE	BORN
(1) Samantha J. Ayres	52	1855
(2)		
(3)		
(4)		
(5)		
(6)		

11. Give names of your father and mother, and your mother's name before marriage:

    Father—English name: Robert Stephens
        Indian name: White man
    Mother—English name: Sarah Jane Ellington Shoe Boots
        Indian name:
        Maiden name:
12. Where were they born?
    Father: Ohio.
    Mother: Georgia, Hightower river.

x

13. Where did they reside in 1851, if living at that time?

    Father: not living,
    Mother: Ohio

14. Date of death of your father and mother:

    Father: 1850 or 1851 on Illinois river bet St Louis + Alton,
    Mother: 1874 near Chetopa, Kans., in Ind. Ter.

15. Were they ever enrolled for money, annuities, land or other benefits? If so, state when and where, and with what tribe of Indians: Do not think was ever enrolled

16. Name all your brothers and sisters, giving ages, and residence if possible:

Name.	Born	Died.
(1) Clarinda		dead
(2) Jacob		dead
(3) Mary		dead
(4) John		dead
(5) Shelby		dead
(6) Sarena / Sarah Jane		dead / dead,

17. State English and Indian names of your grandparents on both father's and mother's side, if possible:

    Mother's ~~Father's~~ Side.   Mother's Side.

    Captain Shoe Boots
    Teaskiyarga full
    blood Cherokee chieftan
    Clarinda Ellington

18. Where were they born? Georgia and Fort Morgan, Ky, respy
19. Where did they reside in 1851, if living at that time? Dead. Died 1827.

20. Give names of all their children, and residence, if possible:

    (1) William Ellington   not living
    (2) John Ellington   not living
    (3)
    (4)
    (5)
    (6)

21. Have you ever been enrolled for money, annuities, land or other benefits? If so, state when and where, and with what tribe of Indians: *no.*

22. To assist in identification, claimant should give the full English and Indian names, if possible, of their parents and grandparents back to 1835: *Given in previous answers so far as is known*

REMARKS.
(Under this head the applicant may give any additional facts which will assist in proving his claim.)

I solemnly swear that the foregoing statements made by me are true to the best of my knowledge and belief.

(Signature) *William Stephens*

Subscribed and sworn to before me this *15th* day of *August* 1907.

Philip H. Cass
Notary Public.

My commission expires *Feby. 17, 1908.*

AFFIDAVIT.
(The following affidavit must be sworn to by two or more witnesses who are well acquainted with the applicant.)

Personally appeared before me *Pete Ayer* and *W. R. Stubblefield*, who, being duly sworn, on oath depose and say that they are well acquainted with *William Stephens* who makes the foregoing application and statements, and have known *him* for *10* years and *25* years, respectively, and know *him* to be the identical person *he* represents *himself* to be, and that the statements made by *him* are true, to the best of their knowledge and belief, and they have no interest whatever in *his* claim.

Witnesses to mark.   Signatures of Witnesses.
Pete Ayer
W. R. Stubblefield

Subscribed and sworn to before me this *15* day of *August* 1907.

My commission expires *Feby. 17, 1908.*

Philip H. Cass
Notary Public.

NOTE.—Affidavits should be made, whenever practicable, before a notary public, or clerk of the court, if sworn to before an Indian agent or disbursing agent of the Indian service, it need not be executed before a notary, etc.

TO THE HONORABLE SELECT COMMITTEE
of the
SENATE COMMITTEE ON INDIAN AFFAIRS.

The undersigned Cherokee Indians by blood respectfully represent that they are a duly selected committee representing certain claimants who deem themselves greatly wronged by the legislation heretofore enacted with regard to the enrollment of the Cherokee people, and, feeling that they have grievances which can only be remedied by congressional action, respectfully ask permission to lay before your honorable committee, and, through it, the Committee on Indian Affairs of the Senate, the following facts:

That, through inadvertence, there has been excluded from the rolls of the Cherokee Nation a number of persons who are Indians in law and in fact, and who have been for from twenty-five to forty years residents in good faith of the Cherokee Nation, with undisputed Indian blood and rights therein, the sole objection to the enjoyment of which has been the fact that they were not enrolled upon any of the tribal rolls, and that thereby a great injustice has been done. This difficulty arose from the following facts:

The Cherokees acquired their title to their home unde the treaty of New Echota of December 29, 1835, and this treaty, while it contemplated the establishment of a Cherok e National Goevernment, also contemplated the enjoyment of equal rights by all Cherokees. After th emigration, repeated invitations were sent to their brethren in the ea t to join them in the west, and the term "brethren in th east" did not apply to those who remained, and are now known as the Eastern Cherokees alone, but to those who were scattered through the country formerly occupied by the nation. In 1841, the Cherokee council extended an inviastion by resolution. The Treaty of 1846, section 8, made provision for transportation for those who would consent to join their people in the west, and Chief Downing issued a general invitation to all of the Cherokee people to come and join with the Nation.

It is true that immediately following the war in 1866 white men who were not Cherokees began to intrude upon the Cherokee lands, and the legislation directed against these people was just and reasonable, but it was so worded that in the end a great advantage was taken over innocent persons who were bona fide Indians and residents. A number of families having Cherokee blood came to the Cherokee Nation from 1866 to 1886. They met no opposition in the occupation of unappropri-

xiii

ated, and unimproved lands.

The Cherokee National government, at various times, appointed commissions to pass upon citizenship, in some cases approving, in others denying, but these claimants whose ancestors were clearly Cherokees were permitted to go before the United States Indian Agent, in early days at Talequah, and subsequently at Muskogee, and there make proof of their Cherokee blood, and were given what is known as "protection papers" i. e., a finding by the Agent to the effect that they had furnished satsifactory proof of their being Cherokees in fact, and that they should not be disturbed until they had an opportunity in some way to secure a trial upon the questions of fact.

Relying upon these protection papers, these men opened up farms, erected houses, built schools and churches, and were the real and actual persons who made the name of Cherokee synonomous with that of the advanced and civilized Indians.

During this time, other persons with no rightful claim to Cherokee blood had also intruded upon the lands of the Nation, and, against such intrusion, the Cherokees rightfully protested. Their protests took form in the ratification of the agreement for the sale of the Cherokee outlet under the act of March 3, 1893, 27th Stats. 641, and therein a great injustice was done in this, that it gave to the Cherokee National authorities a right to say without trial whether or not a man was an intruder. It is true that there were at this time many properly termed "intruders," but a list was immediately prepared containing the names of 2,858 heads of families, and including the names of about 100 heads of families who were fully entitled under every law, treaty, and properly construed enactment.

These men saw that their homes were threatened, that their children were about to be disinherited, and, finding no immediate remedy possible, they sought protection in further legislation, which was secured by a provision contained in the act of March 21, 1895, 28 Stats. 903, directing a suspension of the proceedings until improvements made prior to August 11, 1886, could be appraised, it being believed that those who had migrated to that country prior to that time were entitled to some consideration at the hands of the government and the officials of the Cherokee Nation.

Thereupon, a board of appraisers was appointed, who reported upon a total s number of 315 cases, and allowed awards

(3)

in 117 cases, of a total amount of $74,180.56. This was subsequently modified by deducting certain freedmen claims, leaving a total award in 89 cases of $68,645.36.

The appraisers had no authority to determine the merits of any cases—merely the value of the improvements, afterdeducting the value of the land rental of the land. It was in no sense an adjudication of the rights of the parties.

The authorities of the Cherokee Nation then tendered to each of the parties the amount of the award, accompanying such tender by a receipt, in which they waived their claims to Cherokee citizenship, and all claims of every nature whatever against the Cherokee Nation. In the majority of cases, the parties refused to accept the award if obliged to sign such a receipt, there having been no adjudication of their rights and the tender was not kept good by deposit or otherwise. In 1902, the Cherokee Nation then proceeded at public auction, held at different points, to sell the improvements appraised, and the bidders being confined to Cherokee citizens, it being known that the sale would be contested, trifling sums were bid for valuable homes.

The matter stood in this condition when the Dawes Commission reported to Congress in 1894 and 1895 that the National government was rotten; that citizenship rights therein had been made the subject of barter and sale. That this National government was not competent to make a roll of its citizens, and thereupon Congress authorized the Dawes Commission, under act of June 10, 1896, to prepare a roll of the Five Tribes. Applications to be filed within ninety days from June 10, 1896, and to be passed upon within three months from that time, allowing an appeal from such action to the district court of the proper district.

Under the rights so granted, about 30,000 applications were made. Men with no shadow of right other than that they desired to obtain something of value, made application, but among them a small number of rightful claimants. The result was practically a general denial. No other course was possible, considering the time allowed, while the commission was presentt in the Territory, as, allowing full work by every member for the twenty-four hours of the day, there were about eight minutes to be given each application, and it is fair to say that no decision upon the merits was rendered in any of the disputed cases represented by your petitioners.

Thereupon, appeals were prosecuted to the district court. These appeals were less than 200 in number, and constituted the more meritorious class.

XV

(4)

These people had by this time become poor. They knew they were Indians by blood; they knew that they had been residents for many years in that country; that their children had been born to the allegiance of the nation; that they had exercised every privilege excep that of voting, and that they had been included in what is known as the "intruder roll." In some cases they were striken from the roll after having been enrolled. They sought justice in the court. The judge referred the cases to two masters in chancery to take evidence and render findings of fact. This was done at the expense of the applicants who were appellants, and, in some cases the last cow was sold to pay expenses.

After the master's report had been rendered, finding them to be Indians and residents, the demurrer filed by the Nation was, by the district court, sustained, on the sole ground that they were not upon the approved roll. They knew that in the beginning. The judge of the western district and the Commission to the Five Civilized Tribes were aware of that fact, their sole object being to be placed upon that roll, and we find this condition in the district courts at that time.

Judge Hosea Townsend held in the southern district that the test of citizenship was blood. That the right came from birth, and, where a peal was prosecuted, admitted the applicant.

Judge Clayton, in the Central district held that Indian blood must be accompanied by bona xide residence, and, where both these requirements were shown, admitted the parties.

Judge William M. Springer held that, no matter whether the parties were Indians by blood and bona fide residents of the country or not, they must show that they had been enrolled by the National auth rities prior to June 10, 1896. In other words, the Dawes Commission had no power to add to the rolls of the Cherokee people.

It is believed by your petitioners and applicants that the purpose in creating the Dawes Commission and granting them this power to make rolls was to give them the right to add to the roll where the arty was entitled. Among none other of the nations has it been held to the contrary.

Your petitioners then sought an appeal to the Supreme Court of the United States, and the same was granted, but the act was so worded that the Supreme Court took jurisdiction only for the purpose of passing upon the constitutionality of the act of June 10, 1896, and, while the facsf were proven and admitted, no remedy was granted.

(5)

WE ALLEGE THAT WE REPRESENT THE WHEAT WINNOWED FROM THE CHAFF; that the few hundred persons for whom we speak are BONA FIDE CHEROKEE CITIZENS whose wrongs have not been equalled in the western hemisphere, unless it is by the expulsion of the French from Arcadia. We desire before the closing of the affairs of the Five Civilized Tribes to be allowed a fair presentation, and in proof thereof, we refer to one record as being a complete one, and being a court record, substantiating the facts set forth.

This case of the case of William Stevens (Stephens?). The history of this man is as follows:

Captain Shoe Boots, Teaskiyarga, a full-blood Cherokee Indian chief of a band of Cherokees, captured a white girl named Clarinda Ellington, in Kentucky, and carried her to Georgia, where she became his wife, and there was born to them three children as the issue of this marriage; two sons and a daughter, one of the sons being William Ellington Shoe Boots, and the other John Shoe Boots. William Ellington Shoe Boots' name appears upon the roll of 1851. (He afterwards adopted his mother's name of Ellington.) After the borth of these children, the firends of the wife traced her to her home and induced her to return to her relatives and th home of her childhood. She went with her children, and never returned. The daughter, Sarah, married Robert Stevens, a white man in the southern portion of the State of Ohio, and there was born to them William Stevens, a one-fourth blood Cherokee. William Stevens, in response to Chief Downing's invitation, came to the Cherokee country in 1869, and removed there permanently in 1870. There he reared his family, cleared out farms, built houses, and erected improvements, which, in 1893, amounted to many thousands of dollars, a portion of which only had been made prior to August 11, 1886.

Soon after establishing residence, he made application for his mother and himself for re-admission and enrollment as citizens of the Nation. The Commission which h ard the case was convinced of the genuineness of his claim of Cherokee blood, and so re ported to the Chief, but rejected his application pon a technical ground. Upon this report Chief Mayes, in a message to the general council, stated his confidence in the honesty and genuineness of the claim, and advised the passage of an act recognizing the applic nt as a full citizen, but, for some unknown reason, this was never done.

On the 6th day of December, 1873, he went before the United States Indian Agent at the agency then located at Talequah, in conformity with the practice approved by the Secretary of the Interior, and offered proof showing that he was in fact and law a Cherokee Indian, and was entitled to improve the lands then

(6)

occupied by himself, and, upon such proof, the following paper was issued to him:

United States Agent for the Cherokees, Talequah, C. N., Dec. 6, 1873.

This is to certify that Sarah Dictus and William Stevens have brought proof to show that they have filed their claims for citizenship before Cherokee council through proper channel, but that no action was reached in their case.

I have also information that there is good evidence to show that these parties are Cherokees by blood. They will, therefore, not be interfered with until further notice from this office.

      Jno. B. Jones,
     U. S. Agent for Cherokees.

That at no time, and in no place, have the facts submitted to John B. Jones, Indian Agent, as to the blood of William Stevens ever been controverted by the Cherokee Nation, but, after the passage of the act of March 3, 1893, William Stevens ascertained that his name had been put upon the list of intruders "socalled," or upon the intruders' roll, and that at that time he had improvements of the value of $10,000.PP upon lands which he owned under the title under which Cherokee lands were held and owned by Cherokee citizens.

That later the appraiser appointed by the Honorable Secretary of the Interior appraised said improvements, but refused to appraise any except such as were made prior to August 11, 1886, and did not include any purchased by him or made after that time; that said appraisement was to be found on 234 of the list (See House doc. 54 Congress first session, No. 116) and the value as then found for such improvements was $1,177.50, that the representatives of the Cherokee Nation tendered this amount to him accompanied by a receipt in which he waived his citizenship and claims thereto, and that he replied to the same to the effect that he had never had a trial, nor a hearing upon the merits of his case; that he was a Cherokee in law and fact, and refused to accept such an amount and sign such a receipt.

Thereupon, on October 25, 1902, one John Coody, a representative of the National authorities, collected together a small body of men in the town of Lenepah, and as an officier, of the Cherokee Nation, held a public auction or sale, and sold all the improvements of the said William Stevens for the sum of $382.00.

(7)

That, upon the passage of the act of June 10, 1896, William Stevens made proof of the facts above set forth before the Commission to the Five Civilized Tribes, and upon a denial by them of his claim as a citizen, appealed to the district court. That the case was referred by the judge of the western district to R. P. DeGraffenreid as special master for findings of fact. That said master found each and every allegation of the said William Stevens to be true, and so reported to the court. That after said finding, without any exceptions thereto being filed, the judge of said court sustained a demurrer upon the ground that, not being enrolled by the National authorities, William Stevens was entitled to no relief.

That, thereupon, under the authority granted, this case was appealed to the Supreme Court of the United States, and is reported in 174 U. S. p. 445.

That the court, in passing upon this matter, held that the only proposition before it was the constitutionality of the act of June 10, 1898, said court, however, holding on page 488:

"We repeat that in view of the paramount authority of Congress over the Indian tribes, and of the duties imposed on the Government by their condition of dependency, we cannot say that Congress could not empower the Dawes Commission to determine, in the manner provided, who were entitled to citizenship in each of the tribes and make out correct rolls of such citizens, an essential preliminary to effective action in promotion of the best interests of the tribes. It may be remarked that the legislation seems to recognize, especially the act of June 28, 1898, a distinction between admission to citizenship merely and the distribution of property to be subsequently made, as if there might be circumstances under which the right to share in the latter woud not necessarily follow from the concession of the former."

That, under these decisions and this law, William Stevens has lost the work of a lifetime for the insignificant sum of $382.00, and that this tender has not been kept and made good; but on the contary. has been since expended in some other way.

That his children have been beggared, his property confiscated, in violation of the fundamental law of the land, but without right of recovery by him in view of his dependent condition, due to the wardship of the applicant in the past, and the guardianship of the Government both in the past and present.

RELIEF PRAYED.

Your committee represent that they can furnish records of at least eight or ten cases similar to the case above cited, for the inspection of the members of the Select Committee, if desired. They file herewith the record in the Supreme Court showing the facts set forth, the appraisement record, a plat of ground, and offer nothing which is not capable of direct and positive proof. They ask for no relief which will delay the final closing of the affairs of this Nation. They are only seeking to make effective and just the laws which have heretofore been passed, and ask nothing which a court of equity would not grant were it not for the special plenary authority which Congress possesses over the Indian people.

They do request that the Secretary of the Interior be authorized to add to the roll such persons as are found by the court records to be Indians by blood, residents of the Nation in good faith at the date of the passage of the act of June 10, 1896, and who, under any reasonable construction of the law, were actually entitled to enrollment at that time. This will reopen no case; delay no proceedure; but simply grant the right to those who are entitled. The records are completely made; the number is small. The justice of the application cannot be denied. The masters' reports in every case show the exact status of the people. Only those who are Indians are asking for relief.

Your committee respectfully represent that in closing the affairs of this Nation, their prayer may receive consideration.

They further represent that they each of them have been and are law abiding citizens. That they have never been accused of any crime, nor charged with any violation of law; that they have stood by and seen their homes taken from them, and their children beggared, relying upon the final justice of the great Government of the United States; that the time has now come for final action. They realize that because there were many who had no rights, the few who did have were deprived of that which was theirs, but this condition no longer exists. This can be speedily, easily, and inexpensively granted, and they especially pray for an opportunity to present in a simple and plain manner the facts herein set forth t the full committee of the Senate, and for such further relief as may be deemed proper by your committee.

Respectfully submitted,

35320

State of Kansas,
County of Montgomery, ss.

Personally appeared before me, a Notary Public, within and for the county and State aforesaid, William Stephens, of lawful age, who being duly sworn according to law, deposes and says:

That the name of affiant's maternal grandmother was Clarinda Allen; that she was a resident of Kentucky, near Mount Sterling, that State; that about the year 1807 she was stolen and carried off by the Cherokee Indians; that she was white, and about seventeen years of age; that the band of Cherokees who stole her carried her off to Georgia with them, and their Chief Shoeboots took her as his wife; that they had three children, John, William, and Sarah Allen, the mother of affiant; that the relatives of his grandmother thought she was killed, and did not know of her whereabouts until long after her abduction; that a Kentucky trader who lived near Mount Sterling, Ky., learned, while trading with the Indians of the history of their chief's wife, and recognizing the name and circumstances of her abduction, reported the facts back to her relatives; that thereupon they invited the chief and his family to come and visit them; that this he refused to do, but sent his wife, and children on a visit to Kentucky, with the request that they should return in a certain number of moons; that fearing that some harm might come to them, if they returned, they remained in Kentucky and never went back to Georgia; that affiant's mother married a white man named Stephens and moved to Clark County, Ohio; that affiant does not know the date of such removal; that affiant was born in Clark County, Ohio, December 9, 1837; that affiant resided there until nineteen years old, and then went to Illinois; that affiant lived in Illinois until the Civil War, served in the army, and returned there after his discharge, and continued to reside in Illinois until the Dawes Commission invited all Cherokees to return to the Nation; that affiant went to the Cherokee Nation in 1890; that for the reasons stated, affiant was not enrolled on the roll of 1851; that affiant's mother was with affiant, and died in the Cherokee Nation, about the year 1874; that affiant's mother was never enrolled at any time with the Cherokees; that affiant went to the Agent Jones, when he came to the Cherokee Nation and secured a certificate directing the Cherokees not to molest affiant, as he was a Cherokee Indian; that affiant voted for Chief about 1878 or 1879, and was thereafter and otherwise recognized as a member of the Cherokee tribe until until the Dawes Commission rejected his claim to citizenship; that affiant bought farms and sold them the same as any other Cherokee; that affiant was never held or owned by any person, white or Indian, as a slave; that affiant moved to the west in 1890, as stated, from Fulton County, Illinois; that the facts to which he testifies are within his personal knowledge for the most part, and where hearsay, are well-authenticated family tradition by persons having knowledge of them, and further affiant saith not.

William S. Stephens

Subscribed and sworn to before me, this 10th day of June, A. D., 1909.

Philip H. Cass
Notary Public.

My commission expires, Febr. 17, 1912.

No. 35320.

May 30, 1908.

William Stephens,
    Coffeeville, Kans.
Sir:-

Kindly advise this office why you were not enrolled with the Eastern Cherokees in 1851.

Why were your parents never enrolled with the Eastern Cherokees?

Did you ever live with the Cherokees as a recognized member of their tribe?

Were you held as a slave? If so, were you owned by white people or Indians?

When did you move to the West?

Respectfully,

Special Commissioner.

HWK/AIL

PHILIP H. CASS
ATTORNEY AT LAW
COFFEYVILLE, KANS.

July 31, 1909.

Hon. Guion Miller,
    Washington, D. C.
Dear Sir:

    I am requested by William Stephens, applicant No. 35320 for participation in Eastern Cherokee money, to inclose you to a copy of a report made to Select Committee of the Senate Committee on Indian Affairs several years ago, giving a history of himself and family, and to inform you that he is endeavoring to get the testimony of a full-blood over in the east portion of Oklahoma who had a personal acquaintance with his ancestors.

    The applicant is a very old and feeble man, destitute on account of the wrongs complained of in the report, and disabled now by an injury received in an accident for which a railway company is responsible.

    He has no means with which to get testimony in this case, or properly prosecute it, and my services in this connection are gratis. If there is any way by which he could have the benefit of the evidence referred to in this report in behalf of this application, you would be doing a poor helpless old Indian a good turn which he would appreciate at its full worth, as he is an honest man.

    The copy may have some typographical errors, but is in the main a correct one, and sets out the facts in regard to his history, and which it would seem to one not fully informed, to entitle him to the money asked for.

                  Very respectfully,

                    Philip H. Cass

App. No.35320.

August 4, 1909.

Phillip H. Cass, Atty.,
    Coffeyville,
        Kansas.

Sir:

    I am in receipt of your letter of July 31, 1909, relative to the application of William Stephens, No.35320, for participation in the Eastern Cherokee fund.

    In reply you are advised that from the statements contained in the affidavit made by the said William Stephens it is plain that he and his mother were not members of the Eastern Cherokee tribe in 1835, at the time the rights accrued under this judgment.

    In addition to that you are advised that William Stephens when notified to appear before one of my assistants for examination failed to appear. It does not therefore seem necessary in this case to make any further examination into the facts.

    Very respectfully,

        Special Commissioner.

GM:MLC.

Cherokee Intruder Cases 1901 - 1909

Rec'd	Allottee	Intruder
Feb 19th 1906	746 Lottie Wickett Zena IT	Thos Hall Grove IT EB Hardy Zena IT
Aug 8 -1906	Case set for hearing at Vanita[sic] I.Ty. Aug 21 -1906 All parties notified	
Aug 17 1906	Dfts notified by this office that as they report they have to be at Grove ITy Aug 21 -1906 to then come directly to Vanita ITy	
Aug 21 1906	Case called at Vanita ITy. Pltf appeared and testimony taken.	
Sept 17 1906	Certificate #55998 ret in person & pltf instructed to have land surveyed & report if Dfdts are intruding.	
Oct 18 1906	Eldon Lowe reports that he does not know of papers of Webster Wickett will report again	
Oct 26 1906	Plntf writes that Thos Hall will not give possession	
Jany 22, 1907	" advised to have lands surveyed & report	
Mch 23, 1907	Referred to Robt. R. Bennett for investigation	
Apr 3, 1907	Robt R Bennett encloses request for dismissal Case <u>dismissed</u>	

Notice Sent	Action	Remarks
3/24 06	3/24 Referred to Eldon Lowe for investigation	Mch 20 filed certificate No 55998
Mch 30th 1906	Com^r reports no contests pending and certificates issued	
April 4	Proof of service returned dated Mch 31st 1906	
" "	Answer filed by EB Hardy and Tom Hall	
" 28	Eldon Lowe reports that Dfdts claim that they are not holding Ptf's land and that if they are occupying said land they will surrender same to Allottee as soon as same is proven to them by a competent surveyor	
May 1st	Ptf advise to have land surveyed	
" 14	Plat of the land filed by Plaintiff	

Rec'd	Allottee	Intruder
Mch 16	747 Lizzie Rogers Gdn. for Matt L., Mamie E. and Sylvester A Rogers c/o W.A. Chase Atty Nowata I.T.	Messers Looney Elliott I.T. Josie Looney Defendant is a claimant for citizenship as a Cherokee Freedman
June 12	Com^r reports that citizenship has been denied Defendant	

Cherokee Intruder Cases 1901 - 1909

June 16	Case set for hearing at Claremore June 22/06	
June 22	Answer filed by Defendant in which she states that a motion to reopen her citizenship case is now pending	
June 22	Case called at Claremore both parties present evidence taken. 4 Ex's "A" by Ptfs. 2 certificates filed by Ptf	
July 2	Comr requested to report as to citizenship of Tobe Looney Deceased	
April 30 1907	Com^r reports Josie Looney & children denied enrollment	
May 8 1907	Case reopened and notice sent	
May 22 1907	Proof of service returned dated May 20 -1907 Judgment rendered in favor of plntfs & dfndts given ten days in which to vacate	
June 8/7	Policeman Jas Walker instructed to place plff in possession	
July 11 -07	Police Walker reports today and case <u>Dismissed</u> upon his report	
Jan 15/8	Osborn & Osborn enclose petition of deft to be permitted to remain in possession	
Jan 21/8	Osborn & O. Attys advised that only upon complaint of plff will any further action be taken	

Notice Sent	Action	Remarks
July 17	Com^r reports that citizenship of Tobe Looney has been finally denied by the Dept.	
July 19 1906	Com^r requested to report as to citizenship of Josie and Al Looney	
July 25	Com^r reports motion to review the citizenship cases of Josie Looney and her minors, is now pending before ~~that~~ this office	
July 28	Case dismissed Plaintiff so notified	
July 30	Certificates returned to Plaintiff in care of her Atty	Dismissed
Feby 16 1907	Letters of Gdnship withdrawn to be filed in new case.	
~~May 8 -1907~~	~~Case reopened~~	

Rec'd	Allottee		Intruder
Mch 10	748	Leonord[sic] W Williams for himself, Clem, Viola, Kettie and Tuxie Williams Pryor Creek I.T. R.B. Butz Atty Muskogee I.T.	Joseph Lewis Pryor Creek Wat Mayes Pryor Creek I.T. Ned Campbell Atty Pryor Creek I.T.
Aug 1st 1906	Case called at Muskogee both parties appeared and testimony taken		
Jany 22 1907	Referred to Robt R Bennett for investigation		
Feby 4 1907	Robt R Bennett reports Dfndt not in possession		

Cherokee Intruder Cases 1901 - 1909

	Tuxie Williams told W.W.B. at Claremore ITy 2/8/07 that they ^pintff were in possession. <u>Dismissed</u>	
Sept 6 '07	Plaintiff advised of Action taken by this office in above entitled case.	

Notice Sent	Action	Remarks
3/25'06	3/24 Referred to Eldon Lowe for investigation	Mch 20 Com reports no contests pending
	April 18 Answer filed by Wat Mayes who claims to be the real defendant	
	April 21 Letter from Ptf filed	
	May 4 Proof of service returned dated May 3rd 1906	
	" 5 Answer filed by defendants	
	June 7/06 Case set for hearing at Claremore IT June 20/06	
	" 20/06 Case called at Claremore Dfdt present and his evidence taken, no appearance by Ptf	
	Case to be reset for hearing	
	July 2/06 Report of Eldon Lowe filed, and case dismissed (see carbon in file) (Held up)	
	July 20 " Case set for hearing at Muskogee Aug 1st 1906 1:30 P.M.	

Rec'd	Allottee	Intruder
Mch 21	749 Mrs Mary A Jiles Pryor Creek	vs ~~Wm Jiles and~~ Louis Briggs Pryor Creek
	April 21 Louis Briggs advises that he will remove house occupied by him at once	
	May 5 Louis Briggs requested to advise this office is[sic] house above referred to has been removed	
	" 8 Louis Briggs advises that house has been removed	
	May 21 Plaintiff states that house has been removed and all is satisfactory	
	" 24 case dismissed	
	Certificates returned	Dismissed

Notice Sent	Action	Remarks
3/24 06	3/24 Referred to Eldon Lowe for investigation	Mch 21 Homestead certificate No 13930 and Allotment certificate No 18037
	Mch 30 Com^r reports no contest pending and certificates issued	
	April 10 Plaintiff states that Wm Jiles is not an Intruder. She states that the name of the Intruder is Lewis Briggs. New notices were sent to Ptf.	

Cherokee Intruder Cases 1901 - 1909

April 16th — Eldon Lowe reports (verbaly[sic]) that the house of the Defendant is located upon a portion of the land allotted to Mrs Mary A. Jiles. Defendant was directed to remove said house at once.
April 17 — Answer filed by Dft. April 18 Proof of Service returned
April 21 Eldon Lowe reports Mrs Ada G. Smith is the owner of the house and she was requested to remove it at once

Rec'd	Allottee	Intruder
Mch 12 1906	750 Jennie Bread Hulbert I.T.	vs ~~Mr (Illegible)~~ L. J. Snarr
3/14 06	3/24 Referred to Eldon Lowe	3/12 Homestead Cert No 12921
April 2	Proof of service returned dated Mch 31st 1906 Mch 30 Com^r reports no contest pending and certificates issued	and Allotment certificate No 16509
April 11th	Eldon Lowe reports that they allotment of Ptf Jennie Bread is unoccupied and entirely without with[sic] improvements Plaintiff was requested by this office to take possession of her allotment at once. Certificates returned and case dismissed	
April 18	LJ Snarr appeared at this office and stated that he waived all right to possession	Dismissed

Rec'd	Allottee	Intruder
Mch 23 1906	751 Key Ketcher for John Ketcher c/o J Henry Dick Tahlequah I.T.	Annie Houston Tahlequah I.T.
Notice Sent		
3/28'06	Mch 23 Homestead certificate No 16381 filed	
Mch 28	Referred to Eldon Lowe for investigation	
April 3rd	Com^r reports no contest pending	
April 7th	Withdrawn from Eldon Lowe and referred to Thos Roach, Policeman	
April 19	Policeman Thos P. Roach reports that settlement has been made to the satisfaction of both parties. Case dismissed and certificates returned	Dismissed

Cherokee Intruder Cases 1901 - 1909

Rec'd	Allottee	Intruder
Mch 12 1906	752 Sussanna Allsup nee Morrison for W^m E Morrison Owasso I.T.	W.N. Bleakmore Owasso I.T.
June 7/06	Case set for hearing at Claremore I.T. June 20/06	
" 20 1906	Case called at Claremore Defendant appeared no appearance by Plaintiff	
" 20 "	Case dismissed by order of W.W.B. as this office can take no action till a gdn. is appointed by the U.S. Court Dismissed	

Notice

3/23 1906 Com^r reports, certificates issued and no contest pending. Mch 28 notice sent to ptf to serve on Dft. Mch 28 Matter referred to Eldon Lowe for investigation
April 4   Proof of service returned dated 3/31'06
May[sic] April 30 Answer filed by Dfdt in which he states he is an intermarried citizen and that the Ptf in this case filed on his home and that if he is denied citizenship he has a child that he intends to file on the place
May 10   Eldon Lowe reports that Defendant is in possession by virtue of a rental contract executed by Ptf as Natural Gdn. 5/14 Ptf was advised to be appointed Legal Gdn and forward a copy of the letters of Gdnship to this office at which time further Action will be taken

Rec'd	Allottee	Intruder
Mch 26 1906	753 Mrs Aletha B. Allen nee Ward Mound Valley Kans	Chas McCulloch Afton I.T.

Notice sent

3/30 1906   Mch 26 Homestead certificate No 36118 and Allotment certificate No 59689 filed
  Mch 30th Referred to Eldon Lowe for investigation
  April 3   Com reports no contest pending
  "   "   Proof of service returned dated April 5th 06
  April 10'06 Defendant asked that Action be withheld which was not granted
  April 14   Defendant appered[sic] in person and stated he had filed contest. Com^r requested to advise this office if contest is now pending upon said land and Eldon Lowe advised to take no action until further advised
  April 24 Com^r advises that contest is pending
    Case dismissed and certificates returned to Plaintiff

Cherokee Intruder Cases 1901 - 1909

Allottee	Intruder
Mch 26 1906 754 Youngblood, Reedy father of Oakley Youngblood c/o Thos J Watts Muldrow I.T.	Joanna Taylor and Mr Dickson Neal and London Attys Ft Smith Ark
June 18 1906 Com^r reports motion for review in citizenship case of Dfdt pending, case dismissed	Defendant is a Claimant for citizenship as a Cherokee Freedman Dismissed
(Action)	

Mch 30th Notice sent to Ptf to serve on Dft.
"   "   Referred to Eldon Lowe for investigation
Mch 26   Homestead certificate No 18267 filed by Ptf
April 3   Com^r reports a portion of the land in contest
"   9   Case dismissed as to portion that is in contest
" 18   Attys for Defendant state that Dft is a Claimant for citizenship as a Cherokee Freedman
" 26   Case dismissed do[sic] to all except three acres. See report of Eldon Lowe in file
May 10   In compliance with instructions from the Dept under date of April 19 1906 Com^r is requested to report as to the status of Allotment of Ptf and of citizenship of Dfdt in this case

Allottee	Intruder
Mch 30th 755 Louisa Beam Mother of Murphy Beam Melvin I.T.	(vs) John Ford Melvin I.T.
(Action)	

Mch 30   Homestead certificate No 13829 filed
April 3   Notice sent to Ptf to serve on Dft
"   "   Referred to John Viets for investigation
April 7   Com^r reports no contest pending against homestead
April 10   Proof of service returned
May 28/06   Report of John Vietes[sic] filed and case dismissed upon the request of Plaintiff
   Certificates returned to Plaintiff
                                                                                Dismissed

Cherokee Intruder Cases 1901 - 1909

	Allottee	Intruder
Mch 31 1906	756 Louisa McCrary Kansas I.T.	Ezekiel Perry Dodge I.T.
Action		

Mch 31 Allotment certificate No 18232 filed
April 4th Notice set[sic] to Ptf to serve on Defendant
 "   "   Referred to John Viet for investigation
 "   10 Com^r reports contest pending certificate returned and case dismissed
Dismissed

	Allottee	Intruder
Mch 31 1906	757 Richard D. Foreman Kansas I.T.	Ezekiel Perry Lodge I.T.
Action		

Mch 31 Allotment certificate No 48023 filed April 4th Notice set[sic] to Ptf to serve on Defendant
April 4th Referred to John Viets for investigation
 "   9th Com^r reports no contest pending. Certificates returned and case dismissed
Dismissed

	Allottee	Intruder
April 4 ~~Mch~~ 1904[sic]	758 Emma H. Hamlin Turley I.T. c/o ~~Garfield Buell Atty~~. Muskogee Carroll S. Bucher Atty	I B Cullison Turley I.T. Leeds and Martindale Attys Tulsa I.T.

(Note: continuation from the end of this case) Muskogee I.T.
June 20/06 her evidence was taken. Dfdt did not appear but was represented by Atty DM Martindale
June 20 Case continued until Friday 22nd 10 A.M.
 "   "   Copy of Award of Arbitrators filed by Dfdts
June 22 Case called all parties present evidence taken. Case again continued until June 27 1906
        6/27/06 Case continued Bennett sick
July 24 1906 ~~Com^r~~ Plaintiff requested to report as to status of this case Ptf advises that Dfdts have vacated (by Phone)
 Aug 7 " Ptf reports Defdt damages property & asks redress. Advised to go to US Court. as this office has no jurisdiction
Dismissed

Cherokee Intruder Cases 1901 - 1909

(Action)
April 5th   Notice sent Plaintiff to serve on Dfts
"   4   Com[r] reports no contest pending and certificates issued
April 9th   Garfield Buell advised that he will not be allowed to practice as an Atty before this office until he has paid his Tribal tax which is due the Creek Nation
April 13   Proof of Service returned dated April 4th 1906
"   24   Answer filed
May 22   Plaintiff asks that case be set for hearing at once
June 7/06 Case set for hearing at Claremore IT June 20/06
"   "   "   Attys for Dfdt report that matter has been submitted to a party of arbitrators
" 20 "   Case called at Claremore Plaintiff appeared and
(Note: continued at the beginning of this case)

	Allottee	Intruder
Mch 29 1906	759 Perry Samuel and Amanda	vs M. Simon
	c/o Chas B Rogers Atty	Ramona I.T.
	Vinita	Robison and McKinney
(Note: continuation from the end of this case)		Attys Ramona I.T.

July 10 1906 Answer and Aff. filed by Defendant
"   23   "   Judgment rendered in favor of the Dfdt. both parties so notified and
              a copy of the Judgment sent to each of them
                                                              Case Dismissed
Aug 3-1906 Atty for Plaintiff present application for new hearing
"   8   "   Application for new hearing denied.
Sept 8 1906 CB Rogers for pltf file an appeal from decision of this office.
" 22 1906   CB Rogers advised that he should submit protest & application for appeal
Oct 31, 1906   Submitted to Com[r] Indian Affairs Washington D.C.

(Action)
April 9th   Com[r] reports no contest pending
"   16   Notice sent to Plaintiff to serve on Defendant
"   17   Referred to John Viets for investigation
"   21   Answer and affidavits filed
May 14   Report of John Viets filed and he recommends that case be set for hearing
June 9/06 Case set for hearing at Claremore IT June 20/06
June 20 "   Case called at Claremore I.T. Both parties appear and evidence was taken. Dfdts
Ex "A" a suplimental[sic] contract filed by Dfdts
Ex "B" a rental contract filed by Dfdts
" "C" "   "   "   "   "   "
[sic] 20 "   Atty for Plaintiff asked to be allowed to file brief, request was granted
July 2/06   Rogers, Atty for Plaintiff filed brief   *(Note: continued at the beginning of this case)*
Apr 29-1907 Com[r] of Indian Affairs affirms decision of this office - <u>Dismissed</u>
All parties notified

8

Cherokee Intruder Cases 1901 - 1909

Rec'd	No.	Allottee	Intruder
April 27 1906	760	Margaret Underwood Grove I.T. *(Names Illegible)* Attys Vinita	P F Depriest and W$^{\underline{m}}$ P Mayes Grove I.T.
(Date illegible)		Answer filed	*(Name Illegible)* Atty
(Date illegible)		Attys for ptf request this case be heard at Vinita	Grove IT
(Date illegible)		*(Illegible)* of Eldon Low[sic] filed and case Dismissed as there is a contract in existance[sic] See *(Illegible)* in filed[sic]) Certificates returned	
			Dismissed

(Action)		
April 7	Homestead Certificate No 35714 and Allotment Certificate No 58683 filed		
" 27	Referred to Eldon Lowe for investigation		
" "	Com^r requested to report as to status of Allotment		
" "	Notice sent to Ptf to serve ~~upon~~ on Ptf[sic] Dfdts		
May 5	Com^r reports no contests pending and certificates issued		
" 10	Answer and copy of lease contract filed by Dfdt.		
" 11	Proof of service returned dated May 8th 1906		
June 7/06	Case set for hearing at Claremore I.T. June 20'06		
" 15	Plaintiff advises that on account of condition of her ^health^ she will be unable to attend hearing on June 20 Case is therefore continued and all parties so notified		

Rec'd	No.	Allottee	Intruder
(Date illegible)	761	James Lacey Warner I.T.	Bush Fields Warner I.T.

(Action)
Mch 20 Homestead Certificate No 23748 filed
April 27 Notice sent to Ptf to serve on Dft
"   "   Referred to Eldon Lowe for investigation
May 7 Proof of service returned and ^dismissed^ case as plaintiff states Defendant surrendered possession when he served notice on him, certificates returned
May 5 Com^r reports no contest pending
Dismissed
~~June~~ May 31 06 Eldon Lowe filed report.

Cherokee Intruder Cases 1901 - 1909

Filed	No	Allottee	Intruder
Mch 21 1906	762	L. H. Tackett Gdn. of *heirs of* Chas H. Patton c/o ~~L. G. Elliot Atty~~ Chelsea I.T. Bushyhead I.T.	Jack Jackson and Sam Curtain Tulsa I.T.
		his evidence was taken Dfdt did not appear	
June 15		Proof of Service returned dated June 14 1906	
Mch 21/06		Order of Court filed by Plaintiff	
July 23 "		Judgment rendered in favor of Plaintiff both parties so notified and a copy of the Judgment sent to each of them. Dfdt given 10 days in which to vacate	
Sept 14 -1906		See letter in file from plntf.	
Sept 22 -1906		Instructions issued to policeman W^m M Sunday, of Tulsa ITy to place pltf in possession	
Nov 9 1906		Policeman Sunday requested to report on instructions	
Nov 13, 1906		Policeman Sunday reports that he placed in possession Oct 1, 1906. See #196 Cherokee	
Nov 16 1906		Case dismissed & letter of Gdnship ret to plntf. See file of Cherokee #196 for report of Police Sunday	

Action

Mch 21	Homestead Certificate No 31903, Allotment Certificate No 47831 and letters of Gdnship filed
April 27	Notice sent to Ptf to serve on Dfdt.
" "	Referred to Eldon Lowe for investigation
~~May 3~~	Proof of Service returned dated 5/1 1906
" 8	Com^r reports contest pending *on a portion of the land* Therefore case is dismissed as to that portion
" 9	Report of Eldon Lowe filed
June 6/06	Takett[sic] appeared in person and requested that case be dismissed as to Sam Curtain
" " "	Certificates returned to Plaintiff in person
" " "	Case set for hearing at Claremore IT June 20/06
" 20 1906	Case called at Claremore Plaintiff appeared and Homestead Certificate 32304 No ~~49482~~ and Allotment certificate No 49482

Filed	No	Allottee	Intruder
April 23 1906	763	Alfred Taylor Gdn. of Carl Taylor Pryor Creek I.T.	John R Reeves Pryor Creek I.T.
		A C Brewster Atty.	
June 1/06		Case set for hearing at Claremore I.T. June 21/06	
" 2		Com^r requested to report as to status of citizenship of Defendant	
June 21 "		Case called at Claremore both parties present evidence taken	

10

Cherokee Intruder Cases 1901 - 1909

" 13 Letter from Dept., with *(Illegible)* filed
July 21 1906 Judgment rendered in favor of Plaintiff both parties so notified and a copy of the Judgment sent to each of them. Dfdt requested to vacate within 10 days
Nov 9 1906 Plntf asked to advise if he is in possession
Nov 19 1906 A.C. Brewster Atty for plntf states plntf has possession
Nov 20 1906 Case dismissed & Allottment[sic] certificates returned

Action

April 27 Notice sent to Ptf to serve on Dfdt.
"   "   Referred to Eldon Lowe for investigation
May 3 Proof of service returned dated 5/1 1906
"   8 Com^r reports no contest pending
"   7 Eldon Lowe reports that Dfdt is in possession by virtue of a lease contract from Ashley Norton who is a claimant to citizenship
   12 Plaintiff was advised to be appointed Legal Gdn. of the minor and sent a copy of the Letters of Gdnship to this office and further Action will be taken
"   15 Plaintiff requests that he be placed in possession without be appointed statutory Gdn
"   22 Dfdt requested to file answer if he claims any right to possession

Filed	No	Allottee	Intruder
April 10 1906	764	A. H. Collins Gdn. of Albert H. Jr, Agusta B. and Eli H. Collins Owasso I.T.	vs James Shipman Turley I.T. Harry O Bland Atty Afton I.T.

Action

April 10 Letters of Gdnship filed
"   19 Com^r reports no contest pending
   27 Notice sent to Plaintiff to serve on Defendant
"   Referred to John Veits[sic] for investigation
May 3 Proof of service returned dated 5/1 1906
"   9 Answer filed
May 11 Case set for hearing at Tulsa IT May 17 1906
"   17/21 Report of John Viets filed and case dismissed upon request of Plaintiff Letters of Gdnship returned to Plaintiff
                              Dismissed

Cherokee Intruder Cases 1901 - 1909

Filed	No	Allottee	Intruder
April 10 1906	765	A.H. Collins Gdn of Mary F. Collins Owasso I.T.	James Shipman Turley I.T. Harry O. Bland Atty Afton I.T.

Action	
April 19	Com^r reports no contest pending
" 27	Notice sent to Ptf to serve on Dfdt
" "	Referred to John Veits[sic] for investigation
May 3	Proof of service returned dated 5/1 1906
" 9	Answer files see 764
May 11	Case set for hearing at Tulsa I.T. May 17 1906
" 21	Report of John Viets filed and case dismissed upon request of Plaintiff Dismissed

Filed	No	Allottee	Intruder
April 10 1906	766	Mrs Annie Collins Owasso I.T.	James Shipman Turley I.T. H.O. Bland Atty Afton I.T.

Action	
April 19	Com^r reports no contest pending
" 27	Notice sent to Ptf to serve on Dfdt
" "	Referred to John Viets for investigation
May 3	Proof of Service returned dated 5/1 1906
" 9	Answer filed See #764
May 11	Case set for hearing at Tulsa I.T. May 17th 1906
" 21	Report of John Viets filed and case dismissed upon request of Plaintiff Dismissed

Filed	No	Allottee		Intruder
April 10 1906	767	Albert Ross Evansville Ark	vs	W.D. Hogan Stilwell Watts and Curtis Atty Sallisaw I.T.

(Note: continuation from the end of this case)

Aug 3 1906	Defendant requests a hearing the case is therefore set for hearing at Muskogee Aug 15 1906
Aug 16 1906	Case called & no appearance by either party
Aug 18 "	By request of Watts & Curtis and enclosed statements of pltf requesting withdrawal of complaint, the case is this day <u>dismissed</u>

Cherokee Intruder Cases 1901 - 1909

	Action
April 19	Com.^{r} reports no contest pending
" 27	Notice sent to Ptf to serve on Dfdt
" "	Referred to Thomas P. Roach U.S.I.P. for investigation
May 2̶6̶ 2	Proof of Service returned dated May 2 1906
" 3	Answer filed by W.D. Hogan
" 12	Answer filed by Watts and Curtis Attys for Dfdt
" 12	Report of Thomas P Roach filed
" 22	Dfdt requested to vacate at once otherwise he will be removed
June 8	Plaintiff requested to advise this office if he is now in possession
July 13 1906	Letter from Dfdt filed 7/14 Dfdt requested to make satisfactory settlement at once or vacate
June 9 "	Letter from Ptf filed and July 19 1906. Ptf advised that Dfdt has been requested to vacate
20	Dfdt P̶t̶f̶ states Plaintiff has not made an attempt to settle as agreed.

(Note: continued at the beginning of this case)

(Filed)	(No.)	(Allottee)	(Intruder)
April 26 1906	768	Ben and William Wolf Mayesville[sic] Ark	WP Gillispie Mayesville[sic] Ark

	(Action)
April 26	Certificates of Allotment Nos 7315 and 7316, filed
May 11	Notice sent to Ptf to serve on Defendant
" "	Referred to Eldon Lowe for investigation
" 18	Com.^{r} reports no contest pending
" 23	Report of Eldon Lowe and copy of contract filed case dismissed and certificates returned to Plaintiff Defendant directed to comply with the contract
June 11	Proof of Service returned dated June 5/'06
	Dismissed

(Filed)	(No.)	(Allottee)	(Intruder)
April 26 1906	769	Walter and Lucy Polecat Gdns of Isaac Polecat Long I.T.	Hannah Woods and Sarah Tenney Muldrow I.T.

	(Action)
April 26	Homestead Certificate No 16941 and Allotment certificate No 22967 filed
May "	Notice sent to Ptf to serve on Dfdts
" "	Referred to Eldon Lowe for investigation
" 18	Com.^{r} reports no contests pending

Cherokee Intruder Cases 1901 - 1909

" 25	Eldon Lowe reports that Defendants have vacated. The Plaintiff was instructed goe[sic] into possession and case is dismissed Certificates returned to Plaintiff
	Dismissed

(Filed)	(No.)	(Allottee)	(Intruder)
April 27 1906	770	Hannah M°Waters natural Gdn of Robert Mayes Ft Gibson	Aurthor[sic] Reed Muskogee I.T.

(Note: continuation from the end of this case)

June 22	Answer filed by Defendant
" 27	Case set for hearing at Muskogee IT July 7th 1906
July 7	Case called at Muskogee Ptf present no appearance by Dfdt
" 12	Certified copy of approved roll filed by Com^r
" 9	Dfdt notified to vacate as such or show cause why he should not be removed
Aug 7 -06	Arthur Reid[sic], defendant, notified by reg mail to show cause within ten days, why he should not be removed, otherwise, order will issue to remove him
Aug 9 1906	Reg card to Arthur Reid, showing receipt of notice, returned
Aug 10 -1906	Dfdt appeared in person and agreed to produce proof that Hannah M°Waters, pltf made affidavit that Robt Mayes was over twenty one years of age at time Dfdt purchased land said proof to be submitted within 20 days.
Nov 9, 1906	Dfndt requested to furnish affidavit above mentioned
Jany 28, 1907	Dfndt again requested to furnish evidence
Mch 21, 1907	Judgement[sic] for plntf. Dfndt given ten days to vacate
June 15, 07	Plff. requested to advise in re possession
Aug 14 '07	Husband of Plaintiff appeared in person and stated plaintiff is now in possession certificates returned and case <u>Dismissed</u>

	(Action)
April 27	Homestead certificate No 31926 and Allotment certificate No 47872
May 11	Notice sent to Ptf to serve on Dfdts
" 11	Referred to Eldon Lowe for investigation
" 16	Proof of service returned dated May 15 1906
" 18	Com^r reports no contest pending
" 26	Proof of service returned
June 8 1906	Case set for hearing at Muskogee IT June 15/06
" 15 "	Case called at Muskogee, Plaintiff appeared and her evidence was taken Dfdt did not appear. Defendant was requested to advise this office by what authority he is in possession
June 25 "	Dfdt appeared in person and stated that Ptf had never served papers on him

Cherokee Intruder Cases 1901 - 1909

(Filed)	(No.)	(Allottee)	(Intruder)
April 17 1906	771	Frank Vann nat. Gdn. Jesse Vann Ft. Gibson I.T.	Peggy Wiggins Freedman Santown[sic] I.T.
		(Action)	
April 24	Com[r] reports no contest pending		
May 11	Notice sent to Ptf to serve on Dfdt.		
" "	Referred to Eldon Lowe for investigation		
" 17	Answer filed		
" 26	Eldon Lowe reports that satisfactory settlement has been made both parties so notified and a copy of the contract sent to both of them		
			Dismissed

(Filed)	(No.)	(Allottee)	(Intruder)
April 20 1906	772	Jennie A. Lacie Baptists Westville I.T. S.F. Parris Atty for Pltf Vanita[sic] I.Ty.	W.J.S and W.SL Osborn Collinsville I.T.
Jany 24, 1907	Judgment[sic] for plntf		
June 17 07	Atty for plff requested to advise in re possession		
" 29 "	Plff " " " " " "		
" 20 07	Atty for plff advises J.A. Lacie in possession		
June 24 07	Certs 10887 - 8770 returned to Atty for plff and		
			Case Dismissed
		(Action)	
April 26	Com[r] reports no contests pending		
May 11	Notice sent to ptf to serve on Dfdt		
" "	Referred to Eldon Lowe for investigation		
June 7/06	Case set for hearing at Claremore IT June 21/06		
" 11/06	Report of Eldon Lowe filed in which he stated that Dfdt has agreed to vacate		
June 21 1906	Case called at Claremore W.J. Osborn appeared no appearance by Plaintiff		
" "	Plaintiff advises that it was on account of sickness that she was absent from hearing at Claremore		
Aug 8-1906	Case set for hearing at Vanita[sic] I.Ty. Aug 22 -1906 All parties notified		
Aug 21 1906	Case called at Vanita I.T. Pltf and Atty Mr Parks appeared and testimony taken Certificates #10787 & 8770 filed by pltf Ret card of notice of hearing filed by pltf.		
Aug 20 1906	Motion for continuance filed by defendant accompanied by M.D's		

Cherokee Intruder Cases 1901 - 1909

	certificate stating that the child of defandant[sic] is critically ill. Above motion was forwarded by U.S. Ind Agt at Muskogee I.Ty to W.W. Bennett at Vanita & rec'd there Aug 22 -1906
Sept 26 1906	Case set for hearing at Muskogee I.Ty. Oct 4, 1906 All parties notified
Oct 4 1906	Case called at Muskogee I.Ty. No appearance by either party. Mr. Fogle appeared for plntf
Nov 5 1906	Case set for hearing at Claremore I.Ty. Nov 21, 1906. Dfdt & Pltf Atty notified.
Nov 21 1906	Case called at Claremore. No appearance by dfndt. Plntf represented by Mr. Fogle Atty Vinita ITy.
Jany 24 1907	Plntf requested to advise if possession in 10 das.

(Filed)	(No.)	(Allottee)	(Intruder)
April 18 1906	773	Robt B Williams for Herbert A Williams c/o DeRoss Bailey Atty Muskogee	Mrs Martha J., Albert Morman[sic] and wife ~~Wagoner~~ I.T. Fort Gibson
(Action)			
April 18	Plat and Power of Atty filed by Plaintiff		
" 24	Com^r reports no contest pending on the land discribed[sic] in this case, but some land described in complaint is in contest		
May 12	Notice sent to Ptf to serve on Defendant		
" "	Referred to Eldon Lowe for investigation		
" 17	Mrs Norman states she has filed contest against the land that she notice to vacate		
" 17	Proof of Service returned dated May 15 1906		
June 14	Case set for hearing at Muskogee June 25 1906		
" 25	Case called Ptf appeared No appearance by dfndt		
Nov. 14 1906	Case set for hearing at Muskogee ITy Nov 27, 1906 All notified.		
Nov 27 1906	Case called at Muskogee. All parties present. Dfndt claims possession only of land in contest. Mr. De Ross Bailey for plntf agreed that land is in contest and at request of Mr. Bailey, case continued until contest settled. Same granted.		
Jan 8 08	Case dismissed by order of Mr WW.B.		

Cherokee Intruder Cases 1901 - 1909

(Filed)	(No.)	(Allottee)	(Intruder)
April 19 1906	774	W^m and Caroline Scullawl c/o W J Dodson Claremore I.T.	Watt Mayes Pryor Creek I.T.

(Action)
April 26   Com^r reports no contest pending
May 12   Notice sent to Plaintiff to serve on Dfdt
"   "   Referred to Eldon Lowe for investigation
June 7/06   Case set for hearing at Claremore IT June 21/06
" 20   Dfdt appeared at Claremore and stated that he is not in possession of the land and that Plaintiff may take possession
" 21   Plaintiffs appeared and were advised to take possession of their allotments Case dismissed by order of W.W.B.
7/5/06   Certificates 19477 ∧ 19478 returned
Dismissed

(Filed)	(No.)	(Allottee)	(Intruder)
May 3 1906	775	Larkin Sevenstar Ochelata I.T.	I.T. Wells and Nancy E Rogers Adair I.T. E.B. Lawson Atty Nowata I.T.

(Action)
May 3   Certificate of Allotment no 45489 filed
" 12   Notice sent to Plaintiff to serve on Dfdts Referred to John Viets for investigation
" 18   Com^r reports no contest pending
" 26   Proof of Service returned dated 5/25/06
" 28   Answer filed
June 2   Copy of Rental Contract filed by Nancy E Rogers
June 7/06 Case set for hearing at Claremore IT June 21/06
June 21   Case called at Claremore both parties appeared and evidence taken Complainant requested to appear at Muskogee on June 30 at which time Roy D Palmer was also req. to be present.
" 30   Plff appeared - Mr Palmer did not. Palmer called by 'phone & stated on a/c sickness he was unable to appear but agreed to appear & give evidence within 2 weeks
July 20 1906 R.D. Palmer requested to advise this office when he will appear at this office
Aug 3   "   R.D. Palmer appeared and his testimony taken
Aug 30 1906 Pltf asks to be advised as to status of case

Cherokee Intruder Cases 1901 - 1909

Nov 6 1906	Judgment[sic] rendered in favor of dfndt. Certificate returned to plntf. Lease contract ret to dfndt. <u>Dismissed.</u>

(Filed)	(No.)	(Allottee)	(Intruder)
May 1st 1906	776	Ellen Yates Fort Gibson I.T.	Albert and Louisa Anderson

(Action)
May 12   Notice sent to Ptf to serve on Defendant
" "   Referred to John Viets for investigation
April 28   Com^r reports no contest pending
May 28   Report of John Viets filed and case dismissed upon request of Plaintiff   Dismissed

(Filed)	(No.)	(Allottee)	(Intruder)
April 19 1906	777	Chas M. and Susie E. Ross Tahlequah I.T.	John McDonald Benge I.T. Watts & Curtis Atty Dfdt Claimant for citizenship as a Freedman
(Note: continuation from the end of this case)			

(Action)
Aug 1 1906   Defendant requests Action be withheld as he states he has filed motion for a review of his citizenship case
Aug 1st "   Com^r requested to report
Aug 2 -06   R Lee Wyly reports having placed plaintiff in possession of their allottment[sic] - therefore case is dismissed   Dismissed
Aug 6 1906   Com^r reports a motion for rehearing of citizenship case of Jno McDonald is now pending before his office.
Aug 31 1906   Jno McDonald, dfdnt, notified that complaint filed by him will not be made of record until citizenship case is finally decided.
Oct 3 1906   Watts & Curtis state they are Attys for dfndt & ask status of case
Oct 6 1906   Watts & Curtis advised as to conditions
Nov 30 1906   Dfndt notified that no Action will be taken by this off.

(Action)
April 24   Com^r reports no contests pending
May 12   Notice sent to Plaintiff to serve on Dfdt
" "   Referred to John Veits[sic] for investigation
" 17   Report of Com^r filed from which it appeared that Defendant is a rejected freedman and no motion for review or rehearing is pending

Cherokee Intruder Cases 1901 - 1909

	Papers from case 792 filed in this case
June 7/06	Report of John Viets filed with which 1/06 he transmits a letter from the Com^r in said letter it is set forth that John McDonald is a rejected freedman and that no motion for review of his case is pending
	Defdt was directed to vacate otherwise he will be removed
June 22	Proof of Service returned dated June 13/06
" 19	Dfdt directed to vacate
June 27	Case set for hearing at Muskogee July 6 1906
July 6	Case called at Muskogee Ptf appeared and his testimony taken, no appearance by Dfdt. Case continued in order to give the Dfdt an opportunity to be heard
June 16 1906	Answer filed by Defendant
July 21 "	Judgment rendered in favor of the Plaintiffs both parties so notified and a copy of the Judgment sent to each of them and instructions issued to Policeman R. Lee Wily to place Ptf. in possession

(Note: continued at the beginning of this case)

(Filed)	(No.)	(Allottee)	(Intruder)
April 21	778	Harlin B. Beck Gdn. of Homer, Stella, Ary, Joseph and Jesse Beck c/o S F Parks Atty Vinita I.T.	vs John C Hogan Hiram Hughes and Todd Healton Pryor Creek I.T. A. C. Brewster Atty Pryor Creek I.T.

(Action)	
April 21	Letters of Gdnship filed by Plaintiff
" 27	Com^r reports no contest pending
May 12	Notice sent to Ptf to serve on Defendants
" "	Referred to to[sic] John Viets for investigation
" 19	Answer filed by John C Hogan
" 22	Proof of Service returned dated 5/16 1906
" 26	Answer filed by A.C. Brewster
June 7/06	Case set for hearing at Claremore IT June 21/06
" "	Copy of rental contract and report filed by John Viets
" 14 "	amended answer filed A.C. Brewster Atty for Dfdts
" 21 "	Case called at Claremore, Attys for both parties present neither Ptf nor Dfdts appeared. See Memo in file
July 24 1906	Judgment rendered in favor of Plaintiff both parties s so notified and a copy of the Judgment sent to each of them
	Defendant given 10 day[sic] from date of Judgments with in which to vacate the premises
Aug 22 1906	Richard F West instructed to place pltf in possession at once and

Cherokee Intruder Cases 1901 - 1909

	make report to this office.
Aug 26, 1906	Halin[sic] Beck writes that Intruders will move off of Rutherford Beck's place
Sept 1 1906	US. Ind Policeman Richard F. West reports that he placed Pltf in possession of allottment[sic] of his wards, Aug 23 1906
Sept 5 1906	Letters of Gdnship ret^d to pltf and case dismissed
	<u>Dismissed</u>

(Filed)	(No.)	(Allottee)	(Intruder)
May 5th 1906	779	Pearl M. Miller Starr Vinita I.T. Mr. McCullough Atty Vanita[sic] In. Ty.	P.J. Lawless Dawes I.T. Seymour Riddle Atty for Dfdt.

(Action)	
May 5	Homestead Certificate No 5726 and Allotment Certificate No 7899 filed by Plaintiff
" 12	Notice sent to Ptf to serve on Dfdt.
" "	Referred to John Viets for investigation
" 18	Com^r reports no contest pending
" 25	Proof of Service returned
June 7/06	Case set for hearing at Claremore IT June 21/06
" 7	Report of John Viets filed see report in file
June 21/06	Case called at Claremore neither party appeared
June ~~21~~ 19	Answer filed by P.J. Lawless
July 17 1906	Ptf and Dfdt are both requested to advise this office of the nature of the case that is pending before the Master in Chancery at Vinita (as per answer of PJ Lawless)
Aug 8 1906	Case set for hearing at Vanita[sic] I.Ty. Aug 22 -1906 All parties notified.
Aug 22 1906	Case Called at Vanita I.Ty. Answer filed by Atty for dft. ~~Mr Ri~~ Dfdt being present and testimony taken. Pltf appeared & her testimony taken.
Sept 27 1906	Judgment[sic] rendered in favor of plntf & dfndt given ten days in which to vacate, otherwise orders will issue to remove him.
Oct 3 1906	Plntf states that her contest was decided against dfndt Lawless & asks if he (L)can remove improvements
Oct 15 1906	Plntf advised that redress is in US Court
Jany 22 1907	Referred to Robt R. Bennett for investigation
Feby 4 1907	Robt R. Bennett encloses request for dismissal.
Feb 7 1907	Case dismissed & certificates Nos 7899 & 5726 returned.

Cherokee Intruder Cases 1901 - 1909

(Filed)	(No.)	(Allottee)	(Intruder)
May 7th 1906	780	Emeline Green	W<u>m</u> Campbell
		Vera I.T.	Vera I.T.

(Action)

May 7	Homestead Certificate No 13687 and Allotment certificate No 17731 filed by Plaintiff
" 12	Notice sent to Ptf to serve on Dfdt.
" "	Referred to John Viets for investigation
" 18[sic]	
" 23	Com<u>r</u> reports no contest pending
" 26	John Crittenden appeared in this office and reported that Jane Philip Campbell the wife of the alleged Intruder in this case is a claimant for citizenship as a Cherokee Freedman
" 26	Com<u>r</u> asked to report as citizenship status of ~~citizenship~~ of Dfdt.
June 1st	Proof of Service returned date May 29 1906
" 7/06	Case set for hearing at Claremore IT June 21/06
" 21 1906	Case called at Claremore Ptf appears and her evidence taken. Dfdt did not appear
June 22 "	Dfdt. appeared and stated he had no interest in land, and was requested to surrender possession at once
July 10	Report of Com<u>r</u> filed. Ptf requested to advise this office if possession has been given her.
Jany 22 ~~July~~ 16 1907	Referred to Robt R. Bennett for investigation
Feby 10, 1907	Robt R. Bennett encloses request for dismissal.
Feby 25, 1907	Certificate returned & case dismissed

(Filed)	(No.)	(Allottee)	(Intruder)
May 8	781	William Isreal	Rev. N.L. Nielson
		Oaks I.T.	Oaks I.T.

(Action)

May 8	Homestead Certificate No 27507 and Allotment certificate No 39834 filed by Plaintiff
" "	Surveyor's affidavit filed by Ptf.
" 12	Notice sent to Plaintiff to serve on Dfdt
" 12	Referred to John Viets for investigation
" 23	Defendant appeared in person and Plaintiff was advised that no further Action would be taken by this office until boundry[sic] lines are established by a Gov't Surveyor
May 21	Proof of Service returned dated 5/16 1906
" 18	Com<u>r</u> reports no contest pending
" 24	Defendant appeared in in[sic] person at this office and stated that the

Cherokee Intruder Cases 1901 - 1909

	Mission is located on land segregated by the Com^r for mission purposes and the Plaintiff was requested to advise this office if he thinks it advisable to suspend action until the exterior boundry of the segregation are established and approved by the Government
June 4	Report of John Viets filed with which he submits copy of survey made by Com^r
Jan 8 08	Case dismissed by order of W.W.B.
May 28 09	Case referred to Cusey for investigation

(Filed)	(No.)	(Allottee)	(Intruder)
May 11th 1906	782	Betsy Hildebrand Tahlequah I.T.	Calley Smith Watson I.T.

(Action)
May 11   Certificate of Allotment No 12005 and Certificate
of Homestead   "   "   9789 filed by Dfdt
"   12   Notice sent to Plaintiff to serve on Dfdt
"   "   Referred to Eldon Lowe for investigation
"   17   Proof of Service returned dated May 15, 06
"   18   Com^r reports no contest pending
June 7   Case set for hearing at Claremore IT June 21/06
"   11   Eldon Lowe filed report and rental contract
"   21 1906   Case called at Claremore neither party appeared
"   25 "   Case dismissed as Ptf states that the matter has been settled to her satisfaction
7/3   Certificates returned to Plaintiff
Dismissed

(Filed)	(No.)	(Allottee)	(Intruder)
May 10	783 No 33635	Chas. J. Lynch c/o Starr and Patton Attys Vinita I.T.	Addie Choteau Kansas I.T.

(Action)
May 10   Certificate of homestead filed by Plaintiff
"   14   Notice sent to Plaintiff to serve on Dfdt
"   "   Referred to John Viets for investigation
June 4   Proof of service returned dated 6/1/06
"   7   Case set for hearing at Claremore IT June 22/06
"   22   Case called at Claremore neither party appeared
July 14 1906   Certificate returned to Ptf upon his request and Ptf was requested to advise this office if satisfactory settlement has been made
August 3 "   Defendant advised that case will again be set for hearing

Cherokee Intruder Cases 1901 - 1909

" 8 "   Case set for hearing at Vanita[sic] I.Ty. Aug 22-1906 All parties notified
Aug 22 1906 Case called at Vanita Ind Ty neither party present
Nov 3 1906   Case set for hearing at Claremore I.Ty Nov 19 1906 All notified
Nov 19 1906 Case called at Claremore. No appearance by either party.
Jany 22 1907 Referred to Robt R. Bennett for investigation.
Mch 12 1907 Starr & Patton Atty, enclose request for dismissal.
Mch 15 1907 In view of above, case dismissed
Mch 23, 1907 Robt R. Bennett enclosed request for dismissal.

(Filed)	(No.)	(Allottee)		(Intruder)
May 19 1906	784	D M Marrs for Amanda O. (Wf) and Legal Gdn of David M, Jr., Barney and W^m C Marrs Vinita I.T.	vs	John or Jack Sanders Miles I.T. A.S. McRea[sic] Atty Muskogee I.T.
		(Action)		

May 17   Certificates exhibited
" "   Letters of Gdnship filed by Plaintiff
June 4   Notice sent to Ptf to serve on Dfdts
" 8   Case set for hearing at Claremore IT June 22/06
" 7   Proof is service returned dated June 6/06
" 11 Com^r reports no contests pending
" 14 Com^r reports that a motion for review of the citizenship case of Dfdt has been filed
" 22 Dfdt's Atty states that additional motion has been filed with Hon Secy of the Interior, a copy of which is on file in this case.
June 14 Com^r reports that a motion for review in the citizenship case of the Dfdt is pending
       Case is therefore dismissed Letters of Gdnship returned to Plaintiff
                                                   Dismissed

(Filed)	(No.)	(Allottee)	(Intruder)
April 27 1906	785	Mary Buckner 401 N Cherokee Street Muskogee IT	vs Ellis C Harlin
		(Action)	

May 18   Notice sent to Ptf to serve on Dfdts
" 14   Com^r reports no contests pending
" 21   Dfdts state ~~they~~ he has surrendered possession
June 6   Plaintiff asked to advise this office if she is now in possession

Cherokee Intruder Cases 1901 - 1909

Jany 22 1907   Referred to R.R. Bennett for investigation
Jany 24 1907   C.E. Holderman of Muskogee appeared at office in Muskogee &
               stated Dfndt surrendered possession to plntf
               who delivered possession to him (Holderman)
                                                                    Dismissed
Feby 4 1907   Robt R. Bennett enclosed request for dismissal.
Feby 16 1907   Plntf notified case dismissed

(Filed)	(No.)	(Allottee)	(Intruder)
May 18 1906	786	J.W. Ferguson Gdn. of Mary Sanders Whitmire IT	vs A.P. Terrell Collinsville
		(Action)	

May 18   Letters of Gdnship filed by Plaintiff
"   18   Certificates Nos 27054 and 39208 filed
June 4   Notice sent to Ptf to serve on Dfdts
"   8   Case set for hearing at Claremore IT June 22/06
"   22   Copy of Lease contract filed by Dfdt
"   "   Case called at Claremore Dfdt was present and his evidence was taken
         Plaintiff did not appear. Dfdt stated that he was willing to surrender
         possession at any time that the Plaintiff might demand same
                           returned
July 16 " Certificates ~~referred~~ to L.S. Saunders in person
June 16 " Com^r reports no contest pending
July 9 " Ptf requested to take possession and advise this office when he has done so
"   18 " Plaintiff states that he is now in possession of the Allotment of Mary
          Saunders
          Letters of Gdnship returned and case dismissed
                                                                    Dismissed

(Filed)	(No.)	(Allottee)	(Intruder)
May 17 1906	787	Geo W. Burr, Nat'l Gdn of Alexander Burr Vera I.T.	John Paxton Vera I.T. W.W. Hadley

(Note: continuation from the end of this case)   Vera I.T.
June 22 07   Plff again asks possession stating contest is settled
June 28 07   New notice in duplicate sent plff.
"   "   "   Com^r asked to report
June 29 07   Case set for Vinita, I.T. July 11 1907
July 11 07   Records of U.S. Court Vinita show that Geo. W. Burr was appointed

Cherokee Intruder Cases 1901 - 1909

" " "	Gdn of Alexander Burr Aug. 11/05 Case called, plaintiff appeared and his evidence taken No appearance by defendant.
July 6 07	Ans filed by John Paxton today
July 8/07	Com reports a portion of land not in contest
July 12 -07	defdt appeared today and was informed that his evidence would be taken on 7/19/05 Dfdt informed that he must notify his own witness
July 12 -07	J. George Wright requested that this matter be carefully investigated and that he be advised before Action is taken
July 23 -07	Plff desires possession of land
Aug 27 '07	Com^r advised that WW Hadley has been given 30 days within which to appeal from decision of Com^r requests Action witheld[sic] All parties notified

(Action)

May 25	Com^r reports a portion of the land in contest Case not docketed as to that portion
June 1	Notice sent to Plaintiff to serve on Dfdt
" "	Referred to Eldon Lowe
" 8	Case set for hearing at Claremore IT June 22/06
" 7	Proof of service returned dated June 6/06
" 11	Answer filed
" 13	W.W. Hadley appeared at this office in person and stated that he is the real Defendant and that this matter had been heard and adjusted at a former date. Plaintiff was requested to report.
" 13	W.W. Hadley states he is in possession of 10 acres which is in contest, only
June 22	Case called at Claremore I.T. Both parties appeared and Ptf acknowledged that Dfdts are in possession of only the land which is in contest Case is therefore dismissed

Dismissed

Oct 9 1906	Plntf complains that he cannot get possession of his child's ten acres.
Oct 12 1906	Plntf advised that case was dismissed because of contest & if contest is now settled he may file complaint.
Feby 28 1907	Plntf again asks possession.
Mch 8 1907	Com^r asked to report
30 07	Pltf advised that no further Action will be taken in this matter until 30 days have elapsed or longer as per Com report

(Note: continued at the beginning of this case)

Cherokee Intruder Cases 1901 - 1909

(Filed)	(No.)	(Allottee)	(Intruder)
May 25 1906	788	Lucinda Leader Gdn of David Leader Texanna I.T.	E.E. Williams Texanna I.T.

(Action)	
May 26	Homestead Certificate No 24087 and Allotment Certificate No 34337 filed by Ptf.
June 2	Notice sent to Ptf to serve on Dfdt.
" "	Referred to Eldon Lowe for investigation
" 11	Proof of Service returned dated June 8/1906
" 12	Com^r reports no contests pending by letter
Aug 9 -06	Second request by letter made to Dfdt to vacate or give reasons
Feby 9, 1907	Case set for hearing at Muskogee ITy. Feb 25 1907 All notified
Feby 25, 1907	Case called at Muskogee I.Ty. No appearance by either party.
Feby 19, 1907	Dfndt advises he has given possession.
Feby 20, 1907	Plntf asks dismissal as case has been settled.
Feby 28 1907	Certificates ret'd & case dismissed.

(Filed)	(No.)	(Allottee)	(Intruder)
May 25 1906	789	Emma M. Hopkins c/o Starr and Patton Attys Vinita I.T.	Josie A. Slaughter Bartlesville I.T.

(Note: continuation from the end of this case)

May 2 1907	Judgment rendered in favor of plntf Dfndt given ten days in which to vacate
May 6 1907	Attys for plntf requested to advise if possession is given within specified time
May 11 1907	A.S. McRea[sic] Atty for dfndt serves notice that application for injunction will be heard in the United States Court May 13th 07 at Vinita I.T. See letter in file #991
May 15 1907	Notice served by Atty for Dfndt that application for injunction will be heard at Vinita I.T. May 18[sic] 1907 - at 9 am - See file #991
May 22 1907	Asst U.S. Atty advises injunction granted by U.S. Court at Vinita I.T. See letter file #991
May 23 1907	Restraining order & summons in equity rec'd See file #991
May 24 1907	Com asked if lands in contest & if certificates have been issued
June 29 07	Injunction dissolved
July 6 07	Plff and deft advised of dissolution of injunction
" " "	Instructions issued to Capt John C. west
July 17 07	Capt West encloses agreement of the Slaughters and Wm Gannon to vacate the land, and reports on July 25 that he placed Allottee in possession
August 2 07	Plff advised of report of Capt West and Case Dismissed

26

Cherokee Intruder Cases 1901 - 1909

(Action)

May 25	A copy of the decision of the Secy in a cotest[sic] case, effecting the citizenship of Dfdt filed by Ptf.
June 2	Notice sent to Ptf to serve on Dfdt
" "	Referred to Eldon Lowe for investigation
" 8	Case set for hearing at Claremore I.T. June 22/06
" 12	Com^r reports no contests pending
" 21	Telegram from Agent in which he states that motion for review in the citizenship case of Josie A Slaughter has been filed with Com^r
June 22	Case called at Claremore neither party appear
June 21 1906	Case dismissed as motion to review citizenship of Dfdt is pending Certificates returned to Plaintiff
	Dismissed
Feby 21, 1907	Starr & Patton Atty file motion to reinstate case as Com^r has advised plntf that dfndt denied citizenship
Feby 26 1907	Notices sent c/o Starr & Patton to serve on Josie A Slaughter
Mch 8 1907	Proof of service returned dated March 2, 1907
Mch 11 1907	Dfndt ans & (?) for time. Has Atty in Washington to see President.
Mch 18 1907	Com^r asked to report as to citizenship of Josie A Slaughter
Mch 19 1907	Com^r reports motion for review denied Feby 12, 1906
Mch 20 1907	Dfndt advised to remove This case to be set for hearing.
Apr 6 1907	Case set for hearing at Claremore, I.Ty. Apr 8, 1907
Apr 8, 1907	Case called at Claremore I.Ty. All parties present & testimony taken. See Stenographers notes for motion of dfndt by Atty A.S. McRhea Claims claimant as Cherokee Freedman before Court of Claims now.

(Note: continued at the beginning of this case)

(Filed)	(No.)	(Allottee)	(Intruder)
May 25 1906	790	Jacob Foreman Nat Gdn. for Robby Foreman Santown[sic] I.T.	Emma Wells Santown[sic] I.T.

(Action)

May 25	Certificate of Allotment No 16974
June 2	Notice sent to Plaintiff to serve on Dfdt
" "	Referred to Eldon Lowe for investigation
" 9	Proof of Service returned dated June 8th
" 11	Answer file
" 12	Com^r reports no contests pending
Aug 9 06	Case set for hearing at Muskogee ITy. Aug 17 -06 at 10-A.M.
" "	All parties present

Cherokee Intruder Cases 1901 - 1909

Aug 17 1906 Case called & all parties present. Testimony taken.
It developed that land involved was 3 1/2 acres more or less and agreement was reach in presence of Mr. Bennett that Dfdt should remain in possession until present crop ~~was~~ ^{is} matured & got hired. Dfdt paying to pltf one third of corn & 1/4 of cotton at which time Dfdt is to move her fence back on line & surrender possession of land in controversy.

Case dismissed

(Filed)	(No.)	(Allottee)	(Intruder)
May 11 1906	791	Rachel Christie Tahlequah, I.T.	Robt L. Owen Muskogee I.T.
(Action)			

May 18 Com^r reports no contest pending
June 2 Notice sent to Ptf to serve on Dfdt
"   2 Referred to John Viets for investigation
" 23 Proof of Service returned dated June 18/1906
July 12 1906 Answer filed by R L Owen in which he states that he is in possession by virtue of a Lease contract
" 13 " Ptf. requested to furnish this office with more data
Nov 14 1906 Case set for hearing at Muskogee ITy Nov 28, 1906
Nov 28 1906 Case called. No appearance by either party
Feby 9 1907 Case set for hearing at Muskogee ITy Feby 25 1907
Feby 25 1907 Case called. No appearance by either party
Apr 6 1907 Referred to Robt R. Bennett
Jan 8 1908 Case dismissed by order of W.W.B.

(Filed)	(No.)	(Allottee)	(Intruder)
May 8$^{\underline{th}}$ 1906	792	Charles M. Ross Tahlequah I.T.	vs John McDonald Roland I.T.
(Action)			

May 15 Com^r reports that Dfdt is a rejected Freedman and that there are no contests pending
June 2 Notice sent to Ptf to serve on Dfdt.
"   " Referred to John Viets for investigation
"   " This case dismissed and papers transferred to Case 777.

Dismissed

Cherokee Intruder Cases 1901 - 1909

(Filed)	(No.)	(Allottee)	(Intruder)
(No date given.)	793	Frank R. Akins for self and Robt L Akins Dutch Mills Ark	vs L N Kendrix Pryor Creek I.T. A C Brewster Atty Pryor Creek T.J.P. Thompson Salina I.T.
(Note: continuation from the end of this case)			
Feb 4 1907	Robt. R. Bennett reports dfndt not in possession		
Feby 18 1907	Plntf advised to go into possession & case dismissed		

(Action)
May 21   Certificates Nos 28386, 20405 and 28280 filed by Ptfs.
June 2   Notice sent to Ptf to serve on Dfdts
"   "   Referred to John Viets for investigation
"   8 1906 Case set for hearing at Claremore I.T. June 22/'06
June 12   Com{r} reports no contest pending
"   20   Atty for Dfdt appeared and filed answer in which ~~they~~ ^he^ states that Dfdt is not nor never has been in possession of the land described in the complaint and claims no right thereto
"   22   Case called at Claremore neither party appeared
July 3/06 Proof of service returned
Answer filed by T.J.C. Thompson and he was mad a party defendant
" 23 1906 Proof of Service returned dated July 24 1906
" 23 1906 (This line was left blank)
Aug 8 1906 Case set for hearing at Vanita[sic] I.Ty Aug 22 -1906
All parties notified
Aug 15 1906 Mr. A.C. Brewster Atty for L.N. Kendrix, notified by this office that it will not be nescessary[sic] to appear at Vanita ITy Aug 22 -1906
Aug 18 1906 T.J.C. Thompson writes that ~~he~~ pltf may have land in question.
Aug 22 "   Case called at Vanita I.Ty. neither party present
Aug 30 1906 Pltf directed to take to take possession of allotment[sic].
Sept 17 1906 Pltf requests return of allottment[sic] certificates
" 25 1906 As per request allotment certificates of F R & R L Akins returned
Nov 9 1906 plntf requested to advise if he is in possession
Jany 22 1907 Referred to Robt R. Bennett for investigation.
(Note: continued at the beginning of this case)

Cherokee Intruder Cases 1901 - 1909

(Filed)	(No.)	(Allottee)	(Intruder)
May 10 1906	794	Chas Waters Gdn of vs Jennie, Annie and W<u>m</u> Waters c/o Watts and Curtis Attys Sallisaw I.T.	Silas Edwards Maple I.T.
(Action)			

May 21   Letters of Gdnship and certificates Nos 8923, 11000, 8924, 11101, 8925 and 1102 filed
June 2 1906 Notice sent to Plaintiff to serve on Dfdt.
"   "   "   Referred to John Viets for investigation
"   "   "   Com<u>r</u> reports no contests pending
" 20 "   Proof of Service returned dated June 16 1906
" 18 "   Answer filed by Dfdt
" 26 "   Case dismissed upon request of Attys for Ptf. Certificates and Letters of Gdnship returned
July 5 "   Ptf Ack receipt of certificates and Letters of Gdnship
                                                                                                     Dismissed.

(Filed)	(No.)	(Allottee)	(Intruder)
May 24 1906	795	Lizzie Swimmer Stilwell I.T.	A.P. Terrell Collinsville I.T.
(Action)			

June 6   Com<u>r</u> reports no contest pending
" 15   Notice sent to Ptf to serve on Dfdt
July 18 1906 Proof of Service returned and case dismissed
               Plaintiff states she is in possession of her allotment
                                                                                          Dismissed

(Filed)	(No.)	(Allottee)	(Intruder)
May 25 1906	796	Philo H. Harris Green Brier I.T.	Jess Vann Lyncy I.T. Starr and Patton Attys Vinita I.T.
(Action)			

June 5   Com<u>r</u> reports no contests pending
July 2   Proof of Service returned dated June 27 1906
" 7   Answer filed in which it is stated that Dfdt has an application
         for citizenship as a Cherokee Freedman pending before Com<u>r</u>

Cherokee Intruder Cases 1901 - 1909

"   10   Com^r requested to report
"   14   Com^r advise that he can not report as to citizenship of Jesse Vann as it is not known which Jesse Vann is referred to
July 6 "[sic] Starr and Patton advise that they have filed motion for review
          in citizenship case of Jesse Vann
"   19   "   Status of case given to Plaintiff
"   20   "   Com^r given data by which it is believed he will be able to distinguish between the Jesse Vann in this case and the others whose names appear upon his records
Aug 8 1906   Case set for hearing at Vanita[sic] I.Ty. Aug 22 1906
          Both parties notified
July 30 1906   Com^r advises that application of Jesse Vann & children for enrollment as Cherokee Freedmen, pending in his office
Aug 20 "   In view of above case is this day dismissed and parties notified not to appear in Vanita[sic] I.Ty Aug 22 1906

                                                              Dismissed

(Filed)	(No.)	(Allottee)	(Intruder)
June 7 1906	797	William & Nancy Inlow Grove I.T.	vs Chas Norwood and A. E. Holland Grove I.T.

(Action)
June 7   Certificates Nos 35693, 58649, 58644 and 35692 filed by Plaintiff, allso[sic] plat of land
"   15   Notice sent to Ptf to serve on Dfdts
"   20   Com^r reports a contest pending on a portion of the land Case dismissed as to that portion
"   22   Answer filed by A.E. Holland
"   "   Proof of Service returned dated June 18 1906
August 3 1906   Defendant requested to advise this office if they are in possession of any of the land of W^m and Nancy Inlow which is not involved in contest
Aug 8 1906   Case set for hearing before U.S. Ind Agt at Vanita[sic] I Ty Aug 22nd 1906 All parties notified
Aug 22 1906   Case called at Vanita ITy All parties present Atty Davenport, for dft, showed that dfdt was occupying no lands save those in contest and case dismissed
Dismissed

Cherokee Intruder Cases 1901 - 1909

(Filed)	(No.)	(Allottee)	(Intruder)
June 4 1906	798	Caldonie E Anible Mother of Florence M Tweedle Van Buren Ark.	vs Chas, Bud, and Leonidas R. Johnson
		(Action)	

June 4   Certificate No 42763
" 6   Notice sent to Ptf to serve on Defendant
" 20   Com^r reports no contest pending
" 26   Proof of service returned dated June 19th 1906
" 23   Answer filed by L R Johnson
Aug 8 1906   Case set for hearing at Vanita I.Ty. Aug 22 1906   Both parties notified
Aug 22 1906   Case called at Vanita, I.Ty neither party present
Nov 6 1906   Case set for hearing at Claremore I.Ty. Nov 19 1906 All notified
Nov 19 1906   Case called at Claremore. No appearance by either party.
Jany 22 1907   Referred to Robt R. Bennett for investigation
Jany 22, 1907 Com^r asked to report
Jany 28 1907   Com^r advises no contest
Oct 26 1906   Plntf requests return of certificates.
Feby 27 1907   Robt R Bennett encloses request for dismissal
Mch 7 1907   Certificates returned & case dismissed

(Filed)	(No.)	(Allottee)	(Intruder)
June 14 1906	799	Dora Beck natural guardian of Amy Beck c/o Robertson, King & Kean Attys Muskogee I.T.	vs E. M. Brown Talala I.T.
		(Action)	

June 14 06   Certificates Nos 39643 & 43327
June 20 06   Notice sent to plaintiff to serve on defendant
June 27 06   Commission reports no contest pending
July 5 06   Proof of service returned dated July 2 -06
June 27 06   E.M. Brown filed answer
July 5 06   Case set for hearing at Muskogee I.T. July 27 1906
" 27 "   Case called at Muskogee both parties present evidence
             taken Ex A filed by Plaintiff
Aug 7 06   Judgement[sic] rendered in favor of plaintiff
             both parties so notified & copy of Judgment mailed to both parties
             Defendant given ten days in which to vacate.
Sept 5 1906   Tom B. French U.S. Ind Policeman, instructed to place Dora Beck
             in possession & report to this office.

Cherokee Intruder Cases 1901 - 1909

" 5	Pltf Dora Beck requested to be at Talala I.Ty. to meet Policeman French Friday Sept 7 1906 & there take possession of allottment[sic] of Amy Beck	
Sept 10 1906	Policeman French reports having placed Pltf Amy Beck in possession of her allottment Sept 8" 1906	
Sept 13 1906	Case dismissed and allottments Certificates Nos 43327 & Homestead 29643 ret to pltf	
		Dismissed

(Filed)	(No.)	(Allottee)		(Intruder)
June 1 1906	800	Dollie E Chamberlin	vs	Josie A Slaughter
		c/o Starr and Patton Attys		Dewey, I.T.

(Note: continuation from the end of this case)   Vinita

May 11 1907	A.S. McRea[sic] Atty for dfndt serves notice that an application for injunction will be heard in the U.S. Court May 13 -07 at Vinita I.T. See letter in file #991
May 15 1907	Notice served by Atty for dfndt that application for injunction will be heard at Vinita I.T. May 18th 1907 - See file #991
May 22 1907	Asst U.S. Atty advises injunction granted by Court at Vinita I.T. See letter file #991
May 23 1907	Restraining order & summons in equity rec'd See file #991
May 25 1907	Certificates of Allotment #13720 sent to O.L. Rider Asst U.S. Atty Vinita I.T. See letter in #991
June 10 07	Cert. returned to WW.B. at Vinita upon trial of injunction suit
June 29 07	Injunction dissolved
July 6 07	Plff and deft advised of dissolution of injunction
July 6 07	Instructions issued to Capt Jno C West
July 17 07	Capt West encloses agreement of the Slaughters to vacate allotment
July 25 07	Capt West reports placing Allottee in possession
Aug 2 07	Allotment Cert 13720 returned to plff and Case Dismissed
	(Action)
June 20 06	Notice sent to plaintiff to serve on defendant
June 1 06	Certificate No 13720
" 4 06	Commission asked if any contest is pending
Aug 8 06	Case set for hearing at Vanita ITy Aug 22 -1906 All parties notified
Aug 20 1906	A letter in file from Comr to Soper, Huckleberry & Owens, which states that Josie A. Slaughter has filed a motion for rehearing of her application for enrollment which motion is now under advisement. Under above circumstances, Comr will take no Action towards perfecting title to land involved.
Aug 21 1906	Case called at Vanita ITy Aug 21 -1906. Pltf appeared in person and

Cherokee Intruder Cases 1901 - 1909

	was advised that no Action would be taken until citizenship case of Dfdt is settled
Mch 1 1907	Starr & Patton Attys Vinita I.T. file motion for re-hearing on behalf of plntf.
Mch 4 1907	In compliance with above, notice in duplicate mailed to plntf for service on dfndt
Mch 4 1907	Com^r asked as to contest & citizenship of Josie A Slaughter
Mch 16 1907	Proof of service returned, dated Mch 14, 1907
Mch 18 1907	Com^r advises no contest, also Josie A Slaughter denied citizenship Mch 2, 1906.
	Motion for rehearing denied 2/12/07
Mch 26 1907	Case set for hearing at Claremore, I.Ty. Apr 8, 1907
Apr 8, 1907	Case called at Claremore, I.Ty. Plntf did not appear.
	Husband of dfndt present & testimony taken.
	J.C. Starr Atty, appeared for plntf. Atty A.S. McRhea for dfndt.
	See motion of Dfdnt's Atty. Pending at Court of Claims as Cherokee Freedman
May 1 1907	Judgment rendered in favor plntf - Dfndt given ten days in which to vacate -

(Note: continued at the beginning of this case)

(Filed)	(No.)	(Allottee)	(Intruder)
July 9 1906	801	Martin Ross	Geo Swan
		Vian I.T.	Vian I.T.
		(Action)	
June 5 1906	Report of Com^r filed		
July 11 "	Notice sent to Ptf to serve on Dfdt.		
" 14 "	Proof of Service returned dated July 13 1906		
" 16 "	Answer filed by Dfdt		
Aug 17 1906	Pltf requests that he be placed in possession of his 1 1/4 acres		
Aug 21 1906	Tandy W Adair U.S.I. Policeman of Salisaw[sic] I.Ty instructed to place pltf in possession of land in question		
Aug 27 1906	Tandy W Adair reports that he placed pltf in possession.		
Aug 30 1906	Case dismissed & pltf so notified.		
			Dismissed.

Cherokee Intruder Cases 1901 - 1909

(Filed)	(No.)	(Allottee)	(Intruder)
June 12 1906	802	William R. Johnson	vs Yancy Vinson
(Note: continuation from the end of this case)		Roland I.T.	Roland I.T.
Feby 14 1907		Yancy Vinson letter to Secy in file	
Feby 20 1907		" " advised	

(Action)	
June 23 06	Notice sent plaintiff to serve on defendant
" 21 06	Comm. advises no contest
" 29 06	Proof of service returned dated June 28 -06
July 10 "	Letter from ~~Plaintiff~~ Dfdt. filed
Aug 1st "	Status of case furnished Plaintiff
Aug 7 -06	Case set set[sic] for hearing at Muskogee I.Ty. Aug 17 -1906
Aug 1 1906	Pltf advised, in answer to inquiry, as to status of case.
Aug 17 1906	Case called. Pltf failed to appear. Dfdt present and testimony taken. Dfdt advised that he has no right to land in controversy and he agreed to make satisfactory arrangements with pltf.
Aug 20 1906	Pltf requested to advise this office if satisfactory settlement has been made with dft.
Aug 21 1906	Dfdt, Yancy Vinson requests that this case be held up until his application for citizenship as Cherokee Freedman be dicided[sic]
Aug 23 1906	Receipt of above act.
Aug 28 1906	Pltf advises that can get Vinson to give possession and asks that this office proceed to place him in possession
Aug 31 1906	Pltf advised that the case will be held in abeyance.
" 31 1906	Com^r asked if motion is pending to reopen citizenship of Yancy Vinson
Sept 7 1906	Judgement[sic] rendered in favor of plntf and copy same sent to each
Sept 29 1906	U.S. Policeman instructed to place Allottee in possession
Oct 11 1906	Tandy W. Adair, USIP reports that he placed plntf in possession
	Dismissed.
(Note: continued at the beginning of this case)	

(Filed)	(No.)	(Allottee)	(Intruder)
June 18 1906	803	W. H. Fields, natural gdn Howard Fields & W^m E Fields Vinita I.T.	vs Mrs. Eluja[sic] Hardrick Vinita I.T. Starr and Patton Atty Vinita

(Action)	
June 18 06	Certificate Nos. 49585, 32432, 49583 32431
" 23 06	Notice sent plaintiff to serve on defendant
" 23 06	Comm asked if any contest pending
" 29 06	" reports no contest

35

Cherokee Intruder Cases 1901 - 1909

July 6	"	Proof of Service returned dated July 4 1906
" "	"	Attys for Ptf state that contest has been filed with Com^r
" 10	"	Com^r requested to report
" 14	"	Com^r reports a portion of the land in contest and citizenship of Dfdt pending
		Case is therefore dismissed and certificates dismissed[sic]
		Dismissed

May 10 *(Filed)*	*(No.)*	*(Allottee)*	*(Intruder)*
~~June 12~~ 1906	804	R.W. Hines, administrator vs of the estate of John Fogg dc'd. c/o Watts & Curtis Atty Sallisaw I.T.	Watt Mayes Pryor Creek Ned Campbell Atty Pryor Creek I.T.
		(Action)	
June 12 1906		Complaints & Gdnship papers filed	
June 22 06		Com reports no contest	
" 30 06		Notice sent plaintiff to serve on defendant	
July 14 "		Proof of Service returned dated July 9th 1906	
" 14		Answer filed by dfdt	
Aug 8		Case set for hearing at Vanita ITy. Aug 23-06. All parties notified	
Aug 14 1906		In reply to request of Watts & Curtis Atty's for pltf asking that case be heard in Muskogee, same are notified that no change will be made	
Aug 23 1906		Case called at Vanita ITy. Pltf and Atty present. No appearance by dfdt, but represented by Atty Ned Campbell Atty for pltf introduces letters of Administratorship[sic] as Exhibit "A" also order of U.S. Court Exhibit "B". Atty for dfdt offers in evidence Lease contract from Jno Fogg, dec'd. to Watt Mayes, dfdt. Testimony taken.	
Sept 26 1906		Judgement[sic] rendered in favor of defendant and copy of same mailed to both parties. Case Dismissed	

(Filed)	*(No.)*	*(Allottee)*	*(Intruder)*
June 16 1906	805	Katie Downing *(Names Illegible)* Attys Tahlequah I.T.	John F McClellan Claremore I.T.
		(Action)	
June 23 06		Com reports no contest	
" 30 06		Notice sent plaintiff to serve on defendant	
Aug 9 06		Case set for hearing at Vanita ITy Aug 23-06 All parties notified	
Aug 23 1906		Case called at Vinita I.Ty. neither party appeared	

Cherokee Intruder Cases 1901 - 1909

Aug 24 1906	Attys for pltf file request for dismissal of case, as satisfactory settlement has been made
Aug 28 1906	As per request, case dismissed.
	<div align="right">Dismissed</div>

(Filed)	(No.)	(Allottee)	(Intruder)
June 11 1906	806	Rebecca A. Sanders Cedar, I.T.	Elija Morris Cedar, I.T.

(Action)

June 23 06	Com reports no contest
" 30 06	Notice sent plaintiff to serve on defendant
July 10 "	Proof [sic] Service returned dated July 5 1906
Aug 8 "	Case set for hearing at Vanita ITy. Aug 23 -06 All parties notified
Aug 22 1906	Case called at Vanita I.Ty. Both parties appeared evidence heard but not copied. Case dismissed. Just question of line between filings. Instructed to run lines & set fence on same
	<div align="right">Dismissed</div>

INTRUDER CASE NO. 807
Cherokee NATION

Plaintiff	Geo Meeker Gdn of Mary Hilderbrand Bragg I.T.	Atty.	
	Versus		
Defendant	M.A. Willis Campbell I.T.	Atty.	Hutchings and Murphy Muskogee

Complaint filed June 19 1906 **Commissioner Reports** June 28 1906 **No Contest. Notice Sent** July 3 1906

~~June~~ ~~July~~ 29	1906	Letters of Gdnship and copy of contract filed by Plaintiff
" 16	"	Proof of Service returned dated July 10 1906
" 12	"	Dfdt Willis states he will appear before agent at Muskogee, on July 16th 1906
" 16	"	Defdt and filed answer in which it is set forth that Dfdt is in possession by virtue of a Lease contract executed by Brice Hilderbrand as Legal Gaurdian[sic] of Mary Hilderbrand. A certified copy of the approval of the said Lease contract by the US Court was filed by Dfdts.
" 17	"	Plaintiff advised as to status of case, copy of contract and Letters of Gdnship returned and case dismissed
		<div align="right">Dismissed</div>

37

Cherokee Intruder Cases 1901 - 1909

INTRUDER CASE NO. 808
Cherokee NATION

Plaintiff: Daniel W. Tyner Gdn of Cordelia "   Turley I.T.   **Atty.**

Versus

Defendant: Harve Fenwick   Shiatook I.T.   **Atty.** Robt Smith   Muskogee

Complaint filed July 5 1906   **Commissioner Reports** July 14 1906   **No Contest.**   **Notice Sent** July 9th 1906

July 5 1906	Homestead certificate no 10066 and Allotment certificate no 12390 and Letters of Gaurdianship[sic] filed by Plaintiff
" 16 "	Proof of Service returned dated July 14 1906
" 14 "	Com^r r[sic] *(no other information given)*
" 25 "	Answer filed by Defendant
Aug 9 "	Case set for hearing at Vanita I.Ty. Aug 23 1906 All parties notified
Aug 22 1906	Answer filed by Robert Smith for dfdt in which he states that dfdt is confined to his bed because of sickness & cannot appear but is willing that case be heard and settled on evidence he has already furnished
Aug 23 1906	Case called at Vinita I.Ty neither party appeared
Nov 3 1906	Case set for hearing at Claremore I.Ty. Nov 19 1906 All parties notified.
Nov 19 1906	Case called at Claremore. No appearance by either party
Jany 22 1907	Referred to Robt R Bennett for investigation
Feby 19 1907	Robt R Bennett encloses request for dismissal
Feby 25 1907	Certificate returned & <u>case dismissed</u>

INTRUDER CASE NO. 809
Cherokee NATION

Plaintiff: Geo E Norton Gdn of Jennie Norton   Blunt I.T.   **Atty.**

Versus

Defendant: Dave Willy   Marble I.T.   **Atty.**

Complaint filed July 10 1906   **Commissioner Reports** July 11 1906   **Contest.**   **Notice Sent** July 12 1906

June 21 1906	Certificate of Allotment No 39720 filed by Plaintiff
" 30 "	Proof of Service returned dated July 21 1906
Aug 9 "	Case set for hearing at Vanita I.Ty. Aug 23 -06. All parties notified
Aug 22 "	Case called at Vanita I.Ty. Pltf appeared and his testimony taken.
Aug 25 1906	Letters of guardianship filed by pltf.

Cherokee Intruder Cases 1901 - 1909

Sept 26 1906	Dfdt advised that if he does [sic] surrender land at once, an order will issue to remove him
" 26 1906	Policeman Tandy W. Adair, Sallisaw ITy instructed to place plntf in possession of allottment[sic]
" 26 1906	Pltf instructed to have land surveyed. Allottment[sic] certificates returned.
Oct 4	Tandy W Adair USI Police reports that he placed plntf in possession
" 6	Case dismissed

INTRUDER CASE NO. 810
Cherokee NATION

Plaintiff	James W Dimmons Gdn of David A. Barrick Campbell I.T.	Atty.	Watts and Curtis Sallisaw I.T.	
	Versus			
Defendant	St Louis and Iron Mountain R.R. Ca. Campbell I.T.	Atty.	Oscar L. Miles Genl Atty Ft Smith, Ark.	

Complaint filed July 10 1906 **Commissioner Reports** July 10 1906 **No Contest.** **Notice Sent** July 12 1906

July 10 1906	Letters of Gaurdianship[sic] filed by Plaintiff
" 18 "	Proof of Service returned dated July 16 - 1906
Aug 9 "	Case set for hearing at Vanita I.Ty. Aug 23 -06. All parties notified.
Aug 14 "	In answer to request to change place of hearing, Watts & Curtis Attys for Pltf notified no change in place of hearing
Aug 20 1906	Atty for dft files letter in which he asks thirty days continuance and also states that pltf or party who was at that time in possession has been paid and satisfactory settlement made.
Aug 23 1906	Case called at Vanita ITy. Pltf and attorney Mr. Curtis present Testimony of pltf taken. Allottment[sic] Certificate Nos 31265 & 22247 filed
Sept 21 1906	O.L. Mills[sic] Atty for dfndt notified that the 30 days which was granted him in which to make answer, has passed & he is requested to advise by return mail if he wished to submit any evidence
Sept 17 1906	Attys Watts & Curtis for pltf ask to be advised if any answer or proof has been offered by dfndt
Sept 21 1906	Watts & Curtis advised of letter written to OL Miles 9/21/06 also that they will be advised of reply
" 25 1906	Answer filed by Gen'l Atty Oscar L Miles
Oct 1 1906	Atty Oscar L Miles requested to make satisfactory arrangements with Gdn, or vacate
Jany 22 1907	Referred to Robt R Bennett for investigation
Jany 28 1907	Robt R Bennett reports & encloses request for dismissal signed by Attys
Feby 2 1907	Certificates Nos 22247 - 31265 & case dismissed

Cherokee Intruder Cases 1901 - 1909

INTRUDER CASE NO. 811
Cherokee NATION

Plaintiff: Miss Florence Curry, South West City Mo.
Atty.

Versus

Defendant: Horace Huddleston, South West City Mo.
Atty.

Complaint filed July 13 1906 **Commissioner Reports** July 21 -1906 **No Contest. Notice Sent** July 16 1906

July 13 1906	Certificate of Allotment No 53306 filed by Ptf.
" 23 "	Proof [sic] Service returned July 21, 1906
Aug 9 "	Case set for hearing at Vanita I.Ty. Aug 23/06 All parties notified
Aug 23 "	Case called at Vinita I.Ty. Neither party appeared
Aug 30 "	Pltf notified that no Action will be taken [sic] this office both parties heard.
Nov 3 1906	Case set for hearing at Claremore ITy. Nov 3[sic], 1906. All parties notified,
Nov 19 1906	Case called at Claremore. No appearance by either party.
Jany 18 1907	Case set for hearing at Claremore ITy. Feby 5, 1907 All parties notified.
Feby 5 1907	Case called at Claremore ITy. Neither party appeared.
Feby 11 1907	~~Referred to Robt R. Bennett~~
Feby 4 1907	G.W. Curry advises case has been settled
Feby 11 1907	In view of above certificates returned & <u>case dismissed</u>

INTRUDER CASE NO. 812
Cherokee NATION

Plaintiff: Eli Snell, South West City Mo
Atty.

Versus

Defendant: D. Wilson and Wm Xoley, Dodge I.T.
Atty. Starr and Patton

Complaint filed July 10 1906 **Commissioner Reports** July 21 1906 **No Contest. Notice Sent** July 16 1906

July 10 1906	Certificate of homestead allotment no 32614 and
" 26 "	" " allotment no 50507 filed by Plaintiff
" " "	Answer filed by Dee Wilson
" 25 "	Proof of Service returned dated July 21 1906
Aug 8 "	Case set for hearing at Vanita ITy. Aug 23 -1906. All parties notified
Aug 23 1906	Case called at Vinita I.Ty. All parties present. Dfnt represented by Atty Patton. Satisfactory contract made and case dismissed
	<u>Dismissed</u>

Cherokee Intruder Cases 1901 - 1909

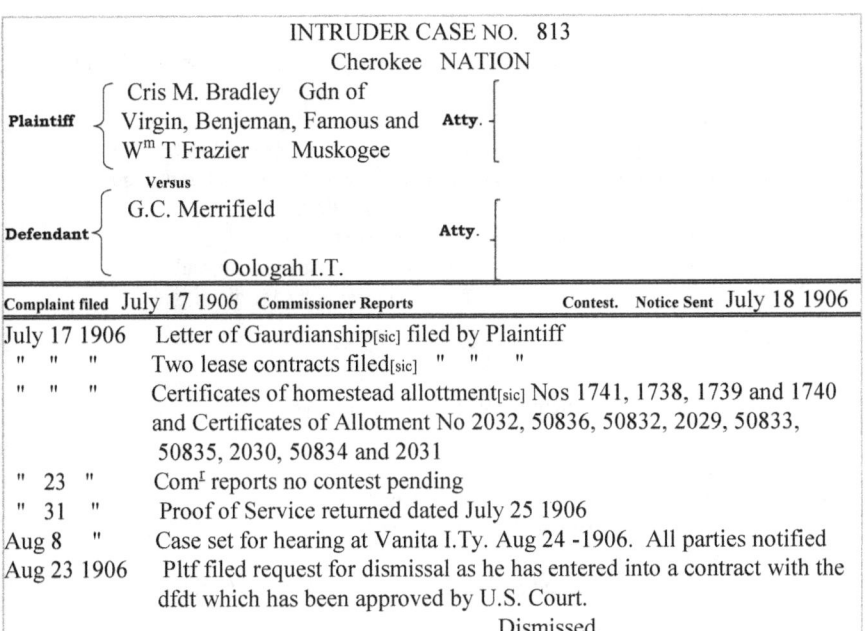

INTRUDER CASE NO. 813
Cherokee NATION

Plaintiff: Cris M. Bradley Gdn of Virgin, Benjeman, Famous and W^m T Frazier   Muskogee
Atty.

Versus

Defendant: G.C. Merrifield   Oologah I.T.
Atty.

Complaint filed July 17 1906 **Commissioner Reports**   **Contest.**   **Notice Sent** July 18 1906

July 17 1906		Letter of Gaurdianship[sic] filed by Plaintiff
" " "		Two lease contracts filed[sic] " " "
" " "		Certificates of homestead allottment[sic] Nos 1741, 1738, 1739 and 1740 and Certificates of Allotment No 2032, 50836, 50832, 2029, 50833, 50835, 2030, 50834 and 2031
" 23 "		Com^r reports no contest pending
" 31 "		Proof of Service returned dated July 25 1906
Aug 8 "		Case set for hearing at Vanita I.Ty. Aug 24 -1906. All parties notified
Aug 23 1906		Pltf filed request for dismissal as he has entered into a contract with the dfdt which has been approved by U.S. Court.

Dismissed.

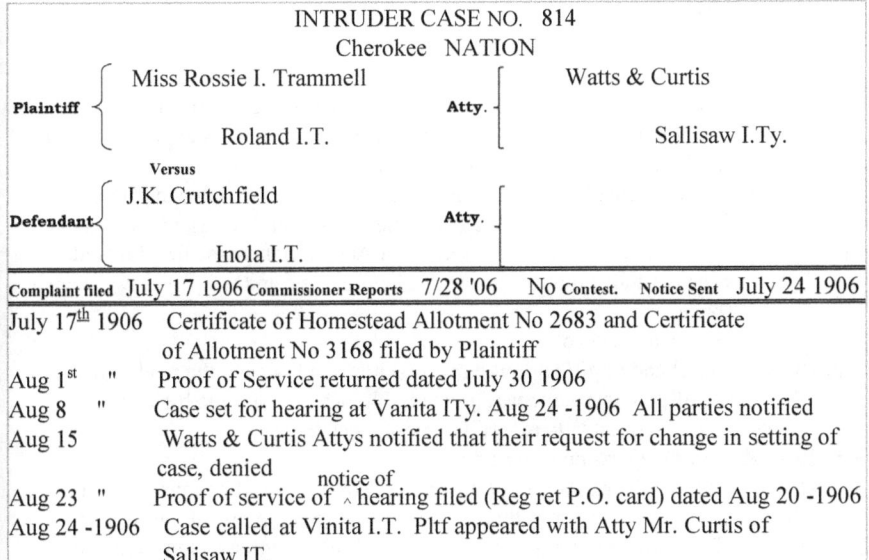

INTRUDER CASE NO. 814
Cherokee NATION

Plaintiff: Miss Rossie I. Trammell   Roland I.T.
Atty. Watts & Curtis   Sallisaw I.Ty.

Versus

Defendant: J.K. Crutchfield   Inola I.T.
Atty.

Complaint filed July 17 1906 **Commissioner Reports** 7/28 '06   **No Contest.**   **Notice Sent** July 24 1906

July 17th 1906	Certificate of Homestead Allotment No 2683 and Certificate of Allotment No 3168 filed by Plaintiff
Aug 1st "	Proof of Service returned dated July 30 1906
Aug 8 "	Case set for hearing at Vanita ITy. Aug 24 -1906 All parties notified
Aug 15	Watts & Curtis Attys notified that their request for change in setting of case, denied
Aug 23 "	Proof of service of notice of hearing filed (Reg ret P.O. card) dated Aug 20 -1906
Aug 24 -1906	Case called at Vinita I.T. Pltf appeared with Atty Mr. Curtis of Salisaw IT.

Cherokee Intruder Cases 1901 - 1909

	Testimony taken.
Sept 25 1906	Judgement[sic] rendered in favor of plntf & copy of same mailed to each party.
	Dfndt given ten days in which to vacate
Nov 9 1906	Plntf requested to advise if possession or settlement has been given.
Nov 17 1906	Atty for plntf advise that plntf is in practical possession of land.
Nov 27 1906	" " " asked to advise more definitely.
Jany 22 1907	Referred to Robt R. Bennett for investigation.
Jany 28 1907	Robt R. Bennett reports & encloses request for dismissal.
Feby 2 1907	Certificates Nos. 3168 - 2683 returned and <u>case dismissed</u>

INTRUDER CASE NO. 815
Cherokee NATION

Plaintiff	Leander Mathews[sic] nee Johnson Braggs I.T.	**Atty.**	
	Versus		
Defendant	Lucy Stantson[sic] and J.T. Elam Keefeton I.T.	**Atty.**	Mr. J. H. Childers Muskogee I.Ty.

Complaint filed July 20 1906 **Commissioner Reports** July 28/06 No **Contest. Notice Sent** July 24 1906

July 20 1906	Certificate of Allotment No 41940 and Certificates of Homestead Allotment No 28858 filed by Plaintiff
Aug 9 1906	Proof of Service rec'd dated Aug 7 -1906
Aug 17 1906	J.T. Elam one of Dfdts, appeared and states that he has made arrangements with pltf to pay rent to him & same is satisfactory.
Aug 20 1906	Lucy Stanton appeared and after having circumstances explained to her, agreed to give possession & not interfere with pltf.
Aug 25 1906	Pltf appeared and asked concerning status of case, same explained and Certificates Nos 41940 & 28858 returned husband JL. Mathes in person
Aug 28 1906	Mr Childers, Atty for dft asked that Action in this case be with held as he is filing a motion for contest before Com^r and will fill answer here at once.
	Same was granted.
Sept 10 1906	Husband of pltf appeared and was informed ~~of~~ as to the request of Atty for dfdt & that same was granted. Pltf advised of same by letter.
" 10 1906	Com^r requested to report if contest is pending
Sept 19 1906	Com^r reports no contest pending.
Sept 25 1906	Mr. Childers, Atty for dfndt, requested to advise if he intends to file contest & answer in this case as per statement in this office Aug 28 -1906.
Sept 29 1906	Pltf notified that this office is now waiting for information from Com^r.

Cherokee Intruder Cases 1901 - 1909

Sept 26 1906	A letter recd from Dpmt addressed to them by Leander Mathes
Nov 1 1906	Mr Childers Atty for dfndt called over telephone & advised that contest would be filed on or before Nov 6, 1906. In return, he was advised that if no contest filed orders will issue
Nov 10 1906	Atty for dfndt files request for suspension of farther Action, together with copy of letter to Com^r
Nov 14 1906	Judgement[sic] rendered for plntf. Instructions issued to Capt Jno C. West to place Allottee in possession
Dec 21 1906	Policeman Jno Barber reports he placed plntf in possession.
Dec 27 1906	Case dismissed

INTRUDER CASE NO. 816
Cherokee NATION

Plaintiff: Sallie Hill mother of Eliza Crossland, Gans I.T. Atty.

Versus

Defendant: Mary McKinney, Muldrow I.T. Atty. Thomas J Watts, Muldrow

Complaint filed July 13 1906 Commissioner Reports July 27 1906 No Contest. Notice Sent July 24 1906

July 13 1906	Certificate of Homestead Allotment No. 21487 filed by Plaintiff
" 30 "	Answer filed by Defendant,
" 27 "	(This line was left blank.)
Aug 1st "	Proof [sic] Service returned dated July 30 1906
" 9 "	Case set for hearing at Vanita I.Ty Aug 24 -1906. All parties notified.
" 14 "	Pltf notified by Atty Mr Watts that Dft claim they do not occupy her land and that if amicable settlement can be made parties need not appear at Vanita I.Ty. Aug 24 -1906
Aug 24 1906	Case called at Vinita I.Ty. No appearance by either party.
Aug 23 1906	Thos. J. Watts, Atty. for Dfdt encloses request from pltf that case be dismissed.
Aug 28 1906	In view of statement by pltf & above request this case dismissed
Jany 7 1907	Plntf requests return of certificates Dismissed
Jany 9 1907	Allottment[sic] certificates returned to plntf.

Cherokee Intruder Cases 1901 - 1909

INTRUDER CASE NO. 817
Cherokee NATION

Plaintiff: Mrs Lizzie Jackson for herself and Osie " Afton I.T. Atty.

Versus

Defendant: W.P. Godard[sic] and Mrs Wasson Wasson I.T. Atty.

Complaint filed July 21 1906 Commissioner Reports 7/28/06 <u>a Portion in</u> Contest. Notice Sent July 24 1906

July 21 1906	Certificates of Allotment Nos 58406, 57114, 57115 and " " Homestead " 34910 and 34911 filed by Pltf.
" 30 "	Proof of Service returned dated July 28th 1906
Aug 3 "	Case dismissed as to that portion of the land which the Com[r] reports in contest.
" 1st "	Answer filed by Defendant Goddard
Aug 9 "	Case set for hearing at Vanita I.Ty. Aug 24 -1906. All parties notified
" 16 "	Dfdts that if they disclaim all right to possession of land in contest, it will not be necessary for them to appear at Vanita Aug 24 -1906.
Aug 24 1906	Case called at Vinita I.Ty. Pltf appeared. No appearance by dfdt. Pltf states that dfdt claims no land except that portion in contest. Certificates Nos. 58406, 57114, 57115, Homestead 34910, 34911 returned to plaintiff in person. Case dismissed

Dismissed

Aug 25 1906 Dfdt Mrs. Wasson notified that case has been dismissed.

INTRUDER CASE NO. 818
Cherokee NATION

Plaintiff: Ada G Smith nee Eaton for herself and John E Eaton Moody I.T. Atty.

Versus

Defendant: J. L. Briggs Pryor Creek - Tipe I.Ty. Atty.

Complaint filed July 23 1906 Commissioner Reports July 28 1906 <u>No</u> Contest. Notice Sent July 24 1906

July 23 1906	Certificates of Allotment No 20892 and 20896 filed by Plaintiff
Aug 9 1906	Case set for hearing at Vanita I.Ty. Aug 24 -1906 All parties notified.
" 7 "	Rec'd proof of service dated Aug 3 1906

Cherokee Intruder Cases 1901 - 1909

Aug 24 1906	Case called at Vinita I.Ty, Both parties taken, testimony taken.
"	Copy of rental contract between pltf & dfdt filed
Sept 24 1906	Judgement[sic] rendered in favor of plntf. Copy of same sent to both parties.
" 24 1906	Plntf. Ada G Smith requested to advise this office if possession is given in ten days
Nov 9 1906	Pntf again requested to advise this office if she is in possession.
Dec 6 1906	Instructions issued to Capt Jno C. West to place plntf in possession.
Jany 21 1907	Plntf states she is now in possession.
Jany 24 1907	In view of above, certificates returned & case dismissed.

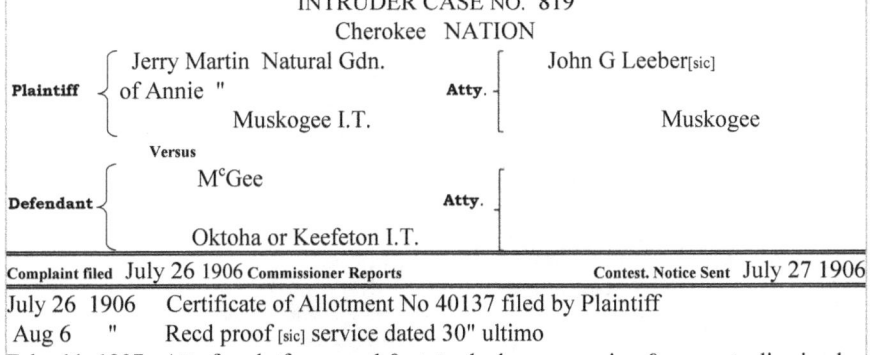

INTRUDER CASE NO. 819
Cherokee NATION

Plaintiff: Jerry Martin Natural Gdn. of Annie " Muskogee I.T.
Atty.: John G Leeber[sic] Muskogee

Versus

Defendant: McGee Oktoha or Keefeton I.T.
Atty.:

Complaint filed July 26 1906 Commissioner Reports   Contest. Notice Sent July 27 1906

July 26 1906	Certificate of Allotment No 40137 filed by Plaintiff
Aug 6 "	Recd proof [sic] service dated 30" ultimo
Feby 11 1907	Atty for plntf appeared & states he has possession & requests dismissal. Certificates returned No 40137. Case dismissed.

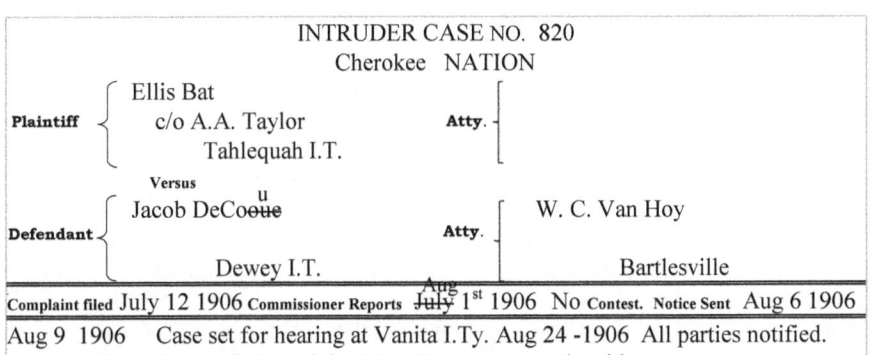

INTRUDER CASE NO. 820
Cherokee NATION

Plaintiff: Ellis Bat c/o A.A. Taylor Tahlequah I.T.
Atty.:

Versus

Defendant: Jacob DeCooue [u above] Dewey I.T.
Atty.: W. C. Van Hoy Bartlesville

Complaint filed July 12 1906 Commissioner Reports July [Aug] 1st 1906 No Contest. Notice Sent Aug 6 1906

Aug 9 1906	Case set for hearing at Vanita I.Ty. Aug 24 -1906 All parties notified.
Aug 24 1906	Case called at Vanita I.Ty. No appearance by either party.
Sept 27 1906	Jacob Decooue[sic] writes that he did not receive his notice in time to

Cherokee Intruder Cases 1901 - 1909

	attend hearing of case at Vinita I.Ty. Aug 24 -1906. Also gives reason for holding land.
Oct 1 1906	Dfndt advised that case will be set for hearing soon
Nov 3 1906	Case set for Claremore ITy Nov 19, 1906. All parties notified.
Nov 12 1906	As per request, copy of complaint mailed to W.C. Van Hoy Atty.
Nov 19 1906	Case called at Claremore. Dfndt & Atty present & testimony taken. No appearance by plntf. Two Lease contracts filed. Dfndt agrees to pay to plntf additional ten cents per acre per annum for remainder of term of lease. Same seems to be only question in controversy.
Nov 24 1906	Plntf advised of the proposition of dfndt & asked to inform this office if he has made satisfactory settlement with dfndt.
Nov 26 1906	N. F. Frazier Jr for dfndt states he has sent $20^{00} Ellis Bat & $10^{00} to Akie Bat which was agreed upon at hearing of case at Claremore. <u>Dismissed</u>
Dec 2 08	Defdt ordered to carry out agreement entered into at hearing, otherwise case will be reopened & further Action taken.

INTRUDER CASE NO. 821
Cherokee NATION

Plaintiff { John B. Acorn for Annie and
Lizzie   "
Stilwell I.T.   **Atty.**

Versus

Defendant { John Barnes   **Atty.**
Gans I.T.

Complaint filed July 20 1906 **Commissioner Reports** July 28 1906 **No Contest.** **Notice Sent** Aug 6 1906

July 20 1906	Certificates No 32123 and 32124 filed by Plaintiff
Nov 12 1906	Proof of service retd dated Nov. 10, 1906
Nov 24 1906	Case set for hearing at Muskogee ITy. Dec 6 1906. All parties notified.
Dec 6 1906	Case called at Muskogee ITy. Dfndt appeared and stated he had no claim on land since he has been rejected by department, only that he owns improvements. House worth $75^{00}, fencing & clearing land. Plntf telephoned that he will be unable to attend hearing because of sickness
Dec 10 1906	Plntf appeared and testimony taken. Certificates returned to plntf and he is instructed to have land surveyed in order to facilitate Action of U.S.I. Police
Dec 31 1906	Jas W. Breedlove, surveyor, of Muldrow ITy. files plats showing allottments[sic] & location of improvements of minors in question.
Jany 3 1907	Plntf instructed to go into possession & advise if molested. <u>Dismissed</u>

Cherokee Intruder Cases 1901 - 1909

INTRUDER CASE NO. 822
Cherokee NATION

Plaintiff: Betsy Bowels for Jennette Bowels, Baron I.T. **Atty.**

Versus

Defendant: Lizzie Terrell - Watts, Baron I.T. **Atty.**

Complaint filed July 23 1906 **Commissioner Reports** July 30 1906 **No Contest.** **Notice Sent** Aug 6 1906

July 23 1906	Plat filed by Plaintiff
Aug 20 "	Pltf requested by this office to have land surveyed.
" 24 1906	Proof of service ret'd dated Aug 13, 1906
Aug 30 1906	Pltf advise to send to this office plat of survey with affidavitt[sic] of surveyor.
Oct 3 1906	Thomas P. Roach I.S.I.P. instructed to place plntf in possession.
Oct 29 1906	Policeman Roach reports that he placed Allottee in possession.
" 29 1906	In view of above case dismissed.

INTRUDER CASE NO. 823
Cherokee NATION

Plaintiff: Noble Denny for self and as Natural Gdn. of Lewis Denny, Hudson I.T. **Atty.**

Versus

Defendant: A.S. Mullslogle Bluff City Kans, C. C. Ranstead, Hudson I.T. **Atty.**

Complaint filed Aug 1st 1906 **Commissioner Reports** Aug 20 1906 **No Contest.** **Notice Sent** Aug 6 1906

August 1st 1906	Two copies of contract and allotment certificates No 9476, 11653, 9477 and 11654 filed by Plaintiff
Aug 9 1906	Case set for hearing at Vanita I.Ty. Aug 24 -1906 All parties notified
" 14 "	Noble Denning[sic] requested to send to this office P.O. registered card by which he got service on Dfdts
" 24 1906	Case called at Vinita I.Ty: Neither party appeared
Aug 21 1906	Noble Denny writes that C C Ranstead has given possession but can not hear from A.S. Mullslogle.
Aug 28 1906	Pltf notified that case is dismissed and certificates No's. 9476, 11653, 9477 and 11654. Dismissed

Cherokee Intruder Cases 1901 - 1909

INTRUDER CASE NO. 824
Cherokee NATION

Plaintiff: Rufus Tadpole for Grover Tadpole, Hulbert I.Ty. Atty.

Versus

Defendant: Chas & Frank Boston ar, Hulbert I.Ty. Atty.

Complaint filed Aug 3 1906 Commissioner Reports Aug 3 1906 No Contest. Notice Sent Aug 7 1906

Aug 13	1906	Proof of Service filed dated Aug 11 -1906
" 15	"	Answer filed by Chas Boston.
" 30	"	Pltf anrs as to status of case.
Sept 5	1906	Case set for hearing Sept 18 -1906 at 2 P.M. both parties notified
" 11	1906	Chas Boston writes that he has given possession to defendant[sic] plntf
" 13	1906	Plntf requested to advise this office if he has possession of land
" 13	1906	Dfdt requested not to interfere with plntf who is instructed to go on land.
Sept 18	1906	Case called at Muskogee ITy. No appearance by either party.
" 14	1906	Pltf states in letter that Frank Barton has surrendered possession of land.
" 19	1906	Plntf states in letter that he has possession of land from Chas & Frank Boston
" 21	1906	In view of above, case h is dismissed.

INTRUDER CASE NO. 825
Cherokee NATION

Plaintiff: Sallie Langley, Lometa I.Ty. Atty.

Versus

Defendant: Wyly Smith, F.M. Booth, Wagoner I.T. Atty.

Complaint filed July 30 1906 Commissioner Reports Aug 3 -1906 No Contest. Notice Sent Aug 10-1906

Aug 15	1906	Rec'd proof of service not dated. Same ret that date of service may be inserted.
Aug 27	1906	Action withheld in this case until until[sic] Com^r reports as to what portion of the allottment[sic] in controversy is segregated.
Aug 27	1906	Proof of service ret'd dated Aug 14 1906
Aug 28	1906	Plntf notified that no further Action will be taken by this office until matter of segregation of a portion of land for church purposes is settled by Com^r
Jan 8	1908	Case dismissed by order of W.W. Bennett.

Cherokee Intruder Cases 1901 - 1909

INTRUDER CASE NO. 826
Cherokee NATION

Plaintiff: Lula Vann
c/o Louis T. Brown
Box #957 Muskogee I.Ty.

Atty.

Versus

Defendant: Robert & Lucinda Horton
Cora Reed & Daisy Reed Alberty
Chetopa, Kans.

Atty. J.C. Starr
Vinita ITy.

Complaint filed Aug 6 1906 **Commissioner Reports** Aug 20 1906 **No Contest. Notice Sent** Aug 10-1906

Aug 6 1906	Certificate of Homestead Allotment #34993 also Surplus Certificate #57271 filed by pltf.
Aug 10 "	Request Com^r to advise of any contest on land
Aug 20 / Sept 4 1906	Answer filed by Dfdt.
Nov 3 1906	Case set for hearing at Claremore ITy Nov. 19 1906. All parties notified.
Nov 7 1906	Cora Reed of Chetopa Kans, states she filed her two daughters, Cora & Daisy Alberty on land & rented same to dfndts in case. See file of #833.
Nov 13 1906	Cora Reed notified of hearing to be held at Claremore ITy Nov 19 1906
Nov 19 1906	Case called at Claremore. Dfndts & Atty Mr. Starr present. No appearance by plntf. It was agreed that if Com^r report shows no application for citizenship pending Judgement[sic] would be found for plntf: otherwise Action would be withheld
Nov 20 1906	Com^r reports citizenship as (freedman) denied & no motion pending to reopen case. Same in #833.
Dec 7 1906	Atty for dfndt notified of report of Com^r & asked to advise his clients (dfndts) to vacate. Same in 833.
Jany 24 1907	Plntf & Atty for dfndt asked if possession has been given.
Jany 31 1907	Atty J.C. Starr for dfndts states plntf may go into possession. See file 833.
Feby 2 1907	Plntf requested to go into possession.
Feby 6 1907	Plntf states dfndts removed improvements. Asks information.
Feby 20 1907	Plntf advised her redress is in U.S. Court
Feby 29 1907	Plntf by her agent J.R. Salter says she has possession.
Mch 13 1907	Certificates return & case <u>dismissed</u>.

INTRUDER CASE NO. 827
Cherokee NATION

Plaintiff: Mrs Sarah Wa.ters Nat'l Gdn of
John Simerson
Afton I.Ty.

Atty. Davis and Mason
Afton & Vinita I.Ty.

Versus

Cherokee Intruder Cases 1901 - 1909

Defendant	Lee Todd of Albia I.Ty. and Wyly Melton Afron I.Ty. ~~Albia~~	Atty.	

Complaint filed Aug 8 1906 **Commissioner Reports** Aug 8 -1906 **No Contest. Notice Sent** Aug 10-1906

Aug 10 1906	Case set for hearing at Vanita I.Ty Aug 24 -1906/ All parties notified.
Aug 24 1906	Proof of Service returned dated Aug 17 -1906 Certificates of Allottment[sic] Nos 27595 Homestead 19816
Aug 24 1906	Case called at Vinita I.Ty, Plntf and her Atty Mr. Mason, appear and asked that case be continued in order that the Natural guardian may take steps towards having lawful guardian apptd as contract had been entered into between her, as nat'l gdn. and the defendant.
Nov 3 1906	Case set for hearing at Claremore ITy Nov 19-1906. All parties notified.
Nov 19 1906	Case called at Claremore. No appearance by either party.
Jany 18 1907	Case set for hearing at Claremore I.Ty. Feby 5, 1907.
Feby 5 1907	Case called at Claremore I.Ty. Neither party appeared.
Feby 13 1907	Referred to Robt R. Bennett
Mch 23 1907	Robt R. Bennett encloses request for dismissal.
Mch 26 1907	Certificates returned & <u>case dismissed</u>.

INTRUDER CASE NO. 828
Cherokee NATION

Plaintiff	Dora M. Holley Coweta I.Ty.	Atty.	G B Denison Jas Davenport, Vinita I.Ty.
Versus			
Defendant	Dr. Dogget, E.E. Also, F.W. Casnor of K.C. Mo. Catoosa I.Ty.	Atty.	Soper, Huckleberry & Owen ~~Jas Davenport~~ ~~Vinita I.Ty.~~

Complaint filed July 21-1906 **Commissioner Reports** Aug 20-1906 **No Contest. Notice Sent** Aug 13-1906

Aug 13 1906	Com^r requested to advise this office if certificate has been issued also as to contest
" 13 "	Case set for hearing at Vanita I.Ty. Aug 24 -1906 All parties notified
Aug 18 "	Proof of Service rec'd dated Aug 16 -1906 Also letter from pltf in which she asks if it is necessary for her to "appear in person". She was requested ~~(illegible)~~ to appear
Aug 24 1906	Case called at Vinita I.Ty. Both parties present. Pltf represented by Atty Denison. Dfdt. filed answer (?). Case continued and set for hearing at Muskogee ITy Aug 28 -1906 at 9 o'clock A.M.
Sept 11 1906	Atty Davenport for pltf filed statement of Clera U.S. Court at Claremore I.Ty. in which he states that no money was deposited by Denison Wichita &

50

Cherokee Intruder Cases 1901 - 1909

	Memphis Ry Co.
Sept 25 1906	Dfndt E E Doggett requested to remove railroad tracks from plntf's land, otherwise orders would issue to remove them. Also a letter to E.G. Wilson enclosed to Doggett to be delivered
Oct 1 1906	Plntf asks as to status of case.
" 1 1906	Pltf advised as to status of case.
Oct 3 1906	Answer filed by Dr. E.E. Doggett in which he says he has referred letter to F.W. Casner K.Cy.
Oct 5 1906	Dfndt requested to vacate at once or orders will issue to remove him
Oct 6 1906	F.W. Casner of K.C. Mo states condemnation proceedings have been commenced.
" 8 1906	Plntf asks to be placed in possession at once.
Oct 15 1906	C[sic].W. Casner letter in file
" 16 1906	Plntf advised that condemnation proceedings have been commenced & that no Action can be taken by this office under circumstances.
" 17 1906	Soper Huckleberry & Owens[sic] requested to furnish this office with evidence of proceedings.
Oct 25 1906	J S Davenport Atty for plntf letter in file.
Oct 30 1906	Jas Davenport Atty advised of Action of Soper Huckleberry & Owens
Nov 15 1906	Plntf notified that Atty for Dfndt has exhibited evidence showing condemnation proceedings have been commenced.
Feby 15 1907	Soper Huckleberry & Owen requested to advise what Action has been taken.
Mch 23 1907	F.W. Casner K.Cy. Mo advised if he does not dep. money with U.S. Clk in 15 da[sic] R.R. will be moved
April 25 1907	Amount of damages fixed by expenses deposited with <u>Clk</u> of U.S. C<u>ourt</u> at Claremore Ind. Ty. and <u>Case dismissed</u>.

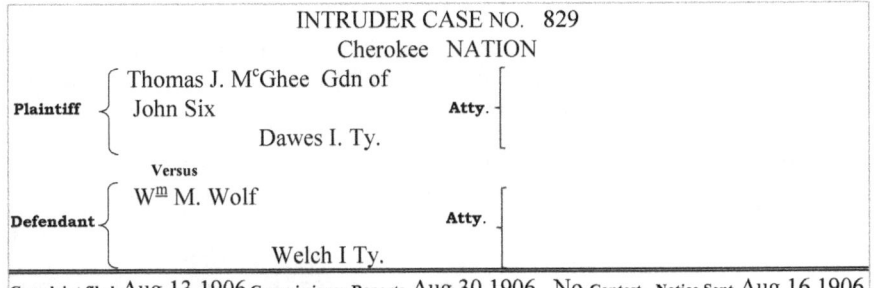

INTRUDER CASE NO. 829
Cherokee NATION

Plaintiff Thomas J. McGhee Gdn of John Six   **Atty**.
Dawes I. Ty.

Versus

Defendant W<u>m</u> M. Wolf   **Atty**.
Welch I Ty.

Complaint filed Aug 13 1906	Commissioner Reports Aug 30 1906	No Contest.	Notice Sent Aug 16 1906

Aug 13 1906	Certificates, Nos. 52338 & 3902 also ~~letter~~ copy of Gdnship papers filed.
" 16 "	Com^r asked by letter if any contest pending.
Aug 21 1906	Proof of service rec'd dated Aug 20" 1906

Cherokee Intruder Cases 1901 - 1909

Aug 31 " (Aug 30 1906 struck through)	S.B. McGee[sic] writes that dfdt is disposing of crop & asks that immediate Action be taken	
Sept 14 1906	S.B. McGee advised by letter that this office can move Intruders from minor's land but for collection of rent, his redress is in U.S. Court	
Sept 11 1906	Pltf states that dfdt is cutting hay on land & urges this office to immediate Action	
Sept 14 1906	Dfdt notified to show cause for his occupancy of land within ten days of orders will issue.	
Nov 27 1906	Plntf requests return of Allottment[sic] certificates & Letters of Gdnship.	
Nov 30 1906	As per request Allottment[sic] certificates & Letters of Gdnship returned and <u>case dismissed</u>	

INTRUDER CASE NO. 830
Cherokee NATION

Plaintiff: Maggie Culver mother of
Maggie Culver
Vian I Ty.   Atty.

Versus

Defendant: Riley Williams and Tom Williams   Atty.
Sandtown Ind. Ter.

Complaint filed Aug 14-1906 **Commissioner Reports** Aug 27-1906 No **Contest.** **Notice Sent** Aug 17-1906

Aug 14 1906	Certificate of Allottment[sic] No 35420 filed.
" 17 "	Com^r ad requested to advise if there is contest pending
Aug 21 1906	Proof of service ret dated Aug 20" 1906
Sept 22 1906	Pltf insists upon being placed in possession of land.
" 25 1906	Pltf advised that dfndts have again been requested to file answer
Oct 5 1906	Riley Williams dfndt filed answer.
Nov 14 1906	Case set for hearing at Muskogee I.Ty. Nov 28, 1906 All parties [sic]
Nov 28 1906	Dfndts appeared & presented report from Com^r showing 20 acres in contest & Dfndt states that he claims no land except that in contest
Nov 30 1906	Com^r asked to report.
Dec 5 1906	Com^r reports land in contest
Dec 10 1906	<u>Case dismissed</u> & allottment[sic] certificate No. 35420 returned.

52

Cherokee Intruder Cases 1901 - 1909

INTRUDER CASE NO. 831
Cherokee NATION

Plaintiff: Myrtle Parker, Dustin I. Ty. **Atty.**

Versus

Defendant: JD Hartfield and Norman Shevose, JA Taylor^(real dfndt) Blackgum ITy., Warner I.Ty. **Atty.**

Complaint filed Aug 13 1906 **Commissioner Reports** Aug 27 1906 **No Contest.** **Notice Sent** Aug 17-1906

Aug 13 1906	Certificates Nos 36437 & 60412 in file.
Aug 17 "	Letter to Com^r asking if there is contest pending on this land.
Aug 25 1906	Proof of service ret dated Aug 23 -1906.
Sept 24 1906	Husband of plntf urges Action in this case. See letter.
" 28 1906	Dfndts given ten days in which to make answer.
" 28 1906	Plntf advised of above.
Nov 2 1906	Case set for hearing at Muskogee Nov. 14, 1906. All parties notified.
Nov 14 1906	Case called at Muskogee. Mr. W. Norman Chavose & J.A. Taylor appeared and stated that J.A. Taylor is the real dfndt. Testimony of same taken No appearance by plntf.
Nov 28 1906	Husband of plntf appeared & stated that his wife is not 18 years of age. He was advised to have curator appointed as this office can do nothing under the circumstances.
Jany 24 1907	Certificates returned & <u>case dismissed</u>

INTRUDER CASE NO. 832
Cherokee NATION

Plaintiff: Alex Buffington, Vinita I Ty **Atty.** F M Smith witness to complaint

Versus

Defendant: J.C. Starr, Vinita I.Ty. **Atty.**

Complaint filed Aug 8-1906 **Commissioner Reports** Aug 20-1906 **No Contest.** **Notice Sent** Aug 25-1906

Nov 3 1906	Case set for hearing at Claremore ITy Nov 19 1906. All parties notified.
Nov 19 1906	Case called at Claremore. No appearance by plntf. Dfndt present & testimony taken. Lease contract filed by Dfndt.
Dec 13 1906	Judgement[sic] for dfndt. Lease contract ret to plntf. <u>Case Dismissed</u>.

Cherokee Intruder Cases 1901 - 1909

INTRUDER CASE NO. 833
Cherokee NATION

Plaintiff: Lula Vann Nat'l Gdn of Willie Vann Box 957 Muskogee I.Ty.

Atty: Louis T. Brown Box 957 Muskogee I.Ty

Versus

Defendant: Robt. and Lucinda Horton Cora Reed for Daisy & Cora Alberty Chetopa, Kans.

Atty: J. C. Starr Vinita I.Ty

Complaint filed Aug 18-1906 **Commissioner Reports** Sept 1 -1906 No **Contest.** **Notice Sent** Aug 25-1906

Aug 18 1906	Certificates of Allottment[sic] No's 57272 & 34994 in file
Aug 25 "	Com^r asked if contest is pending.
Nov 3 1906	Case set for hearing at Claremore I.Ty. Nov 19, 1906 All parties notified.
Nov 13 1906	Com^r asked if citizenship case of dfndt is depending.
Nov 7 1906	Cora Reed of Chetopa Kans writes that she has filed her daughters Cora & Daisy Alberty on land in contest & had rented same to dfndts.
Nov 13 1906	Cora Reed notified that case will be heard at Claremore ITy Nov 19 1906
Nov 19 1906	Case called at Claremore. Lucinda Horton, Cora Reed Alberty & Atty J.C. Starr present No appearance by plntf. It was agreed that if the Com^r's report shows Cora & Daisy Alberta[sic] applicants for citizenship action will be withheld. If not judgement[sic] would be rendered against dfndt.
Nov 20 1906	Com^r reports enrollment denied Cora & Daisy Alberty & no motion pending to reopen case. Same in 826
Dec 7 1906	Atty for dfndt advised as to report of Com^r & asked to advise dfndts to vacate & surrender possession. Same in 826.
Jany 24 1907	Plntf & Atty for dfndt both asked if possession has been given
Jany 31 1907	Atty J.C. Starr for dfndt states plntf may go into possession
Feby 2 1907	Plntf requested to go into possession.
Feby 6 1907	Plntf states Dfndts have removed all improvements & crops
Feby 20 1907	Plntf is advised that her redress is in US Court. See 826
Feby 27 1907	Plntf states thro' her agent J.R. Salter that she has has[sic] possession.
Mch 13 1907	Certificates returned & <u>case dismissed</u>

INTRUDER CASE NO. 834
Cherokee NATION

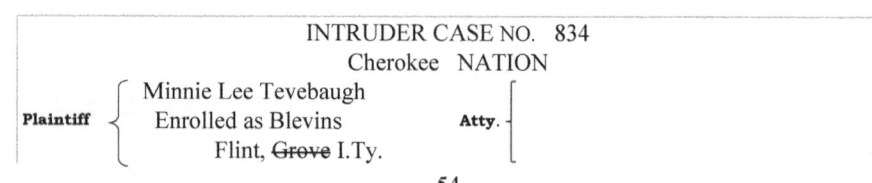

Plaintiff: Minnie Lee Tevebaugh Enrolled as Blevins Flint, ~~Grove~~ I.Ty.

Atty:

54

Cherokee Intruder Cases 1901 - 1909

	Versus	
Defendant	Mrs Val Perry Vinita ITy N.M. Perry Agent Grove ITy.	**Atty.**

Complaint filed Aug 16 1906 **Commissioner Reports** Sept 1 1906   in **Contest.** **Notice Sent** Aug 25 1906

Aug 16 1906	Certificates of Allottment[sic] No's 32105, 48230 & 48229 in file also plat of land
Aug 25 1906	Com^r requested to advise if there is contest pending.
Sept 5 1906	Proof of service returned dated Sept 4-1906
" 6 1906	Answer filed by dfdt. (by O.A. Smith)
" 8 1906	Mr. O.A. Smith for Mrs. Vall Perry, requested to surrender possession of a certain portion of Minnie Lee Tevebaugh's allottment[sic] not in contest.
Sept 18 1906	Pltf asked to advised this office if possession is given of lands not in contest.
Nov 3 1906	Case set for hearing at Claremore ITy Nov 20, 1906. All parties notified.
Nov 9 1906	Dfndt N.M. Perry appeared at Muskogee & claims no right to any of land except that in contest. He was informed that it would not be necessary for him or Mrs Val Perry to appear at Claremore Nov. 20, 1906
Nov 10 1906	In view of above conditions certificates returned & <u>case dismissed</u>

INTRUDER CASE NO. 835
Cherokee NATION

Plaintiff	A Blevins Natural Guardian of Nellie May Blevins Grove ITy.	**Atty.**
	Versus	
Defendant	Nathan M Perry Grove ITy	**Atty.**

Complaint filed Aug 16 1906 **Commissioner Reports** Sept 1 1906   in **Contest.** **Notice Sent** Aug 25 1906

Aug 16 1906	Certificates of allottment[sic] No's 31887 & 48227 & 48228 in file.
Aug 25 1906	Com^r requested to advise if contest is pending
Oct 1" 1906	Answer filed by dfndt.
Oct 4 1906	Proof of service returned, dated Sep 25-1906
Nov 3 1906	Case set for hearing at Claremore ITy. Nov 20 1906. All parties notified.
Nov 9 1906	Dfndt appeared in person at Muskogee ITy. & stated that he did not hold or claim any land involved in this case only that portion in contest. He was then advised that it would be necessary for him to appear at Claremore ITy Nov 20, 1906
Nov. 10 1906	In view of above facts certificates returned & case <u>dismissed</u>

Cherokee Intruder Cases 1901 - 1909

```
                    INTRUDER CASE NO. 836
                        Cherokee NATION
Plaintiff    Simon McKinzey
                                              Atty.
             Pryor Creek ITy.
             Versus
Defendant    Richard C. Adams et al
             Charles Hawkins                  Atty.
             Dr F B Fite   Washington D.C.
```

Complaint filed Aug 7 1906	Commissioner Reports 8/24/06 S2 of NW4 in Contest. Notice Sent Aug 27 1906
Sept 11 1906	Proof of service ret'd dated Sept 5 1906 by Reg Mail.
Sept 11 1906	Answer filed by Richard C Adams in which he states that he has no claim to any land in controversy
Nov 3 1906	Case set for hearing at Claremore ITy Nov 20, 1906 All parties notified.
Nov 17 1906	Dr Fite appeared in person & stated that he claims no right or interest to any portion of land in controversy except that portion involved in contest. He also state that Charles Hawkins one of dfndts will not be able to appear at Claremore on a/c of illness.
Nov. 20 1906	Letter in file from plntf states he will be unable to attend hearing & asks that case be continued.
Jany 18 1907	Case set for hearing at Claremore ITy. Feby 5, 1907. All parties notified
Feby 5 1907	Case called at Claremore ITy. Neither party appeared.
Feby 2 1907	Nev. Campbell Atty Pryor Creek, Foreman ITy. asks that case be heard in Muskogee ITy.
Feby 15 1907	Atty Campbell advised case in hands of field man.
Mch 9 1907	Robert R Bennett reports dfndt claiming only the land in contest.
Mch 20 1907	Case dismissed.

```
                    INTRUDER CASE NO.  837
                        Cherokee NATION
Plaintiff    Susan B Chaney Hawley
                                              Atty.
             Ruby I.Ty.
             Versus
Defendant    Bud Montgomery
                                              Atty.
             Hayden I.Ty.
```

Complaint filed Aug 9 1906	Commissioner Reports Aug 24 1906 No Contest. Notice Sent Aug 27 1906
Sept 5 1906	Proof of service returned dated Sept 1" 1906
Nov 3 1906	Case set for hearing at Claremore ITy. Nov 20, 1906. All parties notified.
Nov 20 1906	Case called at Claremore. W.H. Montgomery, father of dfndt appeared

Cherokee Intruder Cases 1901 - 1909

	& stated that he is real dfndt. He & Bud Montgomery are rejected freedman. He had a fence surrounding land in controversy but plntf is in actual possession. Dfndt advised to not interfere with rights of plntf.
Dec. 12 1906	Plntf advised of statement made by dfndt & instructed to go into possession
Jany 24 1907	Plntf requested to advise if she is in possession
Apr 6 1907	Referred to Robt R. Bennett.
June 25 07	R.R. Bennett reports plaintiff in unrestricted possession of her allmt[sic].
July 5 07	Plff. advised of report of Mr. Bennett and <u>Case Dismissed</u>

INTRUDER CASE NO. 838
Cherokee NATION

Plaintiff: Crawford D. Flying, Muskogee I Ty.   **Atty.**

Versus

Defendant: J.M. Vandiver, Checotah I.Ty.   **Atty.**

Complaint filed Aug 27 1906 Commissioner Reports Sept 18 1906 No Contest. Notice Sent Sept 1 1906

Aug 27 1906	Allottment[sic] certificate No. 37096 in file.
Sept 1 1906	Com^r requested to report as to contest on land.
" 22 "	Proof of service ret'd by pltf in person Same dated Sept 13 1906 Plntf states that dfndt has agreed to surrender possession of land as soon as this year's crop can be removed, and plntf further requests that case <u>be dismissed</u>
Jany 5 1907	Because of verbal complaint made by plntf in which he states dfndt refuses to vacate, dfndt given ten days in which to surrender
Jany 21 1907	Plntf appeared in person & reported possession. Certificate returned.
	<u>Dismissed</u>.

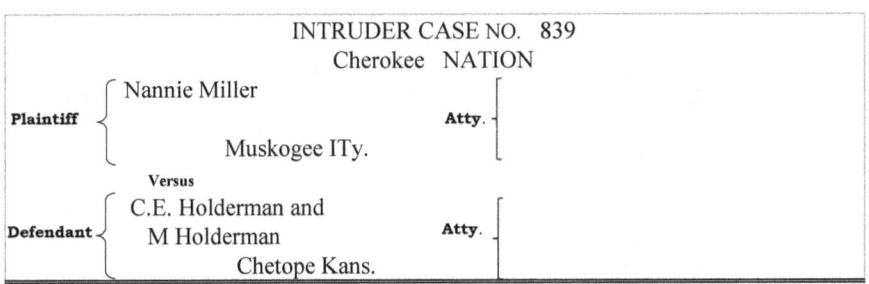

INTRUDER CASE NO. 839
Cherokee NATION

Plaintiff: Nannie Miller, Muskogee ITy.   **Atty.**

Versus

Defendant: C.E. Holderman and M Holderman, Chetope Kans.   **Atty.**

Cherokee Intruder Cases 1901 - 1909

Complaint filed Aug 28 1906 Commissioner Reports Sept 8 1906 No Contest. Notice Sent Sept 1 1906
Aug 28 1906   Allottment[sic] certificates Nos 8175 & 5950 in file.
"   28 1906   Copy of rental contract in file
Sept 1 1906   Com^r asked for a report
Sept 10 1906   Pltf C.C. Holderman appeared in person & states that Nannie Miller has told him, pltf, that the lease on her land given him, pltf, by her husband, Rufus Miller, was satisfactory to her. Pltf exhibited receipt signed by Rufus Miller dated at Muskogee ITy Aug 3-1906 for Thirty (30\underline{^{00}}$/Dollars) in full of a/c as per contract for year 1906 on E^2 SW^4 Sec 16 Twp 29 N. R 20E.
Sept 8 1906   Proof of service ret'd dated Sept 7-1906
Sept 10 1906   Answer filed by Dfdt.
"   14 1906   Dfdt filed additional answer.
"   17 1906   Case set for hearing at Muskogee ITy Sept 27 at 10 o'clock A.M. All parties notified.
Sept 27 1906   Case called at Muskogee ITy. All parties present and testimony taken.
Nov 1   1906   Judgement[sic] rendered in favor of dfndt.
"   1   1906   Certificates returned to plntf & <u>case dismissed</u>

INTRUDER CASE NO. 840
Cherokee NATION

Plaintiff { James A Hibbs Gdn of
Sarah I. Hibbs
Centralia ITy.   Atty. {

Versus

Defendant { Jno Freeman   Freedman
Coodys Bluff   Atty. {
~~Ruby~~ ITy.

Complaint filed Aug ~~30~~ 15 1906 Commissioner Reports Aug 30 1906 ~~in~~ No Contest. Notice Sent Sept 1 1906
Sept 11 1906   Proof of service ret'd dated Sept 10-1906 7-23-08 in contest
Sept 4 1906   Pltf to advise this office if dfdt is in possession of land other than that in
Sept 13 1906   Plntf requested to advise this office if Jno Freeman is in possession of land not in contest
Nov 3   1906   Case set for hearing at Claremore ITy Nov 20, 1906. All parties notified
Nov 20 1906   Case called at Claremore. Dfndt appeared. No appearance by plntf. Dfndt stated that he is willing to surrender possession of land not in contest, which has no improvement except same is *(illegible)* in fence
Dec 10 1906   In view of contest case dismissed.
May 21 1907   Com^r asked to report result of contest
7-11-08   Set for hearing at Claremore on 7-29-08
7-29-08   Case called all parties present evidence taken
3-26 1912   Farm 330 to allottee

Cherokee Intruder Cases 1901 - 1909

INTRUDER CASE NO. 841
Cherokee NATION

Plaintiff: E.E. Lewis father of Estella Lewis — Vian I.Ty. Atty.

Versus

Defendant: Henry Brown — Vian I.Ty. Atty.

Complaint filed Aug 15 1906 **Commissioner Reports** Aug 30 1906 in **Contest. Notice Sent** Sept 1 1906

Sept 11 1906	Answer filed by dfdt
" 12 1906	Proof of service returned dated Sept 9" 1906
" 14 1906	Plntf again asks for possession.
Oct 17 1906	Case set for hearing at Muskogee ITy Oct 30 2 P.M. 1906 All parties notified
Oct 30 1906	Case called at Muskogee; No appearance by either party
Jany 22 1907	Referred to Robt R. Bennett for investigation
Jany 28 1907	Robt R. Bennett reports dfndt claims motion pending to relinquish this ten acres in question.
Feby 11 1907	Plntf asks status of case
Feby 16 1907	Plntf advised that Com^r has been asked to report
Feby 18 1907	Com^r asked to report as to citizenship of Henry Brown and as to motion to relinquish filing on this 10 acres
Feby 27 1907	Com^r reports no contest
Mch 1 1907	Dfndt advised of Com^{rs} report & requested to vacate or order will issue to remove him
June 17 07	Deft requested to advise if he has surrendered possession
June 17 07	Plff requested to advise in re. possession
June 27 07	Plaintiff appeared in person and advised that case had been satisfactorily settle[sic]. Defendant to remain in possession until Jan 1st 1908
June 29 07	Henry Brown advised of plaintiff's statement in re settlement and <u>Case Dismissed</u>

INTRUDER CASE NO. 842
Cherokee NATION

Plaintiff: Jno L Tipton Not Gdn of Lonie Tipton — Talequah[sic] I.Ty. Atty.

Versus

Cherokee Intruder Cases 1901 - 1909

Defendant	Alick McCurry	Atty.	
	Talequah[sic] I.Ty.		

Complaint filed Aug 18 1906 **Commissioner Reports** Aug 30 1906 in **Contest.** **Notice Sent** Sept 1-1906

Aug 18 1906	Plat showing location of land in file.
Nov 28 1906	Referred to U.S.I. Policeman Thos P Roach for investigation
Dec 4 1906	Policeman Thos P Roach's report in file.
Dec 10 1906	Plntf to go into possession of allottment[sic] & notify this office
Jany 22 1907	Referred to Robt R Bennett for investigation
Jan 8 1908	Case dismissed by order of W.W.B.

INTRUDER CASE NO. 843
Cherokee NATION

Plaintiff	Mrs Emma Wallace now Collinsville I Ty	Atty.	
	~~Talequah[sic] I.Ty~~		
	Versus		
Defendant	A.H. Woods	Atty.	H. Jennings
	Collinville I.Ty.		Claremore I.Ty.

Complaint filed Aug 21 1906 **Commissioner Reports** Aug 30 1906 No **Contest.** **Notice Sent** Sept 1-1906

Sept 7 1906	Proof of service ret'd dated September 5 1906
" 14 1906	Answer filed by defendant
Nov 3 1906	To be set for hearing / Case set for hearing at Claremore I Ty Nov 20, 1906 All parties notified
Nov 20 1906	Case called at Claremore. Husband of Emma Wallace present. No appearance by real plntf. Dfndt present & his Atty Mr. Jennings. Testimony taken. Bill of Sale for ~~emp~~ place exhibeted[sic]
Dec 12 1906	Judgement[sic] for plntf & dfndt asked to vacate on or[sic] Jany 1 1907
Jan 3 "[sic]	Com^r Bixby requests that action be witheld[sic] (verbally)
Jany 7 1907	Plntf advised that no action will be taken until citizenship of dfndt is determined
Feby 18 1907	Com^r asked as to citizenship of dfndt
Feby 19 1907	Plntf asks status of case
Feby 25 1907	Plntf advised
Mch 6 1907	Dfndt advised that he has been finally rejected and requested to vacate in ten days
Mch 8 1907	Frank Ertel of Collinsville writes in behalf of dfndt
Mch 13 1907	" " advised
Mch 12 1907	Com^r asked as to reimbursing inter-married whites
Apr 15 1907	Policeman JL Walker, Dewey ITy, instructed to place plntf in possession
Apr 18 1907	Policeman states by "phone" that dfndt is very ill. He is instructed to withhold action for further notice

Cherokee Intruder Cases 1901 - 1909

Apr 30 1907 Pltf asked to advise if she is in possession
May 8 1907 Plntf advises that she is in possession & case <u>dismissed</u>
Oct 4 1907 " " " appraisement of improvements is a matter that
J.G.W. hase[sic] full jurisdiction.

INTRUDER CASE NO. 844
Cherokee NATION

Plaintiff: William Adair Nat'l Gdn
Robert Adair
Coffeyville, Kans
Collinsville ITy.

Atty.

Versus

Defendant: George Ross
Coffeyville, Kans.

Atty. T. L. Brown
Claremore ITy.

Complaint filed Aug 17 1906 **Commissioner Reports** Aug 30 1906 **No Contest.** **Notice Sent** Sept 1 1906

Sept 7 1906 Allottment[sic] Certificates Nos. 38380, 60366 &26455 in file.
" 7 1906 Dft. Geo Ross, appeared in person & states that he is an app claimant as Cherokee Freedman
He was advised that Com^r would be requested to report as to status of his citizenship
Sept 14 1906 Proof of service returned, dated Sept 14 1906
Nov 9 1906 Com^r asked if dfndt has citizenship case pending before him.
Nov 20 1907 Com^r reports citizenship of dfndt denied. No motion pending for review
Jany 18 1907 Case set for hearing at Claremore ITy Feby 5 1907 All parties notified
Feby 5 1907 Case called at Claremore ITy. Dfndt appeared & Atty also Plntf and their testimony taken. Dfndt agreed to move his fence on his own line which is only contention. Certificates returned to plntf & <u>case dismissed</u>
May 4 1907 Dfndt reminded of his agreement to vacate April 5 1907 & instructed to vacate at once or the indian[sic] police will remove him
May 20 1907 Asst U.S. Atty advises injunction granted by U.S. Court at Vinita IT - See letter file #991
May 23 1907 Restraining order & summons in equity rec'd - see file #991
May 24 1907 Com asked if lands in contest & if certificates have been issued -
June 29 07 Injunction dissolved
July 6 07 Judgment rendered in favor of plaintiff copy sent both parties - and deft given ten days in which to vacate. Pltf requested to advise in re possession at end of ten days.
July 13 07 Capt Jno C West instructed to place plaintiff in possession
July 25 07 Capt West reports that deft surrendered possession of the allotment and advises that plaintiff may take possession at any time
August 2 07 Plff advised of report of Capt West and requested to take possession of the land in controversy and <u>Case Dismissed</u>

Cherokee Intruder Cases 1901 - 1909

INTRUDER CASE NO. 845
Cherokee NATION

Plaintiff: Sallie Mabry, Briartown I.Ty. Atty.

Versus

Defendant: A. T. Ingram, Porum I.Ty. Atty.

Complaint filed Aug 13 1906 **Commissioner Reports** Aug 30 1906 No **Contest.** **Notice Sent** Sept 1 1906

Aug 13 1906	A letter & itemised[sic] account in file by pltf.
Sept 11 1906	Proof of service ret'd dated Sept 10-1906
Sept 19 1906	Answer filed by dfndt.
" 22 1906	Case set for hearing at Muskogee I.Ty Oct 4 1906 Both parties notified
Oct 1 1906	Pltf asks that certain witnesses be subpeonied[sic]
Oct 3 1906	Pltf advised that she must arrange about witnesses
Oct 4 1906	Case called, both parties present testimony taken. Pltf advised that this is case for U.S. Court & that this office has no jurisdiction
Nov 1 1906	Judgement[sic] rendered for df<u>ndt</u>.
Nov 1 1906	Contract returned to plntf and <u>case dismissed</u>

INTRUDER CASE NO. 846
Cherokee NATION

Plaintiff: Charlotte E Harris Gdn of John F Harris, Chelsea I Ty Atty. D. G. Elliott, Chelsea I.Ty

Versus

Defendant: Fred Martin et al, Chelsea I.Ty. Atty. Starr and Patton, Vinita I.Ty.

Complaint filed Aug 16 1906 **Commissioner Reports** Aug 30 1906 No **Contest.** **Notice Sent** Sept 1 1906

Aug 16 1906	Letter of Gdnship in file.
Aug 30 1906	Pltf inquires as to status of case.
Sept 4 1906	Pltf advised as to status of case.
Sept 10 1906	Proof [sic] service returned dated Sept 8" 1906
" 10 1906	Answer filed by dfdt.
Sept 21 1906	Pltf advises that dfndt is still in possession & refuses to vacate
" 25 1906	Plntf advised that this case with others will be set for hearing soon.
Nov 3 1906	Case set for hearing at Claremore ITy Nov 20, 1906 All parties notified
Nov 20 1906	Case called at Claremore. Plntf & Atty Mr. D.G. Elliott present. No appearance by dfndt. Testimony of plntf taken.

Cherokee Intruder Cases 1901 - 1909

	Plntf offers finding of Com^r to 5 tribes as Exhibit "A"
Nov 30 1906	Dfndt advised that he may appear at this office Dec 8 1906 & tender testimony if he so desires
Dec 8 1906	No appearance by dfndt.
Dec 12 1906	Judgement[sic] for plntf & dfndt given ten days in which to vacate
Dec 30 1906	Instructions issued to US Ind Policeman Jno Barbee of Afton ITy
Jany 11 1907	Starr & Patton Atty of Vinita file motion to set aside judgement[sic] as they have filed contest proceedings for Elzira Lynch before Com^r on land involved. Elzira Lynch is step daughter of dfndt.
Jany 11 1907	Com^r asked if any contest pending
Mch 21 1907	Com^r asked to report as to contest on land by Elzira Lynch
Jany 12 1907	Com^r reports contest filed by Elzira Lynch
Apr 1 1907	Com^r reports portion of land involved in contest by Elzira Lynch
Apr 15 1907	Plntf advised 50 acres in contest. Asked if dfndts occupy any land in contest
June 10 1907	Plaintiff had failed to reply to letter of April 15 -07 it is presumed that she is in possession of land which is not in contest Case Dismissed

---

INTRUDER CASE NO. 847
Cherokee NATION

Plaintiff: Joe Davis for Chas and Carl Davis, Vinita I Ty
Atty.: Theo D. B. Frear, Vinita ITy.

Versus

Defendant: Samuel Rogers, Coffeyville Kans, Wann I.Ty.
Atty.:

Complaint filed Aug 16 1906 **Commissioner Reports** Sept 1 1906 **No Contest. Notice Sent** Sept 7 1906

Aug 16 1906	Letters of Gdnship in file
Sept 14 1906	Proof of service returned dated Sept 13 1906
Sept 22 1906	Com^r requested to advise if citizenship case is pending before your office
" 18 1906	Dfdnt files answer
Sept 28 1906	Com^r reports that there is no motion pending for review of citizenship of Samuel Rogers, who was denied Aug 19 -1904
Oct 24 1906	Atty for plntf advised that dfndt has not given possession
" 26 1906	Atty for plntf advised that case will be set for hearing soon.
Nov 3 1906	Case set for hearing at Claremore ITy Nov 20, 1906 All parties notified
Nov 20 1906	Case called at Claremore. Plntf & Atty Mr. Frear, present & testimony taken. No appearance by dfndt.
Dec 20 1906	Judgement[sic] rendered in favor of plaintiff. Dfndt requested to vacate on or before Jany 1st 1907
Dec 27 1906	Dfndt states that he was not given a hearing.

Cherokee Intruder Cases 1901 - 1909

Dec 31 1906	Dfndt states that he was not given a hearing.
Jany 14 1907	Dfndt advised that if he claims possession by contract, to furnish copy of same
Jany 28 1907	Instructions issued to Policeman J.L. Walker, Dewey I Ty.
Feby 2 1907	Policeman Walker reports he placed plntf in possession
	Case dismissed

INTRUDER CASE NO. 848
Cherokee NATION

Plaintiff: Ernest G. Perry
Welch I Ty.
Atty.

Versus

Defendant: Dan Dotts
Hollow ITy
Atty.

Complaint filed Sept 4 1906 **Commissioner Reports** Sept 18 1906 **No Contest.** **Notice Sent** Sept 7 1906

Sept 4 1906	Allottment[sic] certificate No 30314 in file.
" 7 "	Com'r requested to report
" 13 1906	Proof of service returned, dated Sept 12 -1906
Sept 24 1906	Pltf advises that dfndt is still in possession
" 29 1906	Dfndt given ten day in which to vacate premises or show cause otherwise order will issue to remove
" 29 1906	Pltf notified of above letter
Oct 6 1906	Dfndt advises that he has given possession
Oct 9 1906	Plntf advised of above & asked to advise this office if he is in possession
Nov 3 1906	Case set for hearing at Claremore ITy Nov 20, 1906 All parties notified
Nov 20 1906	Case called at Claremore. Plntf appear[sic] & stated that dfndt had virtually surrendered premises but still had some hogs & farming implements on place. No appearance by dfndt. Homestead certificate No. 30314 returned to plntf in open court. Dismissed

---

INTRUDER CASE NO. 849
Cherokee NATION

Plaintiff: G. D. Logan Gdn of (Levi L ~~struck~~)
Henrietta and Ernest Garvin
Pryor Creek I.Ty.
Atty.

Versus

Defendant: B A Jarboe
Coffeyville Kans
Atty.

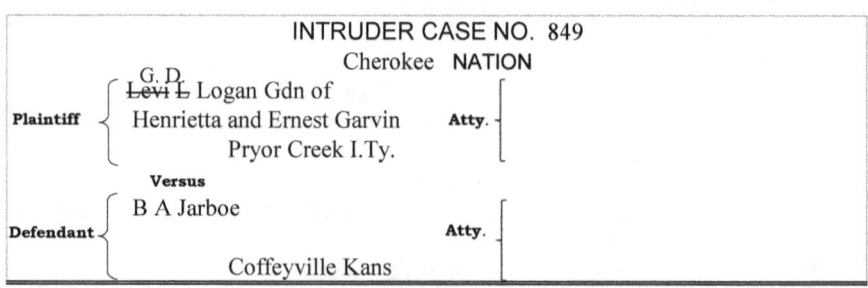

Cherokee Intruder Cases 1901 - 1909

Complaint filed Aug 30 1906 **Commissioner Reports** Sep 8 1906 No **Contest. Notice Sent** Sept 16 1906	
Sept 24 1906	Proof of service returned dated Sept 19 1906 Reg Ret card in file
Oct 1 1906	Pltf writes and asks that certain witnesses to subpeonied[sic].
Oct 3 1906	Pltf advised that it will be necessary for her to arrange about witnesses
Nov 3 1906	Case set for hearing at Claremore ITy Nov 21 1906 All parties notified
Nov 13 1906	Answer filed by dfndt
Nov 21 1906	Case called at Claremore. No appearance by either party
Nov 20 1906	Letter from dfndt enclosing check for $5^{00} to be paid to plntf.
" 24 1906	Check returned to dfndt
Jany 18 1907	Case set for hearing at Claremore ITy Feby 5 1907 All parties notified
Feby 5 1907	Case called at Claremore ITy. Plntf present & testimony[sic] taken
	No appearance by dfndt. Letters of Gdnship filed by plntf
	Certificates exhibited by plntf.
Mch 4 1907	Judgement[sic] found for plntf. Dfndt given ten days to vacate.
Mch 7 1907	Dfndt states he has no claim nor improvements on land in question
Apr 8 1907	Dfndt asks that check $5^{00} be returned to him
Apr 12 1907	Check returned Case Dismissed

INTRUDER CASE NO. 850
Cherokee NATION

Plaintiff   Maggie Poindexter   Atty.
                Wagoner ITy

Versus

Defendant   A.G. Thomas   Atty.
                G.D. Sleeper
                Wagoner ITy.

Complaint filed Sept 18 1906 **Commissioner Reports** Sept 26 1906 No **Contest. Notice Sent** Sept 15 1906	
Sept 8 1906	Allottment[sic] certificate 15993
" 15 1906	Com^r requested to report
Sept 19 1906	Proof of Service returned, dated Sept 17" 1906
Oct 15 1906	Letters from plntf filed
" 17 1906	Above letter answered & asked to advise if she wants G.D. Sleeper made party to dfnse.
Nov 12 1906	At request of plntf. G.D. Sleeper made party of defense
Nov 15 1906	Case set for hearing at Muskogee ITy Dec 4, 1906 All parties notified
Dec 4 1906	Case called at Muskogee ITy plntf & dfndt Sleeper present and testimony taken.
Dec 5 1906	Allottment[sic] certificates Nos 11601-14591-51623 filed by plntf
Feby 16 1907	Allottment[sic] certificates Nos 15993-51623-14591-11601 returned to plntf in person at Muskogee ITy in presence of

Cherokee Intruder Cases 1901 - 1909

Jan 8 1908	Mr. Hadley *(?)*M at Hadley, ITy Case dismissed as defendant has a lease

INTRUDER CASE NO. 851
Cherokee NATION

Plaintiff: George T Welch, Stilwell ITy — Atty.

Versus

Defendant: N.A. Brannon, Stilwell ITy — Atty.

Complaint filed Sept 4 1906 **Commissioner Reports** Sept 26 1906 **No Contest.** **Notice Sent** Sept 17 1906

Sept 4 1906	Allottment[sic] certificate in file No 16860
" 4 "	Lease contract in file
Sept 17 1906	Com^r requested to report
Oct 1 1906	Proof of service returned dated Oct 1, 1906
Oct 9 1906	Plntf states that settlement has been made, requests dismissal return of ∧ certificate
Oct 11 1906	In compliance with above, certificates No 16860 returned &

Case Dismissed

INTRUDER CASE NO. 852
Cherokee NATION

Plaintiff: George ~~McLain~~ Fillmore, McLain ITy — Atty. J.H. Childers, Muskogee I.Ty.

Versus

Defendant: Sam Carpenter, Warner ITy. — Atty. W.J. Crump, Muskogee ITy.

Complaint filed Sep 8 1906 **Commissioner Reports** Sept 26 1906 **No Contest.** **Notice Sent** Sept 17 1906

Sep 8 1906	Allottment[sic] certificate No 24013 in file
" 17 1906	Com^r requested to report
Oct 1 1906	Proof of service returned dated Oct 1" 1906
Oct 10 1906	Answer filed by Atty for dfndt
Oct 20 1906	Case set for hearing at Muskogee Nov 3 1906 10 AM All parties notified
Nov 3 1906	Case called at Muskogee ITy No appearance by either party
Feby 9 1907	Case set for hearing at Muskogee ITy Feby 26 1907 All parties notified
Feby 26 1907	Atty for plntf told W.W.B. over phone & asked that case be dismissed

Cherokee Intruder Cases 1901 - 1909

	as settlement had been made. Dismissed
Oct 24 07	Allottment[sic] certificate No 24013 returned to plaintiff in person.

INTRUDER CASE NO. 853
Cherokee NATION

Plaintiff: Wm Sweetwater for Golda Sweetwater, Zena I.Ty.   **Atty.**

Versus

Defendant: Bill Ballard [Boland struck] and J.A. Mathews   **Atty.**

Complaint filed Sept 1 1906 **Commissioner Reports** Sept 26 1906 **No Contest.** **Notice Sent** Sept 17 1906

Sept 1 1906	Allottment[sic] certificates No. 58112 & 35449
" 17 1906	Com^r requested to report.
Oct 1 1906	Proof of Service returned, dated Sept 28 1906
Oct 5 1906	William Ballard files answer in which he states plntf must be in error as he is living on his own allottment[sic].
Nov 3 1906	Case set for hearing at Claremore ITy 1906 All parties notified
Nov 21 1906	Case called at Claremore Defendant appeared and rendered testimony no appearance by Plaintiff
Dec 12 1906	Plntf advised to take possession as dfndt stated he would remove his fence & vacate. Allottment[sic] certificates returned. Case dismissed

INTRUDER CASE NO. 854
Cherokee NATION

Plaintiff: Wm Sweetwater father of and for John Sweetwater and Viola Sweetwater Zena I.Ty   **Atty.**

Versus

Defendant: Thos J Jordan, Vinita ITy   **Atty.** J.C. Starr, Fogle & Parks, Vinita ITy.

Complaint filed Sept 1 1906 **Commissioner Reports** Sept 27 1906 see below Contest. **Notice Sent** Sept 17 1906

Sept 1 1906	Allottment[sic] certificates Nos 35450-58114, 35448-58111
" 17 1906	Com^r requested to report
Sept 27 1906	Com^r reports a portion of land allotted[sic] to Viola Sweetwater in contest
Oct 1 1906	Plntf advised of Com^r report & that case is dismissed as to that

Cherokee Intruder Cases 1901 - 1909

	portion of the land
Oct 1 1906	Proof of service returned dated Sept 28-1906
Oct 12 1906	Answer filed by dfndt.
Nov 3 1906	Case set for hearing at Claremore ITy Nov 2 1906 All parties notified
Nov 21 1906	Case called at Claremore ITy. No appearance by either party
Jany 18 1907	Case set for hearing at Claremore ITy Feby 5 1907 All parties notified
Feby 5 1907	Case called at Claremore ITy. Plntf appeared & testimony taken. No appearance by dfndt. Plntf is full blood.
Feby 5 1907	Atty for dfndt advises dfndt cannot appear because of sickness in family
Feby 13 1907	Dfndt requested to appear at this office Feby 25 1907 to give evidence
Mch 2 1907	Com^r asked to report.
Mch 6 1907	Dfndt advised that if he does not vacate or show cause, an order will issue to remove him.
Mch 7 1907	Com^r reports no contest on allottment[sic] of Jno Sweetwater.
Mch 26 1907	Case set for hearing at Claremore ITy. Apr 8, 1907.
Apr 8 1907	Case called a Claremore I.Ty. No appearance by either party Mr. Farks[sic] Atty for dfndt states that dfndt confess judgement[sic].
June 18 07	Plff requested to advise in re possession
July 5 -07	Case dismissed as pltf *(illegible)* that matter is settled.
	<center>Dismissed</center>
7/17/07	Certs returned today

INTRUDER CASE NO. 855
Cherokee NATION

Plaintiff — John C. West Adm^r of Elizabeth McElmeele, deceased, Muskogee, I.Ty. **Atty.** — R. P. D^{e}Graffenreid

Versus

Defendant — Harvey Human, Muskogee ITy. **Atty.** — William & Nelson, Muskogee ITy

Complaint filed Sept 22 1906 **Commissioner Reports**   **Contest.**   **Notice Sent** Sept 24 1906

Sept 22 1906	Plat from Com^r in file.
" 25 1906	Proof of service returned, dated Aug 24 1906
Oct 3 1906	Answer filed by dfndt
Oct 5 1906	Case set for hearing at Muskogee ITy Sat Oct 6 1906
Oct 6 1906	Case called all parties present & testimony taken Letters of administration issued to Jno C. West dated April 26 1906 Exhibit "A"
" 1906	Both parties represented by Attys. Agreement made (verbal) whereby dfndt was to atone to plntf Jno C West for all rents according to his agreement with allottee[sic], now deceased, and surrender possession of

Cherokee Intruder Cases 1901 - 1909

Jany 19 1907	premises Jany 1, 1907 Capt West reports possession. <u>Case dismissed</u>

INTRUDER CASE NO. 856
Cherokee NATION

Plaintiff	Runabout Ummarteskee	**Atty.** H.L. Littlefield Peggs ITy.
	Versus	
Defendant	Ed Culver Vian ITy.	**Atty.**

Complaint filed Aug 31 1906 **Commissioner Reports** Sept 18 1906 Portion in **Contest.** **Notice Sent** Sept 27 1906

Oct 8 1906	Proof of service, returned Oct 6, 1906.
Nov 14 1906	Case set for hearing at Muskogee ITy Nov 29 1906 All parties notified
Nov 29 1906	Case called & no appearance by either party
Jany 22 1907	Referred to Robt R. Bennett for investigation.
Jany 28 1907	Robt R. Bennett reports recommends plntf be requested to go into possession
Feby 1 1907	Plntf requested to go into possession. <u>Case dismissed</u>

INTRUDER CASE NO. 857
Cherokee NATION

Plaintiff	Edith Wickett Roberts (nee Wickett) Grove I.Ty.	**Atty.**
	Versus	
Defendant	Earl Hardy Zena ITy.	**Atty.**

Complaint filed Sept 4 1906 **Commissioner Reports** Sep 18 1906 **No Contest.** **Notice Sent** Sept 27 1906

Oct 2 1906	Allottment[sic] certificates Nos 9523 & 778 filed by Eldon Lowe who had same in his possession in a former case. Plntf so notified
Nov 3 1906	Case set for hearing at Claremore ITy Nov 21 1906 All parties notified
Nov 21 1906	Case called at Claremore. No appearance by either party.
Jany 8 1907	Certificates returned as per request of plntf & she is advised that case will again be set for hearing.
Jany 18 1907	Case set for hearing at Claremore ITy Feby 5 1907 All parties notified

Cherokee Intruder Cases 1901 - 1909

Feby 5 1907   Case called at Claremore ITy. Neither party appeared.
Feby 13 1907   Referred to Robt R. Bennett
Mch 23 1907   Robt R. Bennett advises settlement made.
Mch 27 1907   Case dismissed

INTRUDER CASE NO. 858
Cherokee NATION

Plaintiff: Peggie Malvern, Checotah ITy. Atty.

Versus

Defendant: Muskogee Development Co, Muskogee ITy. Atty. Hutchings, Murphy & German, Muskogee ITy.

Complaint filed Sept 6 1906 **Commissioner Reports** Sept 19 1906 No **Contest**. **Notice Sent** Sept 27 1906

Oct 8 1906   Proof of service returned, dated Oct 6, 1906
" 16 1906   Answer filed by Attys for dfndt.
Nov 14 1906   Case set for hearing at Muskogee ITy Nov 29 1906
Nov. 30 1906   Case called at Muskogee ITy. Plntf present & testimony taken. Dfndt represented by Mr. German Atty. Dfndt[sic] have legal contract. Case dismissed See Stenographer's notes in 863.

INTRUDER CASE NO. 859
Cherokee NATION

Plaintiff: Samuel E Gidney Legal Gdn of Willie Porter, Muskogee ITy. Atty.

Versus

Defendant: W.W. Findlay, Watova I.Ty. Atty.

Complaint filed Sept 7 1906 **Commissioner Reports** Sept 19 1906 No **Contest**. **Notice Sent** Sept 27 1906

Nov 3 1906   Case set for hearing at Claremore ITy Nov 21 1906 All parties notified
Nov 21 1906   Case called at Claremore. No appearance by either party.
Nov 19 1906   Proof of Service returned, dated Nov 9 1906
" 19 1906   Letter filed by plntf in which dfndt signifies willingness to surrender and plntf requests dismissal.
Jany 24 1907   In view of above, case dismissed

Cherokee Intruder Cases 1901 - 1909

INTRUDER CASE NO. 860
Cherokee NATION

Plaintiff: Samuel E. Gidney, Legal Gdn of Maud Porter   Atty.

Versus

Defendant: Ed. J. Gottlulp
D.D. Holloway   Atty.
Coffeyville Kans

Complaint filed Sept 7 1906 **Commissioner Reports** Sept 1906 **No Contest. Notice Sent** Sept 27 1906

Oct 30 1906	Answer filed by dfndt
Nov 3 1906	Case set for hearing at Claremore ITy Nov 21 1906 All parties notified
Nov 5 1906	Data furnished dfndt.
Nov 19 1906	Proof of service as shown by reg ret card. Lease contracts & affidavitts[sic] filed by dfndt by mail at Claremore ITy
" 21 1906	Case called at Claremore ITy. No appearance by either party
Dec 12 1906	DD Holloway made party dfndt & case set for hearing at Muskogee ITy Dec 27 1906. All parties notified.
Dec 27 1906	Case called at Muskogee ITy. Plntf appeared & testimony taken No app by dfndt
Jany 30 1907	Judgement[sic] rendered for plntf. Dfndt given ten days in which to vacate
June 18 07	Plff. requested to advise in re. possession
Jan 8 08	Case dismissed by order of W.W.B.

INTRUDER CASE NO. 861
Cherokee NATION

Plaintiff: Rosa Young   Atty.
Fort Gibson ITy

Versus

Defendant: Robert Moore
W.J. Stark   Atty.   Louis T. Brown (nigger)
Turley I.Ty. Tulsa ITy   Muskogee ITy

Complaint filed Sept 8 1906 **Commissioner Reports** Sept 19 1906 **No Contest. Notice Sent** Sept 27 1906

Oct 19 1906	Plntf states she is unable to locate dfndt & can not serve notice
" 22 1906	Plntf advised to return notices & ascertain who is actually in possession & notify this office
Nov 7 1906	Proof of service returned dated Nov 5 1906
Nov 23 1906	Answer filed by W.J. Stark
Nov 27 1906	Case set for hearing at Muskogee ITy Dec 6" 2 PM 1906 All parties notified
Dec 6 1906	Case called at Muskogee ITy. All parties present testimony taken. Atty for dfndt asks 10 days in which to file documentary evidence

Cherokee Intruder Cases 1901 - 1909

Dec 7 1906	Com^r asked to report as to citizenship of Robert Moore, dfndt. *no appeal*
Dec 14 1906	Com^r reports application of Robert Moore a Freedman rejected May 29
Dec 20 1906	Judgement[sic] rendered in favor of plndt[sic]. Dfndt to vacate in ten days.
Jany 12 1907	Instructions issued to Policeman William M Sunday Tulsa I.Ty.
Feby 7 1907	Policeman Sunday appeared at this office & stated plntf had not advised him when she would meet him.
Feb 7 1907	Plntf requested to advise Policeman Sunday when she will meet him
Feby 14 1907	Policeman Sunday reports he placed plntf in possession.
Feby 19 1907	Case dismissed

INTRUDER CASE NO. 862
Cherokee NATION

Plaintiff: S F Parks Legal Gdn of Rufus V Lacey and Charlotte C Lacey Vian ITy
Atty: G. P. Fogle Vinita I.T.

Versus

Defendant: D. Cameron, W J Osborn and Tom Jordon Collinsville ITy.
Atty:

Complaint filed Sept 5 1906 **Commissioner Reports** Sept 19 1906 **No Contest**. **Notice Sent** Sept 28 1906

Sept 5 1906	Letters of Gdnship filed
Oct 4 1906	Proof of service returned, dated Oct 2" 1906
Oct 8 1906	Answer filed by dfndt
Nov 3 1906	Case set for hearing at Claremore ITy Nov 21 1906 All parties notified
" 21 1906	Case called at Claremore IT Atty for Ptf appeared No appearance by Dfdt.
Jany 18 1907	Case set for hearing at Claremore ITy Feby 5 1907 All parties notified.
Feby 5 1907	Case called at Claremore ITy. Plntf appeared and testimony taken. No appearance by any of Dfndts.
Mch 4 1907	Judgement[sic] found for plntf. Dfndt requested to vacate in ten days.
Mch 8 1907	Plntf advised case is settled & he is in possession.
Mch 12 1907	Letters of gdnship returned & case dismissed

INTRUDER CASE NO. 863
Cherokee NATION

Plaintiff: Peggie Malvern Nat Gdn of Lone Butler Checotah ITy
Atty:

Versus

Cherokee Intruder Cases 1901 - 1909

Defendant	Muskogee Development Co Muskogee ITy.	Atty.	Hutchings, Murphy & German Muskogee ITy.

Complaint filed Sept 6 1906 **Commissioner Reports** Sep 19 1906 No **Contest.** **Notice Sent** Sept 28 1906

Oct 9 1906	Proof of service returned dated Oct 6 1906
Nov 15 1906	Case set for hearing at Muskogee ITy Nov 30 1906 All parties notified.
Nov 30 1906	Case called at Muskogee I.Ty. Plntf present and testimony taken. Dfndt represented by his Atty Mr. German. Dfndt exhibited lease signed by natural gdn of minor child. Plntf advised that guardian should be appointed. <u>Dismissed</u>. See statement in copy of testimony.

INTRUDER CASE NO. 864
Cherokee NATION

Plaintiff	Henry W Ziegler Legal Gdn of Samuel, Nancy, Jeremiah and Charlotte Ziegler Vinita ITy	Atty.	S F Parks Vinita ITy.
	Versus		
Defendant	R.L. ~~James~~ England Cleora I.Ty	Atty.	

Complaint filed Sept 5 1906 **Commissioner Reports** Sept 19 1906 No **Contest.** **Notice Sent** Sept 28 1906

Sept 5 1906	Letters of Gdnship filed.
Oct 10 1906	Proof of service returned dated Oct 8, 1906
" 16 1906	Answer filed by R.L. England fndt[sic]
Nov 3 1906	Case set for hearing at Claremore ITy Nov 21 1906 All parties notified
" 21 1906	Case called at Claremore ITy Defendant appeared and rendered testimony Plntf represented by Mr. Fogle no appearance by Plaintiff
Dec 14 1906	Plntf requested to advise if he wishes to be heard.
Dec 26 1906	Judgement[sic] rendered in favor plntf. Dfndt requested to vacate in 10 days
Jany 26 1907	Plntf requested to advise if he is in possession.
Jany 29 1907	Atty for plntf states they understand plntf has made compromise, but if so, without their advise[sic]
Feby 5 1907	Plntf requested to advise if case is settled
Feby 12 1907	Plntf reports he has possession.
Feby 16 1907	In view of above, <u>case dismissed</u>

Cherokee Intruder Cases 1901 - 1909

INTRUDER CASE NO. 865
Cherokee NATION

Plaintiff: Lewis Budding Legal Gdn of Maudie Fallingpot
Eucha ITy.
Atty.: (Illegible) Foegle
Vinita ITy

Versus

Defendant: Rose Vann, Ed Vann, C.D. West
Chaffee ITy
Atty.: Starr & Patton
Vinita ITy.

Complaint filed Sept 6 1906 **Commissioner Reports** Sept 19 1906 **No Contest. Notice Sent** Sept 28 1906

Sept 6 1906	Lease contract & Letters of Gdnship in file.
Oct 13 1906	Proof of service returned dated Oct 5" 1906
Oct 15 1906	Answer filed by dfndt. State that Lula Vann is applicant for enrollment
Oct 25 1906	Com^r reports one Rosa Vann applicant for enrollment. Ed Vann refused, no motion to reopen.
Nov 3 1906	Case set for hearing at Claremore ITy. Nov 21, 1906 All parties notified.
Nov 21 1906	Case called at Claremore. Plaintiff appeared and rendered testimony No appearance by Defendant
Dec 12 1905	Because of application for citizenship pending - Rose Vann - <u>case dismissed</u> & Letters of gdnship & Lease contract ret to plntf
2-11-09	Referred to Cusey for investigation
1-29-09	Pltf advised
1-29-09	Com^r's report requested (furnished)

INTRUDER CASE NO. 866
Cherokee NATION

Plaintiff: William W. Ross, Jr
Talequah[sic] ITy.
Atty.:

Versus

Defendant: S. H. and M.V. Patton
Whitmire ITy.
Atty.:

Complaint filed Sept 10 1906 **Commissioner Reports** Sept 25 1906 **No Contest. Notice Sent** Sept 28 1906

Sept 10 1906	Rental contract filed
Oct 10 1906	Proof of service returned dated Oct 4, 1906 Reg ret card in file
" 10 1906	Answer filed by dfndt
" 16 1906	Case set for hearing Nov 12 1906 at 2 PM All parties notified
Nov 12 1906	Plntf appeared and asked that case be continued pending settlement and agreed to notify this office s to disposition. Granted.
Dec 8 1906	As per request of Plntf <u>case be dismissed</u>

Cherokee Intruder Cases 1901 - 1909

INTRUDER CASE NO. 867
Cherokee NATION

Plaintiff: Andrew Tally, Legal Gdn of Maggie Tally, Ft Gibson ITy. **Atty.**

Versus

Defendant: Arthur Owens, Checotah ITy. **Atty.** Charles R Freeman, Checotah ITy.

Complaint filed Sept 24 1906 **Commissioner Reports** Oct 10 1906 **No Contest.** **Notice Sent** Sept 28 1906

Sept 24 1906	Allottment[sic] certificates Nos 42196 - 29025
" 24 1906	Letters of Gdnship filed.
" 24 1906	Com^r requested to report
Oct 4 1906	Proof of service returned, dated Oct 4 1906
Oct 26 1906	Dfndt again asked to show cause why he should not be removed
" 30 1906	Atty for dfndt states plntf is sick & will file answer soon.
Nov 1 1906	Atty for dfndt advised that more than ten days have elapsed since service
Nov 3 1906	By agreement over telephone case called at Muskogee. Mr E.T. Owen father of Arthur Owen, and Atty C.R. Freeman of Checotah ITy. present Testimony of E.T. Owen, real dfndt taken.
Dec 4 1906	Case set for hearing at Muskogee ITy. Dec 12" 1906. All parties notified
Dec 12 1906	Case called at Muskogee ITy. No appearance. Plntf writes that he is in jail & can not be here.
Dec 29 1906	Case set for hearing at Muskogee ITy Jany 2 1907 2 P.M.
Jany 2 1907	Case called at Muskogee ITy. Plntf present & testimony taken. Letters of gdnship offerred[sic] in evidence. Same were returned to him, also Allottment[sic] certificates Nos 42196 - 29025 Later, Letters of gdnship & certificates No 29025 52196 again in file.
Jany 30 1907	Judgement[sic] for plntf. Dfndt given ten days in which to vacate.
Feby 21 1907	Atty for dfndt asks new hearing. Denied & requested to vacate.
Mch 18 1907	Plntf appeared & stated he has possession. Letters of gdnship & certificates returned to plntf in person & <u>case dismissed</u>

INTRUDER CASE NO. 868
Cherokee NATION

Plaintiff: Ellen C McLane, Owasso ITy **Atty.**

Versus

Defendant: George Prichard, Owasso ITy. **Atty.**

Cherokee Intruder Cases 1901 - 1909

Complaint filed Sept 19 1906	Commissioner Reports Oct 10 1906 No Contest. Notice Sent Sept 28 1906
Sept 19 1906	Allottment[sic] certificates Nos 10580 - 8609
" 28 1906	Com^r requested to report
Oct 19 1906	Proof of service returned dated Oct 18, 1906
Nov 5 1906	Case set for hearing at Claremore ITy Nov 22 1906 All parties notified
Nov 22 1906	Case called at Claremore ITy. Plntf appeared and testimony taken No appearance by Defendant
Nov 27 1906	Lease contracts filed by plntf.
Dec 14 1906	Judgement[sic] in favor of plntf. Dfndt given ten days to vacate.
Dec 31 1906	Plntf states she has possession & asks for certificates.
Jany 4 1907	Certificates Nos 10580 - 8609 returned - <u>Case dismissed</u>

INTRUDER CASE NO. 869
Cherokee NATION

Plaintiff: Tom Sunday for Kelly and Kittie Sunday, Porum I Ty.   Atty.

Versus

Defendant: Monroe and Tom Young, Fannie Starr see 10/4/06 in dkt., Porum ITy   Atty.

Complaint filed Sept 14 1906 Commissioner Reports	Contest. Notice Sent Sept 28 1906
Sept 14 1906	Allottments[sic] certificates Nos 8753-10766-8754-10767
" 14 1906	Com^r requested to report
Oct 4 1906	Proof of service returned dated Oct 2nd 1906
" 4 1906	Pltf requests notice to serve on Fannie Starr.
Oct 13 1906	Pltf advises that detfndt will not surrender premises.
Oct 8 1906	Com^r advises that allottment[sic] certificates of plntfs have been cancelled
" 10 1906	F.C. Starr advises that he is gdn of Eli Bunch and asks if Tom Sunday has filed complat[sic].
" 12 1906	Plntf advised as to report of Com^r. Certificates returned No. 8753-10766-10767 forwarded to Com^r to be cancelled. <u>Case dismissed</u>
Oct 13 1906	F.C. Starr notified of above action.
" 22 1906	Com^r ack. receipt of certificates for cancellation
" 31 1906	Upon request, plntf advised that certificates were forwarded to Com^r <u>Dismissed</u>

Cherokee Intruder Cases 1901 - 1909

INTRUDER CASE NO. 870
Cherokee NATION

Plaintiff: Cornelia C Benge, Talala ITy.
Atty.

Versus

Defendant: Haywood Jones (colored), Talala
Atty.

Complaint filed Sept 27 1906 **Commissioner Reports** Oct 10 1906 portion in **Contest. Notice Sent** Sept 28 1906

Sept 27 1906	Allottment[sic] certificates Nos 34228 - 55490 filed.
" 28 1906	Com^r requested to report
Oct 9 1906	Proof of service returned dated Oct 6, 1906
Nov 3 1906	Case set for hearing at Claremore ITy Nov 22, 1906 All parties notified
Nov 12 1906	Plntf states has possession of place
" 15 1906	In view of above, <u>case dismissed</u> & Allottment[sic] certificates Nos 34228 -55490 returned
~~May 7 1907~~	~~Dfndt advised not to interfere~~
Nov 18 07	Plntf requests information which is furnished and Defendant requested to pay rents as contest is not pending Dismissed
Feb 14 08	*(No other information given.)*

INTRUDER CASE NO. 871
Cherokee NATION

Plaintiff: H.L. Rogers for Beulah E Rogers
Atty. Neal and London, F^t Smith Ark.

Versus

Defendant: William Kirkland and Squire Little, Roland I.Ty.
Atty.

Complaint filed Sept 10 1906 **Commissioner Reports** Oct 8 1906 No **Contest. Notice Sent** Sept 29 1906

Sept 10 1906	Allottment[sic] certificate No 62310 filed.
~~Sept 29~~ Oct 1 1906	Com^r requested to report
Oct 6 1906	Proof of service returned dated Oct 4, 1906
Nov 15 1906	Case set for hearing at Muskogee ITy. Nov 30, 1906 All parties notified
Nov 21 1906	Answer filed by W M Kirkland.
Nov 30 1906	Case called at Muskogee ITy. No appearance by either party. Case set for hearing at Muskogee ITy Dec 5, 1906
Dec 5 1906	Case called at Muskogee ITy. Plntf appeared & testimony taken. No

Cherokee Intruder Cases 1901 - 1909

	appearance by dfndt. Plntf to furnish copy of Letters of Gdnship
Dec 15 1906	Judgement[sic] for plntf. Dfndt given ten days to vacate.
Jany 14 1907	Instructions issued to Policeman Tandy W Adair of Salisaw ITy.
Jan 29 1907	Policeman Adair reports he place allottee[sic] in possession Report misplaced.
Feby 11 1907	Case <u>dismissed</u>
Mch 4 1907	Plntf states he has not been placed in possession. Says TW Adair *(?) (illegible)* to pay 6\underline{^{00}}$.
Mch 9 1907	Plntf asked if he went with Policeman Adair to be placed in possession.
Mch 9 1907	TW Adair Policeman advised of plntf's letter & asked to reply
Mch 14 1907	HL Rogers asks for possession & encloses letter to him from Policeman T.W. Adair.
Mch 20 1907	HL Rogers advised that this office will take no farther action
Mch 26 1907	H.L. Rogers states he has never been in possession.
Apr 12 1907	Policeman T.W. Adair instructed to place plntf in possession.
April 19 1907	Indian Policeman Adair reports pltf placed in <u>possession</u> of land.
April 25 1907	Case <u>dismissed</u> -

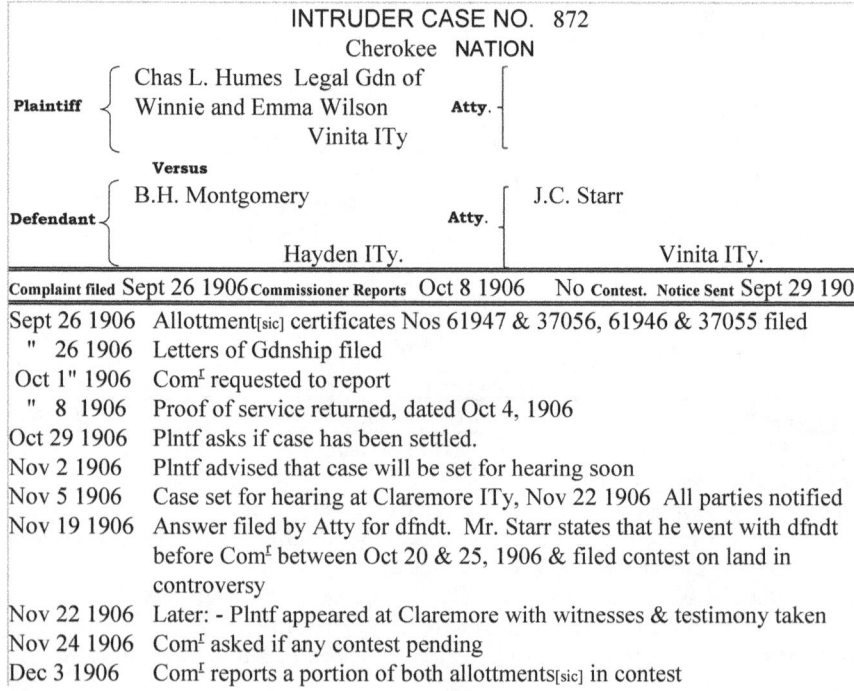

INTRUDER CASE NO. 872
Cherokee NATION

Plaintiff: Chas L. Humes Legal Gdn of Winnie and Emma Wilson
Vinita ITy
Atty.

Versus

Defendant: B.H. Montgomery
Hayden ITy.
Atty. J.C. Starr
Vinita ITy.

Complaint filed Sept 26 1906	Commissioner Reports Oct 8 1906	No Contest. Notice Sent Sept 29 1906

Sept 26 1906	Allottment[sic] certificates Nos 61947 & 37056, 61946 & 37055 filed
" 26 1906	Letters of Gdnship filed
Oct 1" 1906	Com[r] requested to report
" 8 1906	Proof of service returned, dated Oct 4, 1906
Oct 29 1906	Plntf asks if case has been settled.
Nov 2 1906	Plntf advised that case will be set for hearing soon
Nov 5 1906	Case set for hearing at Claremore ITy, Nov 22 1906 All parties notified
Nov 19 1906	Answer filed by Atty for dfndt. Mr. Starr states that he went with dfndt before Com[r] between Oct 20 & 25, 1906 & filed contest on land in controversy
Nov 22 1906	Later: - Plntf appeared at Claremore with witnesses & testimony taken
Nov 24 1906	Com[r] asked if any contest pending
Dec 3 1906	Com[r] reports a portion of both allottments[sic] in contest

Cherokee Intruder Cases 1901 - 1909

Dec 14 1906 Plntf advised that land is in contest & no action can be taken by this office. Allottment[sic] certificates Nos 61947, 37056, 61946, 37055. Also Letters of Gdnship returned to plntf & <u>case dismissed</u>

	INTRUDER CASE NO. 873	
	Cherokee NATION	
Plaintiff	Nannie West	Frank J. Boudinot &
	Atty.	Eiffert
	Fort Gibson, ITy.	Ft Gibson ITy
	Versus	
Defendant	Oma Campbell	W.J. Sullivan
	Atty.	
	F^t Gibson ITy.	Muskogee ITy

Complaint filed Sept 13 1906 **Commissioner Reports** Sept 26 1906 No **Contest. Notice Sent**

Sept 13 1906 Allottment[sic] certificates Nos 24987 & 35800 filed.
Sept 15 1906 Com^r requested to report as to contest
Oct 1 1906 Com^r requested to report if motion to re-hear case of Oma Campbell is pending
Oct 9 1906 Proof of service ret dated Oct 18, 1906
~~Oct 8 1906~~ ~~Com^r reports no contest pending.~~
Oct 6 1906 Com^r states application for citizenship of Oma Campbell refused.
Nov 1 1906 Answer filed by Atty for dfndt.
Nov 10 1906 Case set for hearing at Muskogee ITy Nov. 14, 1906
Nov 14 1906 Case called at Muskogee All parties & Attys present. Testimony taken Exhibit "A" showing status of citizenship of dfndt Exhibit "B" plat of land
Nov 15 1906 Comr reports denial of citizenship of dfndt confirmed by department. Three motions to review have been denied & he, Com^r, is now without authority to consider motion to review.
Dec 3 1906 Judgment for plntf. - dfndts requested to vacate within ten days
Dec 11 1906 Atty for dfndt filed application for appeal from decree of this office go Com^r of Indian Affairs Washington D.C. Same is granted 12/14/06. See carbon
Dec 14 1906 Copy of application for appeal sent to Atty for plntf who is notified that action by this office will be withheld pending action of dpmt.
Dec 18 1906 Submitted to Com^r of Indian Affairs ~~for~~ and asked that judgement[sic] be sustained.
Apr 1 1907 Com^r of Ind Affairs confirms decision of U.S.I. Agent & directs that he place plntf in possession.
Apr 9 1907 Dfndt advised of above & directed to vacate. Plntf asked to advise this office if dfndt vacates.
Apr 16 1907 Policeman R.E. Williams instructed to place plntf in possession
Apr 24 1907 Policeman R.E. Williams reports pltf in <u>possession</u> of land.

<u>Case Dismissed</u>

Cherokee Intruder Cases 1901 - 1909

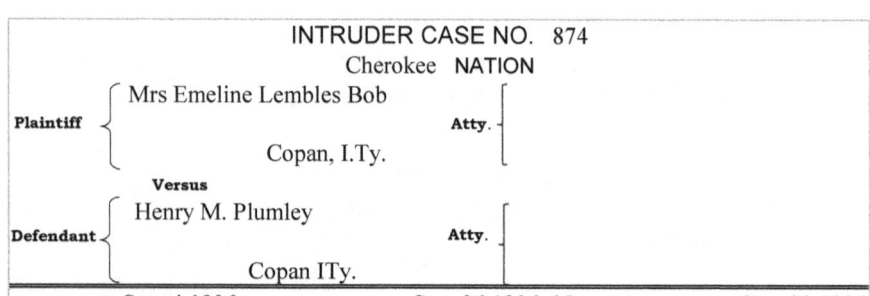

INTRUDER CASE NO. 874
Cherokee NATION

Plaintiff: Mrs Emeline Lembles Bob, Copan, I.Ty.   Atty.

Versus

Defendant: Henry M. Plumley, Copan ITy.   Atty.

Complaint filed Sept 4 1906 **Commissioner Reports** Sept 26 1906 **No Contest. Notice Sent** Sept 29 1906

Sept 4 1906 Plat showing location of land, filed.
Oct 6 1906 Dfndt files answer.
" 8 1906 Return of Proof of service dated Oct 4, 1906
" 8 1906 Plntf complains of dfndt's cattle on her homestead.
" 16 1906 " gives additional data.
Nov 3 1906 Case set for hearing at Claremore ITy Nov 22, 1906 All parties notified
Nov 22 1906 Case called at Claremore ITy. No appearance by either party.
Nov 16 1906 W.H. Nash letter in file, states dfndt has vacated premises.
Nov 30 1906 In view of above letter <u>case dismissed</u>

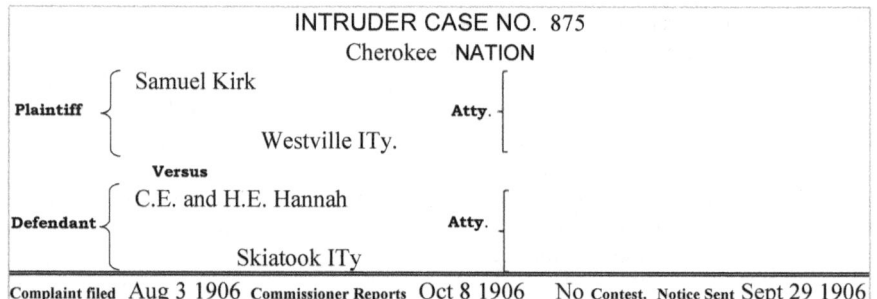

INTRUDER CASE NO. 875
Cherokee NATION

Plaintiff: Samuel Kirk, Westville ITy.   Atty.

Versus

Defendant: C.E. and H.E. Hannah, Skiatook ITy   Atty.

Complaint filed Aug 3 1906 **Commissioner Reports** Oct 8 1906 **No Contest. Notice Sent** Sept 29 1906

Oct 1 1906 Com^r requested to report.
Aug 3 1906 Certificate of allottment[sic] No 8878 filed.
Oct 17 1906 Plntf asks when case will be heard.
" 19 1906 Plntf informed that he will be advised later.
Oct 8 1906 Proof of service returned dated Oct 6, 1906
Oct 22 1906 Answer filed by dfndt
Nov 3 1906 Case set for hearing at Claremore ITy Nov 22 1906 All parties notified
Nov 22 1906 Case called at Claremore. All parties present. Testimony taken. Two lease contracts offerred[sic] by Dfndt C.E. Hannah. Same in file. Allotment[sic] certificate No 10949 filed by plntf.
Dec 14 1906 Judgement[sic] for plntf. Contracts ret to dfndts & they are requested to

Cherokee Intruder Cases 1901 - 1909

               vacate in 10 da.
Jany 6 1907   Plntf requested to advise if he is in possession
June 18 07   Certs 10949 - 8878 returned to plff and he requested to advise in re poss.
Sept 20 07   Plaintiff has failed to reply to letters addressed to him.
               It is presumed that Plaintiff is in possession. Case Dismissed

INTRUDER CASE NO. 876
Cherokee NATION

Plaintiff: William A Cooper, Gdn of Joseph and Pigeon Sanders   Atty.
Adna[sic], Kans

Versus

Defendant: Aaron Webber - Colored.   Atty.
Centralia, ITy.

Complaint filed Sept 29 1906 **Commissioner Reports** Oct 13 1906 All in Contest. **Notice Sent** Oct 5 1906

Sept 29 1906 Allottment[sic] certificates Nos 6586, 8942, 6585 & 8941 in file.
~~Oct 5 1906~~   ~~Com^r requested to report~~
Oct 4 1906   Letters of Gdnship filed.
Oct 6 1906   Com^r requested to report as to any contest.
Oct 25 1906 Proof of Service returned dated Oct 16, 1906
Oct 22 1906 In view of Com^r report certificates & Letters of Gdnship returned and
               Case dismissed

INTRUDER CASE NO. 877
Cherokee NATION

Plaintiff: Ora B Adkison Nat Gdn of Ella M Adkison   Atty.
Catoosa ITy

Versus

Defendant: F.W. Casner owner of Narrow Guage Ry.   Kansas Cy Mo   Atty.
E.E. Doggett, Catoosa, ITy

Complaint filed Sept 27 1906 **Commissioner Reports** Oct 13 1906 No **Contest. Notice Sent**

Sept 27 1906 Allottment[sic] certificates No 62695 in file
Oct 6 1906   Com^r requested to report as to any contest
" 13 1906   Proof of service returned, dated Oct 12, 1906
" 1 1906   Letter from plntf complains because of having to be made legal gdn.
" 13 1906   Pltf states she will not compromise

Cherokee Intruder Cases 1901 - 1909

Oct 25 1906　Plntf asks status of case
Nov 1 1906　Plntf advised that no action can be taken if land is involved in US Court
Nov 23 1906　Upon request of plntf of 11/14/06 Allottment[sic] certificate No 62695
　　　　　　　returned　　　　　　　　　　　　　　　　　　　　　Case Dismissed.

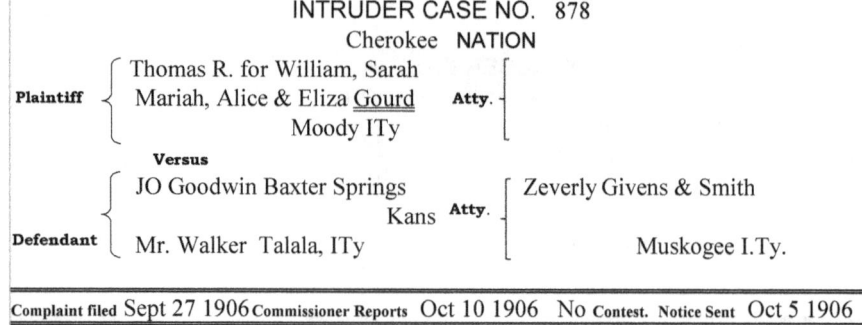

INTRUDER CASE NO. 878
Cherokee NATION

Plaintiff: Thomas R. for William, Sarah Mariah, Alice & Eliza Gourd　Atty. Moody ITy

Versus

Defendant: JO Goodwin Baxter Springs Kans　Atty. Zeverly Givens & Smith
Mr. Walker Talala, ITy　　　　　　　　　　　　Muskogee I.Ty.

Complaint filed Sept 27 1906　Commissioner Reports Oct 10 1906　No Contest.　Notice Sent Oct 5 1906

Sept 27 1906	Allottment[sic] certificates Nos 10343, 12792, 27996, 40575, 10344, 12793,
" 27 1906	12795, &10346 in file
Oct 5 1906	Agricultural rental contract in file.
" 10 1906	Com^r requested to report
Oct 26 1906	Proof of Service returned dated Oct 10 1906 Reg Ret card
Oct 31 1906	Plntf advised that case will be set for hearing soon
Nov 3 1906	Plntf asks that case be set at Muskogee or Talequah[sic].
Nov 9 1906	Goodwin advised that that[sic] he should file answer
Dec 13 1906	Goodwin advises that he has no interest in land in question
	U.S. Policeman J.L. Walker, Dewey ITy requested to investigate and
Dec 22 1906	advise this office as to who is in actual possession of the land in question.
Dec 27 1906	Policeman Walker's report in file.
Jany 2 1907	Mr. Ed Hyatt requested to show cause for occupancy of land
Feby 9 1907	Answer filed by E.A. Hiatt[sic] of Talala, ITy.
Feby 27 1907	Case set for hearing at Muskogee, ITy. Feby 27 1907 All parties notified
	Case called at Muskogee ITy. All parties present. Dfndt rep Smith
	appeared as Atty for dfndt. Five leases filed by Atty for dfndt. Additional
Mch 11 1907	evidence to be offered by dfndt Tuesday Mch 12 1907
	Plntf notified that he need not appear 3/12/07 as dfndt told W.W.B. on
Mch 12 1907	phone he could not get evidence
	Certificates Nos 27996-40575 ret to W^m R Gourd in person in Muskogee
	ITy at which time he appeared & entered into agreement that present
	occupant of land may remain on land as his plntfs tenant. A copy of said
	agreement in file also all parties furnished copy.
	Dismissed

Cherokee Intruder Cases 1901 - 1909

Mch 29 08	Com reports no contest
Mch 26 08	Proof of service filed today
April 17 08	Case <u>dismissed</u> by request of plf as to Mariah R Gourd

INTRUDER CASE NO. 879
Cherokee NATION

Plaintiff: Luvina Latty, Muskogee ITy
Atty:
Defendant: D. H. Burke, Warner ITy
Atty: De Roos Bailey

Complaint filed Sep 20 1906 **Commissioner Reports** Oct 4 1906 **No** Contest. **Notice Sent** Oct 26 1907

Oct 19 1906 Answer filed by Atty for dfndt ~~Reg ret card (supposed to be proof of service in file dated Oct 14, 1906~~
Oct 20 1906 Case set for hearing at Muskogee ITy Nov 2, 1906. All parties notified.
Oct 18 1906 Proof of service returned dated Oct 15, 1906.
Nov 2 1906 Case called at Muskogee. All parties present & testimony taken.
Mr Bailey Atty present for dfndt. No Atty for plntf. Rental contract, statement of acct & receipt offered in evidence. Same returned to dfndt in open court. Lease offered is valid and ample consideration. Certificates in possession of dfndt were delivered to plntf in open court. <u>Case dismissed</u>.
Nov 10 1906 Dfndt D.H. Burke transmitted to this office a warranty deed made by him to plntf for her surplus same to be delivered to plntf. As deed had been recorded by U.S. Cln, it was returned to dfndt to clear title. <u>Dismissed</u>.

INTRUDER CASE NO. 880
Cherokee NATION

Plaintiff: Della Groomer, for her son Willie Groomer, a minor
Atty: W. P. Thompson, Vinita ITy.
Defendant: Henry Stubler and Zeke Clyne
Atty:

Complaint filed Oct 4 1906 **Commissioner Reports** Oct 13 1906 all in **Contest**. **Notice Sent** Oct 8 1906

Oct 18 1906 Proof of service returned, dated Oct. 12, 1906
Oct 8 1906 Com^r requested to report.
Oct 4 1906 Allottment[sic] certificates Nos 62409 & 37241 in file.

Cherokee Intruder Cases 1901 - 1909

Oct 17 1906 Plntf notified that all lands are in contests & in view of this fact the case is <u>dismissed</u> & Allottment[sic] certificates Nos 62409 & 37241 returned

---

INTRUDER CASE NO. 881
Cherokee NATION

Plaintiff: Emma Howard nee Keener
210 North N. St
Muskogee ITy.   Atty.

Versus

Defendant: Andy Hare
Hulbert ITy.   Atty.

Complaint filed Oct 4 1906   Commissioner Reports Oct 4 1906   No Contest. Notice Sent Oct 8 1906

Oct 19 1906	Proof of service returned, dated Oct 12, 1906
Oct 19 1906	Answer filed by dfndt
Oct 29 1906	Proof of service returned dated Oct 16, 1905. Reg ret card.
Nov 15 1906	Case set for hearing at Muskogee ITy Dec 1" 1906. All parties notified.
Dec 1 1906	Case called at Muskogee ITy. Husband of plntf appeared. No appearance by dfndt.
Dec 26 1906	Plntf writes concerning case
Jany 8 1907	Case set for hearing at Muskogee ITy Jany 26 1907 All parties notified.
Jany 26 1907	Case called at Muskogee ITy. Plntf & Atty appered. No appearance by dfndt.
Jany 28 1907	Dfndt requested to appear at this office Feby 11, 1907.
Jany 28 1907	Com^r asked to report
Jany 26 1907	Answer filed by dfndt.
Feby 4 1907	Com^r reports no contest.
Feby 26 1907	Judgement[sic] in favor of plntf. Both parties notified. Dfndt requested to vacate in ten days, otherwise order will issue. Plntf requested to advise.
Mch 4 1907	Plntf advised as to status of case & requested to inform this office if possession is given.
May[sic] 20 1907	Com^r reports no contest
Mch 21 1907	R. Lee Wyly, Policeman, instructed to place plntf in possession.
June 12 07	Policeman Wyly reported in person he could not find plff to accompany him to allotment and it is presumed she is in possession.
June 18 07	Plff advised of Policeman's report and requested to advise in re possession.
May 16 08	<u>Case Dismissed</u>. See carbon in file.

Cherokee Intruder Cases 1901 - 1909

INTRUDER CASE NO. 882
Cherokee NATION

Plaintiff: John Johnson for Redbird Johnson, Hulbert ITy Atty.

Versus

Defendant: Chas Butler, Hulbert ITy Atty.

Complaint filed Oct 6 1906 **Commissioner Reports** Oct 16 1906 **No Contest. Notice Sent** Oct 10 1906

Oct 6 1906	Certificate of Allottment[sic] No 61945
Oct 23 1906	Proof of service returned, dated Oct 21, 1906
Nov 15 1906	Case set for hearing at Muskogee ITy Dec 1" 1906 All parties notified
Dec 1 1906	Case called at Muskogee ITy John Johnson appeared & testimony taken No appearance by dfndt.
Jany 22 1907	Referred to Robt R. Bennett for investigation
Feby 11 1907	Robt R Bennett encloses request for dismissal.
Feby 18 1907	Certificate No 61945 returned & <u>case dismissed</u>

INTRUDER CASE NO. 883
Cherokee NATION

Plaintiff: Oliver Hogg, Nat Gdn, John Hogg, Blackgum ITy. Atty.

Versus

Defendant: Harry Lee, Blackgum ITy Atty.

Complaint filed Sept 24 1906 **Commissioner Reports** Oct 8 1906 **No Contest. Notice Sent** Oct 10 1906

Oct 17 1906	Watts & Curtis Attys of Salisaw ITy request, on authority of plntf, that case be dismissed.
Oct 19 1906	As per above request <u>case dismissed</u> & Watts & Curtis so notified

INTRUDER CASE NO. 884
Cherokee NATION

Plaintiff: John Bulletta, Claremore ITy Atty.

Versus

Cherokee Intruder Cases 1901 - 1909

Defendant	P.W. Shultz & family	Atty.

Complaint filed Sept 27 1906 **Commissioner Reports** Oct 10 1906 **No Contest. Notice Sent** Oct 12 1906	
Nov 3 1906	Case set for hearing at Claremore ITy Nov 22, 1906. All parties notified.
Nov 9 1906	As per request of plntf <u>case dismissed</u> as same has been settled satisfactorily.

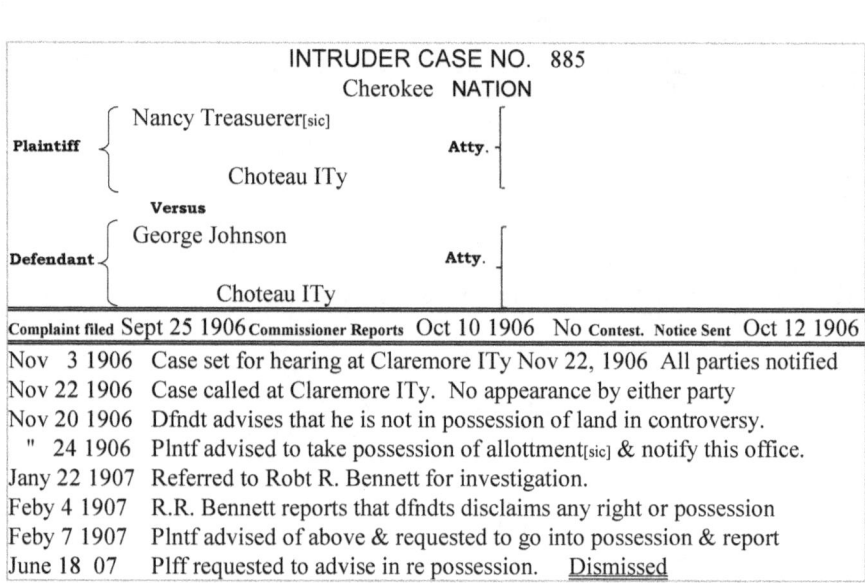

INTRUDER CASE NO. 885
Cherokee NATION

Plaintiff	Nancy Treasuerer[sic] Choteau ITy	Atty.
	Versus	
Defendant	George Johnson Choteau ITy	Atty.

Complaint filed Sept 25 1906 **Commissioner Reports** Oct 10 1906 **No Contest. Notice Sent** Oct 12 1906

Nov 3 1906	Case set for hearing at Claremore ITy Nov 22, 1906 All parties notified
Nov 22 1906	Case called at Claremore ITy. No appearance by either party
Nov 20 1906	Dfndt advises that he is not in possession of land in controversy.
" 24 1906	Plntf advised to take possession of allottment[sic] & notify this office.
Jany 22 1907	Referred to Robt R. Bennett for investigation.
Feby 4 1907	R.R. Bennett reports that dfndts disclaims any right or possession
Feby 7 1907	Plntf advised of above & requested to go into possession & report
June 18 07	Plff requested to advise in re possession. <u>Dismissed</u>

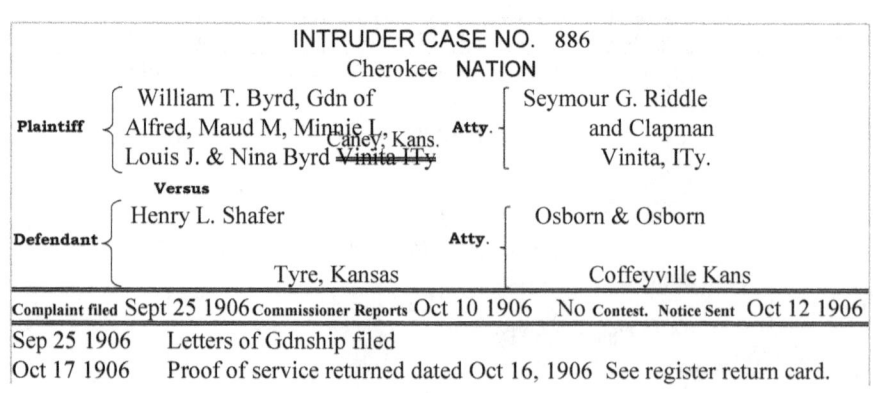

INTRUDER CASE NO. 886
Cherokee NATION

Plaintiff	William T. Byrd, Gdn of Alfred, Maud M, Minnie L, Louis J. & Nina Byrd ~~Vinita ITy~~ Caney, Kans.	Atty.	Seymour G. Riddle and Clapman Vinita, ITy.
	Versus		
Defendant	Henry L. Shafer Tyre, Kansas	Atty.	Osborn & Osborn Coffeyville Kans

Complaint filed Sept 25 1906 **Commissioner Reports** Oct 10 1906 **No Contest. Notice Sent** Oct 12 1906

Sep 25 1906	Letters of Gdnship filed
Oct 17 1906	Proof of service returned dated Oct 16, 1906 See register return card.

Cherokee Intruder Cases 1901 - 1909

Oct 25 1906	Attys for dfndt file answer & states that land is involved in U.S. Court proceeding
Oct 31 1906	Attys for plntf asks when case will be heard
Nov 2 1906	Case set for hearing at Claremore ITy Nov 19 1906 All parties notified.
Nov 6 1906	Order of Master in Chancery, A.M. Etchen, filed by Atty for dfndt.
Nov 8 1906	All parties notified that unless case is heard by Master in Chancery before Oct 19 1906 they need not appear at Claremore Oct 19 1906
Nov 12 1906	Letter from Atty for Dfndt
Jany 12 1907	Copy of order of Master in Chancery A.M. Etchen, in file by Roy T Osborn
Feby 2 1907	Seymour G Riddle Atty for plntf requested to advise of lease is approved
Feby 12 1907	Attys for plntf state IS Court approved Case held by Dfndt
Feby 16 1902	Letters of Gdnship returned & <u>case dismissed</u>

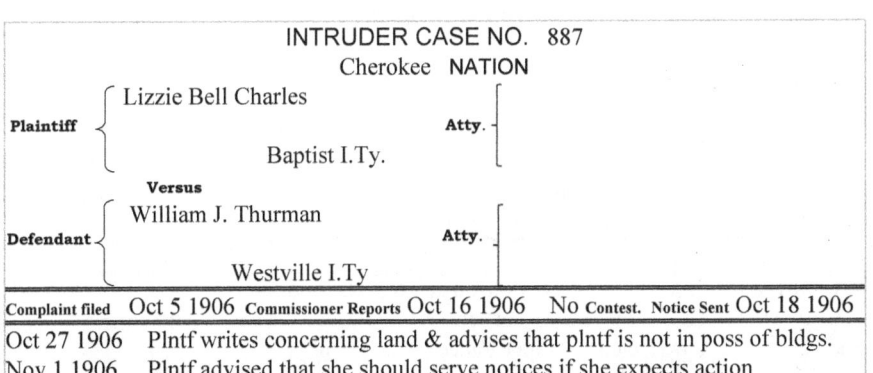

INTRUDER CASE NO. 887
Cherokee NATION

Plaintiff: Lizzie Bell Charles, Baptist I.Ty.
Atty.

Versus

Defendant: William J. Thurman, Westville I.Ty
Atty.

Complaint filed Oct 5 1906 Commissioner Reports Oct 16 1906 No Contest. Notice Sent Oct 18 1906

Oct 27 1906	Plntf writes concerning land & advises that plntf is not in poss of bldgs.
Nov 1 1906	Plntf advised that she should serve notices if she expects action
Dec 22 1906	U.S.I Policeman Thos P. Roach instructed to investigate & report.
Jany 16 1907	Thos P. Roach U.S.I. Policeman reports plntf took possession.
Jan 24, 1907.	In view of above, <u>case dismissed</u>

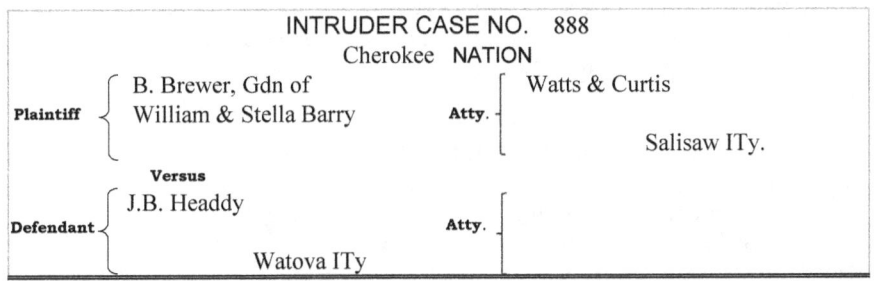

INTRUDER CASE NO. 888
Cherokee NATION

Plaintiff: B. Brewer, Gdn of William & Stella Barry
Atty. Watts & Curtis, Salisaw ITy.

Versus

Defendant: J.B. Headdy, Watova ITy
Atty.

Cherokee Intruder Cases 1901 - 1909

Complaint filed Oct 6 1906	Commissioner Reports Oct 16 1906 No Contest. Notice Sent Oct 18 1906
Oct 6 1906	Letters of Gdnship filed by plntf.
	Proof of service returned dated Oct 22, 1906
Nov 3 1906	Case set for hearing at Claremore ITy Nov 22 1906 All parties notified.
Nov 22 1906	Case called at Claremore ITy. No appearance by either party.
Jany 18 1907	Case set for hearing at Claremore ITy Feb 5 1907. All parties notified.
Jany 24 1907	J P[sic] Heady[sic], dfndt, writes that plntf may go into possession as no one claims land
Jany 26 1907	Plntf requested to go into possession & report
Feby 5 1907	Case called at Claremore ITy. Neither party appeared.
Jany 25 1907	Watts & Curtis, Attys, state they are under impression this case is settled
Feby 20 1907	Letters of Gdnship returned to Watts & Curtis. <u>Case dismissed</u>

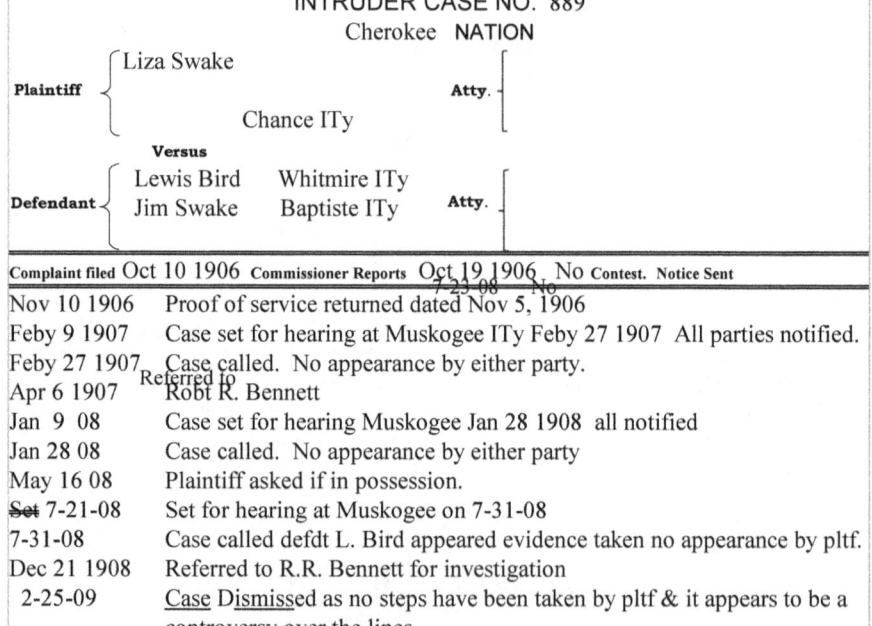

INTRUDER CASE NO. 889
Cherokee NATION

Plaintiff: Liza Swake, Chance ITy

Versus

Defendant: Lewis Bird — Whitmire ITy
Jim Swake — Baptiste ITy

Complaint filed Oct 10 1906	Commissioner Reports Oct 19 1906 7-23-08 No	No Contest. Notice Sent
Nov 10 1906	Proof of service returned dated Nov 5, 1906	
Feby 9 1907	Case set for hearing at Muskogee ITy Feby 27 1907 All parties notified.	
Feby 27 1907	Case called. No appearance by either party. Referred to	
Apr 6 1907	Robt R. Bennett	
Jan 9 08	Case set for hearing Muskogee Jan 28 1908 all notified	
Jan 28 08	Case called. No appearance by either party	
May 16 08	Plaintiff asked if in possession.	
~~Set~~ 7-21-08	Set for hearing at Muskogee on 7-31-08	
7-31-08	Case called defdt L. Bird appeared evidence taken no appearance by pltf.	
Dec 21 1908	Referred to R.R. Bennett for investigation	
2-25-09	<u>Case Dismissed</u> as no steps have been taken by pltf & it appears to be a controversy over the lines.	

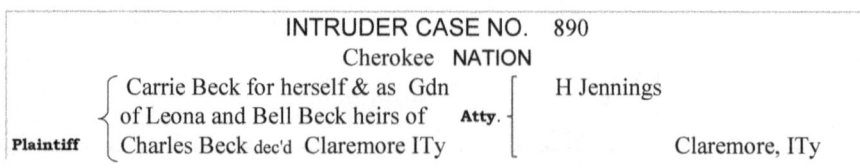

INTRUDER CASE NO. 890
Cherokee NATION

Plaintiff: Carrie Beck for herself & as Gdn of Leona and Bell Beck heirs of Charles Beck dec'd Claremore ITy

Atty: H Jennings, Claremore, ITy

Cherokee Intruder Cases 1901 - 1909

Defendant	Versus Flora ~~Klase~~ Kla~~use~~ SS Chelsea ITy.	Atty.	J.T. Brown Chelsea ITy.

Complaint filed Oct 9 1906 **Commissioner Reports** Oct 19 1906 **No Contest. Notice Sent** Oct 22 1906

Oct 9 1906	Order of U.S. Court in file
Nov 3 1906	Case set for hearing at Claremore ITy Nov 22 1906 All parties notified
Nov 7 1906	Answer filed by dfndt
Nov 22 1906	Case called at Claremore ITy All parties present. Both parties present & testimony taken. Three checks offerred[sic] as Exhibit "B" Allottment[sic] Certificates of Allottment[sic] filed by plntf as Exhibit "A"
Nov 22 1906	Proof of service returned, dated Oct 30 1906
Dec 14 1906	Judgement[sic] in favor of plntf & dfndt requested to vacate with 10 days.
Jany 21 1907	Plntf requested to advise if she is in possession.
Jany 31 1907	Mr. H. Jennings requests return of Allottment[sic] certificates.
Feby 4 1907	As per request, certificates #35444-24822 returned & <u>case dismissed</u>

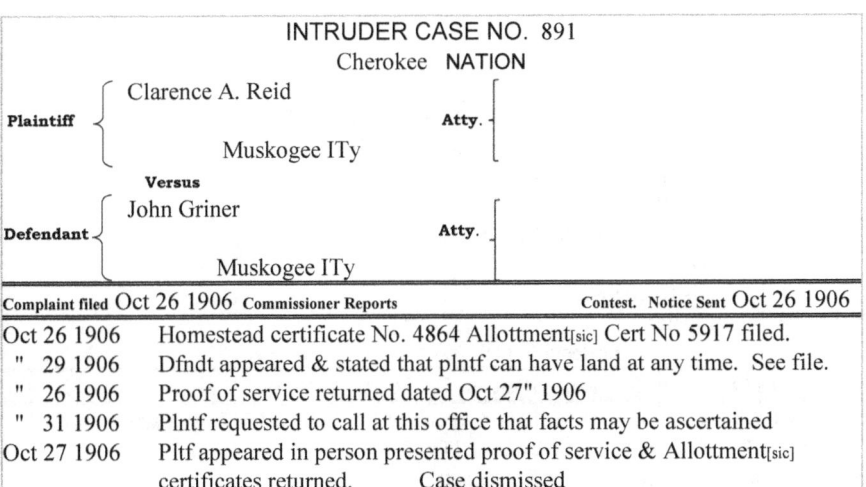

INTRUDER CASE NO. 891
Cherokee NATION

Plaintiff	Clarence A. Reid Muskogee ITy	Atty.	
Defendant	Versus John Griner Muskogee ITy	Atty.	

Complaint filed Oct 26 1906 **Commissioner Reports** **Contest. Notice Sent** Oct 26 1906

Oct 26 1906	Homestead certificate No. 4864 Allottment[sic] Cert No 5917 filed.
" 29 1906	Dfndt appeared & stated that plntf can have land at any time. See file.
" 26 1906	Proof of service returned dated Oct 27" 1906
" 31 1906	Plntf requested to call at this office that facts may be ascertained
Oct 27 1906	Pltf appeared in person presented proof of service & Allottment[sic] certificates returned. <u>Case dismissed</u>

INTRUDER CASE NO. 892
Cherokee NATION

Plaintiff	A.J. Shasteel Gdn of Malinda Harris	Atty.	Chas R. Freeman Checotah, I.Ty

Cherokee Intruder Cases 1901 - 1909

Defendant	Versus M.F. Coon	Atty.	J. Blair Shoenfelt & Sons Muskogee ITy

Complaint filed Oct 25 1906	Commissioner Reports Nov 9 1906	No Contest. Notice Sent Nov 3 1906

Oct 25 1906	Homestead certificate No 23241 Allottment[sic] Cert No 33091 in file.
Nov 3 1906	Com^r requested to report
Nov 14 1906	Answer filed by Atty for dfndt
Nov 20 1906	Case set for hearing at Muskogee ITy Dec 4 1906 All parties notified
Dec 5 1906	Proof of service returned dated November 7 1906
Dec 5 1906	Case called at Muskogee ITy. All parties and counsel present testimony taken. Letters of Gdnship offered[sic] by plntf. Original contract filed[sic] by dfndt. Atty for defense granted 30 days in which to brief & serve Atty for plntf with copy of same
Jany 30 1907	Judgement[sic] for dfndt as this office refused to take action & refers plntf to U.S.P. Gen'l. Allottment[sic] certificates No 23241-33091 returned & case dismissed
Jany 8 08	Original lease contract filed by defendant returned to J.B. Lucas. Atty at Checotah, who called in person today for same. Dismissed.

INTRUDER CASE NO. 893
Cherokee NATION

Plaintiff	Georgia A Ccroggins[sic] - nee Holland Bartlesville, ITy.	Atty.	
Defendant	Versus Louis Keefer and Will Black Bartlesville ITy.	Atty.	

Complaint filed Oct 15 1906	Commissioner Reports Oct 26 1906	No Contest. Notice Sent Nov 12 1906

Jany 18 1907	Case set for hearing at Claremore ITy Feby 5 1907 All parties notified
Feby 5 1907	Case called at Claremore ITy. Neither party appeared.
Feby 14 1907	Referred to Robt R. Bennett
Mch 6 1907	Robt R. Bennett encloses request for dismissal.
Mch 14 1907	Case dismissed

Cherokee Intruder Cases 1901 - 1909

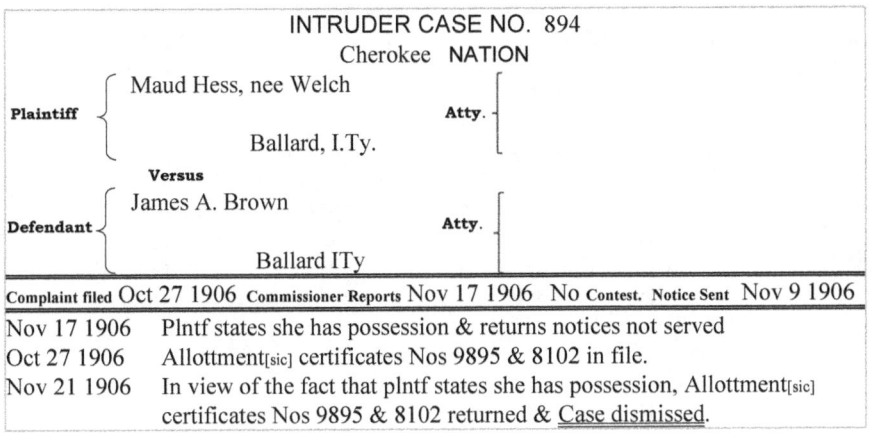

INTRUDER CASE NO. 894
Cherokee NATION

Plaintiff: Maud Hess, nee Welch
Ballard, I.Ty.
Atty.

Versus

Defendant: James A. Brown
Ballard ITy
Atty.

Complaint filed Oct 27 1906 Commissioner Reports Nov 17 1906 No Contest. Notice Sent Nov 9 1906

Nov 17 1906	Plntf states she has possession & returns notices not served
Oct 27 1906	Allottment[sic] certificates Nos 9895 & 8102 in file.
Nov 21 1906	In view of the fact that plntf states she has possession, Allottment[sic] certificates Nos 9895 & 8102 returned & <u>Case dismissed</u>.

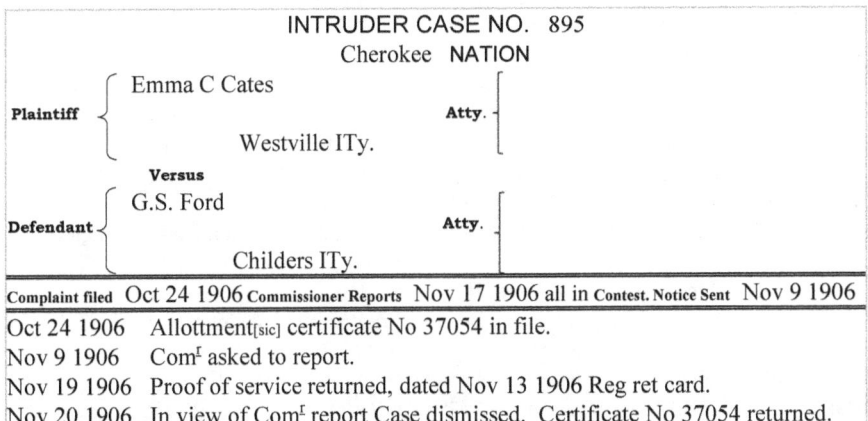

INTRUDER CASE NO. 895
Cherokee NATION

Plaintiff: Emma C Cates
Westville ITy.
Atty.

Versus

Defendant: G.S. Ford
Childers ITy.
Atty.

Complaint filed Oct 24 1906 Commissioner Reports Nov 17 1906 all in Contest. Notice Sent Nov 9 1906

Oct 24 1906	Allottment[sic] certificate No 37054 in file.
Nov 9 1906	Com^r asked to report.
Nov 19 1906	Proof of service returned, dated Nov 13 1906 Reg ret card.
Nov 20 1906	In view of Com^r report <u>Case dismissed</u>. Certificate No 37054 returned.

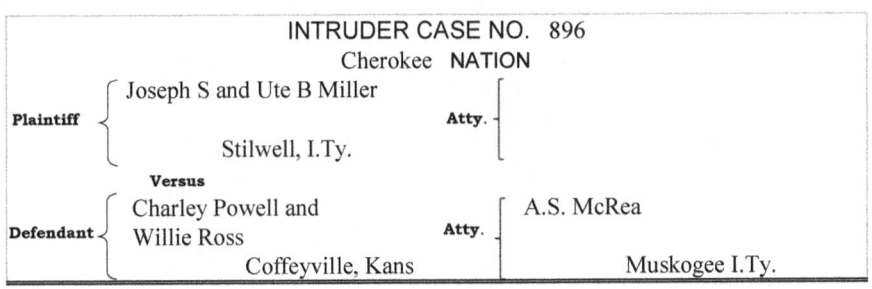

INTRUDER CASE NO. 896
Cherokee NATION

Plaintiff: Joseph S and Ute B Miller
Stilwell, I.Ty.
Atty.

Versus

Defendant: Charley Powell and Willie Ross
Coffeyville, Kans
Atty. A.S. McRea
Muskogee I.Ty.

Cherokee Intruder Cases 1901 - 1909

Complaint filed Oct 25 1906	Commissioner Reports Nov 17 1906 $^{40@\ in}$ Contest. Notice Sent Nov 9 1906
Oct 25 1906	Allottment[sic] certificates Nos 24569, 17938, 24571 & 17937 in file
Nov 9 1906	Com^r asked to report
Nov 15 1906	Proof of service returned, dated Nov 14, 1906
Nov 23 1906	Dismissed as to that portion of land in contest
Jany 19 1907	Case set for hearing at Claremore ITy Feby 6 1907 All parties notified
Feby 6 1907	Case called at Claremore ITy. Plntfs appeared & testimony taken. No appearance by dfndt. Com^r report shows 40 acres in contest.
Mch 2 1907	Notice of hearing returned to this office by Dead Letter office and as evidence of dfndt recieving[sic] notice, this case to be reset for hearing & all parties notified.
Mch 5 1907	Dfndt requested to vacate or show cause.
Mch 5 1907	Com^r asked to report.
Mch 5 1907	Plntf advised that this case will again be set for hearing.
Mch 6 1907	Plntf asks status of case.
Mch 15 1907	Plntf advised case will again be set for hearing.
Mch 13 1907	Com^r report in file showing no contest on land of either plntf
Mch 14 1907	Will Ross files answer.
Mch 26 1907	Case set for hearing at Claremore ITy Apr 8 1907
Mch 27 1907	Com^r reports no contest & encloses status of ~~certificate~~ citizenship & allottment[sic].
Apr 5 1907	Plntfs advise they will not be present at hearing at Claremore I.Ty.
Apr 9 1907	Charles Powell appeared at Claremore I.Ty & testimony taken. No appearance by plntfs or other dfndt. A.S. McRea as Atty for dfndt.
Mar 25 1907	Com^r reports dfndts denied citizenship.
May 1 1907	Judgment rendered in favor of plntf. Dfndts given ten days in which to vacate.
May 14 1907	Plntf requested to advise if in possession
May 22 1907	Asst U.S. Atty advises injunction granted by U.S. Court at Vinita IT See letter in file $^\#$991
May 23 1907	Restraining order & summons in equity rec'd - see file $^\#$991
May 25 1907	Certificates of allotment $^\#$ 17937 & 24569 Joseph S and $^\#$ 17938 & 24571 Ute B. Miller sent to O. L. Rider Asst U.S. Atty at Vinita I.T. See letter in $^\#$991
June 29 - 07	Injunction dissolved. See cases 991 - 1008 etc.
July 6 - 07	Plffs and defts advised of dissolution of injunction
July 6 - 07	Instructions issued to Capt Jno C. West.
July 25 - 07	Capt West reports that on July 17-1907- he placed the allottee[sic] in unrestricted possession.
Aug 2 - 07	Plffs advised of report of Capt West and Case Dismissed
Aug 29 - 07	Letter returned to Pltf today.

Cherokee Intruder Cases 1901 - 1909

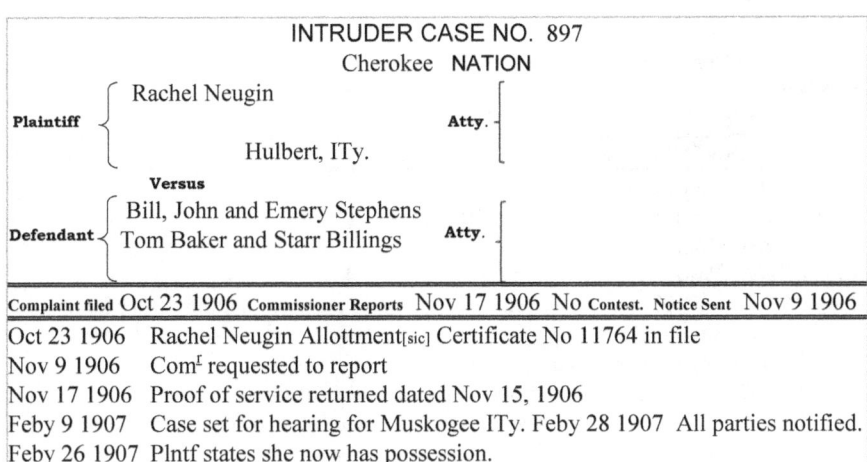

INTRUDER CASE NO. 897
Cherokee NATION

Plaintiff: Rachel Neugin
Hulbert, ITy.
Atty.

Versus

Defendant: Bill, John and Emery Stephens
Tom Baker and Starr Billings
Atty.

Complaint filed Oct 23 1906 **Commissioner Reports** Nov 17 1906 **No Contest.** **Notice Sent** Nov 9 1906

Oct 23 1906	Rachel Neugin Allottment[sic] Certificate No 11764 in file
Nov 9 1906	Com^r requested to report
Nov 17 1906	Proof of service returned dated Nov 15, 1906
Feby 9 1907	Case set for hearing for Muskogee ITy. Feby 28 1907 All parties notified.
Feby 26 1907	Plntf states she now has possession.
Mch 1" 1907	Certificates returned & <u>case dismissed</u>

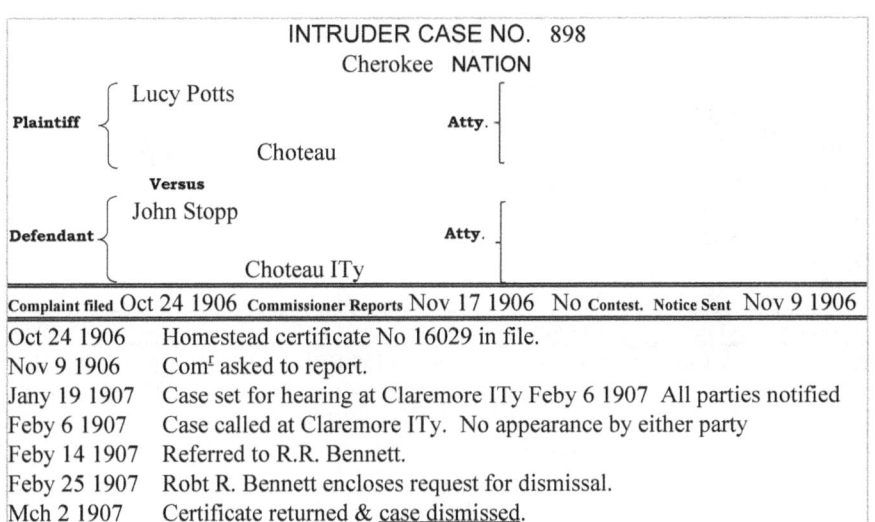

INTRUDER CASE NO. 898
Cherokee NATION

Plaintiff: Lucy Potts
Choteau
Atty.

Versus

Defendant: John Stopp
Choteau ITy
Atty.

Complaint filed Oct 24 1906 **Commissioner Reports** Nov 17 1906 **No Contest.** **Notice Sent** Nov 9 1906

Oct 24 1906	Homestead certificate No 16029 in file.
Nov 9 1906	Com^r asked to report.
Jany 19 1907	Case set for hearing at Claremore ITy Feby 6 1907 All parties notified
Feby 6 1907	Case called at Claremore ITy. No appearance by either party
Feby 14 1907	Referred to R.R. Bennett.
Feby 25 1907	Robt R. Bennett encloses request for dismissal.
Mch 2 1907	Certificate returned & <u>case dismissed</u>.

INTRUDER CASE NO. 899
Cherokee NATION

Plaintiff: Mary J White
Webbers Falls ITy.
Atty.

Cherokee Intruder Cases 1901 - 1909

	Versus	
Defendant	Oscar L. Hayes	Atty.
	Webbers Falls ITy.	

Complaint filed Nov 7 1906 **Commissioner Reports** Nov 24 1907 **No Contest.** **Notice Sent** Nov 16 1906

Nov 7 1906	Certificates No. 44337 filed.
" 15 1906	Certificate returned to plntf in person. (No 44337).
Nov 16 1906	Com^r asked to report.
Nov 26 1906	Proof of service returned dated Nov. 24, 1906
Dec 4 1906	O.L. Hayes and his Atty Thos H Owen appeared and stated that he would surrender possession of land on or before Jany 1 -1907, without any further action
Jany 26 1907	Plntf asked to report if she has possession of land
June 10 1907	Pltf has failed to answer letter and has not advised if she is in possession it is presumed she is in possession and case <u>Dismissed</u>
	(Allottee[sic] is practically white)

INTRUDER CASE NO. 900
Cherokee NATION

Plaintiff	John Foreman	Atty.
	Vinita ITy	
	Versus	
Defendant	Walter Crump	Atty.
	Centralia ITy	

Complaint filed Oct 22 1906 **Commissioner Reports** Nov 9 1906 **No Contest.** **Notice Sent** Nov 16 1906

Jany 19 1907	Case set for hearing at Claremore ITy Feby 6 1907 All parties notified.
Feby 6 1907	Case called at Claremore ITy. No appearance by plntf. Dfndt appeared & states he is not holding any land in SE^4 of Sec 19 or any land in Sec 29 Claims land only in NE^4 of 19
Feby 13 1907	Plntf requested to have land surveyed, go into possession & notify this office
June 18 07	Plff requested to advise if land has been surveyed
Sept 20 07	Plff has failed to reply to letters addressed to him, it is presumed he is in possession. <u>Case Dismissed</u>

Cherokee Intruder Cases 1901 - 1909

INTRUDER CASE NO. 901
Cherokee NATION

Plaintiff: John Watt, Westville ITy. **Atty.**

Versus

Defendant: Frank Cromwell, Vinita ITy. **Atty.**

Complaint filed Oct 24 1906 **Commissioner Reports** Nov 9 1906   No **Contest.** **Notice Sent** Nov 16 1906

Dec 10 1906	Proof of service returned dated Dec 7, 1906
Jany 19 1907	Case set for hearing at Claremore I.Ty Feby 6 1907. All parties notified.
Feby 6 1907	Case called at Claremore ITy. No appearance by either party
Feby 8 1907	Proof of service returned dated not dated.
Feby 14 1907	Referred to Robt R. Bennett.
Mch 23 1907	Robt R. Bennett encloses request for dismissal.
Mch 29 1896	Case dismissed

INTRUDER CASE NO. 902
Cherokee NATION

Plaintiff: James Lowrey for minor son James Fite Lowrey, Muskogee ITy **Atty.**

Versus

Defendant: Mrs. Ruth Kirk, Muskogee ITy **Atty.**

Complaint filed Nov 10 1906 **Commissioner Reports** Nov 24 1906   No **Contest.** **Notice Sent** Nov 6 1906

Nov 10 1906	Allottment[sic] certificates No[sic] 63070 - 37553
" 16 1906	Com^r asked to report
Nov 27 1906	Plntf appeared & states that all the land in question is now in contest Allottment[sic] certificates returned to plntf in person Case dismissed

INTRUDER CASE NO. 903
Cherokee NATION

Plaintiff: Daisy Walker, Braggs ITy. **Atty.**

Versus

Cherokee Intruder Cases 1901 - 1909

Defendant	John McKinney	Atty.	W.T. Hunt	
	Wagoner ITy.		Wagoner ITy.	

Complaint filed Nov 5 1906 Commissioner Reports	Contest. Notice Sent Nov 16 1906
Nov 5 1906	Allottment[sic] certificate No 60227.
" 16 1906	Com^r asked to report.
Nov 26 1906	Proof of service returned dated Nov 22, 1906. Reg Ret card.
Dec 5 1906	Atty for dfndt advises that there is contest on land in question
Dec 17 1906	Plntf writes concerning contest.
Dec 18 1906	Com^r reports case pending on appeal to Com^r of Indian Affairs
Dec 26 1906	Plntf of Com^r's report & <u>case dismissed</u> because of contest.

INTRUDER CASE NO. 904
Cherokee NATION

Plaintiff	Thomas Eaton for Nina, Phil & Johanna Eaton	Atty.	
	Chaffee ITy.		

Versus

Defendant	Mack W Whitney	Atty.	
	Adair ITy		

Complaint filed Nov 7 1906 Commissioner Reports Nov 24 1906 No Contest. Notice Sent Nov 16 1906
Nov 7 1906   Allottment[sic] certificates Nos 38559 - 26626 - 38556 & 26625
" 16 1906   Com^r asked to report
Jany 19 1907   Case set for hearing at Claremore ITy Feby 6 1907 All parties notified.
Jany 29 1907   Answer filed by dfndt.
Feby 6 1907   Case called at Claremore ITy. Both parties present & testimony taken. Dfndt has relinquished all claim to land - certificates returned & <u>Case dismissed</u>

INTRUDER CASE NO. 905
Cherokee NATION

Plaintiff	Hattie Bliss formerly Hattie Phillips	Atty.	
	Spavinaw ITy.		

Versus

Defendant	George Ross	Atty.	T.L. Brown
	Coffeyville Kans		

Cherokee Intruder Cases 1901 - 1909

Complaint filed Nov 19 1906 Commissioner Reports Dec 1 1906 70@ in Contest. Notice Sent Nov 22 1906	
Nov 19 1906	Allottment[sic] certificates Nos 16917, 22933 in file
Nov 22 1906	Com^r asked to report.
Dec 1 1906	Proof of service returned dated Dec 4, 1906
Jany 19 1907	Case set for hearing at Claremore ITy Feby 6 1907. All parties notified.
Feby 6 1907	Case called at Claremore I.Ty. Both parties present & testimony taken. Atty for plntf agreed that if Congress does not furnish some relief for rejected Cherokee Freedman, dfndt Geo Ross will vacate premises on or before Mch 4" 1907. Judgment to be rendered for plntf.
Mch 9 1907	Plntf states dfndt has not vacated.
Mch 12 1907	Dfndt requested to vacated. Plntf advised concerning improvements.
Mch 27 1907	Plntf states dfndt has not vacated.
Apr 12 1907	Dfndt requested to vacate or order will issue to U.S.I. Police.
Apr 23 1907	Com^r asked if control is pending on lands allotted[sic] to Hattie Bliss
May 11 1907	A.S. McRea Atty for dfndt serves notice showing that application for injunction to restrain Agent from removing dfndt from lands involved is at this time pending before the United States court - Application will be heard May 13th 1907 at Vinita I.T. - See letter in file $^\#$ 991 -
May 14 1907	Judgment rendered in favor of plntf - Dfndt given ten days in which to vacate
May 15 1907	Notice served by Atty for dfndt that application for injunction will be heard at Vinita I.T. May 18-1907- See file $^\#$ 991 -
May 22 1907	Asst U.S. Atty advises injunction granted by U.S. Court at Vinita, I.T. See letter in file $^\#$ 991
May 23 1907	Restraining order & summons in equity rec'd - See file $^\#$ 991
May 25 1907	Certificate of allottment[sic] $^\#$ 16917 & 22933 sent to O. L. Rider Asst U.S. Atty at Vinita I.T. - See letter in $^\#$ 991
June 10 '07	Certs returned to W.W.B. at trial of injunction case at Vinita 6/7-6/8.
June 29 07	Injunction dissolved See cases 001 - 1008 - etc.
July 6 07	Plff and deft advised of dissolution of injunction & Instructions issued to Capt West.
July 25 07	Capt West reports placing allottee[sic] in possession - Aug 2/7 Certs returned and Case Dismissed.

INTRUDER CASE NO. 906
Cherokee NATION

Plaintiff { S.R. Lewis Gdn of
Mary E. Osage
Tulsa I.Ty

Atty. { McDougal Walker
and Carrol
Tulsa ITy

Versus

Cherokee Intruder Cases 1901 - 1909

Defendant	R.M. Erwin, etc. Tulsa I.Ty.	Atty.	Leeds & Martindale Tulsa ITy

Complaint filed Nov 19 1906 **Commissioner Reports** Dec 6 1906   **No Contest**. **Notice Sent** Nov 26 1906

Nov 26 1906	Allottment[sic] certificates Nos 10017 & 12477
" 26 1906	Letters of Gdnship in file
" 28 1906	Com[r] asked to report.
Dec 7 1906	Proof of service returned dated December 6 1906
Dec 14 1906	Answer filed by Atty for dfndt.
Dec 31 1906	As per request plntf advised as to status of case.
Jany 19 1907	Case set for hearing at Claremore ITy. Feby 6 1907 All parties notified
Feby 6 1907	Case called at Claremore ITy. Plntf absent but represented by Atty Walker. Dfndt and Atty Mr. Leeds, present. Continued until Friday 7:30 Feby 15, 1907, because of absence of plntf.
Feby 15 1907	Case called at Muskogee ITy. All parties & Attys present. Depositions to be submitted.
Feby 26 1907	Both parties notified to furnish additional evidence if desired.
Mch 30 1907	Attys for plntf ask for decision in this case
Apr. 3 1907	Attys for plntf advised judgement[sic] will be rendered soon.
April 23 1907	Judgement[sic] rendered in favor of pltf - Both parties notified and copy of judgement[sic] sent to each - The dfndt given ten days from date of jdgment[sic] within which to vacate.
May 16 1907	Plntf requested to advise if case has been settled
June 4 1907	Pltf again requested to advise in re possession
July 2nd 07	Case dismissed as pltf writes that matter is settled. Dismissed
7/17 07	Certs & letters of gdn returned to pltf Dismissed

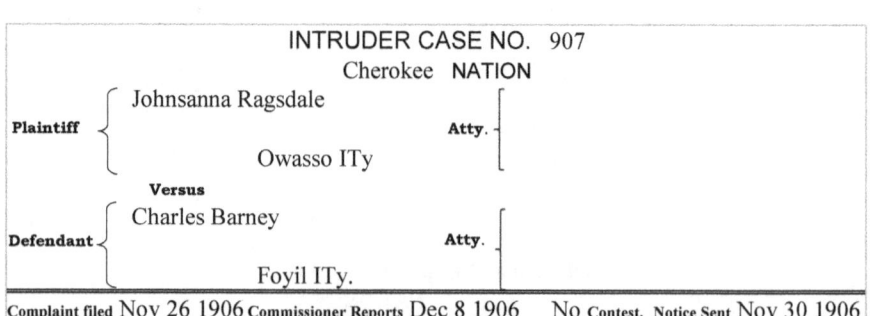

	INTRUDER CASE NO. 907 Cherokee NATION		
Plaintiff	Johnsanna Ragsdale Owasso ITy	Atty.	
	Versus		
Defendant	Charles Barney Foyil ITy.	Atty.	

Complaint filed Nov 26 1906 **Commissioner Reports** Dec 8 1906   **No Contest**. **Notice Sent** Nov 30 1906

Nov 26 1906	Allottment[sic] certificate No 50646 in file
Dec 10 1906	Dfndt, Charles Barney, appeared & stated that he is an intermarried citizen Was married in 1869 & an applicant "on that *(illegible)*." He made all

Cherokee Intruder Cases 1901 - 1909

	improvements on place. His children have all filed on land as Cherokees.
Dec 12 1906	Proof of service returned dated Dec 6 1906
Jany 19 1906	Case set for hearing at Claremore I.Ty Feby 6 1907 All parties notified.
Feby 6 1907	Case called at Claremore ITy. No appearance by plntf. Dfndt appeared & exhibited judgement[sic] by Com^r Jany 23 1907 admitting him to citizenship as an intermarried citizen~~ship~~ of Cherokee Nation.
Feby 5 1907	R.J. Kirksey M.D. Owasso, ITy. advises plntf unable to attend hearing at Claremore
Feby 20 1907	Plntf asks status of case.
Feby 28 1907	Plntf is advised.
May 24 1907	Plff again asks status of case and June 5/7 she was advised
June 10 07	Com^r reports portion of allotment relinquished
June 18 07	Case set for Vinita IT July 8/7. All parties notified.
July 8 07	Case called no appearance by either party.
Sept 20 1907	Case set for hearing at Claremore ITy. Oct 2, 1907. All parties notified.
Oct 2 1907	Case called no appearance by either party.
Jan 8 1908	<u>Case dismissed</u> in accordance with report of Com^r, order W.W.B.

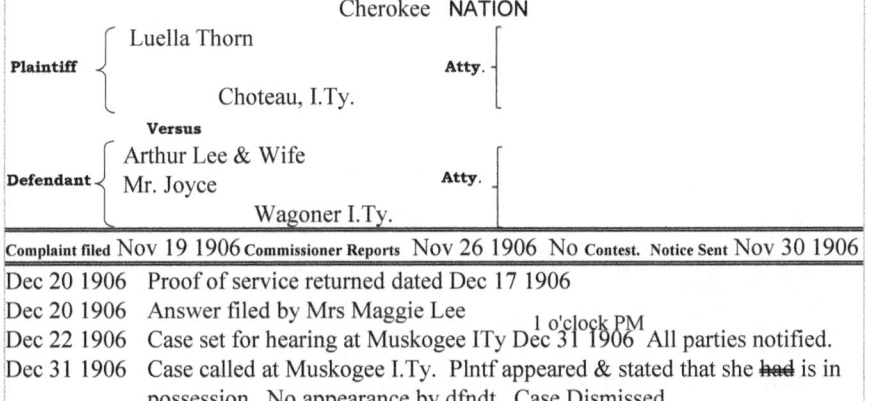

Complaint filed Nov 19 1906	Commissioner Reports Nov 26 1906 No Contest. Notice Sent Nov 30 1906
Dec 20 1906	Proof of service returned dated Dec 17 1906
Dec 20 1906	Answer filed by Mrs Maggie Lee
Dec 22 1906	Case set for hearing at Muskogee ITy Dec 31 1906 1 o'clock PM All parties notified.
Dec 31 1906	Case called at Muskogee I.Ty. Plntf appeared & stated that she ~~had~~ is in possession. No appearance by dfndt. <u>Case Dismissed</u>

Cherokee Intruder Cases 1901 - 1909

Defendant	Sam Walker Moody ITy	Atty.	

Complaint filed Nov 12 1906 **Commissioner Reports** Nov 24 1906 No **Contest. Notice Sent** Dec 11 1906

Dec 11 1906	Proof of service returned, dated Dec 8, 1906
Dec 19 1906	Answer filed by dfndt
Dec 21 1906	Case set for hearing at Muskogee ITy. Jany 3 1907 All parties notified
Jany 3 1907	Case called at Muskogee ITy. Dfndt appeared & testimony taken. No appearance by plntf.
Jany 18 1907	Plntf requested to appear at Muskogee ITy Jany 25 1907 if she wishe[sic] to be heard
Feby 1 1907	Plntf again requested to advise if she will appear & submit evidence
Feby 12 1907	Plntf requested to appear & bring allottment[sic] certificates.
Feby 19 1907	Plntf states certificates with restrictions division.
Feby 20 1907	Allottment[sic] certificate No. 36585 rec'd from Restrictions & filed by P.J. Hurley
Feby 25 1907	Plntf notified of same.
June 21 07	Referred to R.R. Bennett.
Jan 11 08	Plaintiff advised to appear in 15 days and give evidence
May 16 08	Plaintiff requested to appear in 10 days and give testimony or case will be dismissed. Also to advise if in possession or settlement had
7-30-08	Case dismissed as in re possession Dtf has possession
	Dismissed

INTRUDER CASE NO. 910
Cherokee NATION

Plaintiff	Iola M Sult Coffeyville Kans	Atty.	
	Versus		
Defendant	Mrs Aggie Little Lenapah ITy.	Atty.	W.H. Twine McRea, Muskogee Muskogee ITy

Complaint filed Nov 7 1906 **Commissioner Reports** Nov 24 1906 No **Contest. Notice Sent** Dec 1 1906

Nov 24 1906	Com^r reports application of dfndt for enrollment denied. Also a motion for review denied May 2 1906 No motion now pending.
Dec 12 1906	Proof of service returned dated Dec 10 1906
" 12 1906	Answer filed by dfndt.
Jany 19 1907	Case set for hearing at Claremore ITy Feby 6 1907. All parties notified.
Feby 2 1907	Plntf states she is too poor to appear at hearing
Feby 6 1907	Case called at Claremore ITy. No appearance by either party
Feby 8 1907	Later - Dfndt appeared & Atty McRea See stenographer's notes

Cherokee Intruder Cases 1901 - 1909

Mch 5 1907	Judgement[sic] rendered for plntf. Dfndt given ten days to vacate.
Mch 14 1907	Atty for dfndt served notice of application for injunction vs Agent before U.S. Judge Lawrence
Mch 15 1907	W.W.B. appeared in US Court Judge Lawrence denied application of dfndt for injunction
Mch 15 1907	Atty for dfndt served notice of application to Appealate[sic] Court for injunction See #940
May 14 1907	Instructions issued to Capt Jno C West to place plntf in possession
May 20 1907	On acct of health of Capt West instructions transferred to Policeman J. L. Walker
May 27 1907	Policeman Walker reports he placed plntfs in possession.
May 29 1907	The case is this day dismissed
8/9/07	Policeman Walker again instructed to place the pltf in possession
Nov 6 07	James L Walker again instructed to place plaintiff in possession & plaintiff requested to notify Walker when she can receive possession

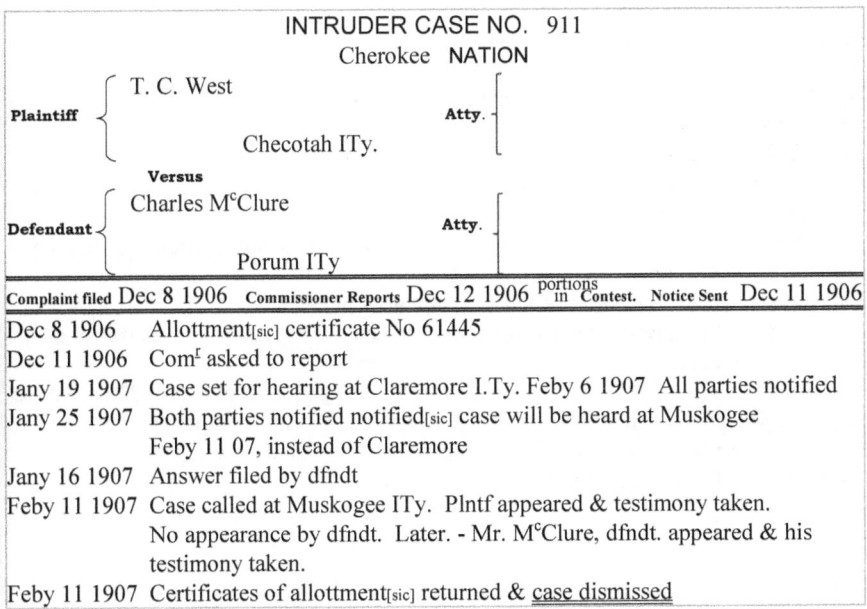

INTRUDER CASE NO. 911
Cherokee NATION

Plaintiff T. C. West
Checotah ITy.
Atty.

Versus

Defendant Charles McClure
Porum ITy.
Atty.

Complaint filed Dec 8 1906 Commissioner Reports Dec 12 1906 portions in Contest. Notice Sent Dec 11 1906

Dec 8 1906	Allottment[sic] certificate No 61445
Dec 11 1906	Com^r asked to report
Jany 19 1907	Case set for hearing at Claremore I.Ty. Feby 6 1907 All parties notified
Jany 25 1907	Both parties notified notified[sic] case will be heard at Muskogee Feby 11 07, instead of Claremore
Jany 16 1907	Answer filed by dfndt
Feby 11 1907	Case called at Muskogee ITy. Plntf appeared & testimony taken. No appearance by dfndt. Later. - Mr. McClure, dfndt. appeared & his testimony taken.
Feby 11 1907	Certificates of allottment[sic] returned & case dismissed

Cherokee Intruder Cases 1901 - 1909

INTRUDER CASE NO. 912
Cherokee NATION

Plaintiff: Cleo D. Duncan
Atty. Baron ITy

Versus

Defendant: Charles Martin
Atty. Catale ITy

Complaint filed Nov 28 1906 **Commissioner Reports** **Contest. Notice Sent** Dec 11 1906

Nov 28 1906	Allottment[sic] certificates Nos 34171 & 23983 in file.
Dec 14 1906	Com^r reports citizenship of Chas Martin, denied. No motion for review.
Dec 20 1906	Proof of service returned dated Dec 17 1906
Dec 22 1906	Policeman Thos P. Roach instructed to investigate & report.
Jany 16 1907	Policeman Roach reports & recommends removal of dfndt.
Jany 24 1907	Dfndt, requested to vacate or make satisfactory settlement.
Feby 23 1907	Plntf's letter asking possession in file.
Mch 5 1907	Plntf requested to ascertain if dfndt is in possession & same is in hands of representative
Mch 2 1907	Referred to Robt R Bennett
Mch 28 1907	Robt R Bennett's report in file.
Apr 2 1907	Plntf requested to go into possession & report.
Apr 3 1907	Plntf states dfndt refuses to pay rent or vacate.
June 21 07	Plff requested to advise in re survey of his allotment and if he has been given possession of same
Oct 21 07	Plaintiff encloses certified plat
Nov 11 07	Plaintiff advised no action can now be taken towards removing Cherokee Freedman
Jan. 19 08	Plff writes desiring some action taken in her case
Jan 23 08	Plff advised deft a Cherokee freedman and no action can be taken at this time
Feb 13 08	Transmitted to Commission of I.F. asking if Freedman should be removed
July 14 1909	Pltf called at office and advised that defdt in this case had vacated. <u>Case Dismissed</u> new complaint made for another defdt
9-23-09	Certs returned to E. Leon in person

INTRUDER CASE NO. 913
Cherokee NATION

Plaintiff: Anna Reed
Atty. Vian ITy

102

Cherokee Intruder Cases 1901 - 1909

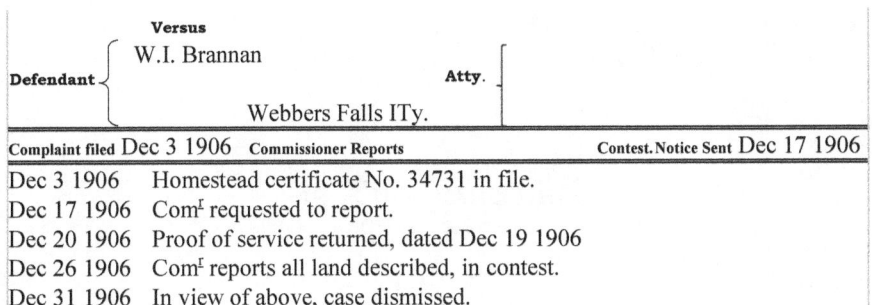

Defendant W.I. Brannan   **Atty.**
Webbers Falls ITy.

Complaint filed Dec 3 1906 **Commissioner Reports**   **Contest. Notice Sent** Dec 17 1906

Dec 3 1906	Homestead certificate No. 34731 in file.
Dec 17 1906	Com^r requested to report.
Dec 20 1906	Proof of service returned, dated Dec 19 1906
Dec 26 1906	Com^r reports all land described, in contest.
Dec 31 1906	In view of above, <u>case dismissed</u>.

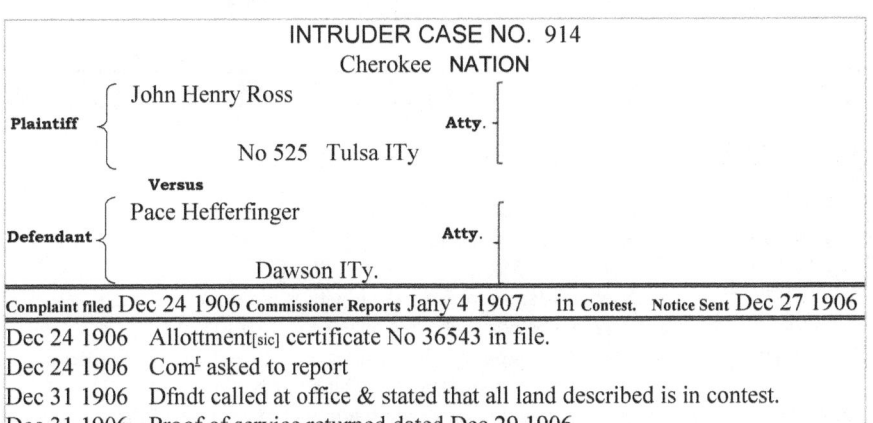

INTRUDER CASE NO. 914
Cherokee NATION

Plaintiff John Henry Ross   **Atty.**
No 525 Tulsa ITy

Defendant Pace Hefferfinger   **Atty.**
Dawson ITy.

Complaint filed Dec 24 1906 **Commissioner Reports** Jany 4 1907 **in Contest.** **Notice Sent** Dec 27 1906

Dec 24 1906	Allottment[sic] certificate No 36543 in file.
Dec 24 1906	Com^r asked to report
Dec 31 1906	Dfndt called at office & stated that all land described is in contest.
Dec 31 1906	Proof of service returned dated Dec 29 1906
Jany 7 1907	In view of Com^r's report, <u>Case Dismissed</u> Certificates returned.

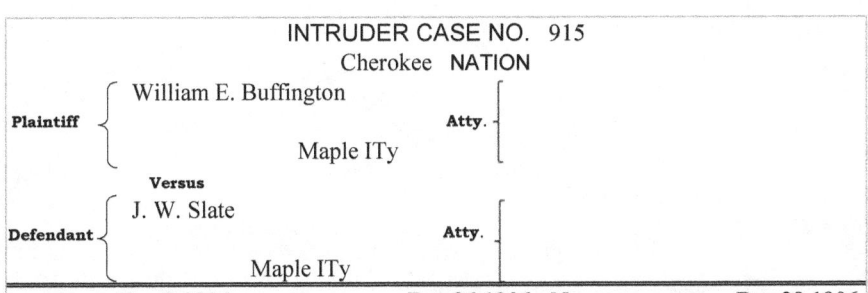

INTRUDER CASE NO. 915
Cherokee NATION

Plaintiff William E. Buffington   **Atty.**
Maple ITy

Defendant J. W. Slate   **Atty.**
Maple ITy

Complaint filed Dec 7 1906 **Commissioner Reports** Dec 26 1906 **No Contest.** **Notice Sent** Dec 29 1906

Feby 9 1907	Case set for hearing at Muskogee ITy. Feby 28, 1907 All parties notified
Feby 14 1907	Dfndt states he has surrendered land & wants nothing to do with it.

Cherokee Intruder Cases 1901 - 1909

Feby 14 1907	Plntf states he has possession & requests dismissal.
Feby 19 1907	Case dismissed

INTRUDER CASE NO. 916
Cherokee NATION

Plaintiff	Annie E White	Atty.	
	Claremore ITy.		
	Versus		
Defendant	Wayne Muller	Atty.	A. F. Mood
	Collinsville ITy		Claremore

Complaint filed Nov 28 1906 **Commissioner Reports** Jany 8 1907   **No Contest. Notice Sent** Dec 29 1906

Nov 28 1906	Copy of lease contract in file.
Nov 28 1906	Allottment[sic] certificates Nos 17769 - 24274 in file.
Dec 29 1906	Com^r asked to report.
Jany 9 1907	Proof of service returned dated Jany 8, 1907
Jany 19 1907	Case set for hearing at Claremore ITy Feby 7 1907. All parties notified
Jany 16 1907	Rental contract & M.D's certificate in file
Feby 7 1907	Case called at Claremore ITy. Both parties present & testimony taken. Continued. To be heard at Muskogee Feby 15 1907
Feby 15 1907	Case called at Muskogee ITy. Dfndt & Atty present. (Atty Walker of Tulsa ITy.) Testimony taken. Deposition to be furnished.
Jan 10 1908	Defendant requested to forward assignment of cont. in 15 days.
6-23-08	Defdt requested to forward assignment of contract in five days otherwise judgement[sic] will be rendered on evidence now on file.
May 11 09	Papers in case referred to Cobb D.A.

INTRUDER CASE NO. 917
Cherokee NATION

Plaintiff	Maggie E Province	Atty.	
	Adair ITy		
	Versus		
Defendant	Harvey Martin	Atty.	Starr & Patton
	Adair ITy		Vinita ITy.

Cherokee Intruder Cases 1901 - 1909

Complaint filed Nov 30 1906 **Commissioner Reports** Jany 8 1907	in **Contest.** **Notice Sent** Dec 29 1906

Nov 30 1906	Allottment[sic] certificates Nos 14775 & 11723 in file.
Dec 29 1906	Com^r asked to report
Jany 2 1907	Proof of service returned dated Jany 1-1907
Jany 7 1907	Answer filed by Atty for dfdt states land is involved in Cherokee contest.
Jany 11 1907	In view of contest, case dismissed and certificates No 14775-11723 returned
Mar 22 1907	Com^r reports Harvey Martin denied enrollment as freedman of Cherokee Nation - See report in Case # 1036
Apr 30 1907	Notice sent
May 4 1907	Proof of service returned dated May 2-1907
May 10 1907	Dfndt requested to appear on this date in Case # 1036, while here his testimony in this case taken
May 10 1907	Plntf requested to appear at this office Muskogee I.T. May 18-1907
May 10 1907	Com^r asked for additional information
May 13 1907	Com^r reports no contest as to land of Maggie Province - Harvey & Gertie Martin denied enrollment by Dept - (Cherokee freedman)
May 18 1907	Husband of plntf appeared & testimony taken
May 23 1907	Judgement[sic] rendered in favor plantf - dfndts given ten day in which to vacate
June 6 07	Capt Jno C West instructed to place plff in poss
June 8, 07	Plff advised that instructions are in hands of Capt West.
June ~~10~~ 07	Capt West reports placing allottee[sic] in poss.
June 14 07	Plff advised of Capt West's report and Case Dismissed

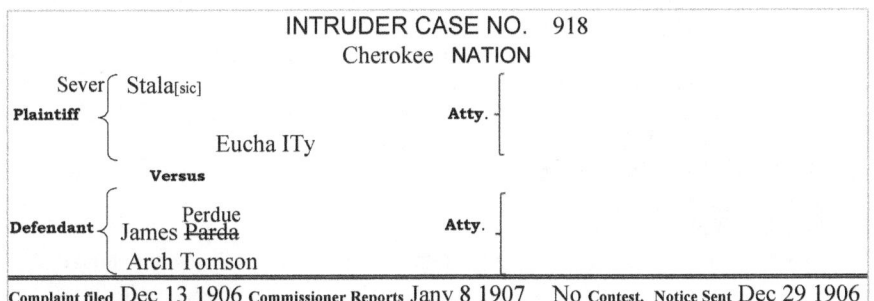

INTRUDER CASE NO. 918
Cherokee NATION

Plaintiff — Sever Stala[sic] / Eucha ITy — **Atty.**

Versus

Defendant — James ~~Parda~~ Perdue / Arch Tomson — **Atty.**

Complaint filed Dec 13 1906 **Commissioner Reports** Jany 8 1907	No **Contest.** **Notice Sent** Dec 29 1906

Dec 13 1906	Allottment[sic] certificates Nos 53251-53252 in file
Dec 29 1906	Com^r asked to report.
Jany 7 1907	Proof of service returned Jany 4 1907
Jany 8 1907	Answer filed by Jas Pardu[sic] one dfndt.
Jany 19 1907	Case set for hearing at Claremore ITy Feby 7 1907 All parties notified
Jany 19 1907	Plntf writes concerning case.
Jany 24 1907	" advised.

Cherokee Intruder Cases 1901 - 1909

Jany 25 1907	Dfndt states he has no improvements on land of plntf.
Feby 7 1907	Case called at Claremore ITy. Neither party appeared.
Feby 13 1907	Referred to Robt R. Bennett
" 26 07	R.R. Bennett reports case settled to satisfaction of plaintiff
July 5 07	Plaintiff advised of Mr. Bennett's report and Case Dismissed
	Entry is an error.

INTRUDER CASE NO. 919
Cherokee NATION

Plaintiff Minzy Rawls, Leg. Gdn of
Winnie D Hatfield   **Atty.**
Whitmire ITy

Versus

Defendant O.M. Millender and
Sam Kinnerman   **Atty.**
Whitmire ITy

Complaint filed Dec 5 1906   **Commissioner Reports** Jany 8 1907   No **Contest.** **Notice Sent** Dec 29 1906

Dec 5 1906	Allottment[sic] certificates Nos 7140 - 6875
Dec 5 1906	Letters of Gdnship in file.
Dec 29 1906	Com^r asked to report
Feby 11 1907	Case set for hearing at Muskogee ITy Mch 1 1907 All parties notified
Jany 21 1907	O.M. Milender[sic] answers & encloses lease contract
Mch 1 1907	O.M. Milender appeared. No appearance by plntf. No testimony taken. Dfndt states Sam Kinnerman is his tenant.
Mch 6 1907	Dfndt's [Plntf] letter in file written from Purcell I.Ty.
Mch 13 1907	Plntf asked to advise when he can appear & give testimony.
June 15 07	Plff requests return of certificate.
June 21 07	Cert 7140 and 6875 returned to plff, Winnie D. Rawls, and she requested to advise in re possession
Jan 11 08	Plaintiff advised that case will be dismissed if she does not appear and give evidence in 10 days.
Jan 14 08	Plff writes case has been settled.
Jan 23 08	In compliance with letter of plaintiff, letters of guardianship returned, and Case Dismissed.

INTRUDER CASE NO. 920
Cherokee NATION

Plaintiff Nannie Miller   **Atty.**
Maysville Ark

Cherokee Intruder Cases 1901 - 1909

	Versus	
Defendant	Jno Adams	Atty.
	Nowata ITy.	

Complaint filed Dec 8 1906 **Commissioner Reports** Dec 21 1906 No Contest. **Notice Sent** Dec 29 1906

Jany 19 1907	Case set for hearing at Claremore ITy Feby 7 -07 All parties notified.
Jany 14 1907	Proof of service returned dated Jany 10 1907
Feby 7 1907	Case called at Claremore ITy. Plntf appeared & her testimony taken. No appearance by dfndt. R.L. Owen has original lease.
Feby 13 1907	Referred to Robt R. Bennett
June 24 07	R.R. Bennett reports matter satisfactorily settled.
July 5 07	Plaintiff advised of Mr Bennett's report and <u>Case Dismissed</u>

INTRUDER CASE NO. 921
Cherokee NATION

	Edward Foster Nat. Gdn.	
Plaintiff	Clem and Quinnie Foster	Atty.
	Cedar ITy	
	Versus	
Defendant	Silas Alberty	Atty.
	Cedar ITy	

Complaint filed Dec 6 1906 **Commissioner Reports** Dec 6 1906 No Contest. **Notice Sent** Dec 29 1906

Jany 4 1907	Proof of service returned dated Jany 2, 1907
Jany 19 1907	Case set for hearing at Claremore ITy Feby 7 1907 All parties notified
Feby 7 1907	Case called at Claremore I.Ty. Both parties present. Tis a matter of lines between two allottees. Understanding between Parties reached & <u>Case dismissed</u>.

INTRUDER CASE NO. 922
Cherokee NATION

	Wallace Ratley	
Plaintiff		Atty.
	Campbell ITy.	
	Versus	
Defendant	Jeff Gilliland	Atty.
	Allottment near Campbell I.Ty.	

Cherokee Intruder Cases 1901 - 1909

Complaint filed Dec 22 1906 Commissioner Reports Jany 8 1907 No Contest. Notice Sent Dec 29 1906
Dec 29 1906   Com^r asked to report
Dec 22 1906   Allottment[sic] certificates Nos 61097 - 61098 in file
Jany 2 1907   Proof of service returned dated Jany 2 1907
Feby 11 1907   Case set for hearing at Muskogee ITy Mch 1 1907 All parties notified.
Mch 1 1907   Case called at Muskogee ITy. Dfndt appeared & testimony taken. No appearance by plntf Dfndt exhibited contract dated since complaint was filed
Mch 2 1907   Certificates returned and <u>case dismissed</u>

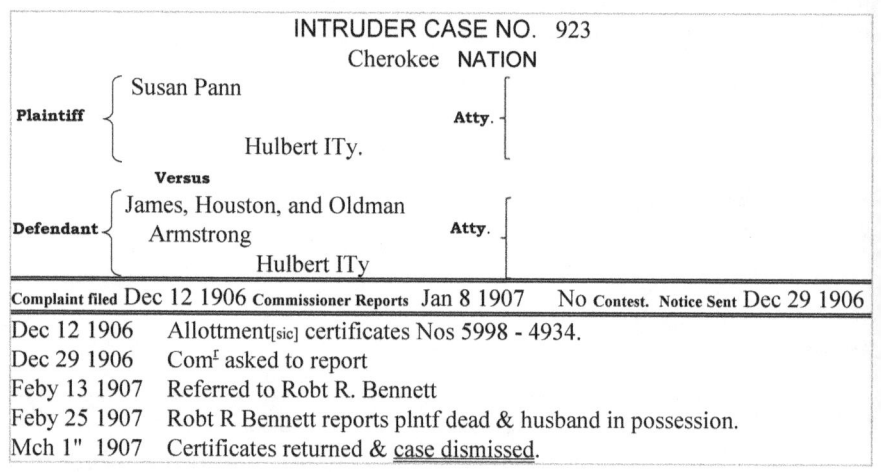

INTRUDER CASE NO. 923
Cherokee NATION

Plaintiff: Susan Pann, Hulbert ITy. Atty. -

Versus

Defendant: James, Houston, and Oldman Armstrong, Hulbert ITy Atty.

Complaint filed Dec 12 1906 Commissioner Reports Jan 8 1907 No Contest. Notice Sent Dec 29 1906
Dec 12 1906   Allottment[sic] certificates Nos 5998 - 4934.
Dec 29 1906   Com^r asked to report
Feby 13 1907   Referred to Robt R. Bennett
Feby 25 1907   Robt R Bennett reports plntf dead & husband in possession.
Mch 1" 1907   Certificates returned & <u>case dismissed</u>.

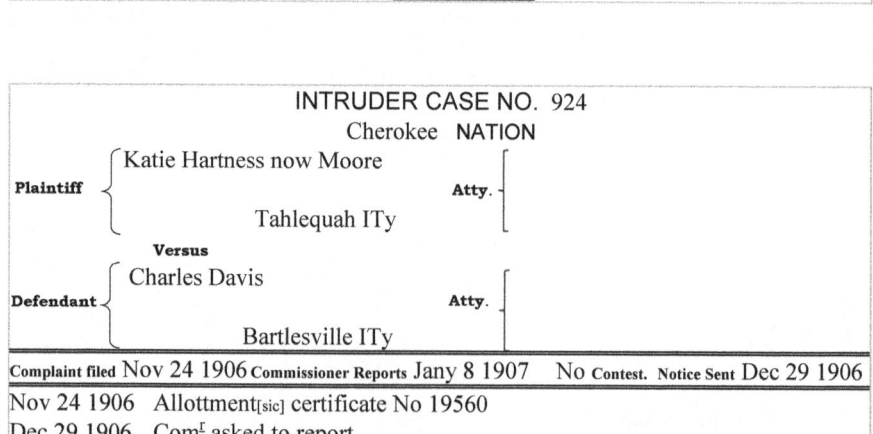

INTRUDER CASE NO. 924
Cherokee NATION

Plaintiff: Katie Hartness now Moore, Tahlequah ITy Atty. -

Versus

Defendant: Charles Davis, Bartlesville ITy Atty.

Complaint filed Nov 24 1906 Commissioner Reports Jany 8 1907 No Contest. Notice Sent Dec 29 1906
Nov 24 1906   Allottment[sic] certificate No 19560
Dec 29 1906   Com^r asked to report.
Jany 19 1907   Case set for hearing at Claremore ITy Feby 7 1907 All parties notified
Jany 14 1907   Proof of service returned dated Jany 12 1907

Cherokee Intruder Cases 1901 - 1909

Jany 29 1907   Dfndt writes in answer to complaint.
Feby 7 1907   Case called at Claremore ITy. Both parties present. Dfndt is not in Possession of land of plntf. Certificates returned & case <u>dismissed</u>.

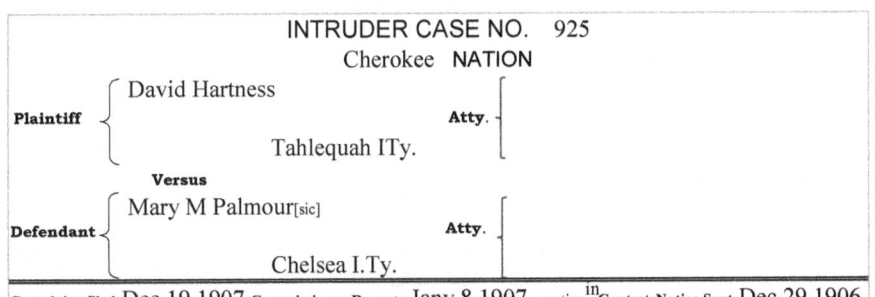

INTRUDER CASE NO. 925
Cherokee NATION

Plaintiff: David Hartness, Tahlequah ITy.   Atty.

Versus

Defendant: Mary M Palmour[sic], Chelsea I.Ty.   Atty.

Complaint filed Dec 19 1907 **Commissioner Reports** Jany 8 1907 portion in Contest. **Notice Sent** Dec 29 1906

Dec 19 1906   Allottment[sic] certificates Nos 50421 - 32603 in file.
Dec 29 1906   Com^r asked to report.
Jany 5 1907   Proof of service returned dated Jany 4 1907
Jany 11 1907   In view of contest on portion of land, case dismissed as to that portion.
Jany 8 1907   D.S. Palmour answers & says portion of land in contest.
Jany 19 1907   Case set for hearing at Claremore ITy Feby 8 1907 All parties notified.
Feby 8 1907   Case called at Claremore ITy. Dfndt appeared. Testimony of husband Taken. No appearance by plntf. Dfndt claims no land save that in contest.
Feby 14 1907   <u>Case dismissed</u> & certificates returned.

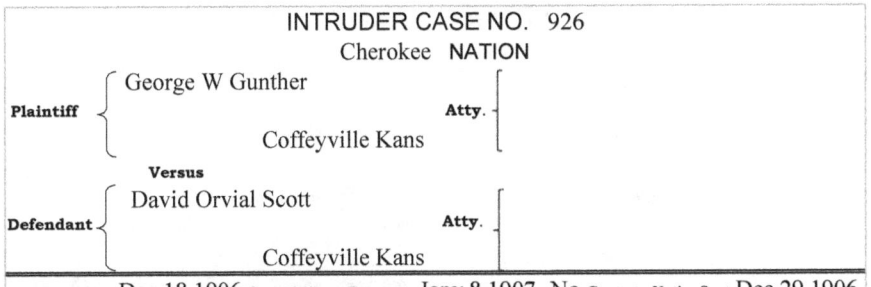

INTRUDER CASE NO. 926
Cherokee NATION

Plaintiff: George W Gunther, Coffeyville Kans   Atty.

Versus

Defendant: David Orvial Scott, Coffeyville Kans   Atty.

Complaint filed Dec 18 1906 **Commissioner Reports** Jany 8 1907 No **Contest. Notice Sent** Dec 29 1906

Dec 18 1906   Allottment[sic] certificate No 15090 in file.
Dec 29 1906   Com^r asked to report
Jany 7 1907   Proof of service returned dated Jany 5 1907
Jany 19 1907   Case set for hearing at Claremore ITy Feby 7 1907 All parties notified
Jany 28 1907   Plntf states dfndt has "moved off" & he now has possession.

Cherokee Intruder Cases 1901 - 1909

Jany 30 1907 In view of above certificate No 15090 returned & <u>case dismissed</u>.
Aug 12 - 07 Com. Reports no contest.

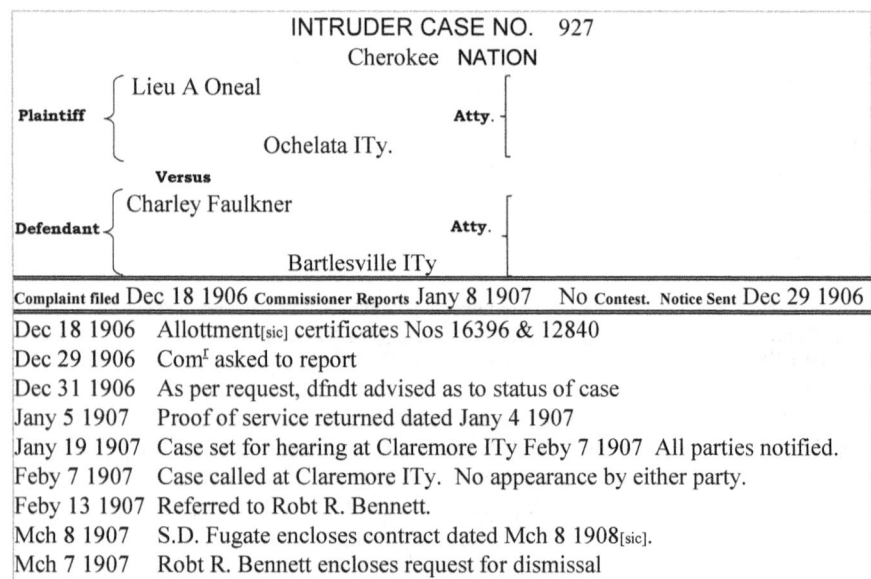

INTRUDER CASE NO. 927
Cherokee NATION

Plaintiff Lieu A Oneal
Ochelata ITy.
Atty.

Versus

Defendant Charley Faulkner
Bartlesville ITy
Atty.

Complaint filed Dec 18 1906 Commissioner Reports Jany 8 1907   No Contest. Notice Sent Dec 29 1906

Dec 18 1906	Allottment[sic] certificates Nos 16396 & 12840
Dec 29 1906	Com^r asked to report
Dec 31 1906	As per request, dfndt advised as to status of case
Jany 5 1907	Proof of service returned dated Jany 4 1907
Jany 19 1907	Case set for hearing at Claremore ITy Feby 7 1907 All parties notified.
Feby 7 1907	Case called at Claremore ITy. No appearance by either party.
Feby 13 1907	Referred to Robt R. Bennett.
Mch 8 1907	S.D. Fugate encloses contract dated Mch 8 1908[sic].
Mch 7 1907	Robt R. Bennett encloses request for dismissal
Mch 14 1907	Certificates returned & <u>case dismissed</u>.

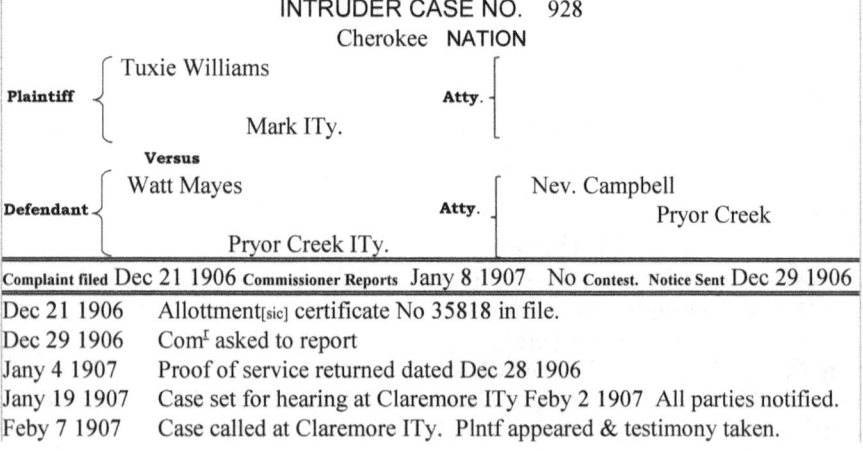

INTRUDER CASE NO. 928
Cherokee NATION

Plaintiff Tuxie Williams
Mark ITy.
Atty.

Versus

Defendant Watt Mayes
Pryor Creek ITy.
Atty. Nev. Campbell
Pryor Creek

Complaint filed Dec 21 1906 Commissioner Reports Jany 8 1907   No Contest. Notice Sent Dec 29 1906

Dec 21 1906	Allottment[sic] certificate No 35818 in file.
Dec 29 1906	Com^r asked to report
Jany 4 1907	Proof of service returned dated Dec 28 1906
Jany 19 1907	Case set for hearing at Claremore ITy Feby 2 1907 All parties notified.
Feby 7 1907	Case called at Claremore ITy. Plntf appeared & testimony taken.

Cherokee Intruder Cases 1901 - 1909

	No appearance by dfndt.
Mch 5 1907	Dfndt asked to advise if he is in possession & by what authority
Apr 6 1907	Referred to Robt R. Bennett.
Apr 11 1907	Ans filed by dfndt
Apr 18 1907	Dfndt advised case in hands of field man
Apr 13 1907	Robt R Bennett report in file.
June 14 07	Plff requested to advise in re. her possession of said land.
July 18 07	Judgement[sic] rendered in favor of pltf.
Aug 1 1907	Nev. Campbell Atty for Defendant appeared in person and stated that it would be necessary to issue an order to remove Defendant and that Plaintiff might go upon his land and take possession thereof and the Defendant will not interfer[sic] with him
Jany 11 08	Plaintiff requested to advise if in possession.
May 16 08	Plaintiff again requested to advise if in possession & advised that if he failed to report in 10 days case would be dismissed
6-22-08	Case is <u>dismissed</u> as it is presumed Dft has possession.
	Dismissed

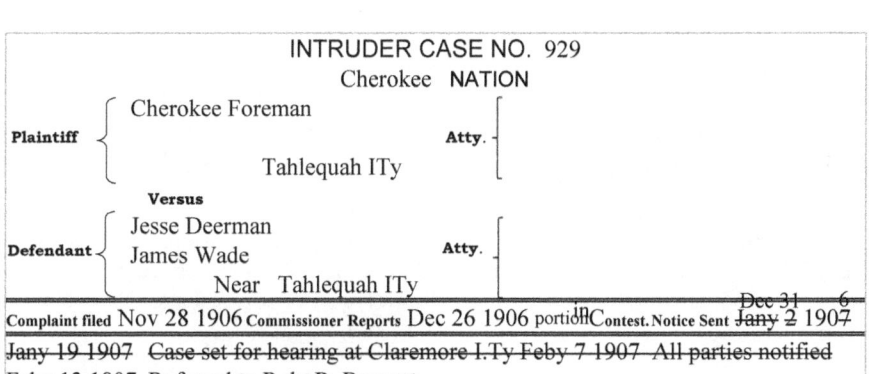

INTRUDER CASE NO. 929
Cherokee NATION

Plaintiff: Cherokee Foreman   Atty.
Tahlequah ITy
Versus
Defendant: Jesse Deerman   Atty.
James Wade
Near Tahlequah ITy

Complaint filed Nov 28 1906 Commissioner Reports Dec 26 1906 portion Contest. Notice Sent ~~Jany 2 1907~~ ~~Dec 31~~ 6
~~Jany 19 1907 Case set for hearing at Claremore I.Ty Feby 7 1907 All parties notified~~
Feby 13 1907 Referred to Robt R. Bennett
Feby 18 1907 Robt R. Bennett reports & recommends dfndt be dispossessed.
Feby 23 1907 Plntf states dfndts have settled.
Mch 4 1907   <u>Case dismissed</u>.

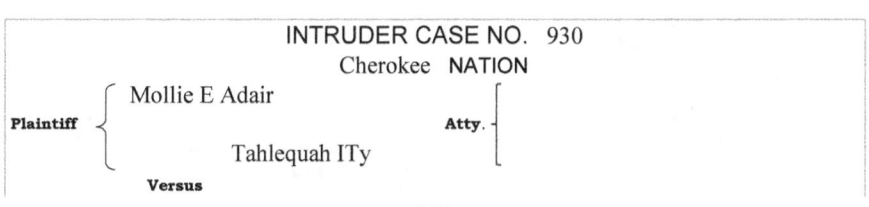

INTRUDER CASE NO. 930
Cherokee NATION

Plaintiff: Mollie E Adair   Atty.
Tahlequah ITy
Versus

Cherokee Intruder Cases 1901 - 1909

| Defendant | J.A. McLain | Atty. | |
| | Bartlesville ITy. | | |

Complaint filed Dec 31 1906 **Commissioner Reports** Jany 21, 07   **No Contest. Notice Sent** Jany 2 1906[sic]

Dec 31 1906	Allottment[sic] certificates Nos 10245 -12648
Jany 2 1906[sic]	Com^r asked to report.
Jany 7 1907	Proof of service returned dated Jany 7 1907
Jany 19 1907	Case set for hearing at Claremore ITy Feby 7 1907 All parties notified.
Jany 28 1907	Answer filed by dfndt.
Jany 26 1907	Plntf states she has possession
Jany 31 1907	In view of above case dismissed.

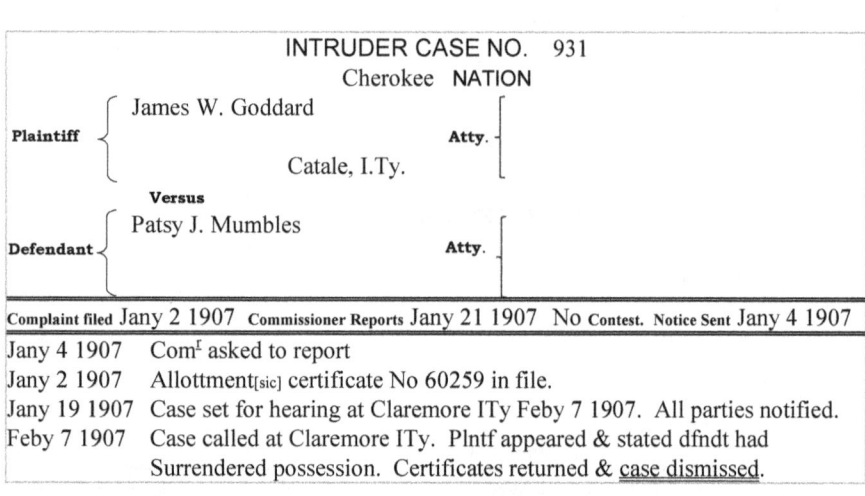

INTRUDER CASE NO. 931
Cherokee NATION

Plaintiff	James W. Goddard	Atty.	
	Catale, I.Ty.		
	Versus		
Defendant	Patsy J. Mumbles	Atty.	

Complaint filed Jany 2 1907 **Commissioner Reports** Jany 21 1907 **No Contest. Notice Sent** Jany 4 1907

Jany 4 1907	Com^r asked to report
Jany 2 1907	Allottment[sic] certificate No 60259 in file.
Jany 19 1907	Case set for hearing at Claremore ITy Feby 7 1907. All parties notified.
Feby 7 1907	Case called at Claremore ITy. Plntf appeared & stated dfndt had Surrendered possession. Certificates returned & case dismissed.

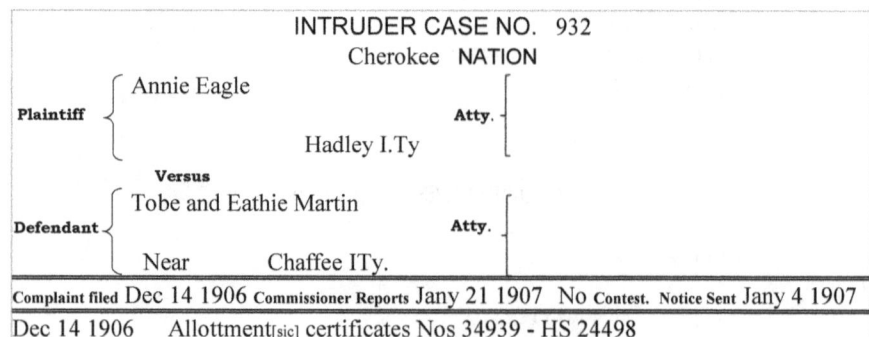

INTRUDER CASE NO. 932
Cherokee NATION

Plaintiff	Annie Eagle	Atty.	
	Hadley I.Ty		
	Versus		
Defendant	Tobe and Eathie Martin	Atty.	
	Near Chaffee ITy.		

Complaint filed Dec 14 1906 **Commissioner Reports** Jany 21 1907 **No Contest. Notice Sent** Jany 4 1907

| Dec 14 1906 | Allottment[sic] certificates Nos 34939 - HS 24498 |

Cherokee Intruder Cases 1901 - 1909

Jany 4 1907	Com[r] asked to report
Jany 10 1907	Case set for hearing at Claremore ITy Feby 8 1907 All parties notified.
Feby 8 1907	Case called at Claremore ITy. Neither party appeared.
Feby 8 1907	Proof of service returned dated Jany 30 1907
Feby 14 1907	Referred to Robt R. Bennett
Feby 22 1907	Plntf *(illegible)* action.
Feby 27 1907	Plntf advised case in hands of field man.
Mch 27 1907	Robt R Bennett's report in file. He found part of land unoccupied & Rachel Vann holding 40 acres.
(Illegible)	Certificates returned & <u>case dismissed</u>.

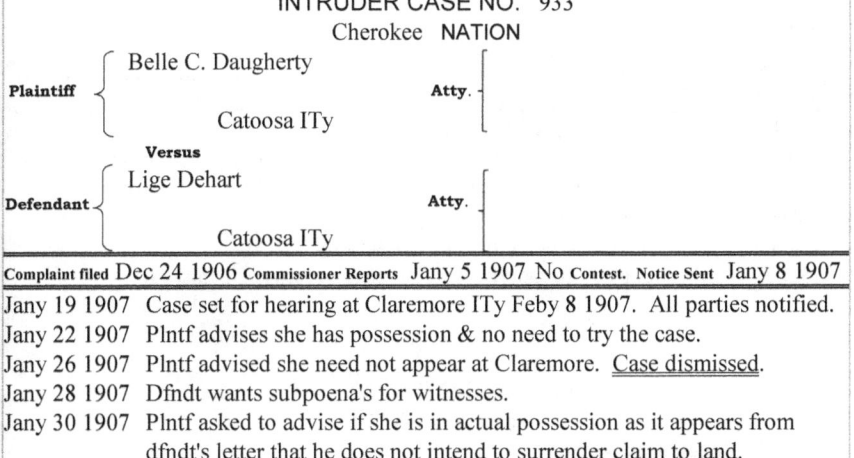

INTRUDER CASE NO. 933
Cherokee NATION

Plaintiff: Belle C. Daugherty, Catoosa ITy Atty.

Versus

Defendant: Lige Dehart, Catoosa ITy Atty.

Complaint filed Dec 24 1906 **Commissioner Reports** Jany 5 1907 **No Contest.** **Notice Sent** Jany 8 1907

Jany 19 1907	Case set for hearing at Claremore ITy Feby 8 1907. All parties notified.
Jany 22 1907	Plntf advises she has possession & no need to try the case.
Jany 26 1907	Plntf advised she need not appear at Claremore. <u>Case dismissed</u>.
Jany 28 1907	Dfndt wants subpoena's for witnesses.
Jany 30 1907	Plntf asked to advise if she is in actual possession as it appears from dfndt's letter that he does not intend to surrender claim to land.

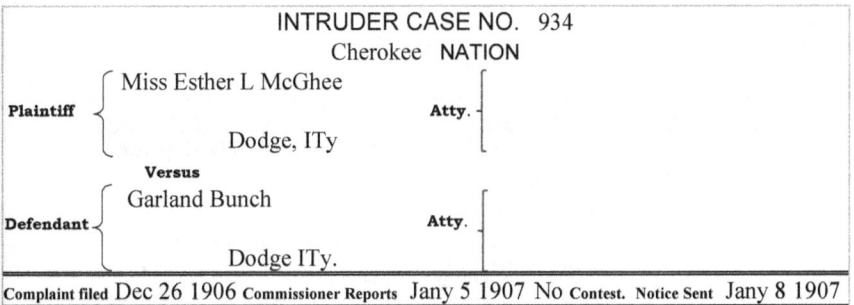

INTRUDER CASE NO. 934
Cherokee NATION

Plaintiff: Miss Esther L McGhee, Dodge, ITy Atty.

Versus

Defendant: Garland Bunch, Dodge ITy. Atty.

Complaint filed Dec 26 1906 **Commissioner Reports** Jany 5 1907 **No Contest.** **Notice Sent** Jany 8 1907

Jany 19 1907	Case set for hearing at Claremore ITy Feby 8 1907 All parties notified

Cherokee Intruder Cases 1901 - 1909

Feby 8 1907	Case called at Claremore ITy Neither party appeared.
Feby 13 1907	Referred to Robt R. Bennett
Mch 23 1907	Robt R. Bennett encloses request for dismissal.
Mch 26 1907	Case dismissed.

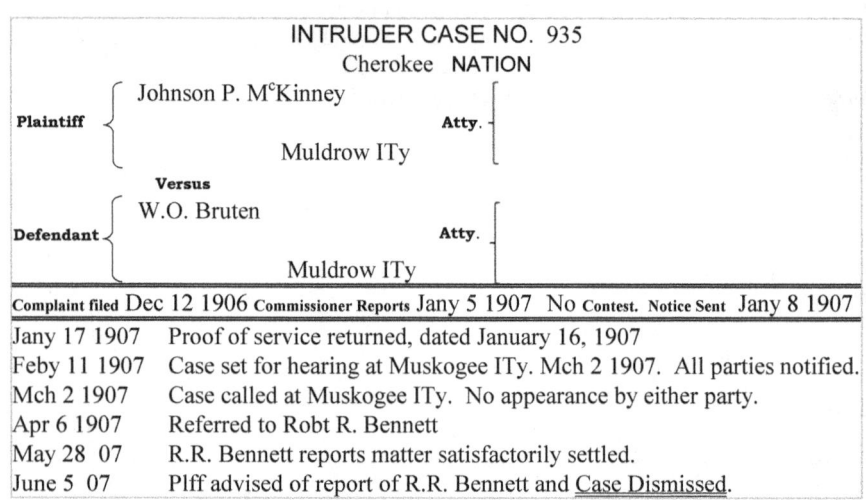

INTRUDER CASE NO. 935
Cherokee NATION

Plaintiff: Johnson P. McKinney, Muldrow ITy Atty.

Versus

Defendant: W.O. Bruten, Muldrow ITy Atty.

Complaint filed Dec 12 1906 **Commissioner Reports** Jany 5 1907 **No Contest.** **Notice Sent** Jany 8 1907

Jany 17 1907	Proof of service returned, dated January 16, 1907
Feby 11 1907	Case set for hearing at Muskogee ITy. Mch 2 1907. All parties notified.
Mch 2 1907	Case called at Muskogee ITy. No appearance by either party.
Apr 6 1907	Referred to Robt R. Bennett
May 28 07	R.R. Bennett reports matter satisfactorily settled.
June 5 07	Plff advised of report of R.R. Bennett and Case Dismissed.

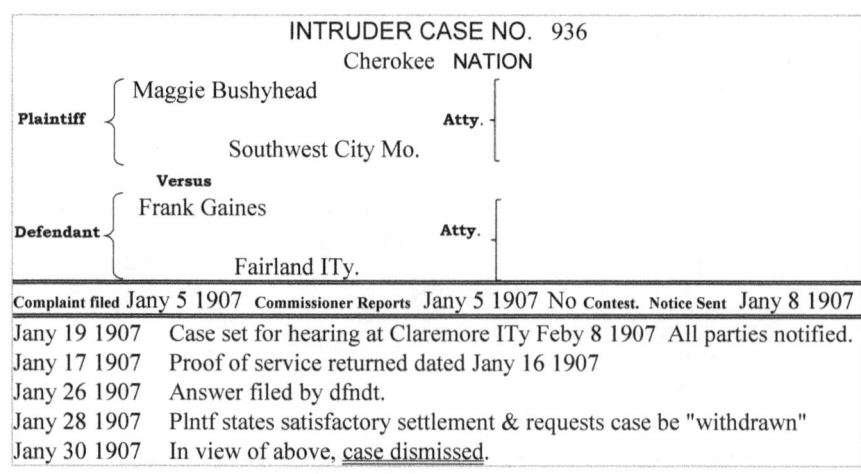

INTRUDER CASE NO. 936
Cherokee NATION

Plaintiff: Maggie Bushyhead, Southwest City Mo. Atty.

Versus

Defendant: Frank Gaines, Fairland ITy. Atty.

Complaint filed Jany 5 1907 **Commissioner Reports** Jany 5 1907 **No Contest.** **Notice Sent** Jany 8 1907

Jany 19 1907	Case set for hearing at Claremore ITy Feby 8 1907 All parties notified.
Jany 17 1907	Proof of service returned dated Jany 16 1907
Jany 26 1907	Answer filed by dfndt.
Jany 28 1907	Plntf states satisfactory settlement & requests case be "withdrawn"
Jany 30 1907	In view of above, case dismissed.

Cherokee Intruder Cases 1901 - 1909

INTRUDER CASE NO. 937
Cherokee NATION

Plaintiff: Luke Witfield[sic]
Wauhillau ITy
Atty.

Versus

Defendant: Lee Wells and Walter Goodridge
Wauhillau ITy.
Atty.

Complaint filed Jany 5 1907 **Commissioner Reports** Jany 16 1907 No **Contest. Notice Sent** Jany 10 1907

Jany 5 1907	Allottment[sic] certificate No 23773.
Jany 10 1907	Com^r asked to report.
Jany 19 1907	Plntf advised he has possession.
Jany 24 1907	In view of above <u>case dismissed</u>.

INTRUDER CASE NO. 938
Cherokee NATION

Plaintiff: Lula Wilson nee Gooden
Maysville Ark
Atty.

Versus

Defendant: Charles Kirby
Maysville Ark.
Atty.

Complaint filed Jany 5 1907 **Commissioner Reports** Jany 16 1907 No **Contest. Notice Sent** Jany 10 1907

Jany 5 1907	Certificate of allottment[sic] No 41188 in file
Jany 5 1907	Copy of contract in file.
Jany 15 1907	Com^r asked to report
Jany 19 1907	Case set for hearing at Claremore ITy Feby 8 1907 All parties notified
Jany 23 1907	Proof of service returned, dated Jany 18 1907
Jany 26 1907	Case set for hearing at Claremore ITy Feby 8 1907 Platf again notified
Jany 24 1907	Answer filed by dfndt.
Jany 30 1907	Receipt of above acknowledged & dfndt requested to appear at hearing
Feby 8 1907	Case called at Claremore ITy. Plntf appeared & testimony taken. No appearance by dfndt.
Mch 5 1907	Judgement[sic] found for plntf and dfndt given ten days to vacate.
Mch 11 1907	Plntf states dfndt has surrendered land.
Mch 10 1907	Certificate returned & <u>case dismissed</u>.

Cherokee Intruder Cases 1901 - 1909

INTRUDER CASE NO. 939
Cherokee NATION

Plaintiff: Sallie Brown — Santown[sic] ITy. **Atty.**

Versus

Defendant: William Taylor — Santown[sic] ITy **Atty.** W.T. McCombs — Sallisaw

Complaint filed Dec 21 1906 **Commissioner Reports** Jany 8 1907 No **Contest.** **Notice Sent** Jany 11 1907

Jany 19 1907	Case set for hearing at Claremore ITy Feby 8 07. All parties notified.
Feby 8 1907	Case called at Claremore I.Ty. All parties present. It is shown that Land is all in contest. Must be a different Sallie Brown. Sallie Brown roll No "F" 606. Wrong land described. <u>Dismissed</u> Land should be 15-11-22

INTRUDER CASE NO. 940
Cherokee NATION

Plaintiff: L.M. Marrs ~~for~~ Legal Gdn of Amanda Olivia, David M Jr, William C and Barney Marrs Vinita ITy **Atty.**

Versus

Defendant: John or Jack Sanders — Miles ITy **Atty.** A.S. McRea — Muskogee ITy.

Complaint filed Jan 9 1907 **Commissioner Reports** Jany 16 1907 No **Contest.** **Notice Sent** Jany 11 1907

Jany 9 1907	Letters of Gdnship in file.
Jany 9 1907	Allottment[sic] certificates Nos 1327-1547-1329-1549-1322-1326-1546 in file
Jany 11 1907	Com^r asked to report
~~Jany 19 1907~~	Case set for hearing at Claremore ITy Feby 8 1907 All parties notified
Jany 15 1907	Proof [sic] service returned dated Jany 14 1907
Jany 22 1907	Plntf advises dfndt has been notified of date of hearing.
Feby 8 1907	Case called at Claremore ITy. All parties present & testimony taken.
Feby 23 1907	Plntf asks immediate action.
Mch 1 1907	Plntf is advised that judgement[sic] will be rendered soon.
Mch 4 1907	Com^r asked asked[sic] as to citizenship of dfndt.
Mch 5 1907	Com^r reports dfndt denied citizenship Oct 26 1905.
Mch 6 1907	Judgement[sic] rendered in favor of plntf. Dfndt requested to vacate in ten days.
Mch 14 1907	Atty for dfndt served notice for application for injunction before Judge

Cherokee Intruder Cases 1901 - 1909

	Wm R. Lawrence.
Mch 15 1907	W.W. Bennett appeared for US Ind Agent before Judge W^m R Lawrence, Dfndt's application denied in US Court.
Mch 15 1907	Atty for dfndt served notice on Agent he would apply to Court of Appeals for injunction See 940
March 22 1907	Policeman Barbee, Afton, ITy. Instructed to place plntf in possession
March 25 1907	Policeman Barbee requested by wire, to withhold action until further instructions.
March 25 1907	Notice of filing of supersedeas bond and appeal served on Agent.
April 23 1907	U.S. Indian policeman John Barbee instructed to carry out original order. All parties notified.
April 25 1907	Policeman Barbee requested by wire to withhold action
April 26 1907	Policeman Barbee wired to carry out original instructions United States Atty advises that the supersedeas does not effect[sic] action of Agent
Apr 29 1907	Policeman Barbee wired to take immediate action
May 1 1907	Policeman Barbee reports (by wire) that he has placed plntfs in possession
May 3 1907	Policeman Barbee advises by phone that dfndts are again in possession - Also advises that when he removed dfndts, plntf was not present to take possession
May 3 1907	Instructions issued to Lennie McIntosh policeman to place plntf in possession
May 8 1907	Policeman McIntosh reports he has paced plntf in possession
	Case dismissed -

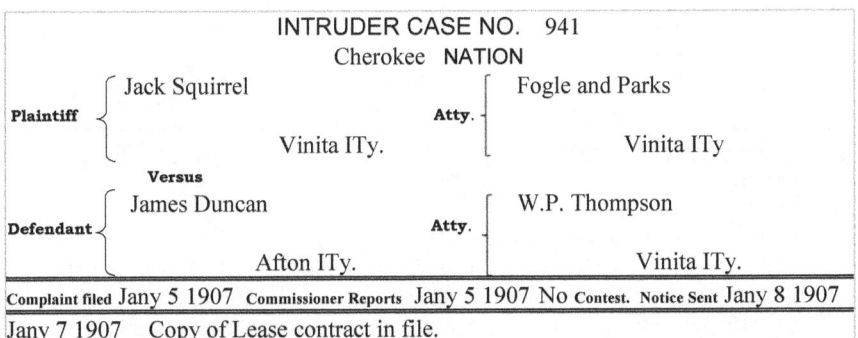

INTRUDER CASE NO. 941
Cherokee NATION

Plaintiff	Jack Squirrel	Atty.	Fogle and Parks
	Vinita ITy.		Vinita ITy
	Versus		
Defendant	James Duncan	Atty.	W.P. Thompson
	Afton ITy.		Vinita ITy.

Complaint filed Jany 5 1907 **Commissioner Reports** Jany 5 1907 No **Contest.** **Notice Sent** Jany 8 1907

Jany 7 1907	Copy of Lease contract in file.
Aug 21 1907	Case set for hearing at Claremore ITy Feby 9 1907 All parties notified
Feby 9 1907	Case called at Claremore ITy. Answer filed by Atty for dfndt. Dfndt present & testimony taken. No appearance by plntf.
Feby 8 1907	Attys for plntf states he is sick & can not appear. Ask continuance. See letters

Cherokee Intruder Cases 1901 - 1909

Mch 6 1907	Plntf advised that case will be set for hearing again in order that his testimony taken.
Mch 26 1907	Case set for hearing at Claremore ITy Apr 8 1907 All parties notified.
Apr 2 1907	Atty for dfndt asks why is case again set for hearing.
Apr 4 1907	Atty for dfndt advised.
Apr 8 1907	Case called at Claremore ITy. Plntf & Atty Parks present. Testimony taken. No appearance by dfndt. Copy of contract filed by plntf also certificates Nos 4532-9647.
May 3 1907	Judgment rendered in favor of plntif - Dfndt given ten days in which to vacate.
May 22 07	Protest filed by deft's Atty and appeal taken to Deptmt.
May 31 07	Plff advises of protest and appeal by deft and requests to file brief if desired
June 13 07	Submitted to Com^r Indian Affairs upon appeal of Deft.
Dec 16 07	Dept affirms decision of this office & orders pltf placed in possession
Dec 21 07	Instructions issued to Capt John C West to place the plaintiff in possession
Jan 18 08	John C West reports that plaintiff was in possession. <u>Case dismissed</u>.

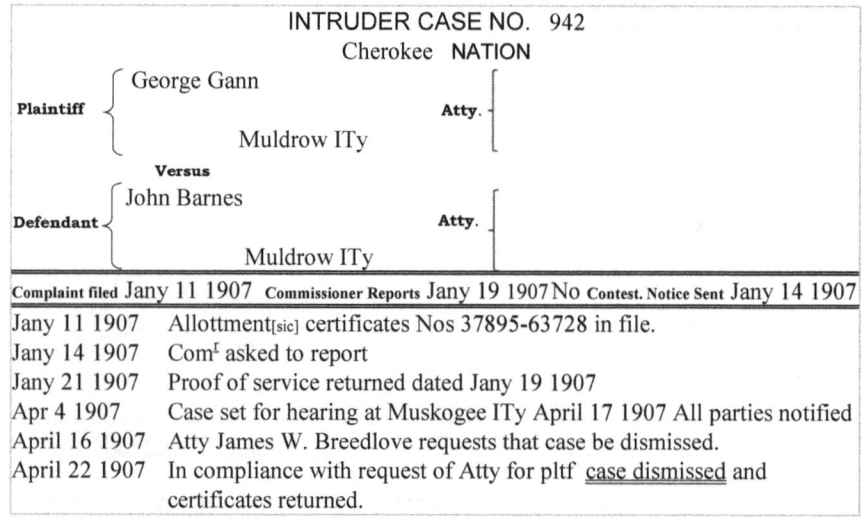

INTRUDER CASE NO. 942
Cherokee NATION

Plaintiff { George Gann Atty. {
Muldrow ITy

Versus

Defendant { John Barnes Atty. {
Muldrow ITy

Complaint filed Jany 11 1907 **Commissioner Reports** Jany 19 1907 **No Contest. Notice Sent** Jany 14 1907

Jany 11 1907	Allottment[sic] certificates Nos 37895-63728 in file.
Jany 14 1907	Com^r asked to report
Jany 21 1907	Proof of service returned dated Jany 19 1907
Apr 4 1907	Case set for hearing at Muskogee ITy April 17 1907 All parties notified
April 16 1907	Atty James W. Breedlove requests that case be dismissed.
April 22 1907	In compliance with request of Atty for pltf <u>case dismissed</u> and certificates returned.

Cherokee Intruder Cases 1901 - 1909

INTRUDER CASE NO. 943
Cherokee NATION

Plaintiff: Henry T Brown, Ketchum ITy — Atty.

Versus

Defendant: Moses Ross, Leger Denning, Ketchum ITy — Atty.

Complaint filed Jany 11 1907 **Commissioner Reports** Jany 19 1907 **No Contest. Notice Sent** Jany 14 1907

Jany 11 1907	Allottment[sic] certificates No 404 in file.
Jany 14 1907	Com^r asked to report
Jany 19 1907	Case set for hearing at Claremore ITy Feby 8 1907 All parties notified
Jany 22 1907	Proof of service returned dated Jany 18 1907
Jany 26 1907	Dfndt Ross answers & says he occupies his own land & Denning is his tenant.
Jany 31 1907	Com^r asked to report as to land allotted[sic] to Plntf.
Feby 8 1907	Case called at Claremore ITy. Plntf appeared & testimony taken. No appearance by dfndt. Certificate No 350 filed by plntf.
Feby 14 1907	Com^r reports no contest.
Feby 16 1907	Letter in file from Moses Ross.
Feby 25 1907	Com^r asked as to citizenship of Moses Ross.
Mch 2 1907	Answer filed by Leger Denning
Mch 2 1907	Moses Ross says he is Cherokee claimant.
Mch 5 1907	" " encloses sundry papers from Com^r to 5 Tribes
Mch 20 1907	Judgement[sic] rendered in favor of plntf. Dfndt requested to vacate in 10 days.
Mch 28 1907	In answer to Mosses[sic] Ross 3/25/07 He is again requested to vacate or order will issue
May 7 1907	Certificate of homestead allotment returned to plntf and ordered to advise if in possession
May 11 1907	A.S. McRea Atty for dfndt serves notice that application for an injunction will be heard in the United States Court May 13th 1907 at Vinita I.T. - See letter in file #991
May 15 1907	Notice served by Atty for dfndt that application for injunction will be heard at Vinita I.T. May 18 - 1907 - See letter file #991
May 22 1907	Asst U.S. Atty advises injunction granted by U.S. Court at Vinita I.T. See letter in file #991
May 23 1907	Restraining order & summons in equity rec'd - See letter file #991
May 24 1907	Com^r asked if lands in contest & if certificates have been issued
May 28 07	Plff advised of restraining order.
July 12 07	Instructions issued to Capt John C. West to place the pltf in possession Injunction was dissolved on June 29 1907

Cherokee Intruder Cases 1901 - 1909

July 25 07	Capt West reports finding plff in possession & therefore he took no action
Aug 2 07	Plff advised of report of Capt West and Case Dismissed.

INTRUDER CASE NO. 944

Plaintiff: Jim Teekahneyeskee   **Agent Atty.:** C.E. Holderman, Muskogee I.Ty.

Defendant: George Ross, Coffeyville Kans   **Atty.:** F.L. Brown, Claremore ITy

Complaint filed Jany 15 1907   **Commissioner Reports** Jany 23 1907   **No Contest. Notice Sent** Jany 16 1907

Jany 15 1907	Allottment[sic] certificates Nos 23098, 17024 in file
Jany 16 1907	Com^r asked to report.
Jany 19 1907	Case set for hearing at Claremore ITy. Feby 8 1907 All notified
Feby 1 1907	Proof of service returned dated Jany 25 1907
Feby 5 1907	Case called at Claremore ITy. Dfndt appeared
Feby 8 1907	Case called at Claremore IT. Both appeared. Dfndt agreed to vacate on or before Mch 4 1907 unless he is permitted to file by Com^r prior to that time, otherwise dfndt agreed to vacate. Certificates returned Dismissed.
May 3 1907	Dfndt reminded of agreement made Feby 8-07 - and given ten days in which to vacate
May 14 1907	Dfndt given ten days in which to vacate. Judgment rendered in favor of plntf - Plntf requested to advise if possession is given.
May 22 1907	Asst U.S. Atty advises injunction granted by U.S. Court at Vinita I.T. See letter in file #991
May 23 1907	Restraining order & summons in equity rec'd; See letter file #991
May 24 1907	Com^r asked if lands in contest & if certificates have been issued
June 29 1907	Injunction dissolved See cases 991-905-1008, etc
July 6 07	Plff and deft advised of dissolution of injunction
July 6 07	Instructions issued to Capt Jno C. West
July 12 07	Instructions issued to Capt J.C. West to place the pltf in possession as injunction was dissolved on June 29-07
July 25 07	Capt West report that on July 20/7 deft surrendered possession and advises that plff may take possession of the place at any time.
August 2 1907	Plff advised of Capt. West's report, requested to take such possession And notified that Case is Dismissed.
Nov 18 1907	Defendant requests to whom to pay rent and he was asked by what authority he again took possession. See carbon.

Cherokee Intruder Cases 1901 - 1909

INTRUDER CASE NO. 945
NATION

Plaintiff: Daniel Snow — Atty.
Vian ITy

Versus

Defendant: Charles Lewis — Atty.
Vian ITy.

Complaint filed Jany 17 1907 **Commissioner Reports** Jany 26 1907 **No Contest. Notice Sent** Jany 19 1907

Jany 17 1907	Allottment[sic] certificate No 16444 in file.
Jany 19 1907	Com^r asked to report.
Jany 28 1907	Proof of service returned dated Jany 26 1907.
Apr 4 1907	Case set for hearing at Muskogee I.Ty Apr 16 1907 All parties notified
Apr 16 1907	Case called Dfndt appeared & testimony taken No appearance by plntf.
May 18 1907	Com^r asked to report as to citizenship of dfndt. & plntf requested to appear as soon as possible
May 29 07	Com^r reports wife and children of deft denied enrollment 12/6/5 no motion pending.
June 12 07	Plf requested to appear at this office for a hearing June 25/7.\
June 25 07	Plff appeared and his testimony taken.
July 23 07	Judgement[sic] rendered in favor of pltf today.
Sept 6 '07	Plaintiff states he has possession of his allotment.
Sept 10 '07	<u>Case dismissed</u> Plaintiff so advised

INTRUDER CASE NO. 946
NATION

Plaintiff: Richard Reese and Annie Reese — Atty.
Proctor I.Ty.

Versus

Defendant: Frank Dowell — Atty.
Oologah I.Ty

Complaint filed Jany 16 1907 **Commissioner Reports** Jany 28 1907 **No Contest. Notice Sent** Jany 21 1907

Jany 16 1907	Allottment[sic] certificates Nos 10195-12567 (Richard) & 10196-12568 (Annie)
Jany 22 1907	Case set for hearing at Claremore ITy. Feby 9 1907 All parties notified
Jany 26 1907	Plntf states she has mailed copy of notice to dfndt.
Feby 9 1907	Case called at Claremore ITy. No appearance by either party.
Feby 13 1907	Referred to Robt R. Bennett
Feby 4 1907	Plntf advises case settled & ask that case be dismissed.

Cherokee Intruder Cases 1901 - 1909

Feby 16 1907	In view of above certificates returned & <u>case dismissed</u>. Letter to R.R. Bennett withdrawn

INTRUDER CASE NO. 947
NATION

Plaintiff	Robert H. Evans Cookson I.Ty.	Atty.	
Defendant	Versus Pearl Smith Nowata I.Ty.	Atty.	W. J. Sullivan Muskogee ITy

Complaint filed Jany 15 1907 Commissioner Reports Jany 29 1907 portion in Contest. Notice Sent Jany 21 1907

Jany 15 1907	Allottment[sic] certificates Nos 23853 - 33951 in file
Jany 21 1907	Com^r asked to report
Jany 23 1907	Case set for hearing at Claremore ITy Feby 9 1907 All parties notified
Feby 1 1907	Proof of service returned dated Jany 31 1907
Feby 4 1907	Plntf advised that case is dismissed as to that portion in contest.
Feby 9 1907	Answer filed W. J. Sullivan.
Feby 9 1907	Case called at Claremore ITy. Both parties present Land shown to be in contest. <u>Dismissed</u>
Aug 21 -07	Com reports no contest
8/20 07	Proof of service filed today
8/13 07	Com^r asked to report

INTRUDER CASE NO. 948
NATION

Plaintiff	Polly Ballard-Spears Talequah[sic] I.Ty	Atty.	
Defendant	Versus Frank Blackwell Nowata I.Ty.	Atty.	

Complaint filed Jany 15 1907 Commissioner Reports Jany 28 1907 No Contest. Notice Sent Jany 21 1907

Jany 15 1907	Allottment[sic] certificates Nos 45530-45528-30904-45529 in file
Jany 21 1907	Com^r asked to report.
Jany 22 1907	Case set for hearing at Claremore I.Ty. Feby 9 1907 All parties notified
Jany 25 1907	Proof of service returned dated Jany 24 1907

Cherokee Intruder Cases 1901 - 1909

Aug 29 1907	Plntf asks that she be heard at Muskogee or Tahlequah I.Ty.
Feby 4 1907	Plntf advised that case will be called at Claremore I.Ty.
Feby 9 1907	Case called at Claremore, I.Ty. Both parties present. Testimony taken. or Sanders
March 6 1907	Com^r asked as to citizenship of Lucinda Thompson now Blackwell
Mch 23 1907	" " " " " "
Mch 29 1907	Com^r reports Lucinda Blackwell as Cher Freedman denied. No motion pending for review.
April 25 1907	Judgment rendered in favor of pltf - Both parties notified and dfndt given ten days in which to vacate
May 9 1907	Dfndt advised that Lucinda Blackwell was denied enrollment by the Dpt - and urged to give possession
June 21 07	Plff requested to advise in re possession
July 26 07	Instructions issued to Capt. John C. West to place pltf in possession & pltf advised
Oct 9 07	John C West reports he placed pltf in possession & pltf advises Case dismissed.
4-14-09	Certs ret'd

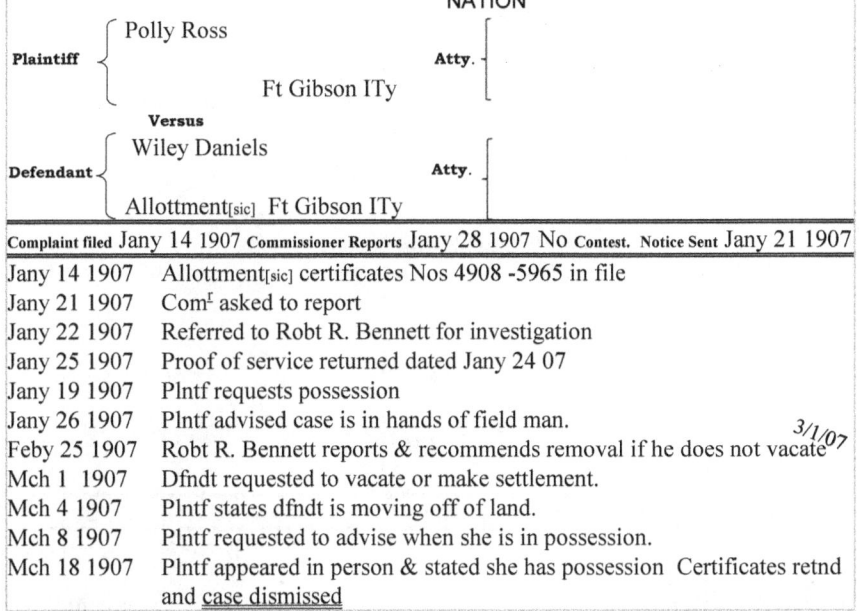

INTRUDER CASE NO. 949
NATION

Plaintiff: Polly Ross
Atty.
Ft Gibson ITy

Versus

Defendant: Wiley Daniels
Atty.
Allottment[sic] Ft Gibson ITy

Complaint filed Jany 14 1907 **Commissioner Reports** Jany 28 1907 **No Contest. Notice Sent** Jany 21 1907

Jany 14 1907	Allottment[sic] certificates Nos 4908 -5965 in file
Jany 21 1907	Com^r asked to report
Jany 22 1907	Referred to Robt R. Bennett for investigation
Jany 25 1907	Proof of service returned dated Jany 24 07
Jany 19 1907	Plntf requests possession
Jany 26 1907	Plntf advised case is in hands of field man.
Feby 25 1907	Robt R. Bennett reports & recommends removal if he does not vacate 3/1/07
Mch 1 1907	Dfndt requested to vacate or make settlement.
Mch 4 1907	Plntf states dfndt is moving off of land.
Mch 8 1907	Plntf requested to advise when she is in possession.
Mch 18 1907	Plntf appeared in person & stated she has possession Certificates retnd and case dismissed

Cherokee Intruder Cases 1901 - 1909

INTRUDER CASE NO. 950
NATION

Plaintiff: Lula Tatum, Vian I.Ty   Atty.

Versus

Defendant: Jay Tatum, Vian ITy   Atty.

Complaint filed Jany 14 1907 **Commissioner Reports** Jany 28 1907 No **Contest.** **Notice Sent** Jany 21 1907

Jany 14 1907	Certificates of Allottment[sic] Nos 36906-25600-36905
Jany 22 1907	Referred to Robt R Bennett.
Jany 21 1907	Com^r asked to report
Jany 24 1907	Proof of service returned dated Jany 24 1907
Jany 21 1907	Plntf states she is 19 years of age Born June 1 1887
Jany 28 1907	Dfndt files answer
Jany 28 1907	Robt R Bennett report in file
Jany 31 1907	Dfndt asked to forward copy of contract
Feby 8 1907	Lease contract filed by dfndt.
Feby 18 1907	Case set for hearing at Muskogee ITy Feby 27 1907 All parties notified
Feb 27 1907	Case called No appearance by either party
Mch 4 1907	Case set for hearing at Muskogee ITy Mch 19 1907 Both parties notified
Mch 19 1907	Case called. No appearance by either party.
Mch 16 1907	Dfndt states plntf may have the land & he has so notified plntf.
Mch 20 1907	Certificates returned to plntf & <u>case dismissed</u>

INTRUDER CASE NO. 951
NATION

Plaintiff: Julia Hall, Ramona ITy   Atty.

Versus

Defendant: William R Swan, Ramona ITy   Atty.

Complaint filed Jany 16 1907 **Commissioner Reports** Jany 28 1907 No **Contest.** **Notice Sent** Jany 21 1907

Jany 16 1907	Allottment[sic] certificates Nos 11328-14178-53636-53645.
Jany 21 1907	Com^r asked to report.
Jany 23 1907	Case set for hearing at Claremore ITy Feby 8 1907 All parties notified.
Jany 25 1907	Answer filed by dfndt. His contract will expire Mch 1 1907

Cherokee Intruder Cases 1901 - 1909

Jany 28 1907	Dfndt requested to vacate. Plntf asked to advise if same is done.
Feby 9 1907	Case called at Claremore ITy. No appearance by either party.
Feby 13 1907	Referred to Robt R Bennett
Jany 24 1907	Proof of service ret dated Jany 23 1907
Feby 6&8 1907	Plntf states she has possession and asks dismissal.
Feby 15 1907	Certificates returned & <u>case dismissed</u> Instructions to Robt R Bennett withdrawn.

INTRUDER CASE NO. 952
NATION

Plaintiff: Alexander Welch, Muldrow ITy — Atty.

Versus

Defendant: Frank M Anderson, Nowata Iy — Atty. J.C. Denton, Nowata Ty

Complaint filed Jany 2 1907 **Commissioner Reports** Jany 17 1907 **No Contest.** **Notice Sent** Jany 21 1907

Jany 2 1907	Copy of Agreement filed.
Jany 23 1907	Case set for hearing at Claremore ITy Feby 9 1907 All parties notified
Feby 9 1907	Case called at Claremore ITy. Both parties present testimony taken.
Feby 5 1907	Proof of service returned dated Jany 29 '07
Feby 12 1907	Atty for dfndt encloses rental contract. $1600.^{00} in promissory notes & Allottment[sic] certificates Nos 11529-9375 which belong to & to be delivered to plntf.
Feby 18 1907	<u>Case dismissed</u> 28 notes of $200.^{00} each, rental contract & certificates returned to plntf.

INTRUDER CASE NO. 953
NATION

Plaintiff: Alfred H. Chaney Gdn of Florence Ellen Chaney, Eureka ITy — Atty.

Versus

Defendant: John and I.B. Brown, Hulbert ITy — Atty.

Cherokee Intruder Cases 1901 - 1909

Complaint filed Jany 3 1907	Commissioner Reports Jany 16 1907 No Contest. Notice Sent Jany 21 1907
Jany 3 1907	Letters of Gdnship in file.
Jany 17 1907	Report of U.S.I Policeman Thos P. Roach in file.
Jany 22 1907	Referred to Robt R. Bennett
Feby 1 1907	Proof of service returned dated Jany 29 1907
Feby 11 1907	Robt R. Bennett encloses request for dismissal.
Feby 19 1907	Letters of Gdnship returned & <u>case dismissed</u>.
Mch 26 1907	Letter from Ida B. Brown complains as to condition of land of Florence E Chaney.
Mch 28 1907	Ida B Brown advises no action to be taken by this office. <u>Dismissed</u>.

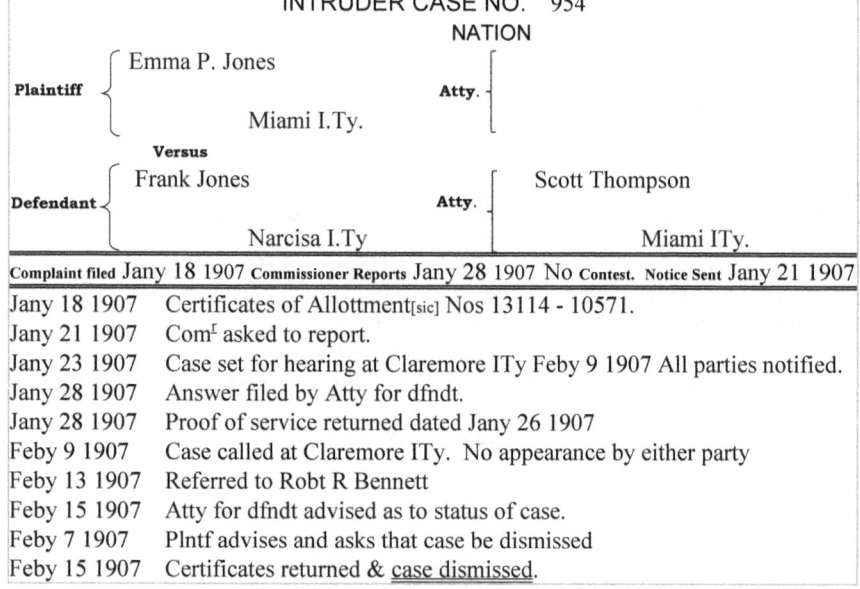

INTRUDER CASE NO. 954
NATION

Plaintiff: Emma P. Jones, Miami I.Ty.
Atty:
Versus
Defendant: Frank Jones, Narcisa I.Ty
Atty: Scott Thompson, Miami ITy.

Complaint filed Jany 18 1907	Commissioner Reports Jany 28 1907 No Contest. Notice Sent Jany 21 1907
Jany 18 1907	Certificates of Allottment[sic] Nos 13114 - 10571.
Jany 21 1907	Com^r asked to report.
Jany 23 1907	Case set for hearing at Claremore ITy Feby 9 1907 All parties notified.
Jany 28 1907	Answer filed by Atty for dfndt.
Jany 28 1907	Proof of service returned dated Jany 26 1907
Feby 9 1907	Case called at Claremore ITy. No appearance by either party
Feby 13 1907	Referred to Robt R Bennett
Feby 15 1907	Atty for dfndt advised as to status of case.
Feby 7 1907	Plntf advises and asks that case be dismissed
Feby 15 1907	Certificates returned & <u>case dismissed</u>.

INTRUDER CASE NO. 955
NATION

Plaintiff: Watson Ketchum
Atty: C. I. Weaver, Nowata ITy
Versus

Cherokee Intruder Cases 1901 - 1909

Defendant: John Poltson Atty.
Bartlesville ITy

Complaint filed Jany 10 1907 **Commissioner Reports** Jany 19 1907 No **Contest.** **Notice Sent** Jany 24 1907

Jany 24 1907	Case set for hearing at Claremore ITy. Feby 9 1907 All parties notified
Feby 9 1907	Case called at Claremore ITy. No appearance by either party.
Feby 13 1907	Referred to Robt R Bennett.
Feby 5 1907	Dfndt advises he has no claim to land in question.
Feby 16 1907	Com^r asked to very[sic] description of land.
Feby 12 1907	Glass & Weaver Attys advises error in description of land. Correct description
Feby 19 1907	Notice in duplicate ∧ furnished Glass & Weaver Attys Nowata ITy.
Feby 21 1907	Com^r furnishes correct description.
Mch 8 1907	Robt R Bennett reports & encloses request for dismissal
Mch 19 1907	Case dismissed.

INTRUDER CASE NO. 956
NATION

Plaintiff: Daniel Sequoyah Atty.
Hadley I.Ty

Versus

Defendant: G.D. Sleeper Wagoner ITy Atty.
A.G. Thomas Sleeper ITy.

Complaint filed Jany 21 1907 **Commissioner Reports** Jany 21 1907 No **Contest.** **Notice Sent** Jany 24 1907

Jany 21 1907	Copy of rental contract in file.
Jany 24 1907	Case set for hearing at Claremore ITy Feby 9 1907 All parties notified
Jany 30 1906[sic]	Proof of service returned dated Jany 28 1907
Feby 9 1907	Case called at Claremore I.Ty. No appearance by either party.
Feby 13 1907	G.D. Sleeper appeared & filed Lease contact & Bill of Sale
Feby 13 1907	Referred to Robt R Bennett
Mch 30 1907	Robt R. Bennett suggests plntfs redress in US Court for fullfilment[sic] of contract
Apr 11 1907	In view of above case dismissed.

Cherokee Intruder Cases 1901 - 1909

INTRUDER CASE NO. 957
NATION

Plaintiff: Estella Page nee Walker.
Seneca Mo.   Atty.

Versus

Defendant: Frank Harele
Miami ITy   Atty.

Complaint filed Jany 23 1907 **Commissioner Reports** Jany 31 1907 **No Contest. Notice Sent** Jany 24 1907

Jany 23 1907	Allottment[sic] certificates Nos. 46667 - 31301 in file.
Jany 24 1907	Case set for hearing at Claremore ITy Feby 9 1907 All parties notified.
Jany 24 1907	Com^r asked to report.
Feby 9 1907	Case called at Claremore ITy. No appearance by either party.
Feby 13 1907	Referred to Robt R. Bennett.
Feby 2 1907	Plntf asks as to possession States house was burned Jany 25 A.M. 1907
Feby 16 1907	Plntf is advised case in hands of field man.
Apr 13 1907	Robt R. Bennett reports plntf in possession.
Apr 17 1907	Certificates returned & <u>case dismissed</u>.

INTRUDER CASE NO. 958
NATION

Plaintiff: Luther A Dunn Gdn of
Henry Joseph Thornton   Atty.
Ramona ITy

Versus

Defendant: Henry Hayden   Ramona ITy
R. W.l Hosley   "   Atty.

Complaint filed Jany 7 1907 **Commissioner Reports** Jany 21 1907 in portion **Contest. Notice Sent** Jany 24 1907

Jany 7 1907	Letters of Gdnship in file
Jany 24 1907	Case set for hearing at Claremore ITy Feby 9 07 All parties notified
Jany 25 1907	Plntf encloses plat of allottment[sic] in question
Feby 9 1907	Case called at Claremore ITy. All parties present. Stipulation filed in which dfndt Hosley agrees to & does surrender all lands except those in contest. <u>Case dismissed</u>.
Feby 12 1907	Letters of Gdnship returned to plntf in person in Muskogee ITy
Feby 18 1907	Plntf advised <u>case dismissed</u>.

Cherokee Intruder Cases 1901 - 1909

INTRUDER CASE NO. 959
NATION

Plaintiff	Ellen Mayberry Muskogee ITy.	Atty.	Alexander Richmond Muskogee ITy
	Versus		
Defendant	Josie Looney Elliott ITy	Atty.	Osborne & Orsborne[sic] Coffeyville Kans

Complaint filed Jany 12 1907 **Commissioner Reports** Jany 23 1907 portion in Contest. **Notice Sent** Jany 24 1907

Jany 2 1907	Case set for hearing at Claremore ITy Feby 9 1907 All parties notified
Feby 7 1907	Answer filed by Attys for dfndt.
Feby 9 1907	Case called at Claremore ITy. No appearance by either party
Feby 13 1907	Com^r asked as to citizenship of Josie Looney.
Feby 8 1907	Answer filed by Atty for dfndt.
Feby 26 1907	Com^r reports Josie Looney denied citizenship Aug 18 1906.
Feby 28 1907	Dfndt advised of Com^r's report & requested to vacate.
Mch 2 1907	Atty for dfndt encloses copy of letter from Com^r which conflicts with his Report to us
Mch 6 1907	Com^r again asked to report because of letter to Atty for dfndt.
Mch 26 1907	Case set for hearing at Claremore ITy Apr 9 1907 All parties notified.
Apr 9 1907	Case called at Claremore ITy. Attys for both parties present and by agreement case continued to be heard at Muskogee ITy Thursday May 9 1907
May 15 1907	Case set for hearing at Muskogee IT May 28-1907 - Both parties notified
May 27 1907	Continued to June 20th '07 by agreement between Attys Richmond and Sullivan
June 30 07	No appearance by either party.
Sept 28 07	Plaintiff requested to advise if case has been settled.
6-30-08	Case dismissed as it is presumed pltf has possession.
7-10-08	Case is reinstated as dfndt is Freedman claimant

INTRUDER CASE NO. 960
NATION

Plaintiff	Samuel L Young Gdn of Katie Webber	Atty.	Geo C. Butte Muskogee I.Ty.
	Versus		
Defendant	Willard Ward Owasso I.Ty.	Atty.	Leeds and Martindale Tulsa I.Ty.

Cherokee Intruder Cases 1901 - 1909

Complaint filed Jany 23 1907 **Commissioner Reports** Feby 4 1907 All in **Contest.** **Notice Sent** Jany 25 1907	
Jany 23 1907	Certificates of Alottment[sic] Nos 46553-31244 in file
Jany 25 1907	Case set for hearing at Claremore ITy. Feby 9 1907 All parties notified.
Feby 9 1907	Case called at Claremore ITy. No appearance by either party
Feby 14 1907	As all the land is in contest, <u>case dismissed</u> Certificates returned.
Apr 18 1907	Geo C. Butte Atty advised case dismissed because of lands involved in contest
Apr 23 1907	Com^r asked for additional information
May 9 1907	Com^r reports no part of plntf's allotment involved in contest William[sic] Ward denied <u>enrollment.</u>
June 12 07	Case set for Muskogee June 26/7. All parties notified
June 25 07	Case called. All parties present and represented by counsel, Butte for plff and Bliss for deft Testimony taken. LB stenog
July 12 07	Judgement[sic] rendered in favor of pltf today
July 19 -07	Instructions issued to Policeman Sunday to place the pltf in possession
July 23 07	Instructions again issued to policeman Sunday today
July 22 07	Ans. Letter Filed by Defdts Atty Jno F Lawrence, Tulsa.
July 27 07	Jno F Lawrence Attorney of Tulsa advised of status of case
July 27 07	Policeman Sunday reports placing allottee[sic] in possession.
July 30 07	Plff advised of report of Policeman Sunday <u>dismissed</u>

INTRUDER CASE NO. 961
NATION

Plaintiff { Joseph T McDaniel
Tahlequah ITy.
Atty. { J A Hensley, Atty
In fact.

Versus

Defendant { Andy Counseler[sic]
Allottment[sic] near Melvin I.Ty.
Atty. {

Complaint filed Jany 15 1907 **Commissioner Reports** Jany 25 1907 No **Contest.** **Notice Sent** Feby 1 1907	
Apr 6 1907	Referred to Robt R. Bennett
Jan 11 1908	Plaintiff requested to make proof of service.
May 16 1908	Plaintiff asked to make return of service & if in possession.
6-23-08	Case dismissed as it is presumed pltf has possession <div align="right">Dismissed</div>
7-9-08	Case re-instated and new notices sent
7-15-08	Proof of service filed
7-28-08	Set for hearing at Muskogee on 8-7-08
Aug 7 08	Case called J.A. Hensley appeared for pltf & his testimony taken no appearance by defdt or pltf

Cherokee Intruder Cases 1901 - 1909

Sept 14 08	Atty-in-fact for pltf advised deft a rejected Cherokee
Nov 24 08	Pltf advised that defdt is a Cherokee freedman - rejected
3-5-09	Mrs J.T. M^cD. advised etc
3-22-09	Letter from Andy Counsel to Dept (referred to Com^r by him to us) answered and he is requested to state whether he is the Deft above.
3/26 1912	Form 330 to allottee

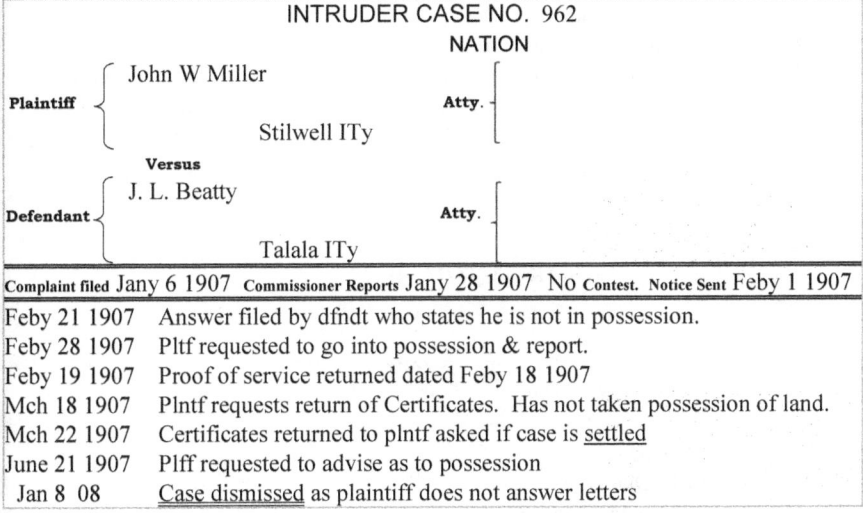

INTRUDER CASE NO. 962
NATION

Plaintiff: John W Miller, Stilwell ITy
Atty.

Versus

Defendant: J. L. Beatty, Talala ITy
Atty.

Complaint filed Jany 6 1907 **Commissioner Reports** Jany 28 1907 **No Contest. Notice Sent** Feby 1 1907

Feby 21 1907	Answer filed by dfndt who states he is not in possession.
Feby 28 1907	Pltf requested to go into possession & report.
Feby 19 1907	Proof of service returned dated Feby 18 1907
Mch 18 1907	Plntf requests return of Certificates. Has not taken possession of land.
Mch 22 1907	Certificates returned to plntf asked if case is <u>settled</u>
June 21 1907	Plff requested to advise as to possession
Jan 8 08	<u>Case dismissed</u> as plaintiff does not answer letters

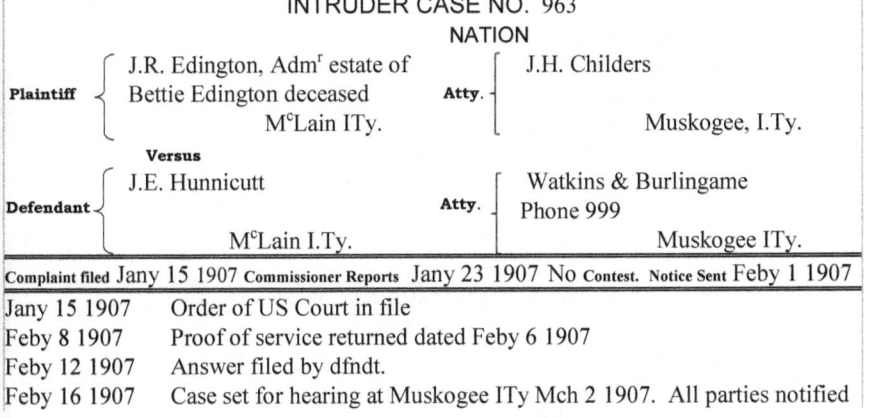

INTRUDER CASE NO. 963
NATION

Plaintiff: J.R. Edington, Adm^r estate of Bettie Edington deceased, McLain ITy.
Atty. J.H. Childers, Muskogee, I.Ty.

Versus

Defendant: J.E. Hunnicutt, McLain I.Ty.
Atty. Watkins & Burlingame, Phone 999, Muskogee ITy.

Complaint filed Jany 15 1907 **Commissioner Reports** Jany 23 1907 **No Contest. Notice Sent** Feby 1 1907

Jany 15 1907	Order of US Court in file
Feby 8 1907	Proof of service returned dated Feby 6 1907
Feby 12 1907	Answer filed by dfndt.
Feby 16 1907	Case set for hearing at Muskogee ITy Mch 2 1907. All parties notified

Cherokee Intruder Cases 1901 - 1909

Mch 2 1907	Answer filed by Atty for dfndt both of whom appeared and asked that case be continued until Monday, Mch 11" 1907
Mch 2 1907	Case called & all parties & Attys present. Case continued to Mch 11" 1907 at request of dfndt.
Mch 11 1907	Case called. All parties present & testimony taken. Exhibits "A", "B" filed by dfndt. Allottment[sic] certificates filed by Plntf. No 37338. Dfndt is to file certified copy of records of US Court showing copy appointment of receiver.
Mch 13 1907	Copy of order of U.S. Court, Wagoner ITy appointing receiver filed by Atty for dfndt.
April 25 1907	Com^r asked for additional information
May 13 1907	Plntf requested to advise as to particular peice[sic] of land in controversy
June 1 1907	Plaintiff appeared and advised that he is in possession of land which is not in contest Certificate No 37338 returned to Plaintiff in person and <u>Case dismissed</u>

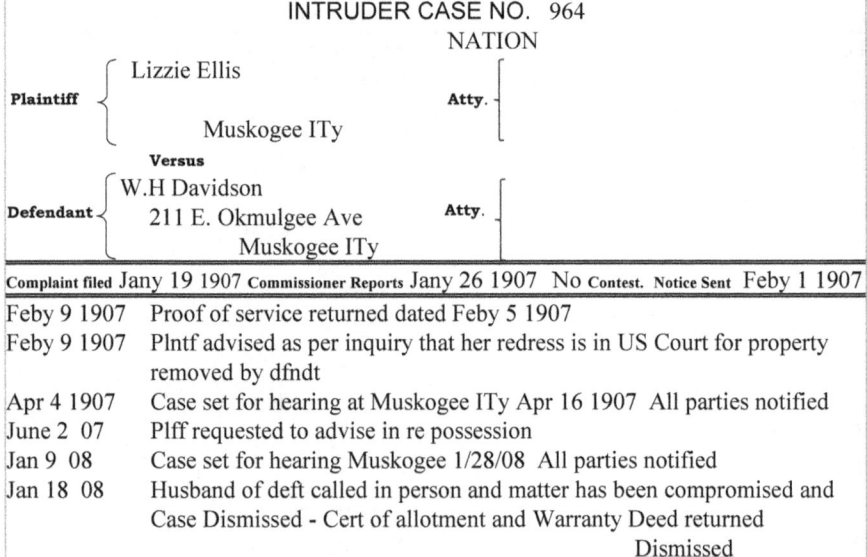

INTRUDER CASE NO. 964
NATION

Plaintiff: Lizzie Ellis, Muskogee ITy **Atty.**

Versus

Defendant: W.H Davidson, 211 E. Okmulgee Ave, Muskogee ITy **Atty.**

Complaint filed Jany 19 1907 Commissioner Reports Jany 26 1907 No Contest. Notice Sent Feby 1 1907

Feby 9 1907	Proof of service returned dated Feby 5 1907
Feby 9 1907	Plntf advised as per inquiry that her redress is in US Court for property removed by dfndt
Apr 4 1907	Case set for hearing at Muskogee ITy Apr 16 1907 All parties notified
June 2 07	Plff requested to advise in re possession
Jan 9 08	Case set for hearing Muskogee 1/28/08 All parties notified
Jan 18 08	Husband of deft called in person and matter has been compromised and Case Dismissed - Cert of allotment and Warranty Deed returned <u>Dismissed</u>

INTRUDER CASE NO. 965
NATION

Plaintiff: Albert Tucker, Tahlequah **Atty.**

Cherokee Intruder Cases 1901 - 1909

	Versus	
Defendant	E.L. Hastings Maysville Ark.	Atty.

Complaint filed Feby 6 1907 **Commissioner Reports** Feby 15 1907 **No Contest. Notice Sent** Feby 9 1907

Feby 6 1907	Allottment[sic] certificate No 4576 in file.
Feby 6 1907	Copy of lease contract in file.
Feby 16 1907	Proof of service returned dated Feby 15 1907.
Mch 8 1907	Plntf asks to be advised as to case.
Mch 13 1907	Plntf is advised.
Mch 13 1907	Dfndt asked to answer.
Mch 23 1907	Referred to Robt E. Bennett.
Mch 23 1907	Plntf advised case in hands of field man.
Aug. 6-07	Case dismissed upon report of Robt B. Bennett.
	<u>Dismissed</u>.

INTRUDER CASE NO. 966
NATION

Plaintiff	James Smith Claremore, I.Ty.	Atty. — c/o John O. Adams Claremore I.Ty.
	Versus	
Defendant	Jack Robinson J.M. Majors C.B. Miller Bushyhead I.Ty.	Atty. — T.L. Brown Claremore I.Ty.

Complaint filed Jany 31 1907 **Commissioner Reports** Feby 15 1907 **No Contest. Notice Sent** Feby 9 1907

Jany 31 1907	Allottment[sic] certificates Nos 3902 - 4616
Feby 9 1907	Com^r asked to report
Mch 2 1907	As per request additional notices furnished to serve on C.B. Miller.
Mch 26 1907	Case set for hearing at Claremore ITy Apr 9 1907 All parties notified.
Apr 9 1907	Case called at Claremore I.Ty. Mr. J.O. Adams appeared for plntf and stated he had been unable to get notice to his client the plntf. One plntf Mrs. Robinson widow of Jack Robinson, now dec'd, and her Atty T. L. Brown appeared. No appearance by plntf. Case continued.
June 18 '07	Case set for Vinita IT. July 8/7. All parties notified.
June 20 07	Plff's Attorney states matter satisfactorily settled
June 24 07	Deft notified of plff's statement and that it will not be necessary to appear at Vinita on July 8
June 24 07	Certs 4616 -3902 returned to plff's attorney and <u>Case Dismissed</u>
Oct 2 07	Plaintiff adv. Certificates were returned June 24 1907
Dec 5 07	Defendant advised that case was <u>dismissed</u> 6/24/07

133

Cherokee Intruder Cases 1901 - 1909

INTRUDER CASE NO. 967
NATION

Plaintiff: Mrs Minnie H. Slagle, Bluejacket I.Ty
Atty.

Versus

Defendant: Won[sic]. Samuel Slagle, Bluejacked ITy
Atty. S.C. Fullerton, Miami, I.Ty.

Complaint filed Jany 19 1907 Commissioner Reports Feby 1 1907 No Contest. Notice Sent Feby 9 1907

Jany 19 1907	Rental contract in file
Feby 13 1907	Proof of service returned dated Feby 11 1907
Feby 14 1907	Answer filed by Atty for dfndt.
Mch 26 1907	Case set for hearing at Claremore I.Ty Apr 9 1907 All parties notified.
Apr 4 1907	Atty for dfndt enclose stipulation & request for dismissal.
Apr 9 1907	Case called at Claremore, ITy. Neither party appeared.
Apr 8 1907	Plntf asked if case is settled to her satisfaction
June 11 1907	No reply from Plaintiff <u>Case dismissed</u> according to terms of stipulation above referred to

INTRUDER CASE NO. 968
NATION

Plaintiff: Narcissus Scarborough, Santown[sic] I.Ty.
Atty.

Versus

Defendant: Jerry Albert, Fort Smith Ark.
Atty.

Complaint filed Jany 22 1907 Commissioner Reports Feby 4 1907 No Contest. Notice Sent Feby 9 1907

Feby 13 1907	Proof of service returned, dated Feby 12, 1907.
Apr 4 1907	Case set for hearing at Muskogee ITy Apr 15 1907. All parties notified.
Apr 15 1907	Case called. All parties present & testimony taken.
Apr 22 1907	Com reports dfndt denied enrollment - See letter in [#]969
May 18 1907	Judgment rendered in favor of plntf - dfndts given ten days in which to vacate -
June 21 07	Plff requested to advise in re possession
June 29 07	Pltf advises that she has possession and case is <u>Dismissed</u>.

Cherokee Intruder Cases 1901 - 1909

INTRUDER CASE NO. 969
NATION

Plaintiff: Delilah Spight for Rachel Spight, Santown[sic] ITy. **Atty.**

Versus

Defendant: Jerry Albert, Fort Smith, Ark. **Atty.**

Complaint filed Jany 21 1907 **Commissioner Reports** Feby 4 1907 **No Contest. Notice Sent** Feby 9 1907

Feby 13 1907	Proof of service returned dated Feby 12-07
Apr 4 1907	Case set for hearing at Muskogee ITy. Apr 15, 1907 All parties notified.
Apr 15 1907	Case called at Muskogee I.Ty. Both parties present. Testimony taken.
Apr 15 1907	Comr asked as to status of citizenship of Jerry Albert.
Apr 22 1907	Com^r reports dfndt denied citizenship in Cherokee Nation. No motion for rehearing pending.
May 15 1907	Judgment rendered in favor of plntf and dfndt given ten days in which to vacate.
June 21 07	Plff requested to advise in re possession
June 28 07	Delilah Spight advises she is in possession.
July 5 07	Plff advised that as she has possession, the Case is Dismissed.

INTRUDER CASE NO. 970
NATION

Plaintiff: Gilbert Stop Gdn, Flora Stop **Atty.** A.C. Brewster, Pryor Creek ITy

Versus

Defendant: Loss Johnson **Atty.**

Complaint filed Jany 23 1907 **Commissioner Reports** Feb 14 1907 E^{2}SE^{4}SE^{1}3° **Contest. Notice Sent** Feby 9 1907

Jany 23 1907	Letters of Gdnship in file.
Feby 15 1907	Proof of service returned dated Feby 14, 1907
Mch 26 1907	Case set for hearing at Claremore ITy Apr 9 1907 All parties notified.
Apr 5 1907	Atty for plntf asks that case be dismissed.
Apr 9 1907	Case called at Claremore ITy. Neither party appeared.
April 4 1907	Atty for pltf reports dismissal of case
April 20 1907	In compliance with request of Atty for pltf case dismissed and letters of gdnship issued to Gilbert Stop returned.

Cherokee Intruder Cases 1901 - 1909

INTRUDER CASE NO. 971
NATION

Plaintiff: Charles T. Mayes Gdn of Cherrie W. Mayes, Pryor Creek I.Ty.   **Atty.**

Versus

Defendant: James Nicodemus, Marn ITy.   **Atty.** Nev Campbell, Pryor Creek ITy.

Complaint filed Jany 30 1907 **Commissioner Reports** Feby 15 1907 **No Contest. Notice Sent** Feby 9 1907

Jany 30 1907	Allottment[sic] certificates Nos 17080 - 23202.
Jany 30 1907	Letters of Gdnship in file.
Feby 9 1907	Com^r asked to report.
Feby 16 1907	Proof of service returned dated Feby 14, 1907.
Feby 25 1907	Case set for hearing at Muskogee ITy. ~~Feby~~ Mch 12-10 A.M. 1907 All parties notified.
Feby 18 1907	Answer filed by Nev Campbell Atty for dfndt.
Feby 25 1907	Plntf says dfndt will not move.
Mch 4 1907	Case set for hearing at Muskogee ITy Mch 12 1907. Served notice to plntf.
Mch 12 1907	Case called. All parties present. Nev Campbell Atty represented dfndt. And filed ~~order~~ copy of ~~Court~~ testimony taken in Probate Court Northern district Probate Dat $^\#$125. Certified copy of findings to be filed by Atty Campbell
Mch 13 1907	Nev Campbell Atty filed order of US Court (Judge L.F. Parker)
Mch 18 1907	Allottment[sic] certificates & Letters of Gdnship returned & case dismissed

INTRUDER CASE NO. 972
NATION

Plaintiff: Hugh M Adair, Stilwell I.Ty.   **Atty.**

Versus

Defendant: A. Crutchfield, Mrs Harriet Oaks   **Atty.**

Complaint filed Feby 2 1907 **Commissioner Reports** Feby 15 1907 **No Contest. Notice Sent** Feby 9 1907

Feby 2 1907	Allottment[sic] certificates Nos 15599 - 20769 in file Proof of service returned dated Feby 13 1907. "same misplaced"
Feby 9 1907	Com^r asked to report.

Cherokee Intruder Cases 1901 - 1909

Feby 12 1907	Proof of service returned dated Feby 9 11907
Apr 4 1907	Case set for hearing at Muskogee ITy Apr 15 1907 All parties notified.
Apr 15 1907	Case called. No appearance by either party.
Apr 9 1907	Plntf states he has possession.
Apr 16 1907	Certificates returned <u>dismissed</u>

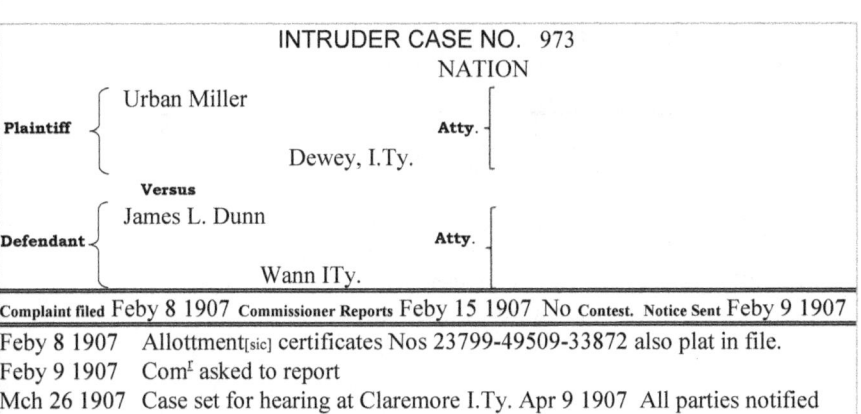

INTRUDER CASE NO. 973
NATION

Plaintiff: Urban Miller
Dewey, I.Ty.
Atty.

Versus

Defendant: James L. Dunn
Wann ITy.
Atty.

Complaint filed Feby 8 1907 **Commissioner Reports** Feby 15 1907 **No Contest.** **Notice Sent** Feby 9 1907

Feby 8 1907	Allottment[sic] certificates Nos 23799-49509-33872 also plat in file.
Feby 9 1907	Com^r asked to report
Mch 26 1907	Case set for hearing at Claremore I.Ty. Apr 9 1907 All parties notified
Apr 9 1907	Case called at Claremore I.Ty. Neither party appeared.
May 3 1907	Plntf appeared in person & stated case satisfactorily settled - Certificates Returned & <u>case dismissed</u>.

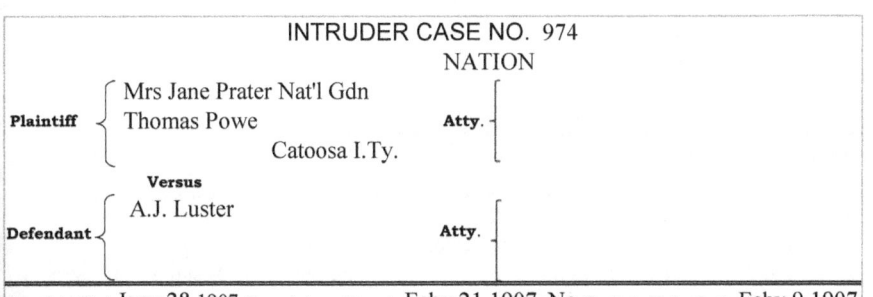

INTRUDER CASE NO. 974
NATION

Plaintiff: Mrs Jane Prater Nat'l Gdn
Thomas Powe
Catoosa I.Ty.
Atty.

Versus

Defendant: A.J. Luster
Atty.

Complaint filed Jany 28 1907 **Commissioner Reports** Feby 21 1907 **No Contest.** **Notice Sent** Feby 9 1907

Jany 28 1907	Allottment[sic] certificates Nos 28258-41020 in file.
Feby 9 1907	Com^r asked to report
Feby 14 1907	Proof of service returned dated Feby 12 1907
Feby 21 1907	Plntf states she has possession.
Mch 4 1907	Certificates returned & <u>case dismissed</u>.

Cherokee Intruder Cases 1901 - 1909

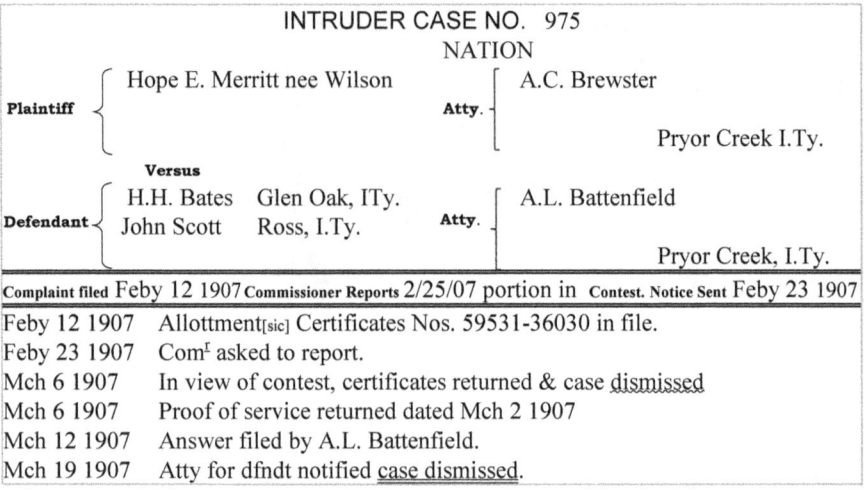

INTRUDER CASE NO. 975
NATION

Plaintiff: Hope E. Merritt nee Wilson
Atty.: A.C. Brewster, Pryor Creek I.Ty.

Versus

Defendant: H.H. Bates — Glen Oak, ITy.; John Scott — Ross, I.Ty.
Atty.: A.L. Battenfield, Pryor Creek, I.Ty.

Complaint filed Feby 12 1907 **Commissioner Reports** 2/25/07 portion in **Contest. Notice Sent** Feby 23 1907

Feby 12 1907	Allottment[sic] Certificates Nos. 59531-36030 in file.
Feby 23 1907	Com^r asked to report.
Mch 6 1907	In view of contest, certificates returned & case dismissed
Mch 6 1907	Proof of service returned dated Mch 2 1907
Mch 12 1907	Answer filed by A.L. Battenfield.
Mch 19 1907	Atty for dfndt notified case dismissed.

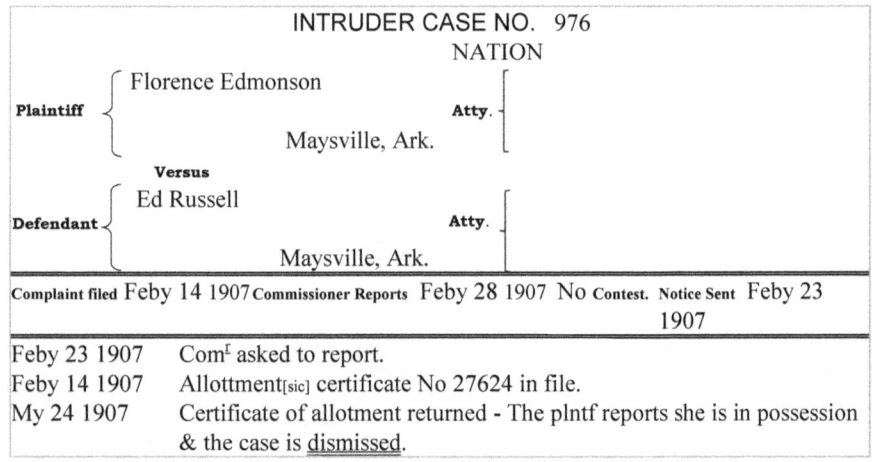

INTRUDER CASE NO. 976
NATION

Plaintiff: Florence Edmonson, Maysville, Ark.
Atty.:

Versus

Defendant: Ed Russell, Maysville, Ark.
Atty.:

Complaint filed Feby 14 1907 **Commissioner Reports** Feby 28 1907 No **Contest. Notice Sent** Feby 23 1907

Feby 23 1907	Com^r asked to report.
Feby 14 1907	Allottment[sic] certificate No 27624 in file.
My 24 1907	Certificate of allotment returned - The plntf reports she is in possession & the case is dismissed.

Cherokee Intruder Cases 1901 - 1909

INTRUDER CASE NO. 977
Cherokee NATION

Plaintiff: William H. White
Fairland, ITy

Atty: Davis, Mason & Bland
Afton
Ind Ter

Versus

Defendant: Winfield S. Nance
Fairland ITy

Atty:

Complaint filed Jany 30 1907 Commissioner Reports Feby 14 1907 in portion Contest. Notice Sent Feby 23 1907

Jany 31 1907	Allottment[sic] certificate No 45898 in file.
Feby 21 1907	Plntf requests return of Allottment[sic] certificates.
Feby 28 1907	Certificates returned & case dismissed because of contest.
Feby 28 1907	Proof of service returned dated Feby 27 1907
May 29 07	Davis, Mason & Bland ask that allottee[sic] be placed in possession Stating deft has been denied citizenship
June 18 '07	Case set for hearing at Vinita, I.T. July 8/7. All parties notified.
June 19 07	Com^r reports allotment selection of W.H. White not involved in contest
July 8 07	Case called at Vinita. No appearance by plaintiff. Defendant appeared and evidence taken.
July 27 07	Plff requested to appear as soon as possible and submit evidence
Aug 7 07	Referred to R.R. Bennett
8/22 07	Pltf advised that matter is in hands of a representative
Jan 13 08	Case set for hearing Claremore 2/3/8 all notified.
Feb 3 08	Case called. No appearance[sic] by plaintiff. Defendant appeared and exhibited a communication from Com^r dated Jan 31/08 together with an order from Com'r dated Jan 30/08 showing that land in controversy is surplus allotment of W^m H White & that his restrictions were removed by Dept, that he subsequently mortgaged said land for $600^{00} In view of above facts case dismissed.

INTRUDER CASE NO. 978
NATION

Plaintiff: C.E. Holderman Gdn of
Simon Bear. Johnson, Polly and
Oscar Bear minors heirs at law
of estate of Johnson Talala Dec'd
Muskogee I.Ty.

Atty:

Versus

Defendant: Mariah Ross

Atty: A.S. McRhea
Muskogee ITy.

Cherokee Intruder Cases 1901 - 1909

Complaint filed Feby 19 1907 Commissioner Reports	Contest. Notice Sent Feby 23 1907
Feby 19 1907	Letters of Gdnship in file.
Feby 19 1907	Order of U.S. Court, Joseph A. Gill, in file.
Feby 19 1907	Two certified copies of Cherokee Roll concerning allottees[sic] in file
Feby 19 1907	One certified copy of Cherokee Freedman Roll " "
Feby 19 1907	Com^r asked to report
Feby 26 1907	Com^r reports Mariah Ross finally rejected no motion pending for review
Mch 4 1907	Proof of service returned, dated Feby 27 1907
Mch 9 1907	Ans filed by Atty for dfndt
Mch 9 1907	Dfndt requested to file answer.
Mch 11 1907	Answer filed by Atty McRhea for dfndt.
Mch 13 1907	All parties advised this case will be heard soon at some point in Cherokee Nation
Mch 26 1907	Case set for hearing at Claremore, I.Ty. Apr 9 1907 All parties notified.
Apr 9 1907	Case called at Claremore, I.Ty. Plntf and Mose Ross son of dfndt appeared & testimony taken. Dfndt Mariah Ross died Mch 26 1907.
May 2 1907	Judgment rendered in favor of plntf - Dfndt given ten days in which to vacate
May 11 1907	A.S. McRea serves notice that application for injunction will be heard May 13th 1907 at Vinita I.T. in the United States Court See file #991
May 14 1907	Order issued to Capt. Jno C. West to place plntf in possession
May 20 1907	On acct. of health of Capt West, instructions were transferred to policeman J.L. Walker.
May 22 1907	Asst U.S. Atty advises injunction granted by U.S. Court at Vinita I.T. See letter in file #991.
May 22 1907	Policeman Walker wired to withhold action
May 23 1907	Restraining order & summons in equity rec'd See file #991
May 24 1907	Com^r asked if land in contest & if certificates have been issued
May 24 1907	Policeman Walker reports he placed plntf in possession
June 27 07	Letters of gdnship returned to plff in person to be filed with Restrictions Division
Sept 14 07	Injunction dissolved and <u>Case dismissed</u>.

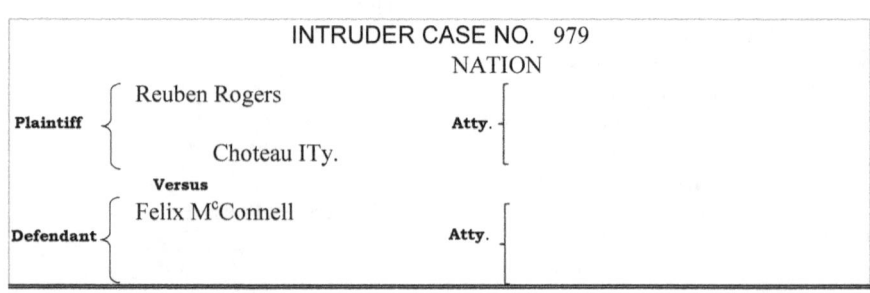

INTRUDER CASE NO. 979
NATION

Plaintiff { Reuben Rogers   Atty. {
          Choteau ITy.

Versus

Defendant { Felix McConnell   Atty. {

Cherokee Intruder Cases 1901 - 1909

Complaint filed Feby 7 1907 Commissioner Reports Feby 15 1907 No Contest. Notice Sent Feby 23 1907	
Mch 16 1907	Proof of service returned dated Mch 12 1907
Mch 26 1907	Case set for hearing at Claremore, I.Ty. Apr 10 1907 All parties notified
Apr 1 1907	Answer filed by dfndt.
Apr 10 1907	Case called at Claremore ITy. Dfndt appeared & testimony taken. Lease filed by dfndt. No appearance by plntf.
May 2 1907	Plntf requested to appear at this office May 9 1907
May 10 1907	Dfndt advised that Judgment will be rendered shortly
May 9 1907	Plntf appeared & testimony taken
May 22 1907	Judgment rendered in favor of dfndt - Contract returned
	Dismissed

INTRUDER CASE NO. 980
NATION

Plaintiff: Walter and Fannie Bigby
(Illegible), I.Ty.
Atty.

Versus

Defendant: Henry Chambers
Bartlesville ITy
Atty. Oscar E Learnard Jr.
Bartlesville, I.Ty.

Complaint filed Feby 20 1907 Commissioner Reports Feby 28 1907 No Contest. Notice Sent Feby 23 1907	
Feby 20 1907	Allottment[sic] certificates Nos 22663, 22664, 32020, 32018 in file
Feby 23 1907	Com^r asked to report.
Mch 25 1907	Proof of service returned, dated Mch 22 1907
Mch 26 1907	Case set for hearing at Claremore, I.Ty. Apr 10 1907 All parties notified.
Apr 4 1907	Atty for ~~plntf~~ dfndt advised of hearing to be held at Claremore I.Ty.
Apr 10 1907	Case called at Claremore, I.Ty. Both parties present. Walter Bigby husband of Fannie Bigby, Fannie B did not appear. Dfndt holding land for his mother Katie Blackwell & Rosie McNier[sic]. He is citizen. They are claimants. Ask Com^r as to citizenship of Katie Blackwell & Rosie McNier
Apr 16 1907	Com^r asked as to citizenship of Henry Chambers, Rosa McNeer or Katie Blackwell
Apr 29 1907	Com^r again asked as to citizenship of dfndt.
May 14 1907	Com^r reports Henry Chambers enrolled as Cherokee freedman. Rosa McNare[sic] and Katie Blackwell denied enrollment.
May 18 1907	Judgment rendered in favor of plntfs - dfndts given ten days in which to vacate
8/17 07	Instructions issued to Policeman Walker to place pltf in possession.

Cherokee Intruder Cases 1901 - 1909

Nov 23 07	Walker reports he placed pltfs in possession. <u>Case Dismissed</u>.
Feb 3 08	Case dismissed as pltf now has possession of land and certificates returned.
	<u>Dismissed</u>

INTRUDER CASE NO. 981
NATION

Plaintiff: Mrs Emeline Walker nee Buttler[sic] Hulbert ITy Atty.

Versus

Defendant: O.S. Skidmore Oolagah ITy Atty.

Complaint filed Feby 11 1907 **Commissioner Reports** Feby 28 1907 **No Contest.** **Notice Sent** Feby 23 1907

Feby 11 1907	Allottment[sic] certificates Nos 5623, 4639 in file.
Feby 23 1907	Com^r asked to report.
Mch 5 1907	Proof of service returned dated Mch 4 1907.
	To be heard in Cherokee Nation April 1907
Mch 11 1903[sic]	Answer filed by dfndt.
Mch 20 1903[sic]	Dfndt advised case will be heard soon. He will be notified.
Mch 26 1907	Case set for hearing at Claremore, ITy Apr 10 1907 All parties notified
Apr 11 1907	Case called at Claremore I.T. Dfndt appeared & testimony taken No appearance by plntf
May 2 1907	Plntf requested to appear at this office May 9 1907
May 9 1907	The husband of complainant appeared and advises that wife is still a minor - and a lease in existence made by the gen[sic] - certificates returned in person - Advised that no further action can be *(illegible)* by this office - <u>Case dismissed</u>

INTRUDER CASE NO. 982
NATION

Plaintiff: Jack Downing Foyil I.Ty. Atty.

Versus

Defendant: Charley G. and Walter F Ross Bushyhead I.Ty. Atty. McCulloch & Probasco Vinita I.Ty.

142

Cherokee Intruder Cases 1901 - 1909

Complaint filed Feby 11 1907 Commissioner Reports Feby 28 1907 50@in Contest. Notice Sent Feby 23 1907	
Feby 11 1907	Allottment[sic] certificates Nos 63863 - 37942 in file.
Feby 23 1907	Com^r asked to report.
Feby 28 1907	Proof of service returned dated Feby 26 1907.
Mch 5 1907	In view of contest, certificates returned & <u>case dismissed</u>
Mch 11 1907	Answer filed by Attys for dfndt
Mch 13 1907	Attys for dfndt advised case is dismissed
Mch 9 08	Blank form of complaint forwarded to pltf by M. Champ with request that same be filled out & ret'd to this office with allotment certificates etc
Mch 17 08	Notice sent
Mch 18 08	Case reinstated.
Mch 21 08	Com reports no contest
Mch 23 08	Proof of service filed today.
Mch 24 08	Ans filed by defdt J.B. Ross today
Mch 28 08	Referred to Frank Robb for investigation
April 9 08	Pltf advised in re status of case
7-11 08	Set for hearing at Claremore on 7-29-08
7-29 08	All parties present
7-29 08	Case called all parties present evidence taken
7-30 08	Further evidence taken
Jan 4 '09	Referred to R.R. Bennett & pltf advised

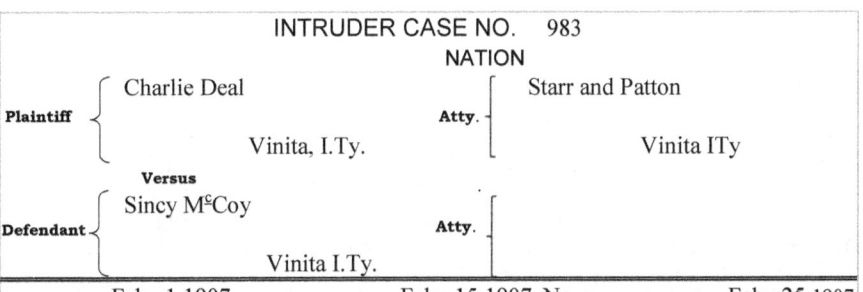

INTRUDER CASE NO. 983
NATION

Plaintiff: Charlie Deal, Vinita, I.Ty.
Atty: Starr and Patton, Vinita ITy

Versus

Defendant: Sincy McCoy, Vinita I.Ty.
Atty:

Complaint filed Feby 1 1907 Commissioner Reports Feby 15 1907 No Contest. Notice Sent Feby 25 1907	
Feby 28 1907	Atty for plntf states plntf has possession & ask that case be <u>dismissed</u>
Mch 6 1907	<u>Case dismissed.</u>

Cherokee Intruder Cases 1901 - 1909

INTRUDER CASE NO. 984
NATION

Plaintiff: Artelia Gilstrap Lg'l Gdn
Albert L and Nora E Gilstrap
Hillside, I.Ty.
Atty.

Versus

Defendant: William Blakeman Hillside I.Ty.
Walter Blakeman Web City Mo.
Atty.

Complaint filed	Commissioner Reports	No Contest. Notice Sent

Mch 5 1907	Proof of service returned dated March 4 1907
Mch 8 1907	G.W. Blakeman files answer
Mch 14 1907	Dfndt advised case will be set for hearing soon
Mch 26 1907	Case set for hearing at Claremore, I.Ty Apr 10 1907 All parties notified
Apr 10 1907	Case called at Claremore I.Ty. Plntf & Mr. A.D. Morton Atty of Bartlesville appeared & stated plntf is in possession by tenant & U.S. Court issued order in Nov. 1906 for plntf to take possession. Dfndt then vacated. <u>Case dismissed</u>.

INTRUDER CASE NO. 985
NATION

Plaintiff: Tyler Chuckluck
Locust Grove, I.Ty.
Atty.

Versus

Defendant: W.A. Chase
Nowata, ITy.
Atty.

Complaint filed Feby 2 1907 **Commissioner Reports** Feby 15 1907 No **Contest.** **Notice Sent** Feby 25 1907

Mch 6 1907	Proof of service returned dated Mch 6 1907
Mch 26 1907	Case set for hearing at Claremore I.Ty Apr 10 1907 All parties notified.
Apr 10 1907	Case called at Claremore, I.Ty. Plntf appeared & testimony taken. No Appearance by dfndt.
Apr 16 1907	Referred to Robt R. Bennett.
May 18 1907	Dfndt asked to advise if he is in possession of land described in complaint.
May 31 07	Ans. Filed by deft. Enclosing copy rental contract.
June 18 07	Case set for Vinita, I.T. July 8/7. All parties notified.
July 8 07	Case called, plaintiff appeared and stated that he executed a lease. No appearance by defendant.
July 26 07	Testimony of the Defendant taken
8/24 07	Judgement[sic] rendered in favor of defdt & <u>case dismissed</u>.

Cherokee Intruder Cases 1901 - 1909

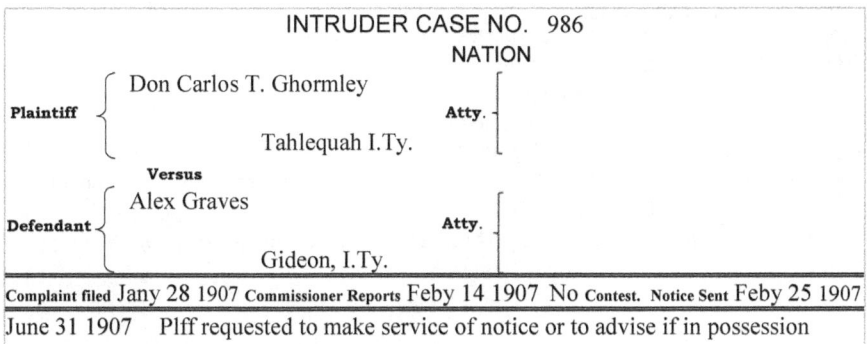

	INTRUDER CASE NO. 986 NATION	
Plaintiff	Don Carlos T. Ghormley Versus Tahlequah I.Ty.	Atty.
Defendant	Alex Graves Gideon, I.Ty.	Atty.

Complaint filed Jany 28 1907 Commissioner Reports Feby 14 1907 No Contest. Notice Sent Feby 25 1907
June 31 1907   Plff requested to make service of notice or to advise if in possession
July 15 07   Case dismissed by request of pltf.

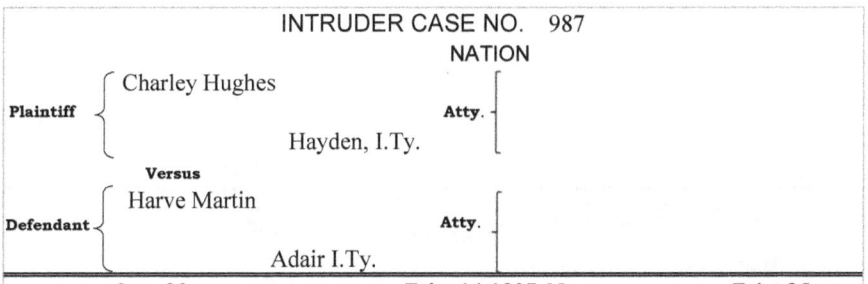

	INTRUDER CASE NO. 987 NATION	
Plaintiff	Charley Hughes Versus Hayden, I.Ty.	Atty.
Defendant	Harve Martin Adair I.Ty.	Atty.

Complaint filed Jany 30 1907 Commissioner Reports Feby 14 1907 No Contest. Notice Sent Feby 25 1907
Mch 26 1907   Case set for hearing at Claremore, I.Ty Apr 10, 1907. All parties notified.
Apr 10 1907   Case called at Claremore I.Ty. Both parties present. It was found that complaint was filed vs wrong party & wrong land described.
Plntf advised to be appointed gdn (as land is for minor 11 yrs) and file new complaint. Case dismissed.

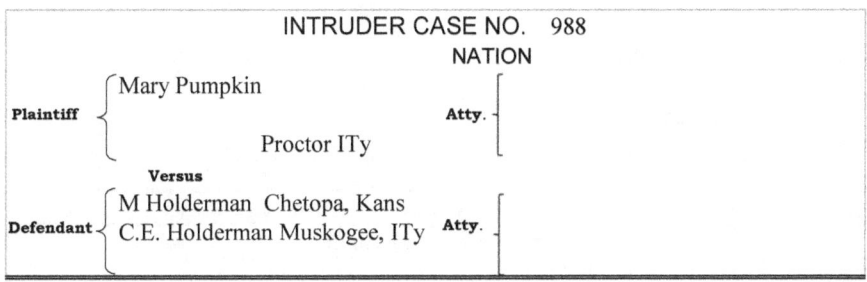

	INTRUDER CASE NO. 988 NATION	
Plaintiff	Mary Pumpkin Versus Proctor ITy	Atty.
Defendant	M Holderman Chetopa, Kans C.E. Holderman Muskogee, ITy	Atty.

Cherokee Intruder Cases 1901 - 1909

Complaint filed Feby 16 1907 Commissioner Reports 3/2/07 No Contest. Notice Sent Feby 25 1907
Feby 16 1907 — Allottment[sic] certificates Nos 6359, 8674 in file.
Feby 16 1907 — Rental contract in file.
Feby 25 1907 — Com[r] asked to report.
Mch 5 1907 — Proof of service returned, dated Mch 4 1907
Mch 26 1907 — Case set for hearing at Claremore ITy Apr 9 1907. All parties notified.
Apr 9 1907 — Case called at Claremore, I.Ty. Both parties present & testimony taken. Dfndt exhibits statement of account.
May 16 1907 — Judgement[sic] rendered in favor of dfndt. Certificates of allottment[sic] returned & case is <u>dismissed</u>.

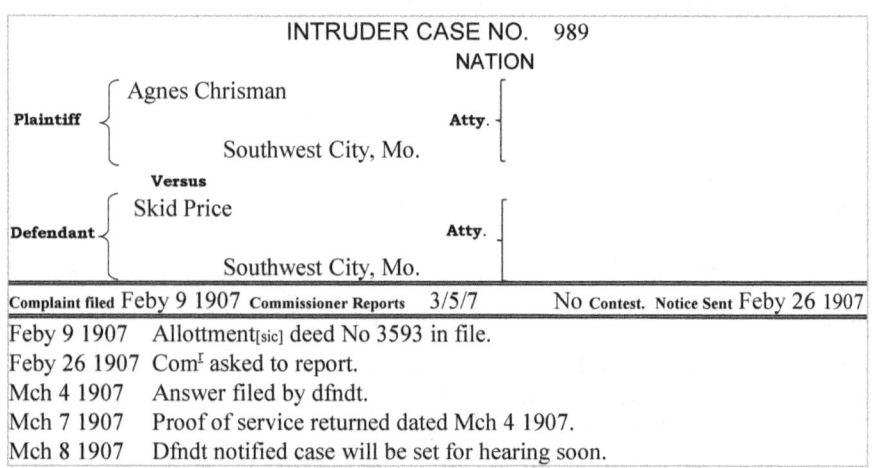

INTRUDER CASE NO. 989
NATION

Plaintiff: Agnes Chrisman, Southwest City, Mo.   Atty.

Versus

Defendant: Skid Price, Southwest City, Mo.   Atty.

Complaint filed Feby 9 1907 Commissioner Reports 3/5/7 No Contest. Notice Sent Feby 26 1907
Feby 9 1907 — Allottment[sic] deed No 3593 in file.
Feby 26 1907 — Com[r] asked to report.
Mch 4 1907 — Answer filed by dfndt.
Mch 7 1907 — Proof of service returned dated Mch 4 1907.
Mch 8 1907 — Dfndt notified case will be set for hearing soon.

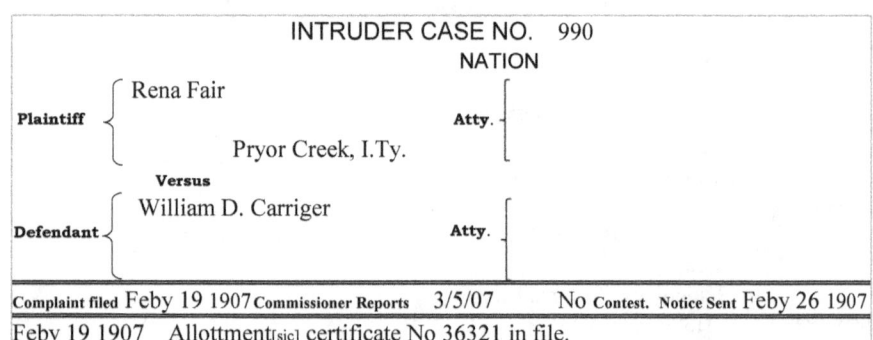

INTRUDER CASE NO. 990
NATION

Plaintiff: Rena Fair, Pryor Creek, I.Ty.   Atty.

Versus

Defendant: William D. Carriger   Atty.

Complaint filed Feby 19 1907 Commissioner Reports 3/5/07 No Contest. Notice Sent Feby 26 1907
Feby 19 1907 — Allottment[sic] certificate No 36321 in file.
Feby 26 1907 — Com[r] asked to report.

Cherokee Intruder Cases 1901 - 1909

Mch 1 1907	Proof of service returned dated Feby 28, 1907.
Mch 4 1907	Answer filed by dfndt.
Mch 11 1907	Plntf states dfndt is still in possession
Mch 15 1907	Plntf advised case will be set for hearing
Mch 26 1907	Case set for hearing at Claremore I.Ty Apr 8 1907 All parties notified.
Apr 8 1907	Case called at Claremore ITy. No appearance by either party.
June 18 07	Case set for Vinita IT. July 8/7. All parties notified.
July 8 07	Case called at Vinita, neither party present.
Sept 20 1907	Case set for hearing at Claremore ITy Oct 2 1907 All parties notified.
Oct 2 1907	Case called and no appearance by either party
Oct 7 1907	Pltf advised <u>case dismissed</u>.
Nov 6 1907	Certificate allotment 35321 returned to plaintiff. <u>Dismissed</u>.

INTRUDER CASE NO. 991
NATION

Plaintiff Mrs Nellie Williamson for Nettie & William F Williamson **Atty.** Welch I.Ty.

Versus

Defendant R. Brown **Atty.** A.S. McRea
Welch I.Ty   Muskogee I.Ty

Complaint filed Feby 15 1907 Commissioner Reports 2/23/7 No Contest. Notice Sent Mch 5 1907

Feby 15 1907	H.S. Certificated[sic] 38131 S.C. 4168. H.S. 38152 S.C. 4207 in file.
Mch 5 1907	Com^r asked to report.
Mch 8 1907	Proof of service returned dated Mch 7 1907
Mch 18 1907	Com^r reports no contest pending.
Mch 20 1907	Dfndt asked to file answer or vacate.
Mch 30 1907	Com^r asked as to status of citizenship of Josie Brown.
Mch 26 1907	Case set for hearing at Claremore I.Ty Apr 8 1907 All parties notified.
Mch 27 1907	Answer filed by Atty for dfndt.
Mch 29 1907	Plntf states we failed to enclose letter.
Apr 3 1907	Plntf requested to be present at hearing.
Apr 5 1907	Com^r reports Josie Brown denied Nov 2, 1906. No motion pending for review.
Apr 8 1907	Case called at Claremore ITy. All parties present and testimony [sic]. Mr. E.N. Williamson appeared as plntf by power of Atty (in file) from plntf, his wife, Nellie Williamson.
May 3 11907	Judgment rendered in favor of plntfs - Dfndt given ten days in which to vacate.
May 11 1907	A.S. McRea serves notice that application for injunction will be heard

Cherokee Intruder Cases 1901 - 1909

	May 13<u>th</u> 1907 in the United States Court at Vinita I.Ty.
May 15 1907	Notice served by Atty for dfndt that application for injunction will be heard at Vinita I.T. May 18<u>th</u> 1907
May 22 1907	Asst U.S. Atty advises injunction granted by U.S. Court at Vinita IT.
May 23 1907	Restraining order & summons in equity received
May 25 1907	Certificates of allotment #38131 & 64158 *(illegible)*; #38152 & 64207 William Williamson sent to O.L. Rider Asst U.S. Atty Vinita I.T. Letter to O.L. Rider filed.
June 8 '07	Certs returned to W.W. Bennett on trial of injunction case at Vinita,
June 29 07	Injunction dissolved. See cases 944-789-800-896-905-1008.
July 6 07	Plff and deft advised of dissolution of injunction - Capt Jno. C. West directed to place plaintiff in possession.
July 25 07	Capt West reports that on July 14/7 he placed gdn. in possession
Aug 1 1907	Certs returned to plff. and *(illegible)* <u>Case Dismissed</u>.

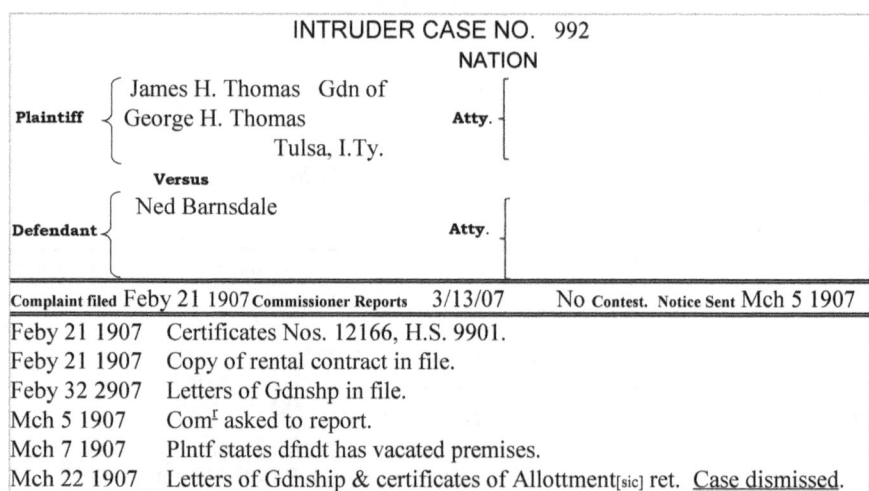

INTRUDER CASE NO. 992
NATION

Plaintiff: James H. Thomas Gdn of George H. Thomas
Tulsa, I.Ty.   Atty.

Versus

Defendant: Ned Barnsdale   Atty.

Complaint filed Feby 21 1907 Commissioner Reports 3/13/07 No Contest. Notice Sent Mch 5 1907

Feby 21 1907	Certificates Nos. 12166, H.S. 9901.
Feby 21 1907	Copy of rental contract in file.
Feby 32 2907	Letters of Gdnshp in file.
Mch 5 1907	Com<u>r</u> asked to report.
Mch 7 1907	Plntf states dfndt has vacated premises.
Mch 22 1907	Letters of Gdnship & certificates of Allottment[sic] ret. <u>Case dismissed</u>.

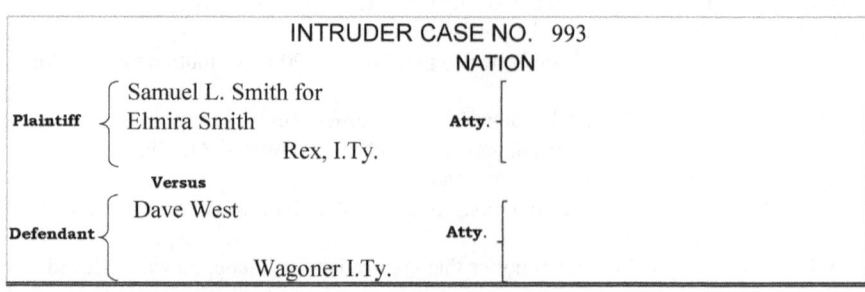

INTRUDER CASE NO. 993
NATION

Plaintiff: Samuel L. Smith for Elmira Smith
Rex, I.Ty.   Atty.

Versus

Defendant: Dave West   Atty.
Wagoner I.Ty.

Cherokee Intruder Cases 1901 - 1909

Complaint filed Feby 27 1907 Commissioner Reports Mch 13 1907 No Contest. Notice Sent Mch 6 1907	
Feby 27 1907	H.S. Certificate No 16344 in file.
Mch 6 1907	Com.r asked to report.
Mch 25 1907	Proof of service returned, dated Mch 23 1907.
Mch 26 1907	Case set for hearing at Claremore, I.Ty Apr 11 1907 All parties notified.
Apr 6 1907	Plntf appeared at office in Muskogee I.Ty stated he had possession. Certificate returned to him in person & case dismissed.

INTRUDER CASE NO. 994
NATION

Plaintiff c/o { Eli Downing / L.R. Johnson ~~for~~ / Dora Ark. }   Atty.

Versus

Defendant { Geo Bell & family }   Atty. { A.S. McRhea }

Muskogee I.Ty.

Complaint filed Dec 20 1906 Commissioner Reports 2/23/7 No Contest. Notice Sent Mch 6 1907	
Jany 3 1907	Com.r reports 40 acres in contest
Mch 12 1907	Referred to Robt R. Bennett
Mch 23 1907	Robt R. Bennett's report in file.
Mch 27 1907	Com.r asked as to citizenship of Geo Bell.
Apr 18 1907	Ans filed by Atty for dfndt
Apr 10 1907	Proof of service returned dated Apr 8" 1907
May 10 1907	Com.r requested to furnish certain information
May 21 1907	Case set for hearing at Muskogee I.T. May 20 1907 Both parties notified.
May 20 1907	Com.r reports application for enrollment of George and July Bell denied by Dpt.
May 29 1907	Case called at Muskogee. Dfdt present No appearance by Plaintiff No testimony taken.
July 17 07	Judgement[sic] rendered in favor of the pltf today.
8/17 07	Instructions issued to Capt John C. West.
Aug 24 '07	Capt West's reports[sic] that he was unable to find Plaintiff to place him in possession but Defendant surrendered possession to him.
Sept 6 '07	Plaintiff advised of Capt West's report and requested to proceed at once to his allotment and take possession Case Dismissed.
Oct. 19 07	Bessie Johnson requests information and is advised status
" 30 07	" " " " " " " in full
Dec 26 07	Bessie Johnson advised we could not place her in possession. Dismissed.

Cherokee Intruder Cases 1901 - 1909

INTRUDER CASE NO. 995
NATION

Plaintiff: Marion F. Wood, Zena, I.Ty.   **Atty.**

Versus

Defendant: John and Lizzie Wooden, Grove, ITy.   **Atty.**

Complaint filed Feby 28 1907 **Commissioner Reports** 3/13/07 portion in **Contest.** **Notice Sent** Mch 6 1907

Feby 28 1907	Certificate No 20146
Mch 6 1907	Com^r asked to report.
Mch 14 1907	Proof of service returned, dated Mch 12, 1907.
Mch 19 1907	Plntf advised that case is dismissed as to portion in contest.
Mch 18 1907	Plntf writes corncerning[sic] case.
Mch 22 1907	Dfndts requested to advise if they are holding any land other than that in contest.
Mch 26 1907	Case set for hearing at Claremore I.Ty. Apr 11 1907 All parties notified.
Apr 1 1907	Answer filed by dfndt.
Apr 2 1907	Dfndt states there is contest on land to be heard May 6 07 before Com^r.
Apr 3 1907	Dfndt advised of hearing & requested to be present.
Apr 4 1907	Dfndt advised no action will be taken while land is in contest.
Apr 3 1907	Plntf requested to advise if dfndt occupy land other than that in contest.
Apr 11 1907	Case called at Claremore I.Ty. Neither party appeared.
Apr 12 1907	Plntf asked to be placed in possession of land not in contest.
Apr 18 1907	Plntf requested to go into possession & notify this office.
June 21 07	Plff again requested to advise in re. possession.
Aug 16 07	Com. reports no contest
Sept 10 07	Certificate returned and Plaintiff requested to advise if case has been settled.
Jan 13 08	Case set for hearing Claremore 2/3/8 all notified.
Feb 3 07	Case called no appearence[sic].
May 16 08	Plaintiff asked if in possession or a settlement made.
6-23 08	Case dismissed as it is presumed that pltf has possession.
7-21 08	Pltf advised in re status of case Dismissed

INTRUDER CASE NO. 996
NATION

Plaintiff: Ada Durall Gdn. Hugh Allen & George Marvin Durall   **Atty.** Welch

Versus

Cherokee Intruder Cases 1901 - 1909

Defendant	Goldie Adair W<u>m</u> Alridge I.Ty[sic]. Redbird ITy. Hudson, ITy.	Atty.	W. J. Sullivan Muskogee I.Ty.

Complaint filed Feby 21 1907 **Commissioner Reports** 3/13/07 portion in **Contest.** **Notice Sent** Mch 6 1907

Feby 28 1907	H.S. Certificates Nos 39147-38148 & S. 64191-64199 in file.
Mch 6 1907	Com<u>r</u> asked to report.
Mch 9 1907	Proof of service returned dated Mch 9 1907
Mch 20 1907	Case dismissed as to portion of Geo Marvin Durall's land that is in contest
Mch 30 1907	Case set for hearing at Claremore ITy Apr 11-07. All parties notified.
Mch 30 1907	Notice sent to & to be served on W<u>m</u> Alridge, Redbird ITy.
Apr 11 1907	Case called at Claremore ITy. B.H. Durall appeared & presented power of Atty from plntf to him. B.H. Durall's evidence taken. No appearance by either dfndt. Letter in file from dfndt W<u>m</u> Alrid[sic] stating he can not appear because of sickness of wife. He enclosed Bill of Sale from J.J. Smith.
Apr 16 1907	Com<u>r</u> asked as to citizenship of dfndts.
Apr 24 1907	Com<u>r</u> reports William Aldrich[sic] enrolled as Cherokee freedman. Goldie Adair denied enrollment.
Apr 29 1907	Com<u>r</u> asked if William Aldrich has filed land or not
Apr 30 1907	Dfndt William Aldrich requested to appear at this office May 8 1907
May 9 1907	William Aldrich dfndt appeared and surrendered possession and this case dismissed as to Aldrich - Judgment to be found as to Goldie Adair
May 9 1907	Com<u>r</u> reports William Aldrich has filed
May 11 1907	Plntf advised that W<u>m</u> Aldrich surrenders possession as to himself.
June 17 '07	Judgment in favor of plff and deft given ten days to vacate.
June 19 07	Letter from plaintiff asking instructions in re leasing land.
June 22 07	Plff requested to advise as soon as matter is satisfactorily settled
June 25 07	Ada Durall forwards contract claimed by Goldie Adair and requests this office to notify A Brown, Goldie Adair and A.J. Ulrey of judgment in her favor thinking this will oliviate[sic] sending policeman
June 29 07	Letters addressed to parties named in plff's letter as per her request
July 17 07	Instructions issued to Capt West to place pltf in possession
July 25 07	Capt West reports placing natural Gdn. in possession on July 22/7.
Aug 1 07	Certs returned to plaintiff and <u>Case Dismissed</u>.

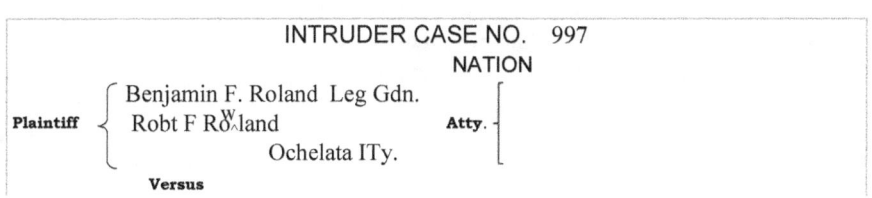

	INTRUDER CASE NO. 997 NATION		
Plaintiff	Benjamin F. Roland Leg Gdn. Robt F Ro<u>w</u>land Ochelata ITy.	Atty.	

Versus

151

Cherokee Intruder Cases 1901 - 1909

Defendant	Charles Harris Oglesby, I.Ty.	Atty.	
Complaint filed Jany 29 1907	**Commissioner Reports** 2/211/7		No Contest. **Notice Sent** Mch 6 1907

Feby 12 1907	Letters of Gdnshp in file.
Mch 26 1907	Case set for hearing at Claremore, I.Ty Apr 11 1907. All parties notified.
Mch 30 1907	Plntf asks letters of Gdnship be returned.
Apr 5 1907	Letters of Gdnship returned.
Apr 11 1907	Case called at Claremore I.T. Neither party appeared.
June 18 07	Case set for hearing at Vinita, I.T. July 8/7. All parties notified.
June 30 07	Plff advises he is in possession.
July 5 07	Deft and plff advised that it is not necessary to appear at Vinita July 8, 1907. and <u>Case Dismissed</u>.

INTRUDER CASE NO. 998
NATION

Plaintiff	Mary A.F. Parker Hulbert, I.Ty.	Atty.	F.L. Brown Claremore ITy.
	Versus		
Defendant	Charles Owens Caney, Kans.	Atty.	
Complaint filed Feby 18 1907	**Commissioner Reports** 2/23/7		No Contest. **Notice Sent** Mch 6 1907

Mch 14 1907	Proof of service returned dated Mch 13 1907 Reg receipt slip.
Mch 15 1907	Answer filed by dfndt
Mch 21 1907	Dfndt advised case will be set for hearing soon.
Mch 22 1907	Reg ret card in file.
Mch 26 1907	Case set for hearing at Claremore, ITy Apr 11, 1907. All parties notified.
Apr 3 1907	Plntf asks case be heard at Nowata or Bartlesville ITy.
Apr 6 1907	Plntf advised case will be heard at Claremore ITy Apr 11 1907
Apr 11 1907	Case called at Claremore ITy. Both parties present & testimony taken. Lease contract & receipt ~~of~~ for $100.^{00} filed by dfndt.
May 4 1907	Judgment rendered in favor of dfndt - Contract returned <u>Case dismissed</u>.

Cherokee Intruder Cases 1901 - 1909

INTRUDER CASE NO. 999
NATION

Plaintiff: Lucy Davis, nee Manning, Porum, I.Ty.
Atty:

Versus

Defendant: J. Smith, Tom Downing, Texanna, ITy.
Atty: Geo C. Butte, Muskogee, I.Ty.

Complaint filed 2/23/7 **Commissioner Reports** 3/13/07 **No Contest. Notice Sent** Mch 6 1907

Feby 23 1907	Certificates No 19955-28056
Mch 6 1907	Com^r asked to report
Mch 11 1907	Proof of service returned dated Mch 9, 1907
Mch 13 1907	Answer filed by J. Smith
Mch 16 1907	Answer filed by Geo C Butte for dfndt.
Mch 22 1907	Case set for hearing at Muskogee, ITy Apr 3 1907. All parties notified.
Mch 26 1907	As per request of plntf. she is advised case set for hearing.
Apr 3 1907	Case called at Muskogee ITy. All parties present & testimony taken.
May 3 1907	Judgment rendered in favor of plntf - Dfndts given ten days in which to vacate.
May 28 1907	Plntf requested to advise if in possession
June 22 07	Plff again requested to advise if she is in possession.
8/17 07	Instructions issued to Capt Jno C. West.
Aug 29 '07	Capt West reports that allottee[sic] has been placed in possession.
Sept 6 07	Certificates returned to Plaintiff and <u>Case Dismissed</u>.

INTRUDER CASE NO. 1000
NATION

Plaintiff: James Sunday, Porum ITy
Atty:

Versus

Defendant: Fred Letcher
Atty: Thomas & Foreman

Complaint filed Feby 18 1907 **Commissioner Reports** 2/23/7 **No Contest. Notice Sent** Mch 6 1907

Mch 30 1907	Plntf returns notices & ask that U.S. I. Agt serve same.
Apr 3 1907	Notices returned to plntf who is instructed to serve same by mail.
Apr 17 1907	Proof of service returned dated Apr 10 1907.
Apr 19 1907	Answer filed by Atty for dfndt,
Apr 23 1907	Case set for hearing at Muskogee Ind. Ty. May 4- 1907

Cherokee Intruder Cases 1901 - 1909

May 7 1907	Contract & receipts in file.
May 20 1907	Judgment rendered in favor of dfndt - Copy of rental contract made by Sunday to Letcher, & copy of rental contract made by Sunday to Fannie C. Starr, two receipts returned to dfndt. Case is dismissed.

INTRUDER CASE NO. 1001
NATION

Plaintiff: Melinda Smith, Ft Gibson, I.Ty.
Atty:

Versus

Defendant: Nat Sauco, Fort Gibson, I.Ty.
Atty: Thomas and Foreman, Muskogee ITy.

Complaint filed Mch 8 1907 **Commissioner Reports** Mch 20 1907 **No Contest. Notice Sent** Mch 14 1907

March 8 1907	Certificate No 16988 in file.
Mch 18 1907	Answer filed by Atty for dfndt.]
Mch 18 1907	Proof of service returned dated Mch 16 1907
Mch 20 1907	Case set for hearing at Muskogee ITy Apr 2, 1907
Apr 2 1907	Case called at Muskogee I.Ty. All parties present & testimony of plntf taken. The fact developed that husband of plntf now decs'd[sic] sold small portion of his on[sic] land but described land of plntf which is now occupied by dfndt. Atty Jno R. Thomas, stated he would file motion in U.S. Court to correct description.
Sept 28 '07	Defendant requested to advise if he had case pending in U.S. C[sic] to correct description.
Mch 25 08	Judgement[sic] rendered in favor of pltf & defdt given ten days.
Apr 13 08	Instructions issued to Capt Jno C. West to-day to place plff in poss.
Apr 15 08	Cert. 16988 returned to Cornelius Nave in person today (Have her son in law)
6-9 08	Capt West reports that he placed pltf in possession & case is Dismissed.

INTRUDER CASE NO. 1002
NATION

Plaintiff: Nellie Jane Chambers, Tiawah, I.Ty.
Atty:

Versus

Cherokee Intruder Cases 1901 - 1909

Defendant	Wayne Mullen	Atty.	A.F. *(Illegible)*	
	Collinsville, I.Ty.		Claremore I.Ty.	

Complaint filed Mch 8 1907 **Commissioner Reports** 3/20/07 No **Contest.** **Notice Sent** Mch 14 1907

Mch 8 1907	Certificates Nos 17785, 24303
Mch 14 1907	Com^r asked to report
Mch 19 1907	Proof of service returned, dated Mch 18, 1907
Mch 26 1907	Case set for hearing at Claremore ITy Apr 11 1907 All parties notified
April 11 1907	Case called at Claremore ITy. Both parties present. Plntf states new contract made for 3 yrs from date. Expires 4/11/1911. Pd $75.<u>00</u> in full. Certificates returned to plntf in person & <u>case dismissed</u>.

INTRUDER CASE NO. 1003
NATION

Plaintiff	Sol Harlan for Walter Harlan Melvin ITy	Atty.		
	Versus			
Defendant	Lee Saunders Melvin ITy	Atty.	J.D. Cox Tahlequah, I.Ty.	

Complaint filed Mch 9 1907 **Commissioner Reports** 3/20/07 No **Contest.** **Notice Sent** Mch 14 1907

Mch 9 1907	Certificates Nos 59179, 35927.
Mch 14 1907	Com^r asked to report
Mch 20 1907	Proof of service returned dated Mch 18, 1907
Mch 27 1907	Answer filed by Atty for dfndt.
Mch 28 1907	Com^r asked as to citizenship of Walter Ferguson.
Apr 5 1907	Com^r advises Waller or Walter Ferguson denied by 1/26/07. see file 1005
June 19 07	Case set for Muskogee, July 6.07. All parties notified
July 6 07	Deft appeared in person and by attorney. It is found the deft is a rejected claimant for citizenship, and owner of improvements on land in controversy. Case continued until appraisement may be completed.
Nov 30/07	Homestead certificate returned
Jan 11 08	Case set for hearing Muskogee Jan 30/8 All notified.
Jan 30 08	Case called. No appearance.
May 16 08	Plaintiff requested to appear and give his evidence and if he is now in possession of land.
6-23 08	Case dismissed as it is presumed pltf has possession.
	Dismissed.

Cherokee Intruder Cases 1901 - 1909

INTRUDER CASE NO. 1004
NATION

Plaintiff: Laura A. Denbo, Catoosa, I.Ty.   Atty.

Versus

Defendant: Thos. J. Daugherty, Catoosa, I.Ty.   Atty.

Complaint filed Mch 6 1907 **Commissioner Reports** 3/25/07 **No Contest. Notice Sent** Mch 14 1907

Mch 6 1907	Certificate No 19401 in file.
Mch 14 1907	Com^r asked to report
Mch 18 1907	Proof of service returned dated Mch 16, 1907
Mch 19 1907	Plntf advises settlement.
Mch 18 1907	Dfndt states he will attend hearing when notified
Mch 23 1907	Certificate returned & <u>case dismissed</u>.

INTRUDER CASE NO. 1005
NATION

Plaintiff: Andrew McCrackin, Melvin, I.Ty.   Atty.

Versus

Defendant: Lee Saunders, Melvin, I.Ty   Atty.   J.D. Cox, Tahlequah ITy.

Complaint filed Mch 5 1907 **Commissioner Reports** 3/20/07 **No Contest. Notice Sent** Mch 14 1907

Mch 5 1907	Certificate No 36428 in file
Mch 14 1907	Com^r asked to report
Mch 20 1907	Proof of service returned dated Mch 18, 1907
Mch 27 1907	Answer filed by Atty for dfndt.
Mch 28 1907	Com^r asked as to citizenship of Walter Ferguson See file 1003
Apr 5 1907	Com^r advises Walter Ferguson denied Jany 26 1907. Same in 1003.
June 19 07	Case set for Muskogee, July 6, 07. All parties notified.
July 6 07	Deft appeared in person and by his attorney. No appearance by plaintiff. It is found that defndant[sic] is a rejected claimant for citizenship and owner of the improvements on the land in controversy. Case continued until appraisement may be completed.
Aug 25 07	<s>C.R. Reynolds reports Defendant has surrendered possession</s>
Sept 5 07	<s>Case dismissed</s>.
Nov 30 07	Homestead certificate returned to plaintiff.

Cherokee Intruder Cases 1901 - 1909

Jan 11 08	Case set for hearing Muskogee Jan 20, 1908 All notified.
Jan 30 08	Case called No appearance.
May 16 08	Plaintiff asked why he did not appear at hearings and give testimony and if he is now in possession or settlement made.
5-29 08	Pltf states case settled & same is <u>Dismissed</u>.

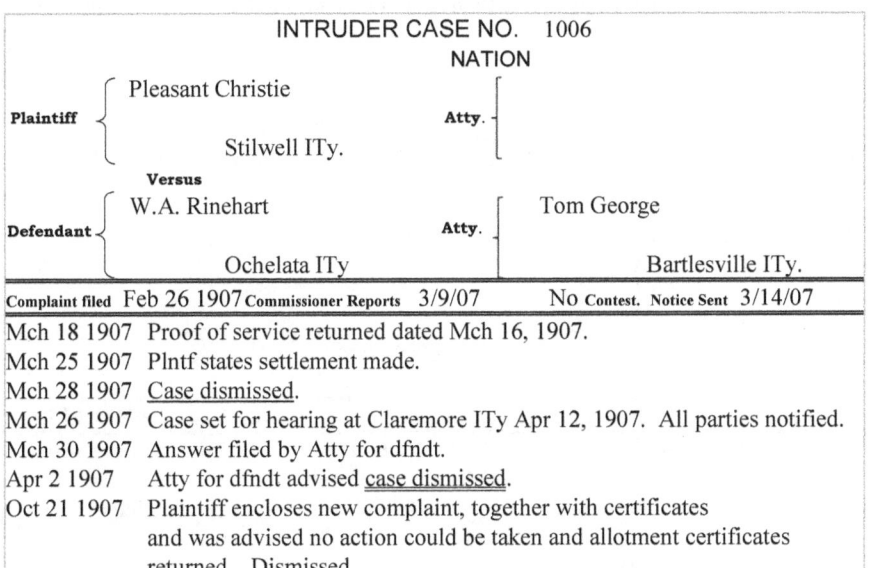

INTRUDER CASE NO. 1006
NATION

Plaintiff: Pleasant Christie, Stilwell ITy.
Atty.:
Defendant: W.A. Rinehart, Ochelata ITy.
Atty.: Tom George, Bartlesville ITy.

Complaint filed Feb 26 1907 Commissioner Reports 3/9/07 No Contest. Notice Sent 3/14/07

Mch 18 1907	Proof of service returned dated Mch 16, 1907.
Mch 25 1907	Plntf states settlement made.
Mch 28 1907	<u>Case dismissed</u>.
Mch 26 1907	Case set for hearing at Claremore ITy Apr 12, 1907. All parties notified.
Mch 30 1907	Answer filed by Atty for dfndt.
Apr 2 1907	Atty for dfndt advised <u>case dismissed</u>.
Oct 21 1907	Plaintiff encloses new complaint, together with certificates and was advised no action could be taken and allotment certificates returned. <u>Dismissed</u>

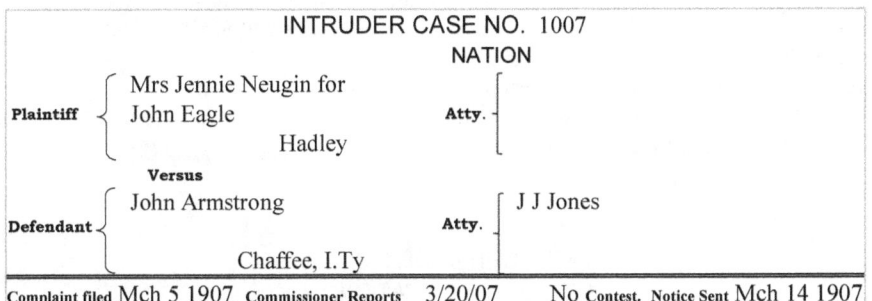

INTRUDER CASE NO. 1007
NATION

Plaintiff: Mrs Jennie Neugin for John Eagle Hadley
Atty.:
Defendant: John Armstrong, Chaffee, I.Ty
Atty.: J J Jones

Complaint filed Mch 5 1907 Commissioner Reports 3/20/07 No Contest. Notice Sent Mch 14 1907

Mch 5 1907	Certificates Nos 24497-34937 in file.
Mch 14 1907	Com^r asked to report.
Mch 26 1907	Case set for hearing at Claremore ITy Apr 12, 1907. All parties notified.

Cherokee Intruder Cases 1901 - 1909

Apr 3 1907	Dfndt states he will be present at hearing.
Apr 12 1907	Case called at Claremore I.Ty. Husband of plntf appeared & testimony taken. Jno Eagle died two weeks ago. Dfndt did not appear but represented by Jones (colored) Atty Vinita. Case <u>dismissed</u>. Certificates returned to husband of plntf. He is stepfather of Jno Eagle
Oct 28 07	Pltf asks to be placed in possession and advised that case has been dismissed and fully advised. See carbon in file.
Nov 8 07	Answer filed by defendant and advised that case has been dismissed & no further action will be taken. <u>Dismissed</u>.

INTRUDER CASE NO. 1008
NATION

Plaintiff: Andrew McAffrey for William Hugh and Cleora McAffrey Afton ITy.

Atty.

Versus

Defendant: Dock Adams   Welch I.Ty.

Atty.

Complaint filed Feby 28 1907 Commissioner Reports 3/9/07 No Contest. Notice Sent Mch 14 1907

Mch 26 1907	Case set for hearing at Claremore, ITy April 12 1907 All parties notified.
Apr 1 1907	Proof of service returned dated Mch 30 1907.
Apr 12 1907	Case called at Claremore ITy. ~~Both parties~~ Plntf only. present. His testimony taken. Plntf states dfndt is also known as R Brown. See report of Com^r in #991 as to citizenship.
May 4 1907	Judgment rendered in favor of pltf - Dfndt given ten days in which to vacate.
May 10 07	Plff notifies this office deft has not vacated in accordance with judgment
June 29 07	Injunction dissolved. See cases 991- 944-789-800-905-896-1008.
July 6 07	Plff and deft advises in re injunction.
July 6 07	Capt John C West instructed to place plff in possession
July 25 07	Capt west reports that on July 23 1907 he placed plff in possession.
Aug 1 07	Plaintiff advised of Capt West's report and <u>Case Dismissed</u>.

INTRUDER CASE NO. 1009
NATION

Plaintiff: Laura Slape Gideon, ITy.

Atty.

Versus

Cherokee Intruder Cases 1901 - 1909

Defendant: G.G. Ingle and A.S. Graves
Gideon, I.Ty.
Atty.

Complaint filed Feby 23 1907 **Commissioner Reports** 3/9/07 **No Contest. Notice Sent** 3/14/07

Mch 23 1907	Case set for hearing at Muskogee, I.Ty. Apr 1 1907 All parties notified.
Mch 23 1907	Proof of service returned dated Mch 19, 1907.
Apr 1 1907	Case called at Muskogee, ITy. Dfndt Graves appeared & exhibited a a[sic] statement signed by plntf that satisfactory settlement had been made No appearance by plntf.
Mch 30 1907	Plntf states settlement has been made.
Apr 2 1907	Case dismissed.

INTRUDER CASE NO. 1010
NATION

Plaintiff: J.B. Burgess
Claremore, ITy.
Atty. C.C. McGee
Tulsa
I.Ty.

Versus

Defendant: G.S. Swift
N.M. Pippin
Keystone, Okla Owasso I.Ty.
Atty. ~~C.C. Gegee~~[sic] Hall
Claremore
~~Tulsa I.Ty.~~

Complaint filed Mch 12 1907 **Commissioner Reports** 3/9/07 **No Contest. Notice Sent** 3/14/07

Mch 21 1907	Answer filed by dfndt
Mch 22 1907	Proof of service returned dated Mch 18 1907
~~Mch 23~~ 1907	~~Proof of service returned dated 19 Mch 190~~[sic]
Mch 26 1907	Case set for hearing at Claremore ITy Apr 12 1907. All parties notified.
Mch 28 1907	N.M. Pippin answers & states he is dfndt. G.S. Swift his tenant.
Apr 1 1907	Dfndt Pippin requested to be present at hearing.
Apr 12 1907	Case called at Claremore ITy. Both parties present. Testimony taken. Exhibits "A" & "B" by plntf. Exhibit by "A" by dfndt.
Apr 15 1907	Two contracts, mutilated note, receipt & certificates no 9327 & 11477 filed by Mrs. Burgess in person.
May 3 1907	Judgment rendered in favor of dfndts - Rental contracts, correspondence & allotment certificates [#'s] 11477 & 9327 returned - Case dismissed -

Cherokee Intruder Cases 1901 - 1909

INTRUDER CASE NO. 1011 NATION		
Plaintiff	Emily J Stranks c/o W. J. Stranks Muskogee, I.Ty.	**Atty.**
	Versus	
Defendant	John Temberlake Chas Smith c/o Jas Dodson Muskogee I.Ty	**Atty.** C. W. Gormly Muskogee, I.Ty.

Complaint filed 3/21/07   **Commissioner Reports** Apr 3 1907   No **Contest. Notice Sent** 3/23/07

Mch 21 1907	Certificates Nos 33-38 in file
Mch 23 1907	Com^r asked to report
Mch 25 1907	Proof of service returned dated Mch 23, 1907.
Apr 11 1907	Case set for hearing at Muskogee, ITy. Apr 18, 1907 All parties notified.
Apr 15 1907	Answer filed by Soper Huckleberry & Owen Atty for dfndt.
Apr 18 1907	Case called. W.J. Strank[sic] husband of plntf appeared & testimony taken No appearance by dfndt
April 22 1907	In compliance with request of Attys for dfdt, judgement[sic] in this case to be withheld for ten days from this date in order that they have opportunity to file evidence showing that motion to review contest is at this time pending.
Apr 25 1907	Atty for <u>dfndt</u> advise that he has nothing further to <u>file</u> in this case
May 18 1907	Judgment rendered in favor of plntf - dfndts given ten days in which to vacate
May 29 07	Capt Jno C West directed to place plff in poss or remove <u>all</u> <u>obj</u>. <u>parties</u>
" 31 07	Capt West reports that on May 30-07 plff placed in possession
June 1 07	Chas. Smith one of defts advised of status of case.
June 5 07	Plff advised of report of Capt West and Case Dismissed.
Sept 21 07	Certificates No 33 & 38 returned to W. J. Stranks in person <u>Dismissed</u>.

INTRUDER CASE NO. 1012 NATION		
Plaintiff	Katie Kernel c/o Sam McCurtain Dawson, I.Ty.	**Atty.**
	Versus	
Defendant	Brewer *(No other name given.)* Mohawk, I.Ty.	**Atty.**

Cherokee Intruder Cases 1901 - 1909

| Complaint filed 3/22/07 | Commissioner Reports | Contest. Notice Sent Mch 23 1907 |

Mch 22 1907   Report of Com^r to Samuel McCurtain in file
Mch 28 1907   Case set for hearing at Claremore, ITy Apr 12, 1907 All parties notified
Apr 2 1907   Proof of service returned dated Apr 1" 1907
Apr 12 1907   Case called at Claremore ITy. Both parties present. It was found that tis
              only a question of lines. Dfndt has abstract of land which he claims. Plntf
              advised to have land surveyed.   Case dismissed.

INTRUDER CASE NO. 1013
NATION

Plaintiff: Geo. B Parks for Margarette Parks, Centralia, I.Ty.
Atty.

Versus

Defendant: Ed Riley, Hayden I.Ty
Atty.

| Complaint filed Mch 15 1907 Commissioner Reports 4/3/7 | No Contest. Notice Sent Mch 25 1907 |

Mch 15 1907   Certificates Ns 37903, 63745-63746
Mch 28 1907   Case set for hearing at Claremore ITy April 12, 1907. All parties notified.
Mch 25 1907   Com^r asked to report.
Apr 2 1907   Proof of service returned dated Mch 29, 1907.
Apr 12 1907   Case called at Claremore, ITy. Both parties present 7 testimony taken.
Apr 16 1907   Com^r asked as to citizenship of Mary Warren nee Thompson.
Apr 24 1907   Com^r reports Mary Thompson denied enrollment
May 4 1907   Judgment rendered in favor of plntf - Dfndt given ten days in which to
              vacate and plntf requested to advise if in possession.
June 22 07   Plff requested to advise in re possession.
July 18 07   Case dismissed by request of pltf, and certs returned.
                                                                        Dismissed.

INTRUDER CASE NO. 1014
NATION

Plaintiff: Emma Alwell for Ruth Alwell, Lenapah, I.Ty.
Atty.

Versus

Cherokee Intruder Cases 1901 - 1909

Defendant	Will Merrill	Atty.	
	Lenapah, I.Ty.		

Complaint filed Mch 20 1907 **Commissioner Reports** 3/3/07   No **Contest. Notice Sent** Mch 25 1907

Mch 20 1907	Certificate No 56603
Mch 29 1907	Proof of service returned, dated Mch 28, 1907
Mch 28 1907	Case set for hearing at Claremore ITy Apr 12, 1907. All parties notified
Mch 25 1907	Com^r asked to report.
Apr 12 1907	Case called at Claremore ITy. Neither party appeared
Apr 10 1907	Plntf states she has possession of land in question.
Apr 16 1907	Certificates returned & case dismissed.
Apr 29 1907	Dfndt advised that case has been <u>dismissed</u>.

INTRUDER CASE NO. 1015
NATION

Plaintiff	Ella Triplett, nee Davis	Atty.	
	Tulsa		
	Tahlequah ITy.		
	Versus		
Defendant	Taylor Goings	Atty.	J.W. Swartz
			Chelsea
	Chelsea, I.Ty		I.T.

Complaint filed Mch 4 1907 **Commissioner Reports** 3/13/7   No **Contest. Notice Sent** Mch 25 1907

Mch 28 1907	Case set for hearing at Claremore ITy April 11 1907. All parties notified.
Apr 11 1907	Case called at Claremore ITy. Neither party appeared.
May 6 1907	Dfndt advised that he will be given hearing
June 18 07	Case set for hearing at Vinita I.T. July 8/7. All parties notified.
July 8 07	Case called at Vinita. No appearance by plaintiff. Dft appeared in person and by attorney. Defendant exhibited letters Gdn. executed to him 1/21/03 by U.S. Court. Dft. also states that the land is leased for this year and thinks Ella Triplett has just arrived at the age of 18 years.
Jan 11 08	Pltf requested to advise if in possission[sic].
April 16 08	Instructions issued to Tom Roach.
4/27 08	Report of Thomas P. Roach filed today.
5-14 08	Pltf appeared today and stated that she now had possession of her land and case is <u>Dismissed</u>.

162

Cherokee Intruder Cases 1901 - 1909

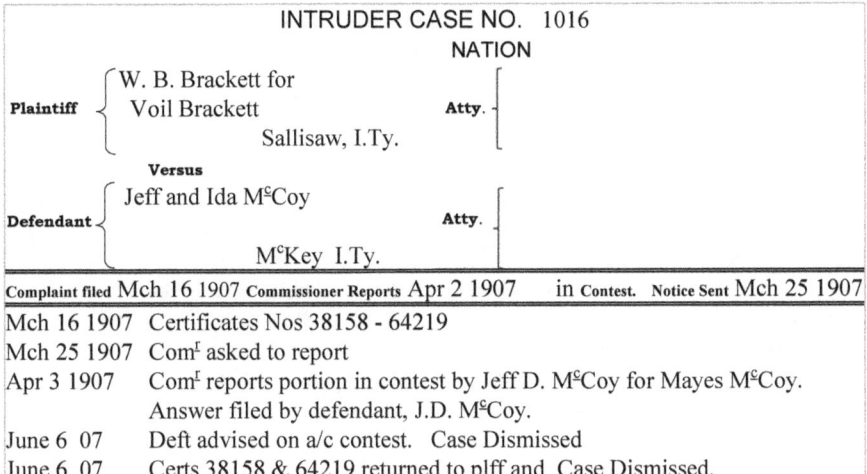

INTRUDER CASE NO. 1016
NATION

Plaintiff: W. B. Brackett for Voil Brackett, Sallisaw, I.Ty.   Atty.

Versus

Defendant: Jeff and Ida McCoy, McKey I.Ty.   Atty.

Complaint filed	Mch 16 1907	Commissioner Reports Apr 2 1907	in Contest. Notice Sent Mch 25 1907

Mch 16 1907   Certificates Nos 38158 - 64219
Mch 25 1907   Com^r asked to report
Apr 3 1907   Com^r reports portion in contest by Jeff D. McCoy for Mayes McCoy. Answer filed by defendant, J.D. McCoy.
June 6 07   Deft advised on a/c contest. Case Dismissed
June 6 07   Certs 38158 & 64219 returned to plff and <u>Case Dismissed</u>.

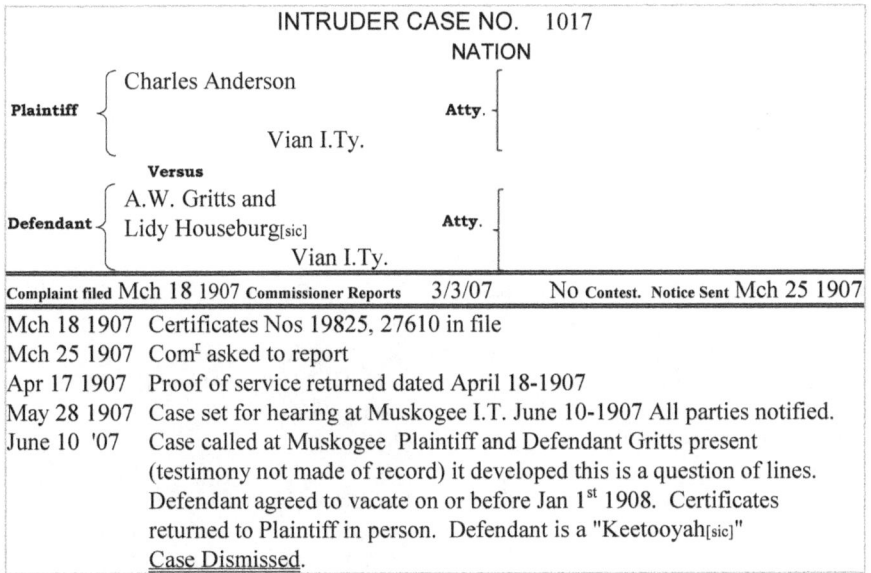

INTRUDER CASE NO. 1017
NATION

Plaintiff: Charles Anderson, Vian I.Ty.   Atty.

Versus

Defendant: A.W. Gritts and Lidy Houseburg[sic], Vian I.Ty.   Atty.

Complaint filed	Mch 18 1907	Commissioner Reports 3/3/07	No Contest. Notice Sent Mch 25 1907

Mch 18 1907   Certificates Nos 19825, 27610 in file
Mch 25 1907   Com^r asked to report
Apr 17 1907   Proof of service returned dated April 18-1907
May 28 1907   Case set for hearing at Muskogee I.T. June 10-1907 All parties notified.
June 10 '07   Case called at Muskogee Plaintiff and Defendant Gritts present (testimony not made of record) it developed this is a question of lines. Defendant agreed to vacate on or before Jan 1st 1908. Certificates returned to Plaintiff in person. Defendant is a "Keetooyah[sic]" <u>Case Dismissed</u>.

Cherokee Intruder Cases 1901 - 1909

INTRUDER CASE NO. 1018
NATION

Plaintiff	Jane Foreman Santown[sic] I.Ty.	**Atty.**	
	Versus		
Defendant	Will H. Hollinger Allottment[sic] near Vian, I.Ty.	**Atty.**	

Complaint filed Mch 1 1907 **Commissioner Reports** 3/15/07 No **Contest.** **Notice Sent** Mch 25 1907

Mch 29 1907 Proof of service returned dated Mch 27 1907
Mch 30 1907 Answer filed by dfndt
Apr 2 1907   Case set for hearing at Muskogee ITy Apr 15 1907 All parties notified.
Apr 15 1907 Case called. Both parties present & testimony taken.
May 11 1907 Plntf advised that judgment will be found as soon as possible.
May 18 1907 Judgment rendered in favor of dfndt. Case dismissed.

INTRUDER CASE NO. 1019
NATION

Plaintiff	Ida Long Vinita I.Ty	**Atty.**	Starr and Patton Vinita, I.Ty.
	Versus		
Defendant	James, Malzy, Sanford, and Aleck Carbin Lee Carbin Freedman Ochelata ITy.	**Atty.**	

Complaint filed Mch 1 1907 **Commissioner Reports** 3/15/7 No **Contest.** **Notice Sent** Mch 25 1907

Mch 12 1907 Atty for plntf ask that case be heard ∧ be added as dfndt
                                             name of Lee Carbin
Mch 28 1907 Case set for hearing at Claremore ITy Apt 10 1907 All parties notified.
Mch 27 1907 Attys for plntf enclose certificates Nos 59657 - 36094.
Mch 30 1907 Atty for plntf ask case be heard 4/8/7
Apr 4 1907   Above request refused
Apr 10 1907 Case called at Claremore ITy. Plntf appeared by Atty Mr. Patton.
             Lee Carben[sic] & one Carben present. It was developed that dfndts are not
             in possession but one John Wood is living in house on land. There by
             authority of Felix Corben[sic] for his decs'd wife who was claimant as
             Cherokee Freedman name Melzy[sic] Corben[sic]. Ask Com^r as to her
             citizenship. Plntf advised to file complaint vs proper parties ie who are
             actually in possession. Dismissed.

Cherokee Intruder Cases 1901 - 1909

Apr 16 1907   Com[r] asked as to citizenship of Malzy Carben.
Apr 24 1907   Com[r] reports Malzy Carbin d<u>enie</u>d enrollment.
July 5   07   Com. reports Lee Carbin denied enrollment

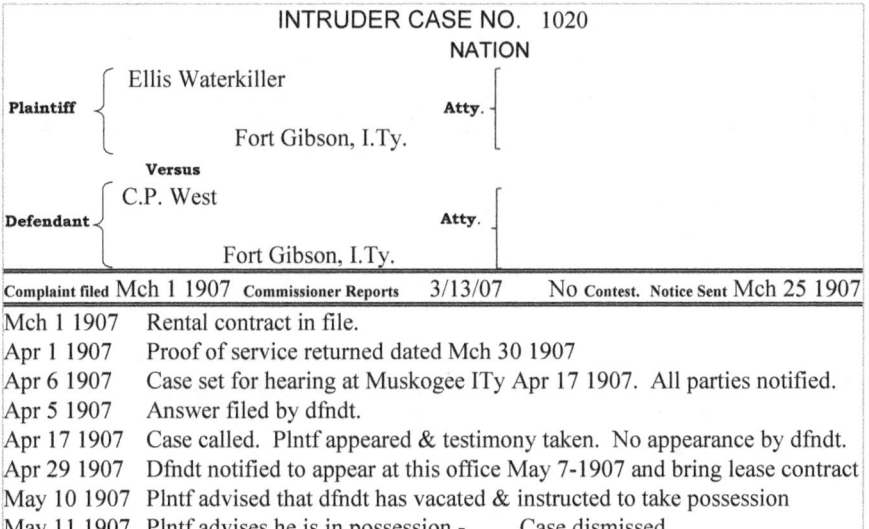

INTRUDER CASE NO. 1020
NATION

Plaintiff — Ellis Waterkiller, Fort Gibson, I.Ty.   Atty. —

Versus

Defendant — C.P. West, Fort Gibson, I.Ty.   Atty.

Complaint filed Mch 1 1907 **Commissioner Reports** 3/13/07 No **Contest. Notice Sent** Mch 25 1907

Mch 1 1907	Rental contract in file.
Apr 1 1907	Proof of service returned dated Mch 30 1907
Apr 6 1907	Case set for hearing at Muskogee ITy Apr 17 1907. All parties notified.
Apr 5 1907	Answer filed by dfndt.
Apr 17 1907	Case called. Plntf appeared & testimony taken. No appearance by dfndt.
Apr 29 1907	Dfndt notified to appear at this office May 7-1907 and bring lease contract
May 10 1907	Plntf advised that dfndt has vacated & instructed to take possession
May 11 1907	Plntf advises he is in possession - <u>Case dismissed</u>.

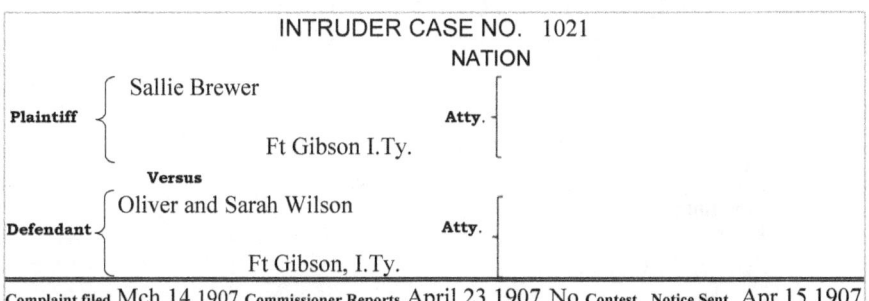

INTRUDER CASE NO. 1021
NATION

Plaintiff — Sallie Brewer, Ft Gibson I.Ty.   Atty. —

Versus

Defendant — Oliver and Sarah Wilson, Ft Gibson, I.Ty.   Atty.

Complaint filed Mch 14 1907 **Commissioner Reports** April 23 1907 No **Contest. Notice Sent** Apr 15 1907

Mch 14 1907	Certificate No 64980 in file.
Apr 1 1907	Certificate returned to husband of plntf in person, in office at Muskogee.
Apr 15 1907	Com[r] asked to report.
June 19 07	Case set for Muskogee, July 2/7. All parties notified.
June 24 '07	Husband of Sally Brewer appeared and stated that the case had been satisfactorly[sic] settled and requested the case be[sic] <u>be Dismissed</u>.

Cherokee Intruder Cases 1901 - 1909

INTRUDER CASE NO. 1022
NATION

Plaintiff: Joel L Baugh, Choteau, I.Ty. Atty.

Versus

Defendant: George and Joanna Cook Atty.

Complaint filed Apr 1 1907 **Commissioner Reports** April 23 1907 **No Contest. Notice Sent** Apr 15 1907

Apr 1 1907	Com' advises application of Joanna Cook a Freedman, denied Feby 27 1907
Apr 1 1907	Certificate No 179 in file.
Apr 15 1907	Com' asked to report
Apr 24 1907	Proof of service returned dated Apr 22-1907
Apr 26 1907	Case set for hearing at Muskogee Ind. Ty. May 6-1907- Both parties notified.
May 6 1907	Case called at Muskogee I.T.; Plntf appeared & testimony taken.
May 7 1907	Dfndts appeared & stated they could not reach Muskogee on the 6th on account of high water - Testimony taken.
May 20 1907	Judgment rendered in favor of plntf - Dfndts given ten days in which to vacate
June 11 07	Capt West directed to ascertain if defts have vacated &, if not, place plff in possession
July 3 07	U.S. Marshal for Northern District requested to send deputy with Capt West on July 6-07 said deputy to arrest the deft if any violence is attempted.
July 25 1907	Capt West reports placing allottee[sic] in possession on July 22, 1907.
Aug 1 1907	Cert returned to plff and <u>Case Dismissed</u>.

INTRUDER CASE NO. 1023
NATION

Plaintiff: Vannie Jordan, Centralia ITy. *Freedman* Atty.

Versus

Defendant: Jordan Looney and Sonny Curray, Centralia, I.Ty. Atty.

Complaint filed Mch 29 1907 **Commissioner Reports** April 23 1907 **No Contest. Notice Sent** Apr 15 1907

Mch 29 1907	Certificates No 32506 - 49936
Apr 15 1907	Com' asked to report

Cherokee Intruder Cases 1901 - 1909

May 16 1907	Com^r asked to report as to citizenship of dfndts.
May 24 1907	Com^r reports George Looney denied enrollment by Dpt. Also impossible to identify Sonny Curray as applicant for enrollment
June 3 07	Reg letter to defts requestg[sic] that they show cause or vacate.
June 12 07	Defendant Geo Looney appeared in person and stated the defendants claim right to possession by virtue of their claim for citizenship case, only.
June 12 '07	Regestry[sic] return receipt received bearing the signature of Geo Looney
Sept 26 '07	Case set for hearing at Claremore 10/3/7 All parties notified.
Oct 3 07	Case called no appearance by either party.
Jan 13 08	Case set for hearing Claremore 2/3/8 all notified.
Feb 3 08	Case called no appearance
May 16 08	Plaintiff asked if in possesseon[sic] of land
5/28 08	Pltf *(illegible)* to advise in in[sic] status of case
Aug 25 08	No response to various letters written her and case <u>dismissed</u>.

INTRUDER CASE NO. 1024 See #492
NATION

Plaintiff James B West
Spavinaw, I.Ty.
Atty.

Versus

Defendant Nicey Vann
Chaffee, I.Ty.
Atty.

Complaint filed Mch 28 1907 **Commissioner Reports**   **Contest. Notice Sent** Apr 1 1907

Mch 28 1907	Certificates No 2463, 2464, 2094 in file.
Apr 1 1907	Com^r asked to report
Apr 5 1907	Referred to Robt. R. Bennett.
Apr 13 1907	Robt. R. Bennett reports dfndt says she is claimant for citizenship.
Apr 6 1907	Com^r reports no contest.
	See 497. Alla Ridge <u>vs</u>. Nicey Vann.
Apr 17 1907	Com^r asked as citizenship of Nicey Vann.
Apr 25 1907	Com^r reports Nicey Vann denied enrollment (as freedman)
May 13 1907	Judgment rendered in favor of plntf - Dfndt given ten days in which to vacate.
May 28 1907	Order issued to J.L. Walker policeman to place plntf in possession.
June 1 07	Policeman Walker reports deft not on James B West allotment
June 5 07	Plff requested to advise if he was with Policeman Walker or if he was placed in poss. on May 31st.
June 5 07	Policeman Walker requested to advise if plff was with him & if he placed plff in possession on May 31st.
June 7 07	Plff advises deft is threatening himself and others.

Cherokee Intruder Cases 1901 - 1909

June 15 07   Plff advised to apply to U.S. Ct. for restraining order and <u>Case dismissed</u>
Jan[sic] 18 07   Plff requests copy of judgment and letter quoting judgment sent him.

	INTRUDER CASE NO. 1025 NATION		
Plaintiff	Elouise M. Clapper Gdn of Carl E and Arthur H Clapper Centralia ITy Versus	**Atty**.	M. L. Paden Centralia I.T.
Defendant	Jack Starr <u>vs</u> Carl E land Monnie Starr <u>vs</u> Arthur H land Centralia I.Ty.	**Atty**.	

Complaint filed Mch 28 1907   Commissioner Reports   7-23-08   No Contest. Notice Sent Apr 1 1907

Mch 28 1907	Letter of Gdnship & certificates Nos 37507-62992, 37506-62991 in file.
Apr 1 1907	Com^r asked to report.
Apr 5 1907	Referred to Robt R Bennett.
April 16 1907	Dfndt files answer
April 22 1907	Receipt acknowledges of answer filed.
April 23 1907	Com^r asked for additional information
May 6 1907	Com^r reports Jack & Monie[sic] Starr denied enrollment
May 10 1907	Certificates of allotment & homestead returned - Plntf advised that case is in hand of representatives.
June 18 '07	Case set for hearing at Vinita, July 8/07. All parties notified.
June 20 07	Letter from plff on file
July 8 07	Case called. All parties present. Testimony taken. Arthur M. Clapper filed power of Attorney authorizing him to act for Elouise M. Clapper.
July 30 07	Judgment rendered in favor of plff. Copy sent both parties. Deft given 20 days.
Aug 22 07	Instructions issued to Capt West to place pltf in possession.
Nov 12 07	Plaintiff requests possession and advised Dept. has instructed us not to remove Freedmen.
" 10 08	H.C. Cusey advised of status.
Dec 5 "	" " " " "
" 28 "	Pltf advised.
April Fool "	H.C. Cusey again advised.
3/26 - 1912	Form 330 to Allottees[sic].

Cherokee Intruder Cases 1901 - 1909

INTRUDER CASE NO. 1026
NATION

Plaintiff: Bunk Coker
903 W 13" St. Coffeyville Kans
Atty.

Versus

Defendant: Bill Beard and Bud Heady
Allottment near Talala & Ramona ITy.
Atty.

Complaint filed Mch 30 1907 Commissioner Reports Apr 12 1907 No Contest. Notice Sent Apr 18 1907

Apr 18 1907	Com' asked to report.
Apr 22 1907	Proof of service returned dated Apr 20-07.
Apr 26 1907	Answer filed by dfndt.
June 4 07	Return of service dated May 27-07, filed.
June 18 07	Case set for Vinita IT July 8/7. All parties notified.
June 22 07	Plff advises notice to be served on defts not enclosed with his notice of hearing.
June 28 07	Notice of hearing again sent plff & defts.
July 8 07	Case called at Vinita. Plaintiff appeared and his testimony taken. No appearance by defendants. Plaintiff admits that he has sold surplus land and defendants have surrendered homestead to him Case <u>dismissed</u>.
Sept 13 '07	Mrs. M. Coker advised of status of case.
" 23 '07	Com' requested to advise if Bunk Coker is a full blood Indian
Oct 1 '07	Com' advised Bunk Coker Cherokee Freedman Roll F 3481 & no contest.
" 11 '07	Plaintiff adv. redress in US Court for recovery surplus land and to Com 57 for issuance of patents. <u>Dismissed</u>.

INTRUDER CASE NO. 1027
NATION

Plaintiff: William McLemore
Stillwell, I.Ty.
Atty.

Versus

Defendant: M. B. Beard
Dawson I.Ty.
Atty.

Complaint filed Apr 15 1907 Commissioner Reports Apr 27-07 No Contest. Notice Sent Apr 18 1907

Apr 15 1907	Certificates Nos 14236 - 11373 in file.
Apr 18 1907	Com' asked to report.
May 4 1907	Proof of service returned dated May 3 1907

Cherokee Intruder Cases 1901 - 1909

June 19 07	Case set for Vinita, July 9-07. All parties notified.
July 9 07	Case called, no appearance by either party.
Aug 8 07	Referred to Robt R. Bennett for investigation.
Jan 13 08	Case set for hearing Claremore 2/3/8 All notified.
Feb 3 08	Case called no appearance.
Feb. 7 - 08	Pltf advise office that it was impossible for him to be present at trial on account of sickness & requests case be continued.
6-23 08	Case dismissed as it is presumed pltf has possession.

Dismissed.

INTRUDER CASE NO. 1028
NATION

Plaintiff: Florence Matthews for Sammie M Matthews, Tahlequah, I.Ty.
Atty:

Versus

Defendant: Moses Hardrick, Chelsea, I.Ty.
Atty: D. G. Elliott, Chelsea, Ind. Ter.

Complaint filed Apr 1 1907 **Commissioner Reports** Apr 27 -07 **No Contest. Notice Sent** Apr 18 1907

Apr 1 1907	Certificates Nos 33638-23632 in file.
Apr 18 1907	Com[r] asked to report
Apr 22 1907	Proof of service returned dated April 21-1907
May 10 1907	Notice again sent.
May 11 1907	Com[r] asked to report as to citizenship of Moses Hardrick
May 20 1907	Com[r] reports Moses Hardrick denied enrollment
June 8 07	Case set for Muskogee, June 24/7. Both parties notified
June 8 07	Answer filed by deft.
June 27 07	Deft's Atty states that deft will give possession without further trouble.
July 19 07	Judgement[sic] rendered in favor pltf
	Andy Kircum has been appearing for the pltf as her agent
8/16 07	Case dismissed by request of pltf & certs returned.

Dismissed.

INTRUDER CASE NO. 1029
NATION

Plaintiff: James Drew, Ft Gibson, I.Ty.
Atty: D M Cupp, Ft Gibson, I.Ty.

Versus

Cherokee Intruder Cases 1901 - 1909

Defendant: Lottie Vanderford and Albert Wimer I.Ty.   **Atty.**

Complaint filed Apr 4 1907	Commissioner Reports Apr 27 -07	No Contest. Notice Sent Apr 18 1907
Apr 4 1907	Certificate No. 36105 in file.	
Apr 29 1907	Com^r asked to report	
July 26 07	Answer filed by defendant.	
Aug 3 07	Com^r asked as to citizenship of defendants	
Aug 10 07	Con[sic]. reports in re citizenship of defdts.	
Sept 20 1907	Case set for hearing at Claremore I.Ty Oct 1 1907 All parties notified.	
Oct 2 1907	Case called no appearance by either party.	
Oct 5 1907	Plaintiff appeared and evidence taken, and it is admitted that he sold his land and had received his pay Case Dismissed	

INTRUDER CASE NO. 1030
NATION

Plaintiff: Joshua Choate, Sallisaw, I.Ty.   **Atty.**

Defendant: Martha Choate & son Frank Hix, Sallisaw I.Ty.   **Atty.** Watts & Curtis, Sallisaw Ind Ty

Complaint filed Apr 10 1907	Commissioner Reports Apr 27 -07	No Contest. Notice Sent Apr 18 1907
Apr 10 1907	Certificates Nos. 28222-40940-40941 in file.	
Apr 18 1907	Com^r asked to report	
Apr 23 1907	Proof of service returned dated April 22nd 1907	
Apr 25 1907	Answer filed by Attys for dfndts	
Apr 29 1907	Case set for hearing at Muskogee Ind. Ty. May 8th 1907 All parties notified.	
May 8 1907	Case called at Muskogee ITy; Both parties present & testimony taken. Parties found to be husband & wife, and Frank Hix, a son of Martha Choate. The dfndt being the wife and having the same right to the property as husband the case is dismissed. Plntf advised that his wife would not be removed.	
June 4 07	Plff requests return of certs.	
June 20 07	Certs 28222-40940-40941 returned to plaintiff at Sallisaw.	
Sept 13 07	Plaintiff asks if his wife has authority to sell timbers	
" 21 07	" advised case is dismissed and his redress is in U.S. Court.	
Oct 24 07	Marriage license returned to Martha Choate. Dismissed.	

Cherokee Intruder Cases 1901 - 1909

	INTRUDER CASE NO. 1031 **NATION**
Plaintiff	William W Foreman Gdn of Bessie J. Foreman Atty. Centralia ITy.
	Versus
Defendant	George and Jane Looney Atty. Centralia I.Ty.

Complaint filed Apr 8 1907 **Commissioner Reports** Apr 27 -07 **No Contest. Notice Sent** Apr 18 1907

Apr 8 1907	Letters of Gdnship in file. Also Certificates Nos. 37454-25889.
Apr 19 1907	Com^r asked to report.
April 25 1907	Proof of services returned dated April 22 -'07
May 16 1907	Com^r asked to report as to citizenship of dfndts.
May 24 1907	Com^r reports Jane & George Looney denied enrollment by Dpt.
May 28 1907	Dfndts requested to advise this office by what authority they claim possession of lands in controversy
June 3 07	Defts requested by registered letter to show cause or vacate.
June 12 '07	Defendant Geo. Looney appeared in person and made verbal answer claimed to be freedman of the Cherokee Nation.
June 12 '07	Registry return receipt received bearing signature of Geo Looney.
June 27 07	Case set for Vinita July 11 '07. All parties notified.
July 11 07	Case called at Vinita. Pltf. appeared his evidence taken. No appearance by defendants
Aug 23 07	Judgement[sic] rendered in favor of pltf & defdt given ten days
8/29 07	Pltf requested to advise in re possession of his land.
Sept 10 '07	Plaintiff requests that he be placed in possession
" 12 '07	Plaintiff advised that Instructions will be issued to a Policeman to place him in possession in the near future.
" 10 07	~~Plaintiff requested to have defendant stop removing timber~~
" 21 07	~~Plaintiff advised that action will be in U.S. Court Case dismissed~~
Oct 1 07	Defendants advised must vacate in accordance with judgment
Nov 29 07	Plaintiff asks status and advised Department has held up removing freedmen until further notice
Jan 17 08	Com^r reports deeds recorded Sept 22/6 and delivered to W.W. Foreman 11/21/6
Jan 5 08	See instructions from dept.
Feb 15 08	Instructions issued to Capt John C West to place pltf in possession & pltf so advised 6-27-08 Policeman French reports placing pltf in possession
6-12-08	Policeman French asked for a report. & case is Dismissed and Certificates ret'd.

Cherokee Intruder Cases 1901 - 1909

INTRUDER CASE NO. 1032
NATION

Plaintiff	Mrs Belle Rush Adm^r estate of Mantie Rice	**Atty.**	Soper Huckleberry & Owen Muskogee, I.Ty.
	Versus		
Defendant	Mr Flippens Claremore I.Ty.	**Atty.**	

Complaint filed Apr 1 1907 **Commissioner Reports**   **Contest. Notice Sent** Apr 18 1907

Apr 1 1907	Letters of Adm^r and certificates No 62090=37104.
Apr 17 1907	Letters of Adm^r & certificates returned to plntf in person.
Apr 19 1907	Com^r asked to report
Apr 27 1907	Com^r reports land in contest - <u>Case Dismissed</u>.

INTRUDER CASE NO. 1033
NATION

Plaintiff	Mrs Minnie Sanders Bunch I.Ty.	**Atty.**	
	Versus		
Defendant	James Huckleberry Muskogee I.Ty.	**Atty.**	

Complaint filed Mch 14 1907 **Commissioner Reports** Apr 3 1907   No **Contest. Notice Sent** Apr 18 1907

Mar 25 1907	Proof of service returned dated April 23-07.
June 5 07	Case set for Muskogee, June 15/7. Both parties notified.
June 19 07	Case set for Muskogee, July 6/7. Both parties notified.
July 6 07	Letter rec'd from pltf today requesting continuance of case
8/10 - 07	Pltf requested to advise if she still wants case continued.
Nov 9 07	" " collection of rent and advised no action could be taken for collection of rent but advised that case will be set for hearing if she desires.
Jan 9 08	Case set for hearing Muskogee 1/28/08 all parties notified.
Jan 28 08	Case called No appearance by either party
May 16 08	Plaintiff asked to advise if in possession.
	6-30-08 <u>Dismissed</u>
6-30 08	Case dismissed defdt does not claim possession

Cherokee Intruder Cases 1901 - 1909

	INTRUDER CASE NO. 1034 NATION	
Plaintiff	Harry McCreary Gdn of Edwin & Thomas L Quinn Oologah I.Ty.	Atty.
	Versus	
Defendant	Mrs L Lane Claremore I.Ty	Atty. Joe M LaHay Claremore I.T.

Complaint filed Mch 18 1907 **Commissioner Reports** Apr 3 1907   No **Contest. Notice Sent** Apr 18 1907

Mch 18 1907	Letters of Gdnship in file
April 25 1907	Proof of service returned dated Apr 23-07
May 6 1907	Answer filed by dfndt.
May 18 1907	Plntf requested to advise if he wants case set for hearing at Muskogee.
May 28 1907	Case set for hearing at Muskogee I.T. June 10 1907 Both parties notified
June 5 07	Letters gdnship returned to plff
June 10 07	Case called All parties in interest present and testimony taken. E.B. stenog. It was agreed by and between the parties that the house supposed to be on alltment[sic] of the minor would be moved by deft within ten days. Otherwise, a survey by a competent engineer must be made and blueprint furnished this office.
June 18 07	Lahay & Shaw Attys for W.H. Flesher, tenant of deft, ask status of case.
June 21 07	Lahay & Shaw Attys of Claremore, advised of status of case.
June 29 07	Deft advised she must comply with agreement to move house at once. Plff advised of letter to deft.
July 27 07	Judgment in favor of plaintiff - copy sent both parties - deft given ten days in which to vacate.
8/7 07	Defdt's Atty requested to advise if his client will vacate as per judgment
Jan 11 08	Plaintiff requested to advise if in possession
Feb 14 08	Pltf advised to make settlement if possible & advise office
6-23 08	Case dismissed as it is presumed that pltf has possession. Dismissed
Jan 28 1910	On request of pltf letters of gdnship sent to Geo W. Wise, at Tahlequah, to be used in re Equalization payment; letter of Pltf also sent.

174

Cherokee Intruder Cases 1901 - 1909

Defendant: J. Ellis, Ochelata, I.Ty.
Atty.:

Complaint filed Mch 14 1907 Commissioner Reports Apr 3 1907 No Contest. Notice Sent Apr 18 1907	
Apr 30 1907	Proof of service returned dated Apr 27-07.
June 19 07	Case set for Vinita July 9/7. Both parties notefied[sic].
July 9 07	Case called neither party appeared.
July 9 07	Case dismissed as pltf. writes that she now has possession of her land
	<u>Dismissed</u>.

INTRUDER CASE NO. 1036
Cherokee NATION

Plaintiff: Mary Welch, Sallisaw, I.Ty.
Atty.: E.M. Frye, Sallisaw, I.Ty.

Versus

Defendant: Harvey Martin, Adair I.Ty.
Atty.:

Complaint filed Mch 26 1907 Commissioner Reports Apr 9 1907 No Contest. Notice Sent Apr 18 1907	
Mch 25 1907	Com^r reports dfndt denied Nov 22 1904. Wife Gurtie Martin denied May 21 1906. No motion pending for review.
Apr 25 1907	Answer filed by dfndt.
Apr 30 1907	Case set for hearing at Muskogee Ind. Ty. May 10-1907 Both parties notified
Apr 26 1907	Proof of service returned dated Apr 23 1907
May 10 1907	Case called at Muskogee - Both parties present. Testimony taken.
May 23 1907	Judgment rendered in favor plntf & dfndt given ten days in which to vacate.
June 3 07	Capt West instructed to place plff in poss and remove obj parties.
June 6 07	Capt West reports plaintiff placed in possession
June 8 07	Allotment certificates and deeds returned to plff direct and plff and Attorney separately advised <u>Case Dismissed</u>.
Jan 11 08	Plaintiff advised that Capt West reported he placed her in possession under date of June 6/08. <u>Case dismissed</u>.

Cherokee Intruder Cases 1901 - 1909

	INTRUDER CASE NO. 1037 NATION	
Plaintiff	John Israel for Phillip Israel Braggs I.Ty. **Versus**	Atty.
Defendant	Redeland Johnson and wife Famous Whitewater and family Allottment[sic] near Braggs I.Ty.	Atty.

Complaint filed Mch 29 1907   **Commissioner Reports** Apr 9 1907   No **Contest**. **Notice Sent** Apr 18 1907

June 5 07	Return of service, dated June 1/7, filed.
June 19 07	Case set for Muskogee, July 8, 07. All parties notefied[sic].
July 8 07	No appearance by either party.
July 16 07	Case set for hearing at Muskogee, I.T. on July 27-07
July 27 07	Case called. Plf appeared. No appearance by deft. Plff's evidence taken. J.E.B. sten.
July 30 07	Defts requested to appear at this office on or b4[sic] Aug 10/7. In case of failure, it will be understood they have no legal claim to premises and an order will issue to U.S. police to remove them.
8/16 -07	Defdts notified to vacate at their earliest convenience.
Aug 31 07	Judgment rendered in favor of Plaintiff a copy sent to each party. Defendant given <u>20</u> days within which to vacate.
Oct 11 07	Instructions issued to John C. West to try to effect settlement
Nov 9 07	John C. Wests reports a settlement had and case <u>dismissed</u>.

	INTRUDER CASE NO. 1038 NATION	
Plaintiff	William Fields for Howard and William E Fields Vinita I.Ty. **Versus**	Atty.
Defendant	Eiza J Hardrick Vinita I.Ty. James Hays Bluejacket I.Ty.	Atty.

Complaint filed Apr 5 1907   **Commissioner Reports** Apr 27 07   No **Contest**. **Notice Sent** Apr 19 1907

Mch 30 1907	Certificate Nos 49583-32432-49585-32431 in file.
Apr 19 1907	Com^r asked to report.
Apr 24 1907	Proof of service returned dated April 23-1907
May 17 1907	Com^r asked as to citizenship of Eliza J. Hardrick.
May 24 1907	Com^r reports Eliza . Hardrick denied enrollment by Dpt.
May 13 1907	Answer filed.
June 10 1907	All Certificates mentioned returned to Plaintiff in person.

Cherokee Intruder Cases 1901 - 1909

June 5 07	Deft states her citizenship case is pending
June 10 07	Deft notified Com^r states she has been denied citizenship.
June 19 07	Case set for Vinita, July 9 1907 All parties notified.
July 8 07	Case called at Vinita, all parties present. Testimony taken.
	Plaintiff admits that he entered into a contract with the defendant Hayes.
	<u>Case Dismissed</u>.

INTRUDER CASE NO. 1039
Cherokee NATION

Plaintiff	Eliza Ratliff Tahlequah	**Atty.**	Tom Williams Siloam Springs Ark
	Versus		
Defendant	James Colbert Bartlesville Ind. Ty.	**Atty.**	A.S. McRae Muskogee I.T. Osborne & Osborne Coffeyville Kns

Freedman

Complaint filed Apr 3 1907 **Commissioner Reports** May 7-07 **No Contest.** **Notice Sent** Apr 30 1907
7-27-08 ~~No~~

Apr 6 1907	Com^r reports James Colbert denied enrollment as Cherokee freedman
Apr 30 1907	Com^r asked to report - Unofficial *(illegible)* filed by pltf showing contest dismissed Apr 29-1907
May 6 1907	Proof of service returned dated May 4 1907
May 21 1907	Dfndt appeared & stated he is claimant for citizenship and He is advised to file answer
June 14 07	Com^r F.T. requested to advise in re citizenship of deft.
June 15 07	Case set for Muskogee, June 26/7. All parties notified
June 26 07	Case called pltf appeared no appearance by defdt. Pltf's evidence taken.
June 19 07	Com^r reports Jas Colbert, an applicant for citizenship as freedman, denied By Sec'y Dec 3 1904 and no motion for review pending
June 25 1907	J.H. Craig appeared in person and filed Homestead and Allotment Certificates issued to Eliza and Ella Ratliff Supplemental
June 24 07	Answer ~~and Supplemental Answer~~ filed by Atty for Deft.
July 30 07	Deft requests more time in which to make arrangements to remain in poss.
Aug 3 07	Plaintiff requested to advise in re. possession.
	(Judgment was rendered in this case on July 22/7. Copy sent both parties And deft given ten days to vacate) 8/5/7
Oct 4 07	Instructions issued to Frank West, and Plaintiff so advised.
Oct 7 07	Certificates 16397, 16398, 22073 & 22074 returned in person to allottees.
Oct 10 07	Deft requested to vacate in 15 days as per agreement with J.C. West & not to tear down improvements.
" 17[sic]	Osborne & Osborne files motion for reopening case & asked to be entered as attorneys for defendants. Osborne called in person

Cherokee Intruder Cases 1901 - 1909

" 24 07	Pltf and defend. notified of above request.	
Nov 6 07	Plaintiff states Colbert ix removing improvements and	
Dec 6 07	defendant is requested not to remove same.	
Jan 10 08	Pltf's Atty advised status of case etc.	
Jan 15 08	Tom ~~Watson~~ Williams advised that he is the Attorney of record.	
Sept 10 08	James Colbert requests protection; advised impossible.	
3/26 - 1912	Form 330 to Allottee.	

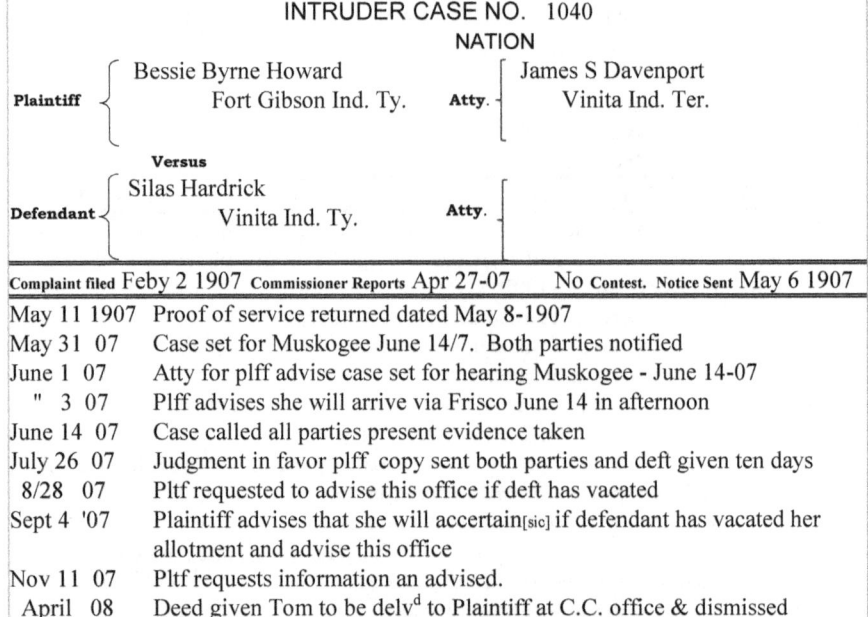

INTRUDER CASE NO. 1040
NATION

Plaintiff: Bessie Byrne Howard, Fort Gibson Ind. Ty.   **Atty.**: James S Davenport, Vinita Ind. Ter.

Versus

Defendant: Silas Hardrick, Vinita Ind. Ty.   **Atty.**:

Complaint filed Feby 2 1907 Commissioner Reports Apr 27-07 No Contest. Notice Sent May 6 1907

May 11 1907	Proof of service returned dated May 8-1907
May 31 07	Case set for Muskogee June 14/7. Both parties notified
June 1 07	Atty for plff advise case set for hearing Muskogee - June 14-07
" 3 07	Plff advises she will arrive via Frisco June 14 in afternoon
June 14 07	Case called all parties present evidence taken
July 26 07	Judgment in favor plff copy sent both parties and deft given ten days
8/28 07	Pltf requested to advise this office if deft has vacated
Sept 4 '07	Plaintiff advises that she will accertain[sic] if defendant has vacated her allotment and advise this office
Nov 11 07	Pltf requests information an advised.
April 08	Deed given Tom to be delv^d to Plaintiff at C.C. office & dismissed

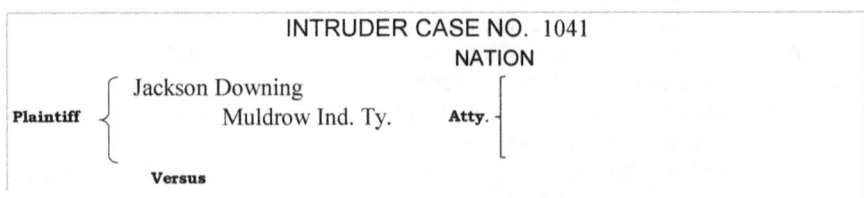

INTRUDER CASE NO. 1041
NATION

Plaintiff: Jackson Downing, Muldrow Ind. Ty.   **Atty.**:

Versus

Cherokee Intruder Cases 1901 - 1909

Defendant: Willie Willace, Muldrow Ind Ty.   **Atty.**

Complaint filed Apr 12 1907 Commissioner Reports Apr 27-07 No Contest. Notice Sent May 6 1907	
May 16 1907	Case set for hearing at Muskogee Ind. Ty. May 27 1907
Apr 24 1907	Answer filed
June 18 07	Case set for Muskogee, July 2/7. All parties notified.
July 9 07	Case set for hearing at Muskogee on Aug. 2-07
Jan 11 08	Plaintiff requested to appear and give evidence
May 16 08	Plaintiff advised that case wold[sic] be dismissed if he did not appear and give his evidence on or before May 26 1908.
6-23 08	Case dismissed as it is presumed pltf has possession.

Dis<u>missed.</u>

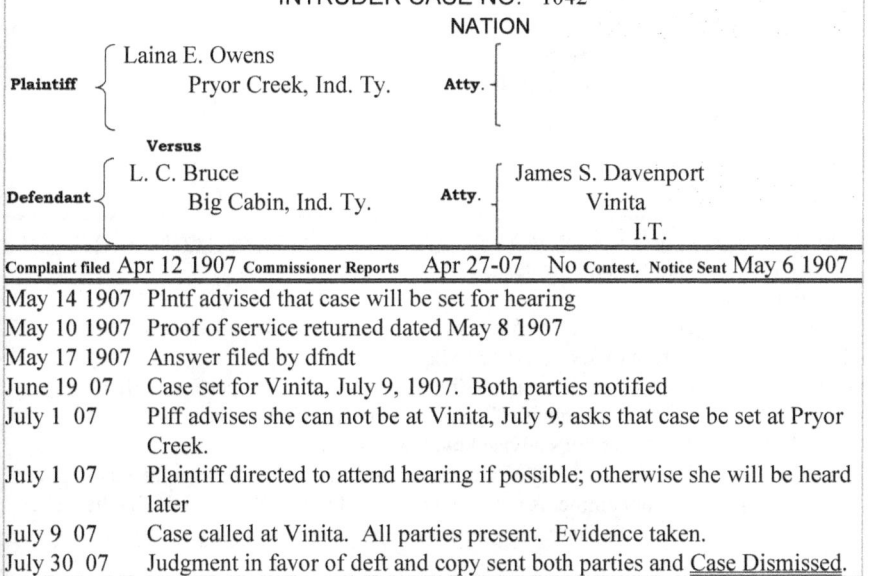

INTRUDER CASE NO. 1042
NATION

Plaintiff: Laina E. Owens, Pryor Creek, Ind. Ty.   **Atty.**

Versus

Defendant: L. C. Bruce, Big Cabin, Ind. Ty.   **Atty.**   James S. Davenport, Vinita I.T.

Complaint filed Apr 12 1907 Commissioner Reports Apr 27-07 No Contest. Notice Sent May 6 1907	
May 14 1907	Plntf advised that case will be set for hearing
May 10 1907	Proof of service returned dated May 8 1907
May 17 1907	Answer filed by dfndt
June 19 07	Case set for Vinita, July 9, 1907. Both parties notified
July 1 07	Plff advises she can not be at Vinita, July 9, asks that case be set at Pryor Creek.
July 1 07	Plaintiff directed to attend hearing if possible; otherwise she will be heard later
July 9 07	Case called at Vinita. All parties present. Evidence taken.
July 30 07	Judgment in favor of deft and copy sent both parties and <u>Case Dismissed</u>.

INTRUDER CASE NO. 1043
NATION

Plaintiff: George B. Keeler, Bartlesville Ind. Ty.   **Atty.**

Cherokee Intruder Cases 1901 - 1909

Defendant	**Versus** Frank Roach et al	Atty.

Complaint filed Apr 9 1907   **Commissioner Reports** Apr 27 -07   No **Contest.** **Notice Sent** May 4 1907

May 11 1907	Proof of service returned dated May 10-1907
May 12 1907	Plntf requested to notify if in possession after ten days.
May 25 1907	Dfndt's again given ten days in which to vacate.
June 19 07	Case set for Vinita, July 9- '07. All parties notified.
June 21 07	Plff advises case settled
June 26 07	Plff notified he need not appear at Vinita and <u>Case Dismissed</u>.

INTRUDER CASE NO. 1044
NATION

Plaintiff	Penny Knott nee Annie P. Malone Tulsa Ind. Ty.	Atty.
Defendant	**Versus** M. R. Glascow Tulsa Ind. Ty.	Atty.

Complaint filed Apr 3 1907   **Commissioner Reports** Apr 23 -07   No **Contest.** **Notice Sent** May 4 1907

May 14 1907	Notice in duplicate sent.
" 26 07	Deft filed ans.
" 31 07	Deft requested to file copy of Case contr under which he claims poss.
May 23 07	Return of service, dated May 19$^{\underline{th}}$ filed
June 19 07	Case set for hearing at Vinita, July 9 1907. All parties notified
June 18 07	W$^{\underline{m}}$ A. Cummings of Catoosa requests information.
June 23 07	Mr. Cummings advised of status of case.
July 9 07	Case called. Plaintiff appeared and stated that she executed a contract & that contract is not being complied with. Pltf. advised that her relief is in U.S. Court. No appearance by Deft. <u>Case Dismissed</u>.

INTRUDER CASE NO. 1045
NATION

Plaintiff	Oliver Wilson gdn of Robert Wilson Fort Gibson Ind. Ty.	Atty.

Cherokee Intruder Cases 1901 - 1909

Defendant	Versus Alex Nivens Fort Gibson Ind. Ty.	**Atty.**

Complaint filed Apr 20 1907 **Commissioner Reports** May 15 -07 **No Contest.** **Notice Sent** May 4 1907

Apr 20 1907	Certificate of homestead allotment #4556
May 4 1907	Com' asked to report
May 10 1907	Proof of service returned & dated May 9 1907 Plntf advises that case has been satisfactorily settled.
May 14 1907	In compliance with request of plntf, case is this day <u>dismissed</u>.

INTRUDER CASE NO. 1046
NATION

Plaintiff	Fred B. Duncan Natrl gdn of Inola Josephine Duncan RFD #3 Chetopa Kansas	**Atty.**
Defendant	Versus James Guthrie James William & John Hackleman Chetopa Kas.	**Atty.**

Complaint filed Apr 9 1907 **Commissioner Reports** Apr 23 '07 **No Contest.** **Notice Sent** May 4 1907

May 9 1907	Proof of service returned dated May 8th 1907
May 10 1907	Dfndt files Answer.
June 19 07	Case set for Vinita, July 9/7. All parties notified.
June 23 07	Deft. forwards letter from Com' F.C.T. directing him to appear before that office July 5th and requests information in re appearing on date of hearing at Vinita.
June 29 07	Jas. Guthrie advised to appear on July 9th at Vinita.
July 9 07	Case called at Vinita. All parties present evidence taken.
Aug 30 07	Com' reports improvements on NE/4 of SE/4 of NW/4 - 13 - 29 -20 appraised to Grace Guthrie at $20.00 and Fred B Duncan is enrolled under Act of Apr 26/06 "new born baby"
6-23 08	Case is dismissed as allottee[sic] is a new-born. Dismissed.

INTRUDER CASE NO. 1047
NATION

Plaintiff	George Washington Natrl gdn of Clifford Washington Vinita, Ind. Ty.	**Atty.**	Gaylord N. Bebont Vinita

Cherokee Intruder Cases 1901 - 1909

Defendant	**Versus** Joe White & family White Oak Ind. Ty.	Atty.	

Complaint filed Apr 9 1907 **Commissioner Reports** Apr 27-07 No **Contest.** **Notice Sent** May 4 1907

June 19 07	Case set for Vinita, July 9 1907. All parties notified.
July 9 07	Case called. No appearance by either party.
July 10 07	G.N. Bebont called and stated he thought plaintiff was in possession will advise office later.
8/24 07	Com asked for report.
Jan 13 08	Case set for hearing Claremore 2/3/8 All parties notified
Jan 15 08	Plaintiff advises case settled & <u>same is dismissed</u>.
Jan 22 08	Plff again advises he is in possession.

INTRUDER CASE NO. 1048
NATION

Plaintiff	Jim Harlin Evansville Ark	Atty.	
Defendant	**Versus** Mr. Cobbs Wimer Ind. Ty.	Atty.	

Complaint filed Apr 22 1907 **Commissioner Reports** May 15 '07 No **Contest.** **Notice Sent** May 4 1907

May 4 1907	Com^r asked to report
Apr 22 1907	Certificates of allotment #58589-58601 in file.
May 17 1907	Proof of service returned dated May 15 1907.
June 18 07	Case set for Muskogee, July 2, 1907. All parties notified
July 3 07	Case called at Muskogee Neither party appeared
8/28 07	Case again set for hearing at Muskogee on Sept 9 -07
Sept 9 08 [sic]	Case called no appearance by either party
5-8 08	Pltf requested to advise in re status of case
6-23 08	Case Dismissed as it is presumed pltf has possession <div align="right">Dismissed.</div>

Cherokee Intruder Cases 1901 - 1909

INTRUDER CASE NO. 1049
NATION

Plaintiff: Ida Long, Vinita, Ind. Ty. **Atty:** Starr & Patton, Vinita

Versus

Defendant: John Wood, Phelix Carbin, Ochelata, Ind. Ty. **Atty:**

Complaint filed Apr 15 1907 Commissioner Reports Mar 15-'07 No Contest. Notice Sent May 4-1907

May 11 1907	Attorneys for plff advise that Ida Long is now in possession.
May 17 1907	Attorneys for plff advised that Case is Dismissed

INTRUDER CASE NO. 1050
NATION

Plaintiff: Jane Mizer for James A Krigbaum, Sallisaw I.T. **Atty:**

Versus

Defendant: James E. Krigbaum, Claremore I.T. **Atty:**

Complaint filed Apr 8 1907 Commissioner Reports May 3 1907 No Contest. Notice Sent May 10 1907

June 18 07	Case set for Muskogee, July 2, 1907. All parties notified
June 27 07	Plaintiff advises she will be unable to appear on July 2-07.
July 2 07	Plff advised to appear any day within next ten days
Sept 11 07	Plaintiff appeared and testimony taken Defendant to be requested to appear or file answer.
" 20 07	Defendant advised to appear at Claremore 10/4/07 and render testimony if he desires.
" 14 07	Pltf encloses letters of guardianship.
Oct 4 07	Case called no appearance by either party
Sept 14 07	Letters of guardianship filed issued to Geo W. Mizer
Nov 8 07	Judgment in favor plaintiff all parties notified defendant given ten days.
Dec 30 08[sic]	Plaintiff states he is in possession and asks return of letters of guardianship which is done Case Dismissed.

Cherokee Intruder Cases 1901 - 1909

INTRUDER CASE NO. 1051
NATION

Plaintiff: Lewis Budder, Eucha, I.T.   Atty.

Versus

Defendant: Clarence Custer, Eucha, I.T.   Atty.   C.B. Rogers, Vinita, I.T.

Complaint filed May 7 1907   **Commissioner Reports** May 22 -'07   **No Contest.**   **Notice Sent** May 10-1907

May 7 1907	Certificate of homestead allotment #3136 in file
May 10 1907	Com^r asked to report
May 22 1907	Proof of service returned dated May 20th 1907
May 25 07	Answer filed by deft.
June 19 07	Case set for Vinita July 9-07. All parties notified.
July 9 07	Case called. All parties present. Testimony taken. Case dismissed as plaintiff's restrictions have been removed and land conveved[sic]. Homestead certificate returned in person. **Dismissed.**

INTRUDER CASE NO. 1052
NATION

Plaintiff: Charley Hughes Jr., Emmett Hughes, Higden I.T.   Atty.   *Settled*

Versus

Defendant: Harve Martin *Freedman*   Atty.

Complaint filed Apr 25 1907   **Commissioner Reports** May 9 '07   **No Contest.**   **Notice Sent** May 21 1907
                                                      7-23-08   No

June 1 07	Return of service, dated May 29-07 filed
June 19 07	Case set for Vinita July 10, '07. All parties notified.
July 10 07	Case called at Vinita. All parties present. Evidence taken.
Aug 24 07	Judgment rendered in favor of plaintiff
Sept 18 07	Plaintiff advised that instructions will be issued to a policeman as soon as possible.
3-25 1912	Form 330 to Allottee Letter #24456-1912
4-25 "	Received letter from Mrs. Martha Hughes to effect controversy settled^

Cherokee Intruder Cases 1901 - 1909

INTRUDER CASE NO. 1053
NATION

Plaintiff: Rufus Cochran gdn
Josie & Dora Cochran
Stillwell, I.T.   **Atty.**

Versus

Defendant: Andrew Clark
Talala
I.T.   **Atty.**

Complaint filed Oct 26 '06 **Commissioner Reports** May 9 '07 No Contest. Notice Sent May 2 1907

Apr 22 1907	Letter of gdnship filed
June 4 07	Return of service, dated May 25/7, filed. Answer filed by deft.
June 5 07	Deft requested to advise if he will surrender poss to plff.
June 7 07	Deft states he is not in poss.
June 11 07	Plff directed to take possession and advise when he has done so.
Jan 11 08	Plaintiff requested to take possession & notify office when done so.
Apr 10 08	Deft again writes in re. payment of rent and is advised.
Apr 18 08	Andrew Clark telephones he will be in Monday the 20th inst.
April 14 08	Judgement[sic] rendered in favor of pltf.
4/22 08	Pltf advised in re status of case Letters of gdn ret'd and case <u>Dismissed</u>

INTRUDER CASE NO. 1054
NATION

Plaintiff: Sarah Brown for
Luther & Clyde Brown
Coffeyville Kas.   **Atty.**

Versus

Defendant: Geo Lane gdn
Chlora Measles Nicholas Miller   Landrum **Atty.**
Seminole I.T.

Complaint filed Apr 23 1907 **Commissioner Reports** May 9 '07 No Contest. Notice Sent May 21st 1907

May 28 07	Return of service dated May 27/7 filed
June 19 07	Case set for Vinita, July 10 1907. All parties notified.
July 10 07	Case called at Vinita. Pltf appeared and evidence taken. No appearance by defendant.
July 22 07	Lease contract filed by pltf today
8/24 07	Judgement[sic] rendered in favor of Pltf.
Oct 19 07	New notice sent as requested by plaintiff.
" 30 07	Proof of service returned dated Oct 21/07.
Nov 5 07	Answer filed by defendant.

Cherokee Intruder Cases 1901 - 1909

" 23 07	Role March files answer for defendant and requests certain information which is furnished.
Dec 5 07	Plaintiff requested if possession is still withheld and if she still desired to be placed in possession
Dec 6 07	Plaintiff called in person and stated she wanted possession right now
Dec 21 07	Instructions issued to Policeman Jas. L. Walker to place pltf in possession
Dec 26 07	Com^r encloses letter of Nicholas Landrum and reports he has been denied enrollment etc.
Jan 2 08	James L Walker reports he placed pltf in possession. Case <u>Dismissed</u>.
Jan 7 08	Pltf asked if in possession & reports on 1/8/8 some as of 1/2/08.

INTRUDER CASE NO. 1055
NATION

Plaintiff — Charles and Annie Dirteater
Moody
Ind, Ty.
Atty.

Versus

Defendant — L.J. Snarr
Oologah
I.T.
Atty.

Complaint filed May 1 1907 **Commissioner Reports**   **Contest. Notice Sent** May 21 1907

May 1 1907	Patents filed with Complaint
May 27 1907	United S. Indian policeman Thomas P. Roach sent instructions to investigate & report
June 4 07	Plffs requested to advise how service was made.
June 18 07	Case set for Muskogee, July 1, 1907. All parties notified.
June 12 07	Plff advises that notice sent by mail <u>was</u> <u>not</u> <u>registered</u>
Jan 10 07[sic]	Case set for hearing Muskogee 1/28/08 All notified
Jan 11 08	Plaintiffs advised date of hearing.
Jan 28 08	Case called. Plffs appeared. No proof of service made but under instructions of C.C. testimony of plff taken L.B. stenog.
Febr 10 08	Deeds of Chas & Annie Dirteater returned to Chas Dirteater in person
Jan 28 08	Pltf stated that he did not know wheather[sic] or not anyone was on land.
Mch 13 -08	Pltf requested to advise in re status of case.
May 16 08	Plaintiff again asked if in possession.
June 22 08	Case Dismissed by order Mr. WWB as plaintiff states he does not know if anyone is in possession Dismissed

Cherokee Intruder Cases 1901 - 1909

INTRUDER CASE NO. 1056
NATION

Plaintiff: Philip B Hopkins, John Doyle, John Leiber, Executors of the este of John W Gleason   Muskogee Ind. Ty.

Atty: John G. Leiber   Muskogee   I.T.

Versus

Defendant: Lige Kelly & One Cooper   Muskogee   I.T.

Atty:

Complaint filed May 11 1907 Commissioner Reports June 4/7 No Contest. Notice Sent May 25-07

May 11 1907	Copy of Letter testamentary & homestead & allottment[sic] certificates filed with complaint
May 25 1907	Com asked to report
June 6 07	Return of service dated June 4/7 filed
June 17 07	Defts requested to file answer within five days, otherwise judgment will render for plff - letters registered
June 27 07	Judgment rendered in favor of plffs. Copy enclosed to each party. Defts given five days to vacate.
July 3 07	Certificates returned to Plaintiff's Atty in person
July 3 07	Instructions issued to Capt Jno C. West to place plffs in poss.
" 6 07	Capt West reported that he had carried out instructions <u>Case Dismissed</u>.

INTRUDER CASE NO. 1057
NATION

Plaintiff: Annie Eagle   Hadley   I.T.

Atty:

Versus

Defendant: Rachel Vann   Chaffee   I.T.   *Freedman*

Atty:

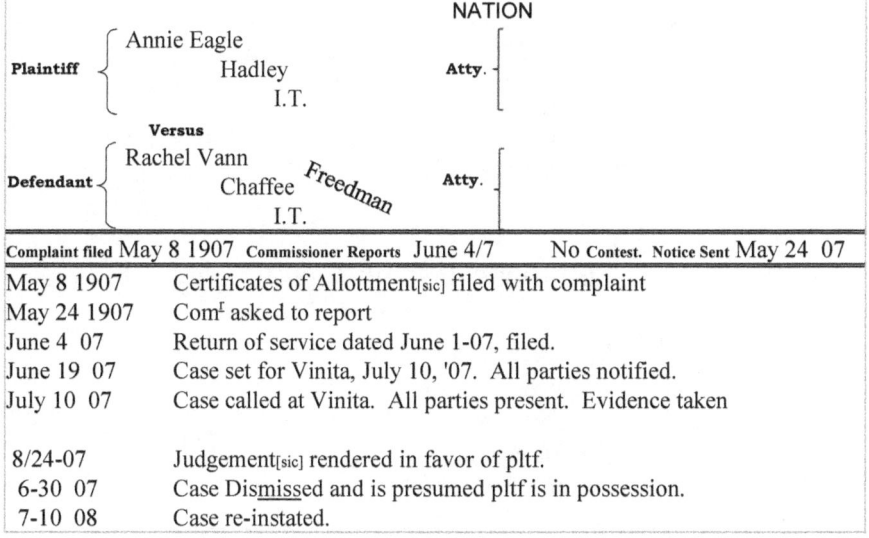

Complaint filed May 8 1907 Commissioner Reports June 4/7 No Contest. Notice Sent May 24 07

May 8 1907	Certificates of Allottment[sic] filed with complaint
May 24 1907	Com^r asked to report
June 4 07	Return of service dated June 1-07, filed.
June 19 07	Case set for Vinita, July 10, '07. All parties notified.
July 10 07	Case called at Vinita. All parties present. Evidence taken
8/24-07	Judgement[sic] rendered in favor of pltf.
6-30 07	Case Di<u>smissed</u> and is presumed pltf is in possession.
7-10 08	Case re-instated.

Cherokee Intruder Cases 1901 - 1909

INTRUDER CASE NO. 1058
NATION

Plaintiff: George W Patrick for Fannie Patrick, Wann I.T. **Atty.**

Versus

Defendant: Robt J. Miles **Atty.**

Complaint filed Apr 27-07 **Commissioner Reports** May 15- '07 **No Contest. Notice Sent** May 24 1907

June 19 07	Case set for Vinita, July 10, 1907. All parties notified.
July 10 07	Case called no appearance by either party.
July 6 -07	Case dismissed by written request of pltf.

<u>Dismissed</u>

INTRUDER CASE NO. 1059
NATION

Plaintiff: Emma M. Hibbs, Muskogee I.T. **Atty.**

Versus

Defendant: Geo W. Mayes, Pryor Creek I.T. **Atty.**

Complaint filed May 15 1907 **Commissioner Reports** June 4/7 **No Contest. Notice Sent** May 24 1907

May 15 1907	Certificates of allotment filed with complaint
May 24 1907	Com^r asked to report
June 5 07	Upon verbal request of plff certif 13523 & 17507 returned to Emma Hibbs and <u>Case Dismissed</u>.

INTRUDER CASE NO. 1060
NATION

Plaintiff: Mrs Peggie Thornton, Wauhillau I.T. **Atty.**

Versus

Defendant: Dr. F.B. Fite & Mr. Hawkins, Muskogee I.T. **Atty.**

Cherokee Intruder Cases 1901 - 1909

Complaint filed May 9 1907 **Commissioner Reports** May 22 '07 No **Contest.** **Notice Sent** May 24 1907	
June 18 07	Case set for Muskogee, July 1, 1907. All parties notified
July 1st 07	Case called at Muskogee Husband of Plaintiff appeared no appearance by Dfdt. Plaintiff states he has not served notice and that matter will probably be adjusted without any action by this office. The Plaintiff is to notify agent when matter has been settled.
July 27 07	Plff asks if she may send notice by mil.
Sept 9 07	Proof of service returned, Registry Ret card in file.
Oct 10 07	Case set for hearing at Muskogee Oct 24, 1907 All parties notified.
" 24 07	Case called Plaintiff appeared no evidence taken no app by defendant but answer is filed by Dr Fite in which he does not claim possession of land but improvements. He was advised to remove improvements & pltf requested to take possession and <u>case dismissed</u>.

INTRUDER CASE NO. 1061
NATION

Plaintiff { Hester & W<u>m</u> Christie / Etta / Ind. Ty.   **Atty.** {

Versus

Defendant { Joe Wealy / Etta / I.T.   **Atty.** {

Complaint filed May 18 1907 **Commissioner Reports** June 4/7 No **Contest.** **Notice Sent** May 25 1907	
May 18 1907	Certificates of allotment filed with complaint
May 24 1907	Com<u>r</u> asked to report
June 3 07	Return of service, dated May 11/7, filed.
June 18 07	Case set for Muskogee, June 29/7. All parties notified.
June 29 07	Case called. All parties present & testimony taken. JEB stenog. Agreement dis by PJH. to stenog. Certs 16955-22991-22993 returned to plff in person.
Jan 11 08	Plaintiffs requested to advise if in possession.
6-23 08	Case dismissed as it is presumed pltf has possession. <u>Dismissed</u>.

Cherokee Intruder Cases 1901 - 1909

INTRUDER CASE NO. 1062
NATION

Plaintiff: Sarah Thompson Nat gdn
Annie Thompson
Lenapah I.T.   **Atty.**

Versus

Defendant: Harrey Martin Adair I.T.
Joshua & Mose Fontleroy
Lenapah I.T.   **Atty.**

Complaint filed May 22 1907 **Commissioner Reports** June 4/7 **No Contest. Notice Sent** May 25 1907

May 22 1907	Certificates of allotment filed with complaint
May 24 1907	Com^r asked to report
May 29 07	Return of service, dated May 28/7, filed
" " "	Answer filed by defts Fountleroy[sic]
June 19 07	Case set for Vinita, July 10-1907. All parties notified.
July 10 07	Case called at Vinita. All parties present. Evidence taken.
Aug 21 07	Judgement[sic] rendered in favor of pltf today & all parties notified.
Aug 31 07	Plaintiff advised that instructions will be issued to a policeman in the near future.
Oct 11 07	Instructions issued to John C. West and plaintiff advised and certificates 34577 & 56357 returned.
Nov 16 07	John C. West reports he went to allotment and give defendant 10 days & at end of ten days plaintiff stated she was in possession and <u>case is dismissed</u>.

INTRUDER CASE NO. 1063
NATION

Plaintiff: Katie Callies
Braggs
I.T.   **Atty.**

Versus

Defendant: Isabel Brown *Freedman*   **Atty.**

Complaint filed May 20 1907 **Commissioner Reports** June 4/7 **No Contest. Notice Sent** May 25 1907

May 20 1907	Certificates of allotment filed with complaint
May 24 1907	Com^r asked to report.
June 1 07	Return of service, dated May 31-07, filed.
June 3 07	Ans filed by defendant.
" 7 07	Com^r asked as to citizenship of Isabel Brown.
June 18 07	Case set for Muskogee, June 29/7. All parties notified.

Cherokee Intruder Cases 1901 - 1909

June 19 07	Com[r] reports Isabella[sic] Brown, an applicant for enrollment as Cherokee freedman, was denied by Sec'y Nov. 22-04; no motion for review pending.
June 29 1907	Case called both parties present testimony taken (RPJ and JEB Stenog's)
July 25 07	Judgment favor of plff. Copy sent both parties. Deft given 20 days.
Nov 6 07	Instructions issued to John C West to place pltf in possession and pltf advised & request to advise Capt West when she can go to allotment. Later instructions withdrawn as Dept has instructed to take no steps now to dispose Cherokee freedmen. Pltf so advised.
3-15 09	Certs #23337 & 33194 returned pltf.
3-25 1912	Form 330 to Allottee[sic].

INTRUDER CASE NO. 1064
NATION

Plaintiff: Mrs Bell Rush Violet, Muskogee, Ind. Ty.   **Atty.**

Versus

Defendant: Jake Looney Elliott, *Freedman*, I.T.   **Atty.**

Complaint filed May 24 1907   **Commissioner Reports**   **Contest. Notice Sent** May 28 1907

May 24 1907	Deeds filed with complaints
June 30(?) 07	Service made on deft by registered mail Reg return card on file
June 20 07	Case set for hearing at Vinita on July 10, 1907. All parties notified
July 10 07	Case called. No appearance by either party.
July 31 07	Deft advised make answer within ten days, otherwise an order will issue to U.S. Indian police to remove him.
July 31 07	Testimony of Plaintiff taken
Aug 26 07	Judgement[sic] rendered in favor of pltf & defdt given ten days
6-30 08	Case dismissed as it is presumed pltf has possession.
7-10 08	Re-instated
Aug 26 08	Instructions issued to Jno C West policeman
Sept 12 08	" carried out and case <u>Dismissed</u>.

Cherokee Intruder Cases 1901 - 1909

INTRUDER CASE NO. 1065
NATION

Plaintiff: James M. and Ethel Walkingstick, Stilwell Ind. Ter. **Atty.**

Versus

Defendant: M. A. Moore, Valeda, Kansas **Atty.**

Complaint filed May 31- 07 **Commissioner Reports** June 11/7 **No Contest. Notice Sent** June 1 -07

	1907	Certificates 21364-30014, James; 21365-30015, Ethel, filed with complaint
June	1	Com^r asked as to contest, etc.
June	20	Case set for Vinita, July 10, '07. All parties notified.
July	10	Case called. Neither party appeared.
July 11	07	Ans filed by defdt today
July 24	07	Judgment
Sept 21	1907	Case set for hearing at Muskogee ITy. Oct 9, 1907. All parties notified.
Oct 8	1907	No appearance by either party.
Jan 10	1908	Case set for hearing Muskogee 1/30/08 All notified.
Jan 30	08	Case called. No appearance by either party.
May 30	08	Plaintiff asked if in possession.
5-25	08	Pltf states case is settled & same is Dismissed and Certificates returned.

INTRUDER CASE NO. 1066
Cherokee NATION

Plaintiff: Thomas J White, Stilwell, Ind. Ter. **Atty.**

Versus

Defendant: Miller Martin, Long, Ind. Ter. **Atty.**

Complaint filed June 4/07 **Commissioner Reports** June 11/7 **No Contest. Notice Sent** June 6/7

	Cert 27210-19577 filed with comp
June 6 07	Com^r asked to report.
June 18 07	Case set for Muskogee, June 29, 1907. All parties notified.
June 18 07	Mrs Millie Morton[sic] makes answer.
June 26 07	Com^r asked to advise in re a seeming discrepancy in their former letter.
June 26 07	Mrs. Morton requested to surrender pos.

Cherokee Intruder Cases 1901 - 1909

June 29 07	Case called. Plff appeared and his testimony taken. Certs returned to plff in person.
July 5 07	Com report filed today. See same in file.
July 28 07	Judgment in favor of complainant, copy sent both parties. Deft given twenty days.
8/24 07	Com^r asked for report.
Aug 30 07	Com^r reports application of Defendant to have improvements appraised <u>denied</u>
Jan 10 08	Pltf requested to advise if in possession.
Jan 14 08	Plaintiff advises he is in possession.
Jan 18 08	As per letter of plff of 14th inst., <u>Case Dismissed</u>.

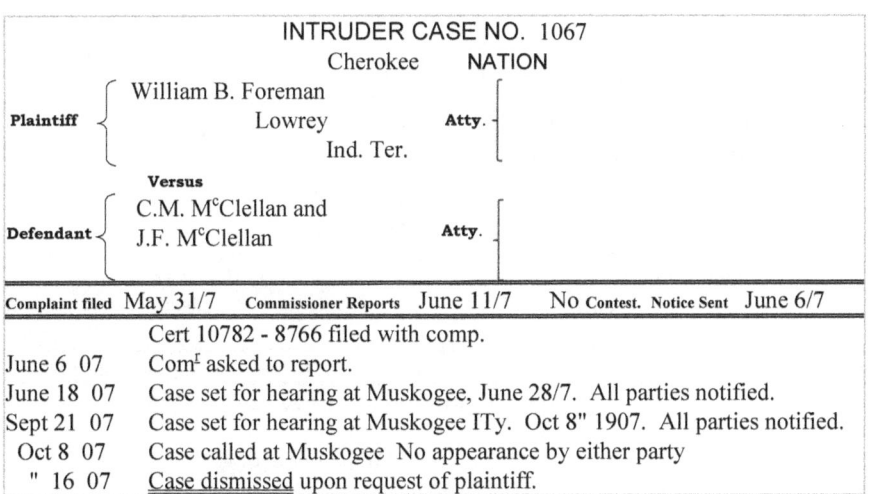

INTRUDER CASE NO. 1067
Cherokee NATION

Plaintiff: William B. Foreman, Lowrey, Ind. Ter. **Atty.**

Versus

Defendant: C.M. McClellan and J.F. McClellan **Atty.**

Complaint filed May 31/7 **Commissioner Reports** June 11/7 No **Contest. Notice Sent** June 6/7

	Cert 10782 - 8766 filed with comp.
June 6 07	Com^r asked to report.
June 18 07	Case set for hearing at Muskogee, June 28/7. All parties notified.
Sept 21 07	Case set for hearing at Muskogee ITy. Oct 8" 1907. All parties notified.
Oct 8 07	Case called at Muskogee No appearance by either party
" 16 07	<u>Case dismissed</u> upon request of plaintiff.

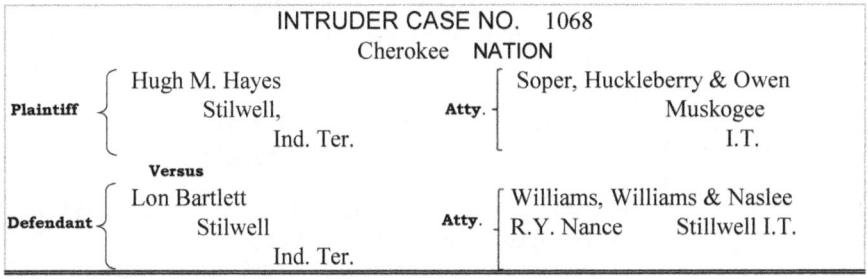

INTRUDER CASE NO. 1068
Cherokee NATION

Plaintiff: Hugh M. Hayes, Stilwell, Ind. Ter. **Atty.** Soper, Huckleberry & Owen, Muskogee I.T.

Versus

Defendant: Lon Bartlett, Stilwell, Ind. Ter. **Atty.** Williams, Williams & Naslee, R.Y. Nance, Stillwell I.T.

Cherokee Intruder Cases 1901 - 1909

Complaint filed May 29/7	Commissioner Reports June 11/7	No Contest. Notice Sent June 6/7
June 6 07	Com^r asked to report.	
June 18 07	Case set for Muskogee, June 28/7. All parties notified.	
June 20 07	Proof of service, dated June 18/7 made.	
June 28 07	Answer filed by deft's attorneys.	
June 28 07	Case called. All parties present and represented by counsel. Testimony taken. E.B. stenog.	
July 26 07	Judgment favor of plaintiff, copy sent both parties. Deft given twenty days	
Jan 10 08	Pltf requested to advise if in possession	
5/4 08	Referred to Thos P. Roach	
5-15 08	Report of Thos P. Roach filed stating pltf now has possession and case is <u>Dismissed</u>.	

INTRUDER CASE NO. 1069
NATION

Plaintiff: J.W. Rider natural gdn of Tip P, Austin W, Augustus and Thos. N. Rider

Atty: Watts & Curtis, Sallisaw, Ind. Ter.

Versus

Defendant: John Rose, Lenapah, Freedman, Ind. Ter

Atty: A.S. McRae, Muskogee, Ind. Ter.

Complaint filed June 6/7	Commissioner Reports June 19/7	No Contest. Notice Sent June 11/7
	Certs 37399-18561-14264-18562-14265-18563-14266-18565 filed	
June 11 07	Com^r asked to report.	
June 20 07	Case set for Vinita July 10, 1907. All parties notified	
June 14 07	Com^r reports John Rose, an applicant for enrollment as intermarried freedman, denied Apr 14,'05; no motion for review on file.	
June 25 07	Answer filed by deft's attorney	
June 26 07	Return of service, dated 6/15/7, made.	
July 10 07	Case called, James S. Davenport, Atty Vinita exhibited a letter from Watts & Curtis. Plaintiff's Attys stating that plaintiff was unable to attend on account of sickness. No appearance by defendant.	
July 15 07	Case set for hearing at Muskogee, I.T. on July 26-07.	
July 24 1907	Mr. Curtis Atty for Plaintiff appeared in person and filed motion for continuance - Case continued	
July 26 1907	Atty for defendant appeared and was advised that case has been continued	
Aug 8 07	Case set for hearing at Muskogee on Aug 22-07	
Aug 22 07	Case called. Atty for Plaintiff appeared No appearance by Plaintiff.	

Cherokee Intruder Cases 1901 - 1909

	Defendant appeared and remained in Muskogee until Aug 23 '07 Atty for the Plaintiff did not appear at this office after the morning of the 22nd - Aug 23 '07 Dfdt requested that the case be continued and that he be notified 30 days in advance of the time of hearing. - Request granted.
8/24 07	Pltf requested to notify this office when he will appear.
8/28 07	Case set for hearing at Muskogee on Sept 27-07
Sept 27 07	Case called Plaintiff telephoned that his baby died and is unable to appear. Defendant appeared and requested that he be given 30 days notice before case is again set. Same granted.
Sept 28/07	Pltf filed motion for cont. Granted and requested to advise 30 days before date wished for hearing so as to notify defendant.

Department of Justice,
Washington.

IN REPLY REFER TO
INITIALS AND NUMBER

Musk 11/20/7
Oct 14/07 Case set for hearing all parties present[sic]
Nov 20/07 Case called all parties present evidence taken
Jan 16/08 Plaintiff advised status of case.
3-27-09   Jess W Watts advised in re status of case
11-26-09   "   " again "
3-25-1912 Form 330 to Allottee[sic].

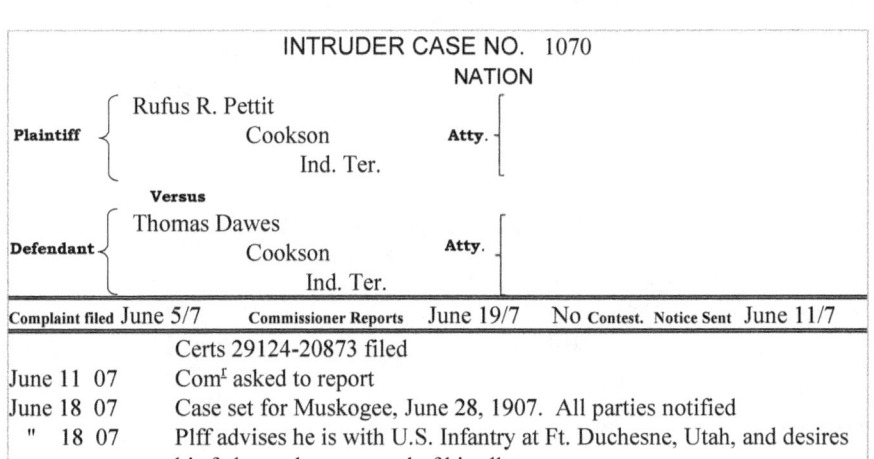

INTRUDER CASE NO. 1070
NATION

Plaintiff   Rufus R. Pettit
              Cookson   Atty.
              Ind. Ter.

Versus

Defendant Thomas Dawes
              Cookson   Atty.
              Ind. Ter.

Complaint filed June 5/7   Commissioner Reports June 19/7   No Contest. Notice Sent June 11/7

	Certs 29124-20873 filed
June 11 07	Com^r asked to report
June 18 07	Case set for Muskogee, June 28, 1907. All parties notified
" 18 07	Plff advises he is with U.S. Infantry at Ft. Duchesne, Utah, and desires his father to have control of his allotment

Cherokee Intruder Cases 1901 - 1909

June 29 07	Rufus R Pettit advised to give his father a power of attorney
July 12 07	Plff advised that case would be further investigated as soon as notice had been served upon the defdt.
July 19 07	Rental contract and affidavit filed by defdt. today
Jan 10 08	Case set for hearing Muskogee 1/29/08 all parties notified
Jan 29 08	Case called. No appearance by either party.
May 16 08	~~Cas~~ Plaintiff asked if in possession or settlement had
6-23 08	Case dismissed & certificates returned as it is presumed that pltf has possession. <u>Dismissed.</u>

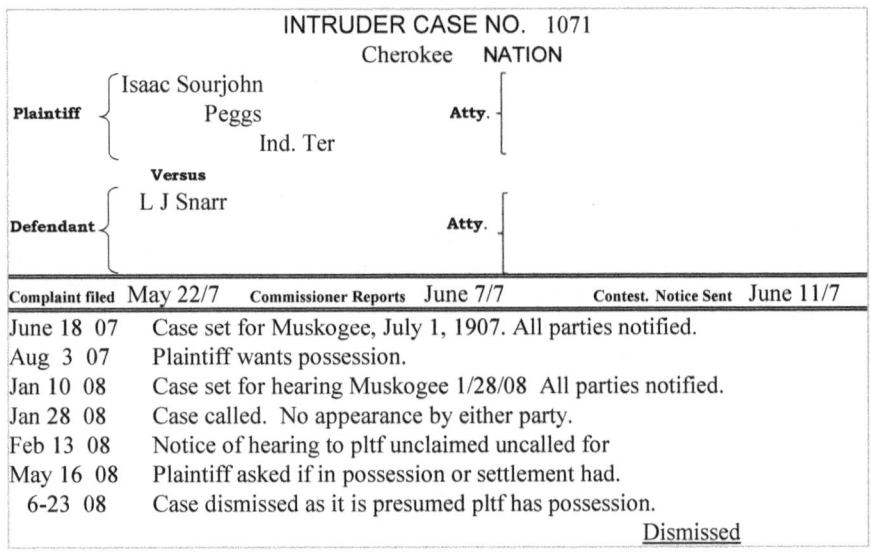

INTRUDER CASE NO. 1071
Cherokee NATION

Plaintiff: Isaac Sourjohn, Peggs, Ind. Ter.   **Atty.**

Versus

Defendant: L J Snarr   **Atty.**

Complaint filed May 22/7   **Commissioner Reports** June 7/7   **Contest. Notice Sent** June 11/7

June 18 07	Case set for Muskogee, July 1, 1907. All parties notified.
Aug 3 07	Plaintiff wants possession.
Jan 10 08	Case set for hearing Muskogee 1/28/08 All parties notified.
Jan 28 08	Case called. No appearance by either party.
Feb 13 08	Notice of hearing to pltf unclaimed uncalled for
May 16 08	Plaintiff asked if in possession or settlement had.
6-23 08	Case dismissed as it is presumed pltf has possession. <u>Dismissed</u>

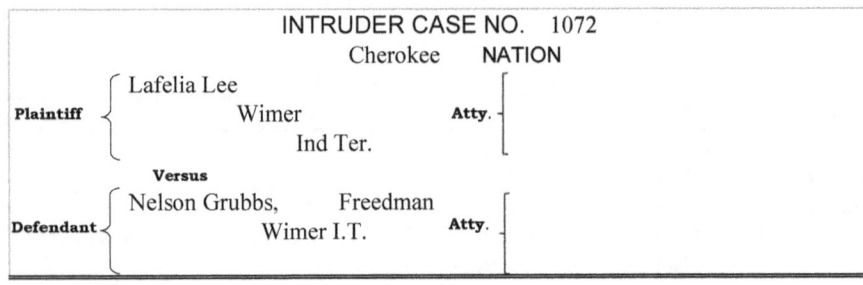

INTRUDER CASE NO. 1072
Cherokee NATION

Plaintiff: Lafelia Lee, Wimer, Ind Ter.   **Atty.**

Versus

Defendant: Nelson Grubbs, Freedman, Wimer I.T.   **Atty.**

Cherokee Intruder Cases 1901 - 1909

Complaint filed June 10 1907 Commissioner Reports	6/28/7 ~~7-27-08~~ ~~No~~ No Contest. Notice Sent June 15 1907
	Certs 63947-38031 filed with complaint
June 15 '07	Com^r asked relative to contest
June 20 07	Return of service made.
July 15 07	Com^r reports application of Nelson Ross[sic] for enrollment as Cherokee Freedman was denied 4/2/10 also that motion for rehearing was denied on Jan 31, 07
July 3 07	Answer filed by Nelson Grubbs Ross
Sept 20 1907	Case set for hearing at Claremore ITy. Oct 2" 1907 All parties notified
Oct 2, 1907	Case called Plaintiff appeared in Person. Evidence taken No appearance by defendant.
7-1 08	Certs ret'd to pltf.
3-26 1912	Form 330 to Allottee[sic].

INTRUDER CASE NO. 1073
Cherokee NATION

Plaintiff { Joe Dirteater
Leach
Ind. Ter. **Atty.**

Versus

Defendant { J. D. Cox
Tahlequah
I.T. **Atty.**

Complaint filed May 27 1907 Commissioner Reports June 11 '07	No Contest. Notice Sent June 15 '07
	Rental contract filed with complaint
July 15 07	Proof of service filed today
July 22 07	Case set for hearing at Muskogee on July 31-07.
July 31 07	Case called at Muskogee I.T. Defendant appeared and his testimony taken no appearance by Plaintiff
Aug 26 07	Pltf requested to appear & submit evidence
Jan 10 08	Pltf requested to appear within 10 days & give evidence
May 16 08	Plaintiff again advised that case would be dismissed if he did not appear and and[sic] give testimony in 10 days.
6-23 08	Case dismissed as it is presumed pltf has possession. Dismissed.

Cherokee Intruder Cases 1901 - 1909

INTRUDER CASE NO. 1074
Cherokee NATION

Plaintiff: Elnora Ross, Muskogee, I.T.
Atty: Howell Parks, Muskogee, I T

Versus

Defendant: Charlotte French *Freedman*
Atty: A S. McRea, Muskogee, IT

Complaint filed May 25 1907 Commissioner Reports June 7/7-07 (7-23-07 all in) No Contest. Notice Sent June 15 '07

Sept 21 1907	Case set for hearing at Muskogee, I.Ty. Oct 9 1907 All parties notified
Oct 9 1907	Case called plaintiff appeared and stated service had not been had and requested case continued. Granted.
" 19 07	A.S. McRea appeared and asked to be entered at Attorney for defendant and that service could be had on him
Jan 13 08	Case set for hearing Claremore 2/3/8 all notified.
Feb 3 08	Case called no appearance by either plaintiff or her Attorney Defendant present, answer filed and evidence taken. Defendant claimant for citizenship
7-23 08	All in contest
3-26 1912	Form 330 to Allottee[sic].

INTRUDER CASE NO. 1075
Cherokee NATION

Plaintiff: Joseph W and Turie Chambers, c/o W.E. Chambers, Claremore, I.T.
Atty:

Versus

Defendant: Mrs. Crutchfield
Atty:

Complaint filed May 31/7 Commissioner Reports June 7/7 No Contest. Notice Sent June 15 1907

Sept 20 1907	Case set for hearing at Claremore I.Ty. Oct 2" 1907 All parties notified
Oct 3 1907	Case called. Plaintiff renders testimony. Power of Atty filed; Def not present
Nov 12 1907	Judgment in favor plaintiff. All parties notified Defendant given ten days
Jan 10 08	Pltfs asked to report if they have possession
May 16 08	Plaintiff requested again to advise if in possession
6-23 08	Case dismissed as it is presumed pltf has possession. <u>Dismissed</u>

Cherokee Intruder Cases 1901 - 1909

INTRUDER CASE NO. 1076
Cherokee NATION

Plaintiff	Hannah E. Jackson, nee Harrison Porum Ind Ter	**Atty.** Mont T. Sharp Muskogee I.T.
	Versus	
Defendant	Webb Wyatt, J S Emerson and Chas McClure Porum, I.T.	**Atty.**

Complaint filed June 19-07 **Commissioner Reports** **Contest. Notice Sent** June 20-07

	Homestead and allotment deeds filed; also copy of lease contract
June 25 07	Return of service made.
July 2 07	Case set for Muskogee, July 17-07 All parties notified
July 2 07	Answer filed by deft Chas McClure.
July 8 07	Case set for hearing at Muskogee on July 17-07
7/19 07	Defdt Mr McClure requested to appear at this office within the next ten days & submit evidence.
July 27 1907	Chas McClure appeared and his testimony was taken.
Aug 13 ✓	J.H. Childers witness for Defendant appeared and rendered testimony
8/26 07	Judgment rendered in favor of defdts and case Dismissed
12/12/07	Lease contract ret^d to Dft who filed same. _Dismissed_
Oct 7 08	A. T. Ingram request return of certain contract claimed to have been filed in this case; advised same never filed.

INTRUDER CASE NO. 1077
NATION

Plaintiff	Price Mouse Eucha I.T.	**Atty.**
	Versus	
Defendant	William L. Trott Vinita, I.T.	**Atty.**

Complaint filed June 14-07 **Commissioner Reports** **Contest. Notice Sent** June 30 1907

	Certs 11937-9727 filed with complaint.
June 20 '07	Com^r asked in re. contest.
June 21 07	E.P. Wolfe, advised of status of case, he having written on behalf of plff
June 24 07	Return of service made -Aug 31-07 Plaintiff requests return of certificates
Sept 5 '07	Plaintiff requested to allow certificates to remain in file until

Cherokee Intruder Cases 1901 - 1909

	investigation has been completed.
Sept 20 1907	Case set for hearing at Claremore ITy Oct 2 1907. All parties notified.
Oct 2 1907	Case called at Claremore. Plaintiff's[sic] renders testimony. Def not present
5-15 08	Defdt notified to surrender possession to pltf & pltf so notified.
6-24 08	Case dismissed as it is presumed that pltf has possession
7-7 08	Certs returned <u>Dismissed</u>

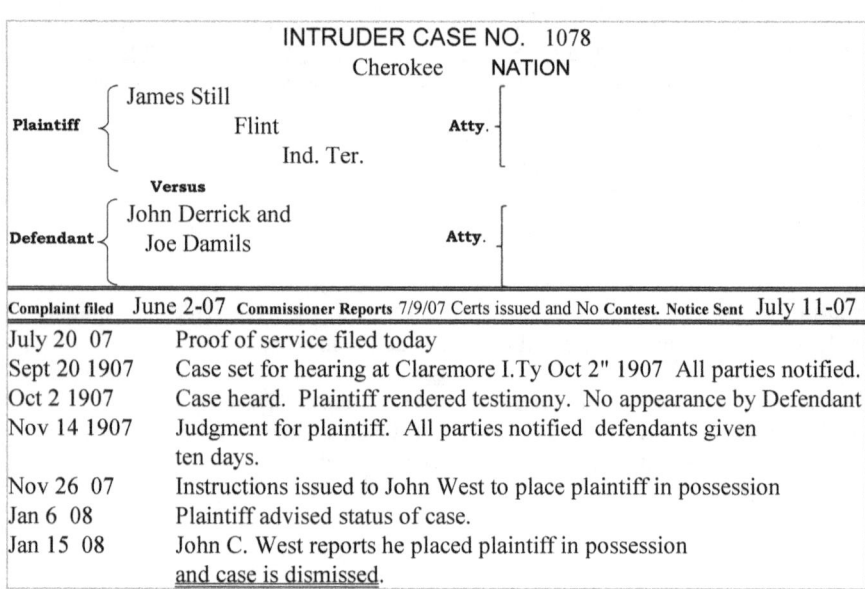

INTRUDER CASE NO. 1078
Cherokee NATION

Plaintiff: James Still, Flint, Ind. Ter.   Atty.

Versus

Defendant: John Derrick and Joe Damils   Atty.

Complaint filed June 2-07   **Commissioner Reports** 7/9/07 Certs issued and No Contest. **Notice Sent** July 11-07

July 20 07	Proof of service filed today
Sept 20 1907	Case set for hearing at Claremore I.Ty Oct 2" 1907 All parties notified.
Oct 2 1907	Case heard. Plaintiff rendered testimony. No appearance by Defendant
Nov 14 1907	Judgment for plaintiff. All parties notified defendants given ten days.
Nov 26 07	Instructions issued to John West to place plaintiff in possession
Jan 6 08	Plaintiff advised status of case.
Jan 15 08	John C. West reports he placed plaintiff in possession <u>and case is dismissed</u>.

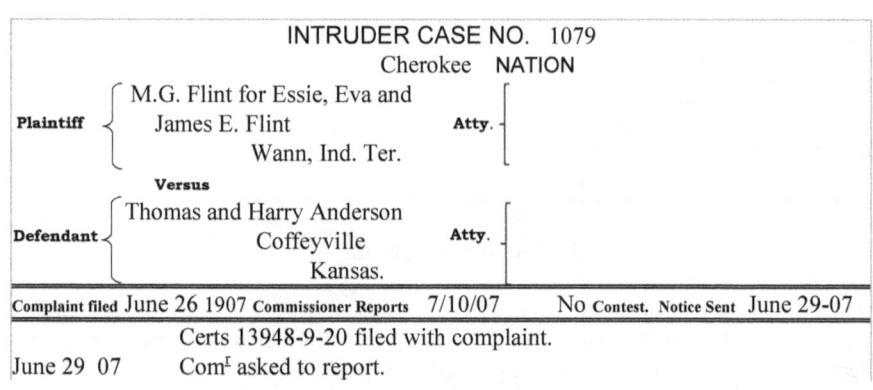

INTRUDER CASE NO. 1079
Cherokee NATION

Plaintiff: M.G. Flint for Essie, Eva and James E. Flint, Wann, Ind. Ter.   Atty.

Versus

Defendant: Thomas and Harry Anderson, Coffeyville, Kansas.   Atty.

Complaint filed June 26 1907   **Commissioner Reports** 7/10/07   No **Contest.** **Notice Sent** June 29-07

	Certs 13948-9-20 filed with complaint.
June 29 07	Com^r asked to report.

Cherokee Intruder Cases 1901 - 1909

July 12 1907	Service returned today
Sept 20 1907	Case set for hearing at Claremore I.Ty. Oct 2" 1907 All parties notified.
Oct 2 1907	Case called. Plaintiff's testimony taken: Plaintiff states he is in possession. Certificates ret. Case <u>dismissed</u>.

INTRUDER CASE NO. 1080
Cherokee NATION

Plaintiff: Sarah Mundis for Nellie and Arrell Mundis Atty.
Coody's Bluff I.T.

Versus

Defendant: Nancy Smith and Bill Reynolds *Freedman* Atty.
Centralia I.T.

Complaint filed June 28-07 **Commissioner Reports** July 25/7 **No Contest. Notice Sent** July 10-07

	Certificates in file.
July 20 1907	Nancy Smith appeared in person and stated that Bill Reynolds is her tenant and that she is a claimant for citizenship as a freedman of the Cherokee Nation
July 29 07	Plaintiff requests immediate action
Aug 3 07	Plff informed case will be set in the near future
Sept 20 1907	Case set for hearing at Claremore I.Ty. Oct 2, 1907 All parties notified.
Oct 2 1907	Case heard. All parties present. Testimony taken.
Nov 27 1907	Pltf asks for possession and is advised no judgment has been rendered as Department has instructed officer not to remove freedmen until further notice
Jan 18 08	Plff again requests to be advised status of case and is advised.
5-23 08	Pltf advised in re status of case
3-3 09	" " " " " " & certificates ret'd.
4-8 09	Dept (Land 22944) thru Com^r's refers letter from pltf for ap. action
4-22 09	Pltf advised
3-26 1912	Form 330 to Allottees[sic].

INTRUDER CASE NO. 1081
Cherokee NATION

Plaintiff: Mary B. Beagles, nee Cordray
4th and Denison Sts. Atty.
Muskogee I.T.

Versus

Cherokee Intruder Cases 1901 - 1909

Defendant: L.J. Snarr, Oologah, I.T. **Atty.**

Complaint filed June 17-07 **Commissioner Reports** 7/3/07 certs issued & No **Contest. Notice Sent** July 10-07

July 15 07	Return of service filed today.
August 3 07	Case set for Muskogee, August 14/7. All parties notified.
8/24 07	Defdt requested to file ans or vacate
Aug 24 07	Plaintiff appeared and her testimony was taken.
Sept 5 07	Letter, with two deeds, which was sent to Plaintiff returned to this office "<u>unclaimed</u>"
Sept 10 07	Deeds returned to Plaintiff in person
" 9 07	Judgment rendered in favor of Plaintiff a copy of judgment sent to each party Defendant given 10 days in which to vacate the allotment
Jan 11 08	Plaintiffs again requested to take possession & advise office Plaintiff requested to advise at once if in possession at once or case will be dismissed upon *(illegible)*
6-17 08	<u>Dismissed</u> as it is presumed pltf has possession

Dismissed

INTRUDER CASE NO. 1082
Cherokee NATION

Plaintiff: Lillie M Conseen for Ella W. Wright, Locust Grove, I.T. **Atty.**

Versus

Defendant: John C. Hogan, Pryor Creek, I.T. **Atty.**

Complaint filed June 17 -07 **Commissioner Reports** 6/20-07 certs issued & No **Contest. Notice Sent** July 10-07

July 18 07	Return of service filed today.
Sept 20 1907	Case set for hearing at Claremore I.Ty Oct 2 1907. All parties notified.
Oct 2 1907	Case called No appearance by either party.
Jan 13 1908	Case set for hearing Claremore 2/3/08. All notified.
Feb 3 1908	Case called no appearance.
Mch 19 08	Notice of hearing to both parties ret'd unclaimed.
May 16 08	Plaintiff advised to report if in possession in 10 days as case will be <u>dismissed</u>.
6-24 08	Case dismissed as it is presumed pltf has possession.

Dismissed

Cherokee Intruder Cases 1901 - 1909

INTRUDER CASE NO. 1083
Cherokee NATION

Plaintiff: Nelson Murphy, Muskogee, I.T. **Atty.** C.E. Holderman, Muskogee, I.T.

Versus

Defendant: Pleasant Alexander, Coffeyville Kasns[sic] *Freedman* **Atty.**

Complaint filed June 20 07 **Commissioner Reports** 7/3/07 certs issued & No Contest. **Notice Sent** July 10-07

July 24 1907	Return of service, dated July 18/7, filed
Sept 18 1907	C.E. Holderman requests that this case be set for hearing at Muskogee
Sept 21 1907	Case set for hearing at Claremore I.Ty Oct 3 1907. All parties notified.
Oct 3 1907	Case called no appearance by either party.
" 11 1907	Defendant states did not receive notice & advised case will again be set for hearing.
Jan 13 08	Case set for hearing Claremore 2/3/8 all notified
Feb 3 08	Case called. All persons present evidence taken. Defendant claimant for citizenship.
Feb 11 08	Com asked if defdt is claimant for citizenship & if rejected.
Feb 15 08	Commission reports motion for rehearing denied.

INTRUDER CASE NO. 1084
Cherokee NATION

Plaintiff: Sallie Brown, Santown[sic], I.T. **Atty.**

Versus

Defendant: William Taylor Vian I.T. and John Taylor and Maud Moore Santown[sic] I.T. **Atty.**

Complaint filed July 2nd 07 **Commissioner Reports** *(Illegible)* No **Contest. Notice Sent** July 10-07

July 10 07	Return of service filed today
July 17 07	Ans filed today
July 22 07	Case set for Muskogee IT for July 30 1907 All parties notified
July 30 07	Case called. Plaintiff appearing but no appearance being made by deft. Plff states Wm Taylor has agreed to pay rents to her and requests that as to Wm Taylor the Case be Dismissed Testimony of plff taken. JEB stenog.
July 31 07	Defts requested to appear at this office not later than Aug 1-07 otherwise an order will issue to remove them

Cherokee Intruder Cases 1901 - 1909

8/17 07	Defdt notified that until he has *(illegible)* he must make satisfactory arrangements with the pltf or vacate
Jan 10 08	Judgment for pltf defendant given 10 days
Jan 15 08	Sallie Brown advises she is in possession
Jan 23 08	In accordance with statement of plaintiff above, <u>Case Dismissed</u>
April 18 08	Com advised in re status of case.
7-9 08	*(Entry completely illegible)*

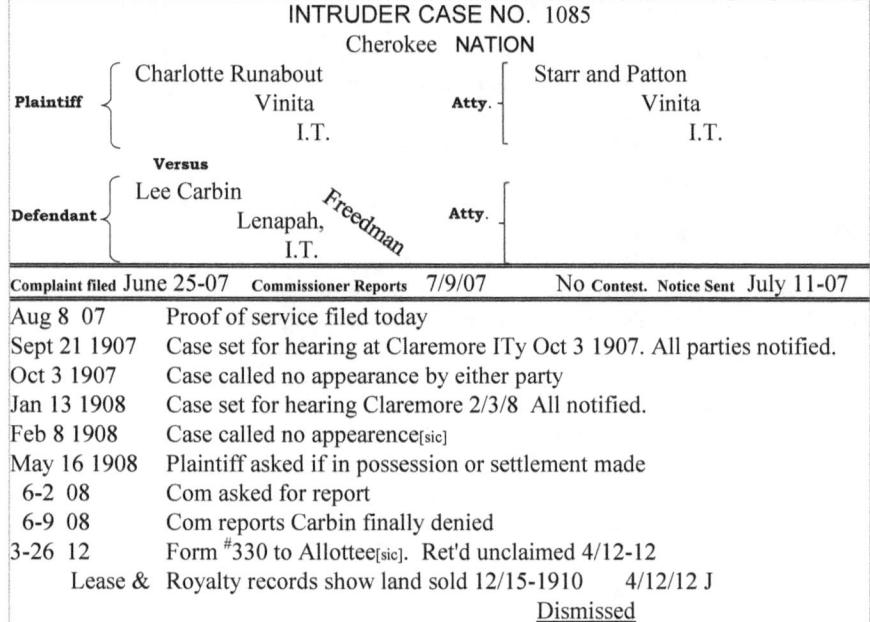

INTRUDER CASE NO. 1085
Cherokee NATION

Plaintiff: Charlotte Runabout, Vinita, I.T.
Atty: Starr and Patton, Vinita, I.T.

Versus

Defendant: Lee Carbin, Lenapah, I.T. *Freedman*
Atty:

Complaint filed June 25-07	Commissioner Reports 7/9/07 No Contest. Notice Sent July 11-07
Aug 8 07	Proof of service filed today
Sept 21 1907	Case set for hearing at Claremore ITy Oct 3 1907. All parties notified.
Oct 3 1907	Case called no appearance by either party
Jan 13 1908	Case set for hearing Claremore 2/3/8 All notified.
Feb 8 1908	Case called no appearence[sic]
May 16 1908	Plaintiff asked if in possession or settlement made
6-2 08	Com asked for report
6-9 08	Com reports Carbin finally denied
3-26 12	Form #330 to Allottee[sic]. Ret'd unclaimed 4/12-12
Lease &	Royalty records show land sold 12/15-1910 4/12/12 J Dismissed

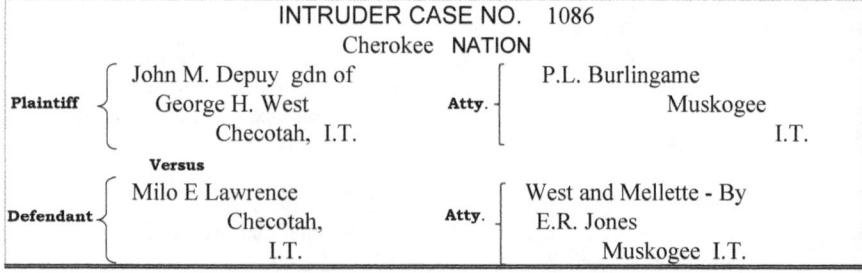

INTRUDER CASE NO. 1086
Cherokee NATION

Plaintiff: John M. Depuy gdn of George H. West, Checotah, I.T.
Atty: P.L. Burlingame, Muskogee I.T.

Versus

Defendant: Milo E Lawrence, Checotah, I.T.
Atty: West and Mellette - By E.R. Jones, Muskogee I.T.

Cherokee Intruder Cases 1901 - 1909

Complaint filed July 9-07	Commissioner Reports Sept 3 '07	No Contest. Notice Sent July 15 -07
	Letter of Gdn in file	
July 22 07	Proof of service filed today	
8/29 07	Case set for hearing at Muskogee on Sept 6-07	
Sept 6 07	Case called at Muskogee Plaintiff and Defendant present and represented by Attys Testimony taken by R.E. Sample stenog!	
Nov 13 07	Judgment in favor of defendant. All parties notified <u>Case dismissed</u>.	

INTRUDER CASE NO. 1087
Cherokee NATION

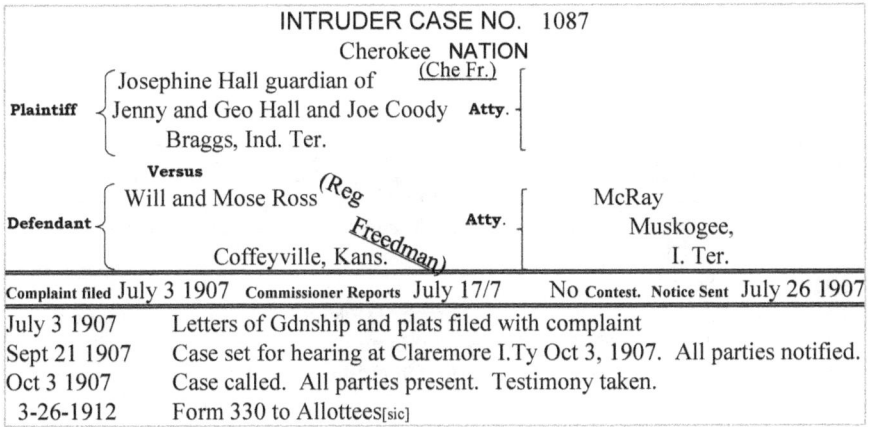

Plaintiff: Josephine Hall guardian of Jenny and Geo Hall and Joe Coody (Che Fr.)
Braggs, Ind. Ter. **Atty.**

Versus

Defendant: Will and Mose Ross (Reg Freedman)
Coffeyville, Kans. **Atty.** McRay
Muskogee, I. Ter.

Complaint filed July 3 1907	Commissioner Reports July 17/7	No Contest. Notice Sent July 26 1907
July 3 1907	Letters of Gdnship and plats filed with complaint	
Sept 21 1907	Case set for hearing at Claremore I.Ty Oct 3, 1907. All parties notified.	
Oct 3 1907	Case called. All parties present. Testimony taken.	
3-26-1912	Form 330 to Allottees[sic]	

INTRUDER CASE NO. 1088
Cherokee NATION

Plaintiff: Robert Groom, gdn of Leeot[sic] Groom Chetopa, Kansas **Atty.** C.E. Holderman Muskogee Ind. Ter.

Versus

Defendant: Frank Wall and Ira Thomas Chetopa Kans **Atty.**

Complaint filed July 23 07	Commissioner Reports	Contest. Notice Sent July 27/7
	Letters of gdnship and Cert 8263 filed with complaint	
Sept 31 1907	Case set for hearing at Claremore ITy. Oct 3 1907. All parties notified.	
Oct 3 1907	Case called. Plaintiff renders testimony. Def not present.	
" " 1907	Proof of service returned dated Oct 3, 1907.	
Nov 12 1907	Judgment in favor plaintiff. All parties notified.	

Cherokee Intruder Cases 1901 - 1909

	Defendant given ten days.
Jan 11 1908	Plaintiff requested to advise if in possession.
May 16 1908	Plaintiff again requested to advise if in possession
5-26 08	Pltf states he has possession & case is Dismissed and Certs ret'd

INTRUDER CASE NO. 1089
Cherokee NATION

Plaintiff	James E Bell for James E Bell, Jr. and Mark R. Bell Oologah, I.T.	Atty.	
	Versus		
Defendant	F.P. Mitchell and A.C. Schnoy Oologah, I.T.	Atty.	W.H. Kronga Vinta I.T.

Complaint filed July 30 1907 **Commissioner Reports** 8/8/07   7-23-08 No.   **No Contest. Notice Sent** July 31-07

July 31 07	Com^r asked to report. Certs 435-437-502 having been filed with complaint Letters of gdn in file & parties in interest notified that case will be set for hearing.
8/15/07	Ans filed
8/26 07	Case set for hearing at Claremore ITy Oct 3 1907. All parties notified.
Sept 21 1907	Certificate No 500 filed by plntf in person.
Sept 21 1907	Certificate no 500 filed by plntf in person
Oct 3 1907	Case called & all parties present: Testimony taken; Cers 437-502 Ret Plaintiff
Oct 4 07	Com^r rept[sic] no contest. Imp appraised to rejected Int. Married whites
Oct 5 1907	Pltf file Com^r report showing S 20: 54 acres Lot 1. S 30 T. 23 N 15E is in contest, and advised that no action can be taken for that land until improvements are appraised and paid for. Defendant claims no right to any land except that appraised to Int. Married citizens. Deft also disclaims as to land of Mark Bell. Case Dismissed as to him. (W.W.B. makes entry)
Nov 9 07	Copy of testimony sent defendant
6-24 08	Case dismissed & certificates ret'd for it is presumed pltf has possession.
7-11-08	Judgment rendered in favor of pltf and defdt given ten days
7-25-08	Instructions issued to Capt West
Aug 17 08	Capt West reports placing pltf in possession excepting a certain house; controversy over lines: & case is Dismissed
Aug 24 08	Jas E Bell transmits certs $^\#$435-500 of Jas E. Jr together with certified plat showing location of house. Capt West verbally instructed to place in poss.
Sept 26 "	Pltf advised of above.
Oct 6 08	Jas E Bell's certs returned
" " "	Capt West places him in pos. of remainder of land.

Cherokee Intruder Cases 1901 - 1909

	INTRUDER CASE NO. 1090	
	Cherokee NATION	
Plaintiff	Jno C Dannenberg, Attorney in fact for Daniel E. Dannenberg Tahlequah, Ind. Ter.	Atty.
	Versus	
Defendant	L.H. and Elizabeth Harrington Jno and Cynthia Morgan Coffeyville Kans	Atty.

Complaint filed July 10 1907 **Commissioner Reports** July 20 1907 **No Contest. Notice Sent** July 31 1907

Aug 20 '07	John C Dannenberg appeared in person and stated that he is now in unrestricted possession of allotment Case Dismissed
Nov 20 07	Defendant files answer and is advised case was <u>dismissed as</u> plaintiff states he was in possession.
Jan 17 08	J C Dannenberg writes asking removal of Geo Kniseley
" 21 08	Mr. Dannenberg advised that having once placed him in possession, this office can take no further action. <u>Dismissed.</u>

	INTRUDER CASE NO. 1091		
	Cherokee NATION		
Plaintiff	Mary A. Gillman, gdn. of Henrietta Gillman Catoosa Ind. Ter.	Atty.	
	Versus		
Defendant	Wylie Brown Catoosa Ind. Ter.	Atty.	Wade S Stanfield Claremore I.T.

Complaint filed July 30 1907 **Commissioner Reports**   **Contest. Notice Sent** Aug 1-07

	Letters of guardianship, certs 39230-27074 and Case filed with complaint
August 2 1907	Com^r asked to report
" 7[sic]	Proof of service filed today
" 14 '07	Action with held upon request of Judge L.T. Parker See letter from W.S. Stanfield, Atty.
" 14 '07	See copy of Petition filed in U S Court. filed in this case by Atty for Defendant
Aug 27 07	Judge Parker advised that this office will take no further action in this matter until he has hearing in Probate case
Aug 28 07	Wade S Standfield[sic] requested to report the date of hearing of the action pending in the US Court which envolves[sic] the land which is

Cherokee Intruder Cases 1901 - 1909

	envolved in this case.
Sept 5 '07	Plaintiff advised of status of case
" 14 "	" " " " " "
" 28 "	" requested to advise as to status of case
" 28 "	" advised that U.S.C. requested to withhold action
Oct 14 07	Contract returned to plaintiff.
Nov 7 07	Plaintiff asked status & advised no action can now be taken.
Mc 18 08	Pltf advised in re status of case.
6-9 08	" " " " " " "
6-24 08	Pltf advised in re status of case & same is dismissed & *(illegible)* & certificates ret'd. <u>Dismissed</u>

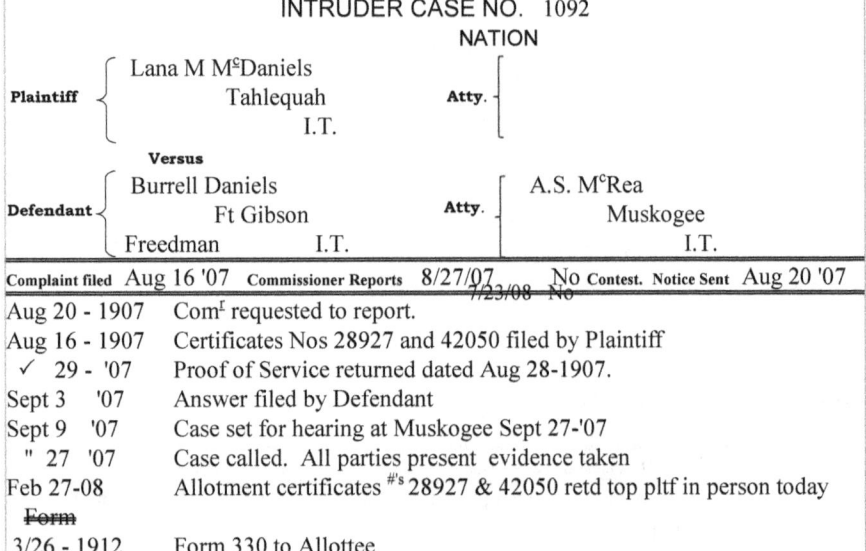

INTRUDER CASE NO. 1092
NATION

Plaintiff: Lana M McDaniels, Tahlequah, I.T.   Atty.

Versus

Defendant: Burrell Daniels, Ft Gibson, Freedman, I.T.   Atty. A.S. McRea, Muskogee, I.T.

Complaint filed Aug 16 '07   Commissioner Reports 8/27/07 7/23/08 ~~No~~ No Contest. Notice Sent Aug 20 '07

Aug 20 - 1907	Com^r requested to report.
Aug 16 - 1907	Certificates Nos 28927 and 42050 filed by Plaintiff
✓ 29 - '07	Proof of Service returned dated Aug 28-1907.
Sept 3 '07	Answer filed by Defendant
Sept 9 '07	Case set for hearing at Muskogee Sept 27-'07
" 27 '07	Case called. All parties present evidence taken
Feb 27-08	Allotment certificates ^{#s} 28927 & 42050 retd top pltf in person today
~~Form~~ 3/26 - 1912	Form 330 to Allottee

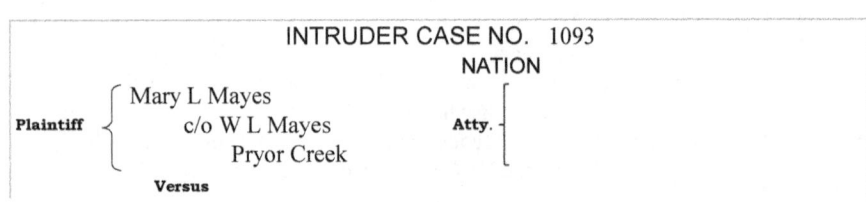

INTRUDER CASE NO. 1093
NATION

Plaintiff: Mary L Mayes, c/o W L Mayes, Pryor Creek   Atty.

Versus

Cherokee Intruder Cases 1901 - 1909

Defendant	Mary Beck Bartlesville IT	Atty.	Chas C. Julian Bartlesville I.T.

Complaint filed Aug 17 '07 **Commissioner Reports** 8/27/07, 4/23-08 **No Contest.** **Notice Sent** Aug 20 '07

Aug 20 '07	Com^r requested to report.
✓ 17 '07	Certificates Nos 38734 and 64149 filed by Plaintiff
Sept 10 '07	Proof of Service returned dated Sept 9 - '07
Sept 13 '07	Com^r requested to report as to citizenship of Mary Beck
	Answer filed by Chas C. Julian for Defendant
Sept 21 1907	Case set for hearing at Claremore I.Ty. Oct 3, 1907. All parties notified.
" 25 1907	Com^r reports Mary Beck rejected freedman and no motion to reopen or review pending.
Oct 3 "	Motion filed by Deft for continuance & Denied
" 3 1907	All parties present, testimony taken.
Jan 14 1908	Allotment Certfs returned to plaintiff's husband in person.
3-26-1912	Form 330 to Allottee

INTRUDER CASE NO. 1094
NATION

Plaintiff	Jess Robertson Nat Gdn of W^m H Robertson Manard I.T.	Atty.	

Versus

Defendant	Jennie Cross Freedman	Atty.	A S McRea Muskogee I.T.

Complaint filed Aug 15 '07 **Commissioner Reports** 8/27/07 **No Contest.** **Notice Sent** Aug 20 1907

Aug 20 '07	Com^r requested to report.
✓ 15 '07	Certificates Nos 34983 and 24527 filed by Plaintiff
29 '07	Proof of Service returned dated Aug 27 - '07
Sept 10 '07	Case set for hearing at Muskogee I.T. Sept 26 - '07
✓ 3 '07	Answer filed by Defendant
✓ 10 07	Com^r requested to report status of citizenship case of defendant
" 20 07	Com^r reports defendant denied enrollment
" 26 07	Case called all parties present evidence taken.
" 18 08	Letter from pltf asking status of case
" 26 "	" answered
2-11- 09	Deft advised no action can be taken to assist her
Nov 3 1909	Jennie Cross writes dept.
Nov 17 1909	Report to Dept made.
3-26 1912	Form 330 to Allottee

Cherokee Intruder Cases 1901 - 1909

INTRUDER CASE NO. 1095
NATION

Plaintiff: Arthur King Nat Gdn. of Geo W. and Pauline M King, Hollow I.T.   **Atty.**

Versus

Defendant: Dock Brown   **Atty.** A S McRea, Muskogee I.T.

Complaint filed Aug 8 '07   **Commissioner Reports** 8/27/07 portion in **Contest.**   **Notice Sent** Aug 20 '07

Aug 20 '07	Com^r requested to report
✓ 8 07	Certificates Nos 64125, 38110, 64127 and 38111 filed by Plaintiff
Sept 10 '07	Answer filed by defendant's Atty.
Sept 21 07	Case set for hearing at Claremore ITy Oct 3 1907. All parties notified.
Oct 3 07	Case called: Evidence taken. Def not present.
" 18 07	Pltf advised Judgment will be rendered as soon as possible.
Nov 9 07	Plff advised that allottees[sic] are New-born children enrolled under Act of April 26/6 and no action can be taken by this office pending the determination of the "Cherokee Baby" case in Supreme Court.
6-24 08	Case dismissed as pltf is a N.B. & allotment certs returned.

Dismissed.

INTRUDER CASE NO. 1096
NATION

Plaintiff: Wm P. Rider Nat Gdn of Jennie May Rider, Ruby I.T.   **Atty.**

Versus

Defendant: Chas Walker, Ruby I.T.   **Atty.**

Complaint filed Aug 13 '07   **Commissioner Reports** 8/27/07   No **Contest.** of New Born **Notice Sent** Aug 20

Aug 20 07	Com^r requested to report.
✓ 13 '07	Certificates Nos 63314 and 37677 filed by Plaintiff.
Aug 29 07	Proof of Service date 8/27/7 returned - unsigned
Sept 6 07	" " " " " " to Plaintiff for Signature
" 16 07	Case set for hearing at Claremore ITy Oct 3, 1907. All parties notified.
Oct 3 07	Proof of Service returned signed.
" 9 07	Case called No appearance by either party.
Jan 13 08	Pltf asked said in col. rent & advised office has no jurisdiction.
Feb 3 08	Case set for hearing Claremore 2/3/8 all parties notified.

Cherokee Intruder Cases 1901 - 1909

	Case called Plaintiff appeared his evidence taken. He admits that allottee[sic] is a "new born" and defendant a Rej Freedman. He was advised no action could be taken until case of Court Claims was decided. No appearance by defendant.
6-28 08	Case dismissed as pltf is a N.B. & allotment acts. set'd. <u>Dismissed</u>.
Nov 24 08	Pltf advised in re status of case.

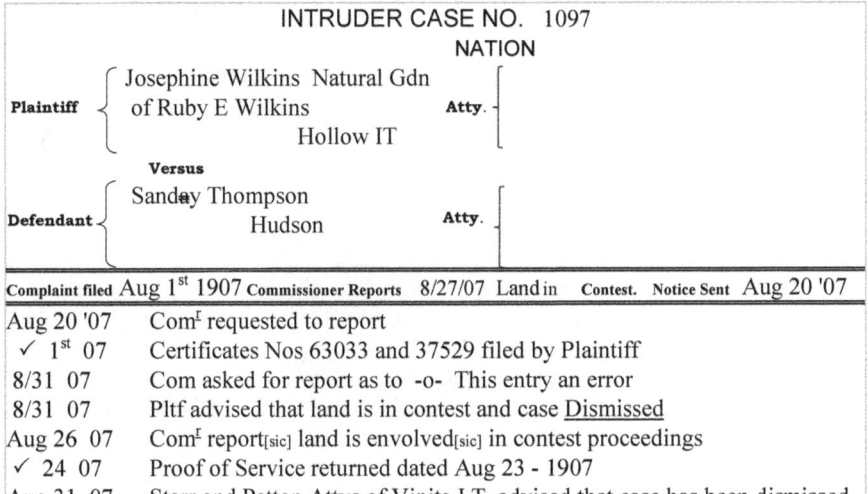

INTRUDER CASE NO. 1097
NATION

Plaintiff: Josephine Wilkins Natural Gdn of Ruby E Wilkins — Hollow IT   Atty.

Versus

Defendant: Sanday Thompson — Hudson   Atty.

Complaint filed Aug 1st 1907   Commissioner Reports 8/27/07 Land in Contest. Notice Sent Aug 20 '07

Aug 20 '07	Com^r requested to report
✓ 1st 07	Certificates Nos 63033 and 37529 filed by Plaintiff
8/31 07	Com asked for report as to -o- This entry an error
8/31 07	Pltf advised that land is in contest and case <u>Dismissed</u>
Aug 26 07	Com^r report[sic] land is envolved[sic] in contest proceedings
✓ 24 07	Proof of Service returned dated Aug 23 - 1907
Aug 31 07	Starr and Patton Attys of Vinita I.T. advised that case has been <u>dismissed</u>

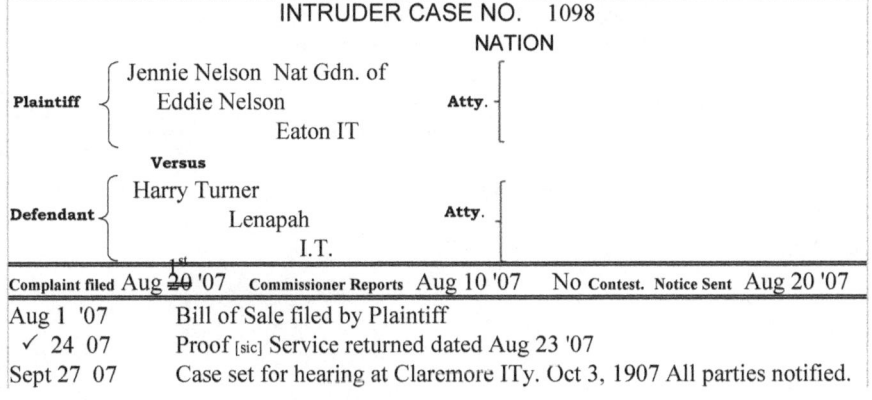

INTRUDER CASE NO. 1098
NATION

Plaintiff: Jennie Nelson Nat Gdn. of Eddie Nelson — Eaton IT   Atty.

Versus

Defendant: Harry Turner — Lenapah I.T.   Atty.

Complaint filed Aug 1st '07   Commissioner Reports Aug 10 '07   No Contest. Notice Sent Aug 20 '07

Aug 1 '07	Bill of Sale filed by Plaintiff
✓ 24 07	Proof [sic] Service returned dated Aug 23 '07
Sept 27 07	Case set for hearing at Claremore ITy. Oct 3, 1907 All parties notified.

Cherokee Intruder Cases 1901 - 1909

Oct 3 07	Case called. Defendant present. Case continued.
Jan 13 08	Case set for hearing Claremore 2/4/07 all notified.
Feb 4 08	Case called. No appearance by plaintiff. Defendant appeared and disclaimed any right to plaintiff's land, but states he has filed his minor child on N 1/2 of NW 1/4 of NW 1/4 of Sec 15-78-15. Case dismissed.

INTRUDER CASE NO. 1099
NATION

Plaintiff: Lizzie W. Trammell
c/o Watts and Curtis
Sallisaw IT

Atty. Watts & Curtis
Sallisaw
I.T.

Versus

Defendant: J. K. Crutchfield
Claremore
I.T.

Atty.

Complaint filed Aug 5 1907 **Commissioner Reports** Aug 13 '07, 7-23-08 No **No Contest. Notice Sent** Aug 20 '07

Aug 23 '07	Notice returned for correction in name
Aug 28 07	Corrected Notice sent to Plaintiff
Sept 3 07	Proof of Service returned dated Aug 31 '07
Sept 21 1907	Case set for hearing at Muskogee ITy Oct 9 1907. All parties notified.
Oct 9 1907	Case called. Plaintiff appeared evidence taken. No appearance by defendant
" 14 07	Ptf requests status of case and advised. Deft given 12 days to appear and give testimony.
" 21 07	Pltff requests action taken & advised defendant had been given 10[sic] days to appear and render evidence
" 24 07	Geo L. Struble asks status of this case and advised. (See carbon)
Nov 14 07	Judgment in favor of plaintiff, all parties notified and defendant given 10 days.
Jan 11 08	Plaintiff requested to advise if in possession
Feb 12 08	Instructions issued to Capt John C West to place pltf in possession
4/28 08	Referred to Thomas P. Roach
5-15 08	Report of Thos P Roach filed
6-22 08	Pltf advised.
July 2 08	Case <u>Dismissed</u> on advice from Pltf's Attys.

Cherokee Intruder Cases 1901 - 1909

INTRUDER CASE NO. 1100
NATION

Plaintiff: Don Akins, Sallisaw IT   Atty.

Versus

Defendant: O. U. Freeman, Nowata I.T.   Atty.

Complaint filed Aug 14 '07 **Commissioner Reports** 6/27/07 No **Contest. Notice Sent** Aug 20 '07

Aug 20 '07	Com[r] requested to report
✓ 13 07	Certificate of Allotment No 57848 filed by Plaintiff
Sept 9 07	Proof [sic] Service returned dated Sept 2nd '07
✓ 7 07	Com[r] requested to report as to citizenship of Defendant.
Sept 27" '07	Case set for hearing at Muskogee ITy Oct 10, 1907. All parties notified.
" 23 '07	Com[r] reports that name of O. U. Freeman cannot be identified on applicant for citizenship. Osa Freeman has been finally denied and no motion pending
Oct 10 07	Case called. All parties present Evidence taken.
3/26 1912	Form 330 to Allottee[sic]
4-25 "	Acting Dist Agt advised that Oce Freeman had appeared before him
" " "	and advised him that he has relinquished all claim to land Letter #25007

INTRUDER CASE NO. 1101
NATION

Plaintiff: Strange W. Akin, Tulsa I.T.   Atty.

Versus

Defendant: Thos D Bard, Chelsa[sic] I.T.   Atty.

Complaint filed Aug 12 07 **Commissioner Reports** 8/27/07 No **Contest. Notice Sent** Aug 20 '07

Aug 20 - 07	Com[r] requested to report.
✓ 12 - 07	Certificates Nos 32053 and 46206 filed by Plaintiff
Sept 9 '07	Proof [sic] Service returned dated Sept 4 '07
✓ ✓ ✓	Com[r] requested to report as appraisment[sic] of improvements
Sept 21 1907	Case set for hearing at Claremore I.Ty. Oct 3, 1907. All parties notified.
" 20 1907	Com[r] reports Thomas D. Bard is a rejected ~~freedman~~ intermarried citizen and that the improvements upon SW^4 NW^4 & *(illegible)* MW[sic] "SW" have been appraised to him.

Cherokee Intruder Cases 1901 - 1909

Oct 3 - 07	Platf appeared and exhibited motion from Commission showing improvements were *(illegible)* to Deft and $150^{00} and states he has not paid for same
	Def appeared, advised no action until imp paid for
Jan 13/08	Case set for hearing Claremore 2/4/08 All parties notified
Feb 4/08	Case called No appearence[sic].
May 16/08	Plaintiff asked if in possession or settlement had.
5-22-08	Referred to R. Short for investigation
5-26-08	Report of R. Short filed & case[sic]
6-24-08	Case dismissed as Short reports Pltf has possession
	Dismissed

INTRUDER CASE NO. 1102
NATION

Plaintiff: Ana Ridge, Eucha

Atty.: J. B. West, Spavinaw I.T.

Versus

Defendant: Nicy Vann, Chaffee I.T. *Freedman*

Atty.:

Complaint filed Aug 10 '07 Commissioner Reports 8/27/07 7-23-8 No Contest. Notice Sent 8/20 07

Aug 10 07	Certificate No 15843 filed by Plaintiff
✓ 20 07	Com^r requested to report
Sept 6 07	Plaintiff requested to make return of Service
Aug 30 07	" asks that action be taken as once
Sept 21 1907	Case set for hearing at Claremore ITy Oct 4, 1907. All parties notified.
" 18 1907	Proof of Service returned
Oct 2 1907	Application for continuance file by McRay[sic].
Oct 1 1907	Plaintiff requested to appear at Claremore Oct 4 1907
" 4 1907	Case called No app by either party.
Nov 6 1907	Pltf adv. case will again be set for hearing.
" 19 1907	Pltf requested to be placed in possession and advised that Dept has instructed not to remove rejected freedman
Mch 13 08	Pltf advised in re status of case.
3/26 1912	Form 330 to Allottee

Cherokee Intruder Cases 1901 - 1909

INTRUDER CASE NO. 1103
NATION

Plaintiff: David Hughes, Halbert, I.T.
Atty.: (Name Illegible), Claremore OK.

Versus

Defendant: H.A. Hills, H[sic]
Atty.:

Complaint filed Aug 8 07 **Commissioner Reports** 8/7/07 **No Contest. Notice Sent** Aug 20 '07

Jan 13 08	Case set for hearing Claremore 2/4/08 all parties notified
Feb 4 08	Case called. Plaintiff appeared evidence taken. No appearance by defendant. Plaintiff files certified copy of W.P.
Feb 27 08	Lease contract filed by O.M. Hollingsmith today.
Apr 15 08	Com F.C.T. requested to advise in re degree of blood of plff.
April 18 08	Com report Pltf is 1/2 blood.
4/27 08	Submitted to J.G. Wright to have proceedings instated in U.S. Court and <u>Case Dismissed</u>.

INTRUDER CASE NO. 1104
NATION

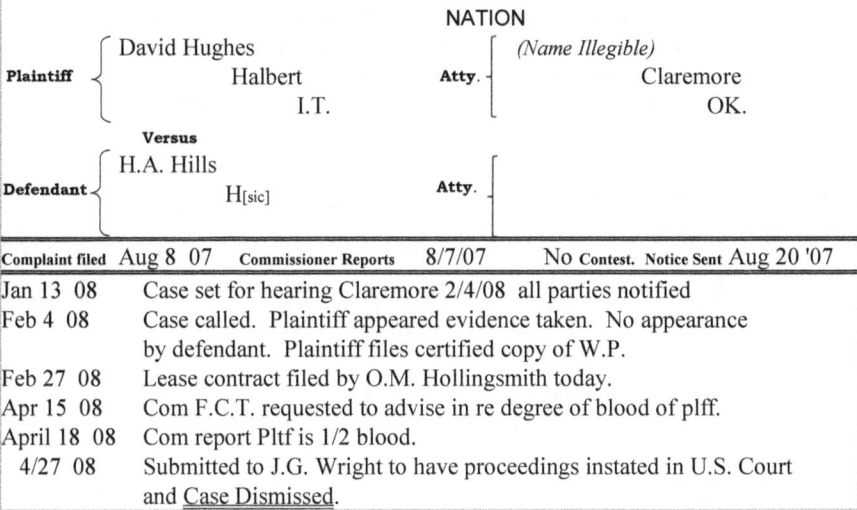

Plaintiff: Mrs Lizzie Rogers for herself and as legal Gdn of Malt Lee, Mamie E and Sylvester A Rogers Heirs of T L Rogers Dec'd.
Atty.:

Versus

Defendant: Maggie Willis Elliott Freedman I.T.
Atty.: Roy T. Osborn, Coffeyville Kans.

Complaint filed July 24 '07 **Commissioner Reports** 7-23-08 **No Contest. Notice Sent** Aug 20 '07

July 24 07	Order of U.S. Court and Letters of Gdnship filed by Pltf.
Aug 26 07	Proof of Service returned dated Aug 23 - 1907
✓ 30 ✓	Answer filed by Plaintiff [sic]
Sept 5 ✓	Com^r requested to report as to citizenship of Defendant.
Sept " "	Com^r states M.W. denied enrollment and no motion for review pending.
Sept 21 1907	Case set for hearing at Claremore ITy. Oct 4 1907. All parties notified.
" 20 1907	Plaintiff requests to be put in possession.
" 23 1907	Plaintiff advised case set for hearing Oct 4/07.
Oct 4 1907	Case called: Plaintiff gives testimony. Defendant not present
Oct 2 1907	Defendant files motion for continuance
" 9 1907	Defts request for continuence[sic] denied and advised to appear within ten days and give testimony

215

Cherokee Intruder Cases 1901 - 1909

"	16 07	Defendants state ~~they~~ she will appear and give testimony with set time.
"	17 07	Roy T Osborne called in person and filed affidavits of Maggie Willis & Charles C. Smith and requests that same receive con. as defendant is without means to appear & render evidence.
Nov 6 07		Pltf advised no action can now be taken to remove freedmen
Dec 2 07		Plaintiff advised fully status case.
2-15 09		Pltf " " " "
3-26 1912		Form 330 to Allottee

INTRUDER CASE NO. 1105
NATION

Plaintiff Cinderella Reynolds Manard I.T. Atty.

Versus

Defendant C. F. McElhney Manard I.T. Atty.

Complaint filed	July 25 07	Commissioner Reports	8/6 '07	No Contest. Notice Sent	Aug 20 '07
Aug 27 07	Proof Error				
Sept 5 07	Case dismissed upon request of Plaintiff				

INTRUDER CASE NO. 1106
NATION

Plaintiff Martin Hopper c/o W.A. Chase Atty Nowata I.T. Atty. W A Chase Nowata I.T.

Versus

Defendant John Johnson Childers I.T. Atty.

Complaint filed	Aug 12 '07	Commissioner Reports	8/20 '07	Contest. Notice Sent	Aug 20
Aug 29 07	Proof of Service returned dated Aug 26th 07				
Sept 21 1907	Case set for hearing at Claremore ITy Oct 4, 1907. All parties notified				
Oct 4 1907	Case called No appearance by either party				
Jan 13 08	Case set for hearing Claremore 2/4/8 All notified				
Feb 4 08	Case called. Plaintiff appeared evidence taken. No appearance by defendants.				
Feb 1 08	Registry return receipt filed by Pltf's Atty today.				

Cherokee Intruder Cases 1901 - 1909

Mch 9 08	Pltf's Atty advised in re status of case
April 9 08	Judgement[sic] rendered in favor of Pltf & defdt given ten days.
5/1 08	Pltf's Atty returned copy of judgment showing that copy of same was served on Defdt.
May 15 08	Plaintiff asked to report if in possession of land.
5-25 08	Instructions issued to Capt West
6-3 08	Capt West reports that he placed pltf tenant in possession and case is _Dismissed_

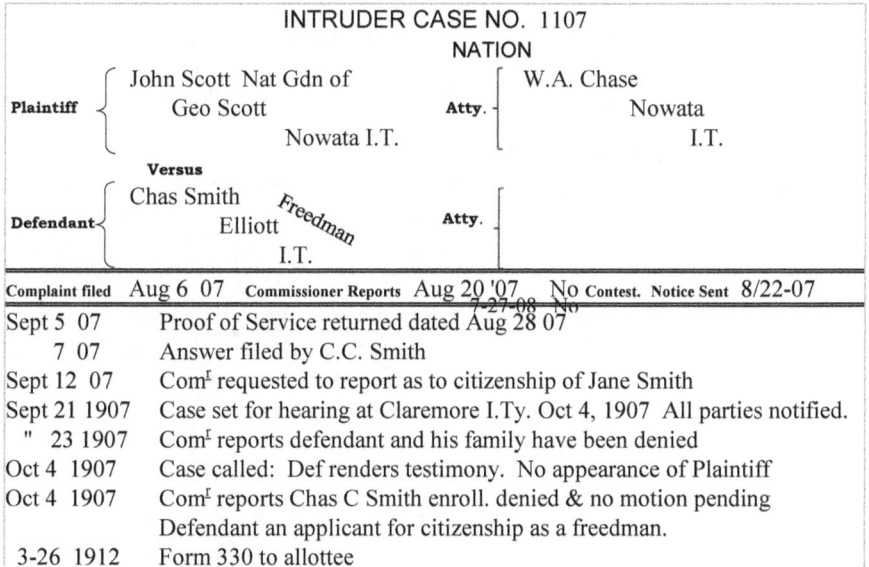

INTRUDER CASE NO. 1107
NATION

Plaintiff: John Scott Nat Gdn of Geo Scott, Nowata I.T.
Atty. W.A. Chase, Nowata I.T.

Versus

Defendant: Chas Smith, Elliott I.T. *Freedman*
Atty.

Complaint filed Aug 6 07   Commissioner Reports Aug 20 '07   No Contest. Notice Sent 8/22-07
7-27-08 No

Sept 5 07	Proof of Service returned dated Aug 28 07
7 07	Answer filed by C.C. Smith
Sept 12 07	Com^r requested to report as to citizenship of Jane Smith
Sept 21 1907	Case set for hearing at Claremore I.Ty. Oct 4, 1907 All parties notified.
" 23 1907	Com^r reports defendant and his family have been denied
Oct 4 1907	Case called: Def renders testimony. No appearance of Plaintiff
Oct 4 1907	Com^r reports Chas C Smith enroll. denied & no motion pending Defendant an applicant for citizenship as a freedman.
3-26 1912	Form 330 to allottee

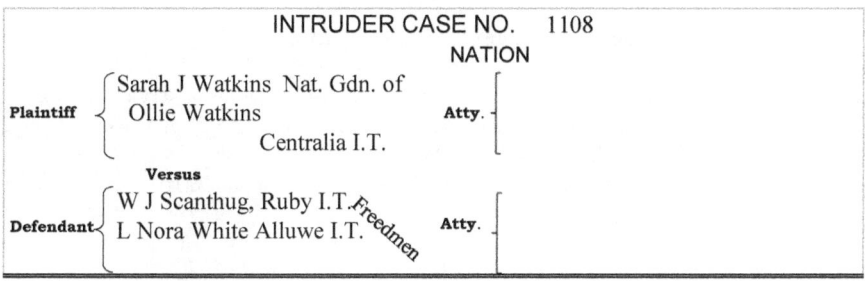

INTRUDER CASE NO. 1108
NATION

Plaintiff: Sarah J Watkins Nat. Gdn. of Ollie Watkins, Centralia I.T.
Atty.

Versus

Defendant: W J Scanthug, Ruby I.T., L Nora White Alluwe I.T. *Freedmen*
Atty.

Cherokee Intruder Cases 1901 - 1909

| Complaint filed | Aug 23 | Commissioner Reports | Aug 20 '07 | No Contest. Notice Sent | 8/27-07 |

Aug 23 07	Certificate No 61672 filed by Plaintiff.
07	Proof of Service returned dated Aug 30-07
Sept 10 07	Answer filed by defendant White
Sept 21 1907	Case set for hearing at Claremore I.Ty. Oct 4 1907. All parties notified.
Oct 4 1907	Case called. Def's rendered testimony: Plaintiff not present
Nov 7 1907	Defendant White is a claimant for citizenship as as[sic] a freedman
Nov 9 1907	Pltf requested to notify office why she did not appear at Claremore when case was set for hearing
Nov 19 1907	Plaintiff advised case will be set for hearing again
Jan 13 08	Case set for hearing Claremore 2/4/8 All notified.
Jan 24 08	Plaintiff asks for a continuance which is granted & all parties notified.
Feb 4 08	Case called plaintiff appeared evidence taken No appearance by defendants.
April 8 08	Com asked for report
Apr 9 08	Com F.C.T. reports L. Nora White does not appear on rolls.
3/26 1912	Form 330 to allottee

INTRUDER CASE NO. 1109
NATION

Plaintiff	Amos White White Oak I.T.	**Atty.**	Bert Van Lewan ~~H.G. Sawyer~~ Nowata OK
Versus			
Defendant	Goldie Starbuck Chanute I.T.	**Atty.**	J.H. Huckleberry Muskogee Okla.

| Complaint filed | Aug 16 07 | Commissioner Reports | Aug 26 07 | No Contest. Notice Sent | Sept 3 '07 |

Sept 21 1907	Case set for hearing at Claremore I.Ty Oct 4, 1907. All parties notified.
" 30 1907	Com^r reports SW^4 NE^4 NE^4 MW^4[sic] SE^4 NE^4 26-77-17 East is in contest
Oct 4 07	Case called no appearance by either party
Jan 13 08	Case set for hearing Claremore 2/4/08 All notified.
Jan 30 08	Plaintiff's Attorney called in person and stated proof of service has not been made & asked that case be continued to be heard at Muskogee Feb 11, 1908 which was done. All parties notified.
Feb 11-08	Attys for both parties appeared and agreed to submit brief within ten days On file
Mch 23 08	Pltf's Atty requested to file brief

Cherokee Intruder Cases 1901 - 1909

6-2 08	W.T. Sawyer advised in re status of case.
5-4 08	Brief filed by Pltf's Atty.
6-11 08	Defdt's Atty requested to file brief
7-29 08	Trans to Com.

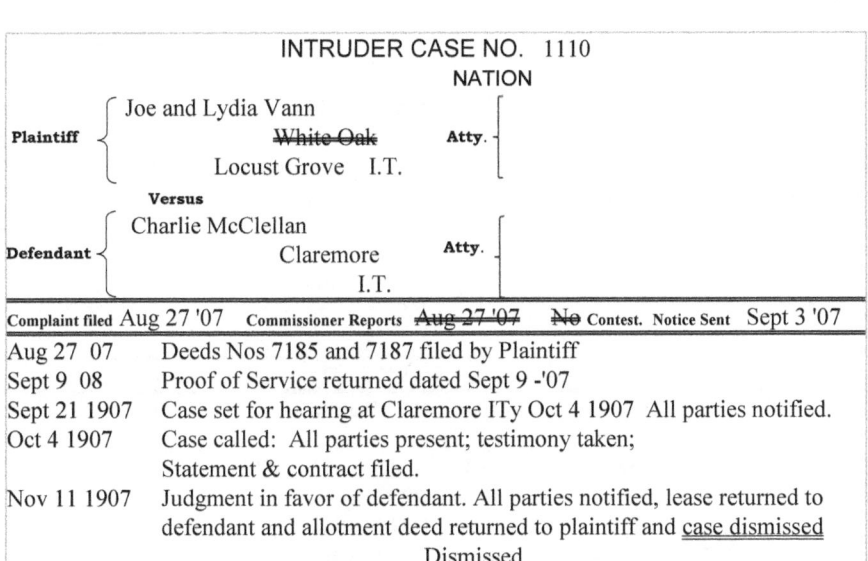

INTRUDER CASE NO. 1110
NATION

Plaintiff: Joe and Lydia Vann, ~~White Oak~~ Locust Grove I.T. **Atty.**

Versus

Defendant: Charlie McClellan, Claremore I.T. **Atty.**

Complaint filed Aug 27 '07 **Commissioner Reports** ~~Aug 27 '07~~ ~~No~~ **Contest. Notice Sent** Sept 3 '07

Aug 27 07	Deeds Nos 7185 and 7187 filed by Plaintiff
Sept 9 08	Proof of Service returned dated Sept 9 -'07
Sept 21 1907	Case set for hearing at Claremore ITy Oct 4 1907 All parties notified.
Oct 4 1907	Case called: All parties present; testimony taken; Statement & contract filed.
Nov 11 1907	Judgment in favor of defendant. All parties notified, lease returned to defendant and allotment deed returned to plaintiff and <u>case dismissed</u>
	Dismissed

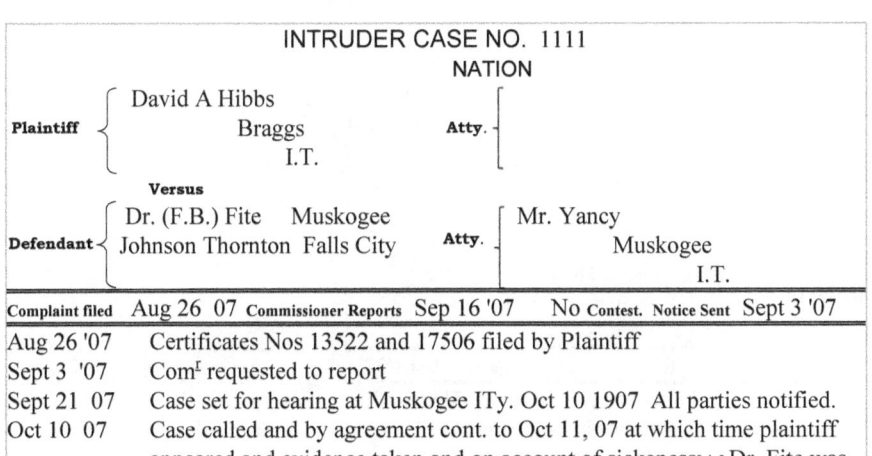

INTRUDER CASE NO. 1111
NATION

Plaintiff: David A Hibbs, Braggs I.T. **Atty.**

Versus

Defendant: Dr. (F.B.) Fite Muskogee, Johnson Thornton Falls City **Atty.** Mr. Yancy Muskogee I.T.

Complaint filed Aug 26 07 **Commissioner Reports** Sep 16 '07 **No Contest. Notice Sent** Sept 3 '07

Aug 26 '07	Certificates Nos 13522 and 17506 filed by Plaintiff
Sept 3 '07	Com^r requested to report
Sept 21 07	Case set for hearing at Muskogee ITy. Oct 10 1907 All parties notified.
Oct 10 07	Case called and by agreement cont. to Oct 11, 07 at which time plaintiff appeared and evidence taken and on account of sickness[sic] Dr. Fite was

Cherokee Intruder Cases 1901 - 1909

	unable to appear and permitted to give evidence later.
Nov 9 07	Defendants requested to appear and render testimony.
Jan 10 08	Defendant requested to appear in 5 days & give testimony
July 31 08	Certs returned in person.
Aug 29 08	Pltf advised he had possession
Sept 4 08	Case dismissed

INTRUDER CASE NO. 1112
NATION

Plaintiff	Mary Waters c/o W.H.H. Clayton Muskogee	Atty.	W.H.H. Clayton Muskogee
	Versus		
Defendant	Arthur Reid Warner I.T.	Atty.	

Complaint filed Sept 4 '07	Commissioner Reports 9/14/7	No Contest. Notice Sent Sept 7 '07

Sept 4 '07	Certificates No 568 and 505 filed by Plaintiff.
" 7 ✓	Com.r requested to report.
Sept 21 07	Case set for hearing at Muskogee I.Ty Oct 11, 1907.
" 20 07	Proof of Service returned dated 9/17/07
Jan 11 08	Case set for hearing Muskogee 1/27/8 all parties notified
Jan - 08	Plff's Attorney writes that plff states she has possession
Jan 25 08	In accordance with statement of plff's attorney Ezra Brainerd- Certs 505 and 561[sic] returned to plaintiff and Case Dismissed

INTRUDER CASE NO. 1113
NATION

Plaintiff	James K Landrum - Gdn of Hiram W and Arkansas Landrum Grove I.T.	Atty.	Ad[sic] V. Coppedge Grove I.T.
	Versus		
Defendant	Dan Robertson, Henry Kiefer *Fairland I.T.* and J L Courtney Afton I.T.	Atty.	

Complaint filed Sept 3 '07	Commissioner Reports 9/12/07 7-23-08 No	No Contest. Notice Sent Sept 7 '07

Sept 3 '07	Letters of Guardianship filed by Plaintiff
✓ ✓ 07	Certificates No 35615, 35613, 24901 and 24901[sic] filed by Plaintiff.
✓ 7 '07	Com.r requested to report.

Cherokee Intruder Cases 1901 - 1909

Sept 21 1907	Case set for hearing at Claremore I.Ty Oct 4, 1907. All parties notified
" 12 1907	Com. reports no contest.
" 18 1907	Proof of service returned.
Oct 4 1907	Case called. All parties present; Testimony taken
Nov 4 1907	Plaintiff asks status and advised judgment will be rendered soon as possible.
Nov 9 1907	Dan Robertson requested to advise if petition has been filed in U.S.C.
Jan 10 1907[sic]	Defendant ~~to~~ requested to furnish copies of court papers within 5 days
Feb 21 08	Judgment rendered in favor of pltf & defdt given ten days
Mch 25 08	Instructions issued to Capt J C West to place pltf in possession.
April 1 08	Jas. S. Davenport, Atty, Vinita, writes asking status of case and for a copy of proof of service upon defendant Kiefer.
" 1 08	Capt West reports that on Mch 30-31st he placed plff in possession
Apr 4 08	Atty Davenport furnished desired information
" " "	Plff advised of report of Capt. West. Certs. returned, also letters of Gdnship; and <u>Case Dismissed</u>.
6-15 08	Atty J.S. Davenport files motion for rehearing
6-18 08	Motion for rehearing denied.
7-8 08	*(Illegible)* to Dept on appeal
10-12 08	Dept asks for citation of decision of court in re nat. gdn.
" " "	Referred to p 134 - Vol 79 SW Reprtr.
3-27-09	Copy of Dept's letter affirming decision of this office received & defts given 10 days to vacate
3-3-09	<u>Pltf advises Robertson has lease for 1909</u>: matter of rent for 1908 will come up in Ottawa
	Cty Crt Ap 8-09: receiver has been appointed. <u>Dismissed</u>.
Apr 20 09	letter rec'd from defdts.

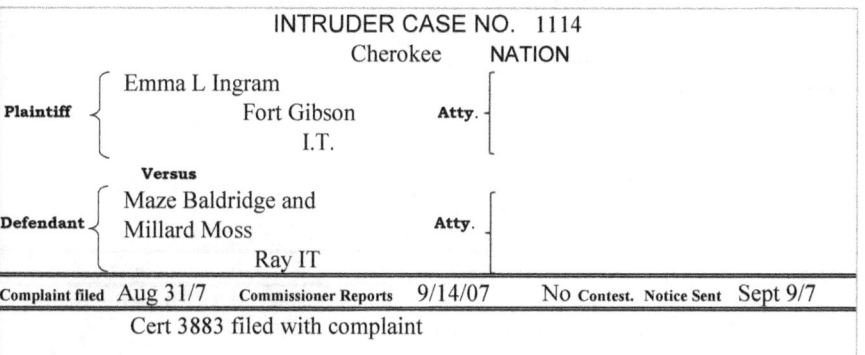

INTRUDER CASE NO. 1114
Cherokee NATION

Plaintiff: Emma L Ingram, Fort Gibson, I.T.   **Atty.**

Versus

Defendant: Maze Baldridge and Millard Moss, Ray IT   **Atty.**

Complaint filed Aug 31/7   Commissioner Reports 9/14/07   No Contest. Notice Sent Sept 9/7
Cert 3883 filed with complaint

Cherokee Intruder Cases 1901 - 1909

Sept 9 07	Com^r asked to report in re contest etc.
Sept 21 07	Case set for hearing at Muskogee ITy Oct 11, 1907. All parties notified.
" "	*(Blank line)*
Oct 11 07	Case called. All parties present. Dft. Baldridge, surrendered possession and Dft Moss agrees to pay Pltf rents. No one being on the land. Cert 3883 returned to Pltf in person. <u>Case dismissed</u>.

INTRUDER CASE NO. 1115
Cherokee NATION

Plaintiff	Mike Bluejacket Bluejacket, I.T.	Atty.	H. Jennings Claremore OK
	Versus		
Defendant	M. K. & T. Railway Co.	Atty.	C. C. Jackson Muskogee IT. for Deft

Complaint filed Sept 11/7 **Commissioner Reports** 9/20/7 No **Contest. Notice Sent** Sept 13/7

	Cert 960 Letter from M. K.& T Ry. filed with complaint
Sept 13 07	Com^r asked to report in re. status of land.
Sept 21 1907	Case set for hearing at Claremore I.Ty. Oct 4, 1907. All parties notified
" 26 1907	Proof of service returned dated Sept 25, 1907.
Oct 2 "	Answer filed with blue prints
Oct 4 1904[sic]	Case called. Plaintiff renders testimony: No appearance by Defendant.
Jan 15 1908	Plaintiff advised status of case.
May 18 09	See letter from the Com^r to the 5 Civilized Tribes and hold case accordingly.

INTRUDER CASE NO. 1116
Cherokee NATION

Plaintiff	Lizzie Caywood for Thomas P Caywood Row, Ind. Ter.	Atty.	
	Versus		
Defendant	Mrs Sarah Scales Row, Ind. Ter.	Atty.	

Complaint filed Aug 31/7 **Commissioner Reports** Sept 7/7 No **Contest. Notice Sent**

Sept 21 1907	Case set for hearing at Claremore I.Ty. Oct 4, 1907. All parties notified.
" 26 1907	Proof of service returned dated Sept 23, 1907

Cherokee Intruder Cases 1901 - 1909

" 26 07	Answer filed by defendant
Oct 4 07	Case called no appearance by either party.
" 11 07	Plaintiff advised of defendants statement to vacate January 1 07 and requested to advise if same will be satisfactory
Jan 13 08	Case set for hearing Claremore 2/4/08 All notified
Jan 21 08	Plff advises that deft has given her possession.
Jan 27 08	In accordance with statement above of plff. Case Dismissed

INTRUDER CASE NO. 1117
Cherokee NATION

Plaintiff: Charley and Dochie Simmons, Dustin, Ind. Ter. **Atty.**

Versus

Defendant: Thomas Brown, Bristow, Ind. Ter. **Atty.**

Complaint filed Sept 11/7 **Commissioner Reports** **Contest. Notice Sent** Sept 3/7

	Certs 16693 - 16692 filed with complaint
Sept 13 07	Com^r asked to report
Sept 21 1907	Case set for hearing at Claremore ITy Oct 4 1907. All parties notified.
" 21 1907	Proof of service returned dated 9/20/07 Case erroneously made up made up as Cherokee when in reality it is a Creek Case. Notice of entered above was not mailed. See Creek #1965.

INTRUDER CASE NO. 1118
Cherokee NATION

Plaintiff: Benjamin W. Williams Gdn Robt L Williams, Maydalen, Wallie G Williams **Atty.** R.L. Butts, Muskogee I.T.

Versus

Defendant: J.T. Stallings Lamar Ark; J.A. Nourse Muskogee I.T.; G.C. Robertson Keeflen I.T.; W.J. Williams " " **Atty.** Cravens & Cravens, Muskogee I.T.

Complaint filed Sept 18 1907 **Commissioner Reports** **Contest. Notice Sent** 9/18/07

Sept 18 07	Letters of guardianship filed.
" 18 07	Com^r asked to report if land is in contest, if certificates have been issued

Cherokee Intruder Cases 1901 - 1909

" 27 07	and also nation & blood allottee[sic] is Proof of service returned.
" 28 07	Com reports land has been allotted[sic] to Plaintiffs
Oct 7 07	Case set for hearing at Muskogee IT 10/21/07 all parties notified
" 21 07	Case called all parties present evidence taken. 3 lease contracts filed by defendants. Defendants move that action be withheld pending suit in US Court & agree to file a written motion in a few days.
" 23 07	Case called all parties present more evidence offered
" 25 07	Motion which defendants filed at hearing was returned to be signed & requested to return same to office when signed.
" 27 07	Above motion is returned signed.
Nov 11 07	Com^r requested to advise if certificates have been issued.
" 20 07	Com^r reports certfs issued.
5-18 08	Pltf's Atty advised that his redress is in district or *(illegible)* court and case is Dismissed

---

INTRUDER CASE NO. 1119
Cherokee NATION

Plaintiff: Runaway Bridge for himself and Nellie Bridge — Locust Grove IT   Atty.

Versus

Defendant: Dr. J. E. Bristow — Pryor Creek I.T.   Atty.

Complaint filed Sept 9/07   Commissioner Reports 9/18/7   No Contest. Notice Sent 9/23/07

Sept 23 07	Case set for hearing at Claremore I.T. 9/23/07 10-3-07. All parties present[sic]
Oct 1 07	Proof of service returned dated Sept 30 '07,
Oct 3 07	Case called. No appearance by either party.
Oct 11 07	Plaintiff requests case heard at Vinita, and advised case will again be set for hearing at some point Cherokee Nation
" 10 07	Deft files answer and lease contract.
Jan 13 08	Case set for hearing Claremore 2/4/8 All notified
Jan 28 08	Plaintiff requested to advise if she signed a request for dismissal transmitted to this office
Feb 4 08	Case called No appearance[sic]
Mch 14 08	Pltf advises in re status of case
May 15 08	Plaintiff asked if in possession or settlement made
6-24 08	Case dismissed at pltf request of 1-28-08.
	Dismissed

224

Cherokee Intruder Cases 1901 - 1909

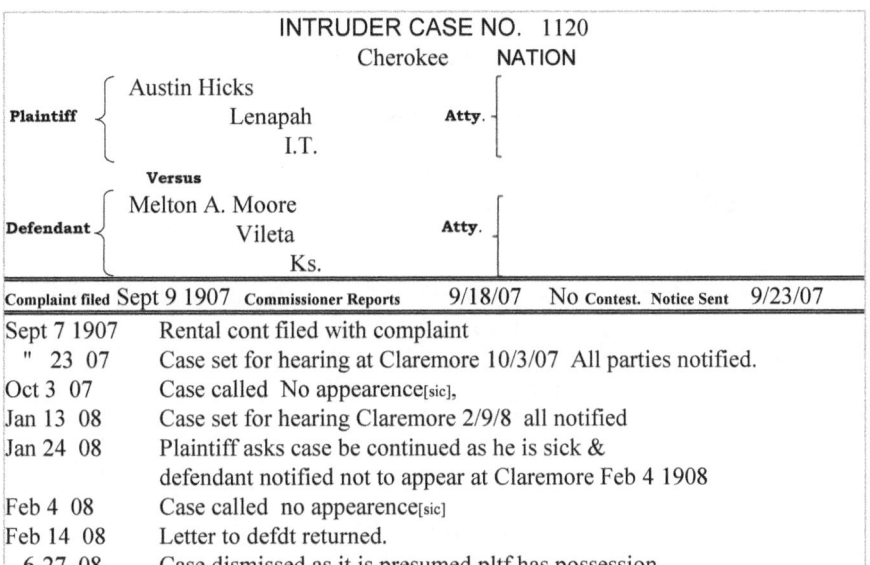

INTRUDER CASE NO. 1120
Cherokee   NATION

Plaintiff: Austin Hicks, Lenapah, I.T.   Atty.

Versus

Defendant: Melton A. Moore, Vileta, Ks.   Atty.

Complaint filed Sept 9 1907 Commissioner Reports 9/18/07 No Contest. Notice Sent 9/23/07

Sept 7 1907	Rental cont filed with complaint
" 23 07	Case set for hearing at Claremore 10/3/07 All parties notified.
Oct 3 07	Case called No appearance[sic],
Jan 13 08	Case set for hearing Claremore 2/9/8 all notified
Jan 24 08	Plaintiff asks case be continued as he is sick & defendant notified not to appear at Claremore Feb 4 1908
Feb 4 08	Case called no appearance[sic]
Feb 14 08	Letter to defdt returned.
6-27 08	Case dismissed as it is presumed pltf has possession.

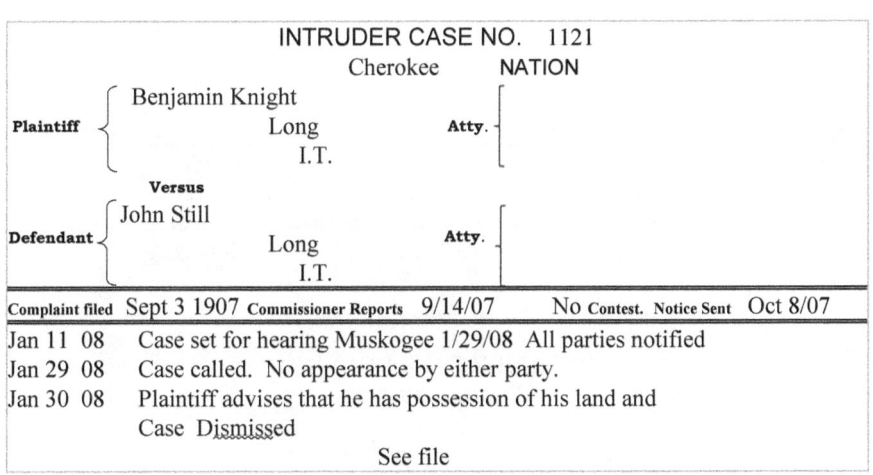

INTRUDER CASE NO. 1121
Cherokee   NATION

Plaintiff: Benjamin Knight, Long, I.T.   Atty.

Versus

Defendant: John Still, Long, I.T.   Atty.

Complaint filed Sept 3 1907 Commissioner Reports 9/14/07 No Contest. Notice Sent Oct 8/07

Jan 11 08	Case set for hearing Muskogee 1/29/08 All parties notified
Jan 29 08	Case called. No appearance by either party.
Jan 30 08	Plaintiff advises that he has possession of his land and Case Dismissed

See file

Cherokee Intruder Cases 1901 - 1909

INTRUDER CASE NO. 1122
Cherokee   NATION

Plaintiff: Sara England, Stilwell, I.T.   Atty.

Versus

Defendant: T.B. Tanner, Albuquerque, New Mex.   Atty.

Complaint filed Sept 6 1907   Commissioner Reports Sept 14/07   No Contest. Notice Sent Oct 8/07

| Jan 13 08 | Case set for hearing Claremore 2/4/08 all notified |
| Feb 4 08 | Case called No appearance[sic] by plaintiff. Defendant appeared and filed request for dismissal signed by plaintiff. Dismissed. |

INTRUDER CASE NO. 1123
Cherokee NATION

Plaintiff: John Hickory, Choteau, I.T.   Atty.

Versus

Defendant: C. S. Perry, Redland, I.T.   Atty.

Complaint filed Sept 19 1907   Commissioner Reports Oct 1/07   No Contest. Notice Sent Oct 8 1907

| Jan 13 08 | Case set for hearing Muskogee 1/27/8 All parties notified |
| Jan 27 08 | Case called. All parties present and testimony taken. L.B. Deft gave plff $35^{00} to balance the $110^{00} consideration in the lease and this being satisfactory to plff. Case Dismissed. |

INTRUDER CASE NO. 1124
Cherokee NATION

Plaintiff: Henry C Phillips, Catoosa, I.T.   Atty.

Versus

Defendant: J. W. Bridges, Catoosa, OK.   Atty. Anderson & Ertel, Claremore, OK.

Cherokee Intruder Cases 1901 - 1909

Complaint filed Sept 10 1907 Commissioner Reports Sept 21/07 No Contest. Notice Sent Oct 8/07	
Oct 16 07	Answer filed by defendant
Jan 13 08	Case set for hearing Claremore 2/5/8 all notified
Feb 5 08	Case called all parties present. Defendant files a demurrer which was sustained as plaintiff acknowledges he is a minor Case dismissed.

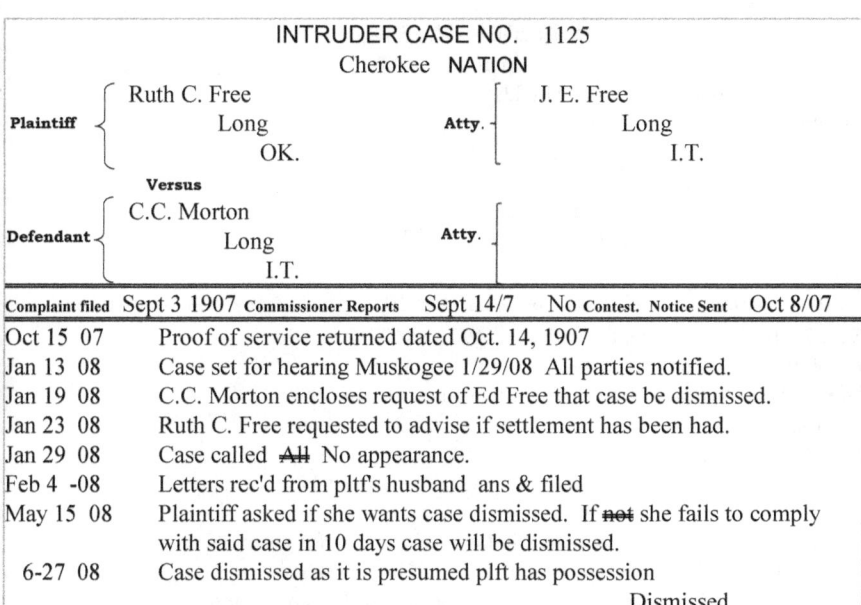

INTRUDER CASE NO. 1125
Cherokee NATION

Plaintiff: Ruth C. Free, Long, OK.   Atty:
Versus: J. E. Free, Long, I.T.
Defendant: C.C. Morton, Long, I.T.   Atty:

Complaint filed Sept 3 1907 Commissioner Reports Sept 14/7 No Contest. Notice Sent Oct 8/07	
Oct 15 07	Proof of service returned dated Oct. 14, 1907
Jan 13 08	Case set for hearing Muskogee 1/29/08 All parties notified.
Jan 19 08	C.C. Morton encloses request of Ed Free that case be dismissed.
Jan 23 08	Ruth C. Free requested to advise if settlement has been had.
Jan 29 08	Case called A̶l̶l̶ No appearance.
Feb 4 -08	Letters rec'd from pltf's husband ans & filed
May 15 08	Plaintiff asked if she wants case dismissed. If n̶o̶t̶ she fails to comply with said case in 10 days case will be dismissed.
6-27 08	Case dismissed as it is presumed plft has possession
	Dismissed

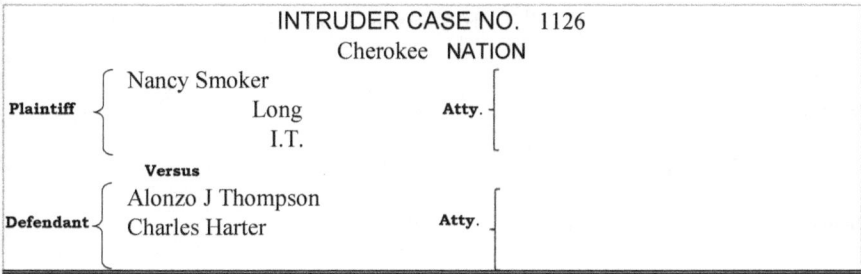

INTRUDER CASE NO. 1126
Cherokee NATION

Plaintiff: Nancy Smoker, Long, I.T.   Atty:
Versus
Defendant: Alonzo J Thompson, Charles Harter   Atty:

227

Cherokee Intruder Cases 1901 - 1909

Complaint filed Sept 18 1907 Commissioner Reports Sept 26/7 No Contest. Notice Sent Oct 8/7	
Jan 13 08	Case set for hearing Muskogee 1/29/08 All parties notified
Jan 29 08	Case called. No appearance.
May 9 08	Plaintiff requested to advise if in poss or if settlement has been made
6-27 08	Case dismissed as it is presumed pltf has possession
	Dismissed

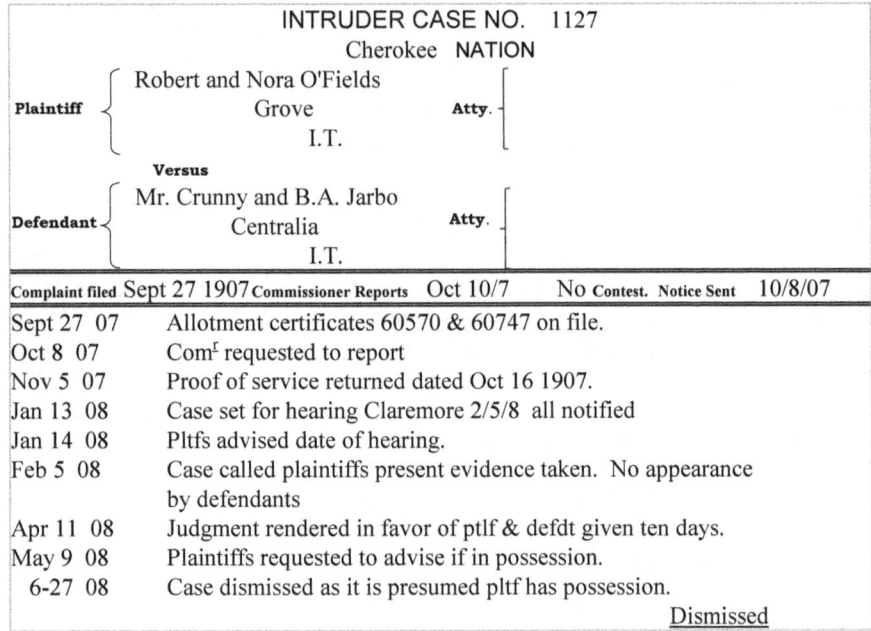

INTRUDER CASE NO. 1127
Cherokee NATION

Plaintiff: Robert and Nora O'Fields, Grove, I.T.   Atty.

Versus

Defendant: Mr. Crunny and B.A. Jarbo, Centralia, I.T.   Atty.

Complaint filed Sept 27 1907 Commissioner Reports Oct 10/7 No Contest. Notice Sent 10/8/07	
Sept 27 07	Allotment certificates 60570 & 60747 on file.
Oct 8 07	Com'r requested to report
Nov 5 07	Proof of service returned dated Oct 16 1907.
Jan 13 08	Case set for hearing Claremore 2/5/8 all notified
Jan 14 08	Pltfs advised date of hearing.
Feb 5 08	Case called plaintiffs present evidence taken. No appearance by defendants
Apr 11 08	Judgment rendered in favor of ptlf & defdt given ten days.
May 9 08	Plaintiffs requested to advise if in possession.
6-27 08	Case dismissed as it is presumed pltf has possession.
	Dismissed

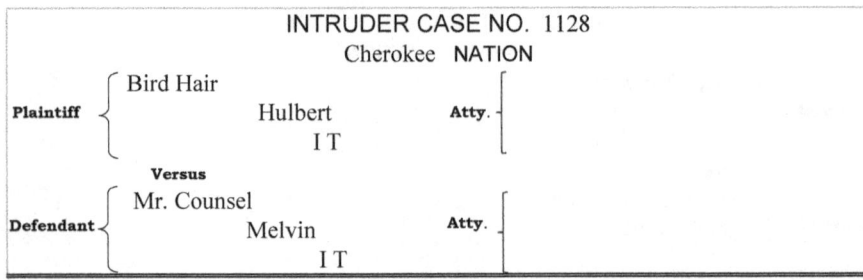

INTRUDER CASE NO. 1128
Cherokee NATION

Plaintiff: Bird Hair, Hulbert, I T   Atty.

Versus

Defendant: Mr. Counsel, Melvin, I T   Atty.

Cherokee Intruder Cases 1901 - 1909

Complaint filed	Sept 28/07	Commissioner Reports	Oct 17/7	No Contest. Notice Sent	Oct 8/07
Sept 28 07	Allot. Cert # 15215 and Home S. C. 11059 on file					
Oct 8 07	Com^r requested to report.					
" 17 07	Proof of service returned dated October 15, 1907					
Jan 13 08	Case set for hearing Muskogee 1/29/08 All parties notified					
Jan 29 08	Case called Pltf failed to appear. Deft appeared. Was advised no further action would be taken pending instructions from Dept in re claimants to citizenship					
Mch 14 08	Pltf advised in re status of case					
4/27 08	Case dismissed by personal request of pltf & certs ret'd.					
					Dismissed

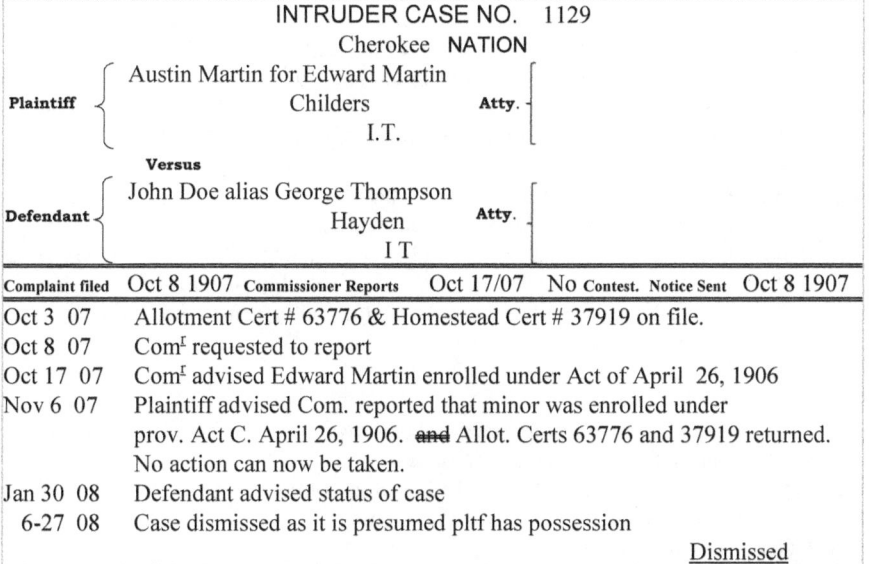

INTRUDER CASE NO. 1129
Cherokee NATION

Plaintiff: Austin Martin for Edward Martin
Childers   **Atty.**
I.T.

Versus

Defendant: John Doe alias George Thompson
Hayden   **Atty.**
I T

Complaint filed	Oct 8 1907	Commissioner Reports	Oct 17/07	No Contest. Notice Sent	Oct 8 1907
Oct 3 07	Allotment Cert # 63776 & Homestead Cert # 37919 on file.					
Oct 8 07	Com^r requested to report					
Oct 17 07	Com^r advised Edward Martin enrolled under Act of April 26, 1906					
Nov 6 07	Plaintiff advised Com. reported that minor was enrolled under prov. Act C. April 26, 1906. ~~and~~ Allot. Certs 63776 and 37919 returned. No action can now be taken.					
Jan 30 08	Defendant advised status of case					
6-27 08	Case dismissed as it is presumed pltf has possession					
					Dismissed

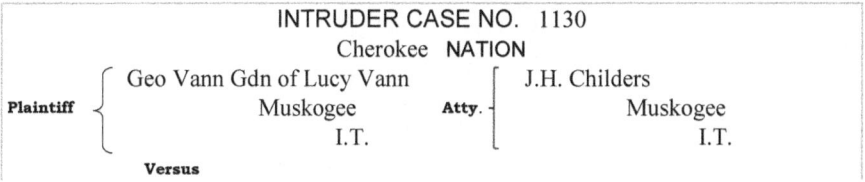

INTRUDER CASE NO. 1130
Cherokee NATION

Plaintiff: Geo Vann Gdn of Lucy Vann
Muskogee   **Atty.**
I.T.

J.H. Childers
Muskogee
I.T.

Versus

Cherokee Intruder Cases 1901 - 1909

Defendant	Henry Brown Vian I.T.	Atty.	Stewart & Stewart Muskogee
Complaint filed Oct 8 1907	**Commissioner Reports** 10/17/7		**No Contest. Notice Sent** Oct 8 1907

Oct 8 07	Allotment Cert. 63125 on file.
" 8 07	Com⁺ requested to report
" 12 07	Answer filed by defendant
" 14 07	Proof of service dated Oct. 12, 1907
" 17 07	Answer filed by defendant
Nov 20 07	Plaintiff asks for possession and advised case will be set for hearing in near future and prompt action then taken.
Jan 13 08	Case set for hearing Muskogee 1/29/08 All parties notified
Jan 29 08	Case called. Pltf did not appear either in person or by Atty: Deft appr. and testimony taken. L Long Stenog.
Feb 21 08	Pltf requested to call & give evidence.
Mch 14 08	Pltf advised in re status of case and Cert # 63125 returned
May 9 08	Plaintiff requested to appear in 10 days and give evidence or case will be dis.
6-27 08	Case dismissed as it is presumed pltf has possession.
	" Re-instated Dismissed
Sept 14 08	Geo Vann appeared and stated has been ill asked to be heard in re case: evidence taken
Oct 12 08	Geo Vann asked that Lucy's cert be returned advised same has been return'd
Oct 28 08	Defdt's Attys advise that they desire to give notice of appeal if decision has been rendered against defd; Defd given 10 days to give additional testimony.
Oct 28 08	Pltf requested to for'd gdnship papers
Nov 6 08	Testimony taken
Nov 9 08	Jane Brown given registered call to show cause why should not be removed
Nov 30 08	Jane app'd and more testimony taken
Dec 9 8[sic]	Com⁺ advised this office verbally that no contest is pending & that deed had been issued to Lucy Vann
Dec 9 08	Judgment in favor of pltf; all parties notified
Dec 11 08	Notice of appeal filed by defdt' Attys.
Dec 15 08	Record trans- to Department on appeal (1-2-09) Copy of test Dec 28 furnished Deft Pltf advised
" 28 " 1-8- 09	Appeal papers sent to Dept
1-20- 09	George Vann advised of status.

Cherokee Intruder Cases 1901 - 1909

INTRUDER CASE NO. 1131
Cherokee NATION

Plaintiff: James Burney for Willie Burney, Centralia, I.T. **Atty.**

Versus

Defendant: Will Williams *Freedman*, Centralia, I.T. **Atty.**

Complaint filed Sept 17 1907 **Commissioner Reports** Sept 18/07 **No Contest. Notice Sent** Oct 14 1907

Oct 24 07	Answer filed by defendant.
" 28 07	Proof of service returned dated Oct 19, 1907.
Jan 13 08	Case set for hearing Claremore 2/5/8 All notified
Jan 15 08	Com^r requested to advise if patents have been delivered
Jan 17 08	Com^r reports deeds recorded Sept 22/6 & delivered Error see 103
Feb 5 08	Case called no appearance by plaintiff, Defendant appeared evidence taken. Rejected freedman.
Mch 10 08	Pltf requested to appear & give evidence.
9-19 08	Pltf advised in re case
Oct 23 08	Pltf files new complaint; advised that no action can be taken pending instructions; complaint returned; also gdnship papers
3/26 1912	Form 330 to Allottee

INTRUDER CASE NO. 1132
Cherokee NATION

Plaintiff: Mrs. Annie Waters, Muskogee, IT **Atty.** *(Name Illegible)*

Versus

Defendant: V. Dodge *(Illegible)*, M E Lawrence **Atty.** Millette West & Jones, Muskogee, I.T.

Complaint filed Oct 4 1907 **Commissioner Reports** 10/19/07 **No Contest. Notice Sent** Oct 14 1907

Oct 4 07	Allotment Certificate No *(illegible)* filed
" 12 07	*(Entry illegible)*
" 29 07	Proof of service returned dated Oct 26 1907
Nov 7 07	Answer filed for defendant
Jan 13 08	Case set for hearing Muskogee 1/27/08 all notified
Jan 27 08	Case called. Plff and deft Lawrence present and represented by attorneys and case continued until Feb 6/8 at which time deft states if he has no legal contract he will vacate

Cherokee Intruder Cases 1901 - 1909

May 9 08	Plaintiff asked if in possession of if she wanted case presented to its *(illegible)*
5-15 08	Case dismissed by request of pltf's Atty
	Dismissed
5-18 08	Allotment certificate ret'd to pltf.

INTRUDER CASE NO. 1133
Cherokee NATION

Plaintiff: James E Bell guardian of Martin A Bell *(Illegible)*
Atty: *(Illegible)* Anderson, Claremore OK

Versus

Defendant: Bruce Mitchell, Oologah I.T.
Atty: W.H. Kornegay, Vinita I.T.

Complaint filed Oct 4 1907   **Commissioner Reports** Oct 19/07   **No Contest. Notice Sent** Oct 14 1907

Oct 4 07	Allotment Certificate 567 & Homestead 437
" 12 07	Com^r requested to report
" 14 07	Proof of service returned dated October 16 1907
" 24 07	Answer filed by defendant himself
" 30 07	Answer filed by defendant by attorney
Jan 13 08	Case set for hearing Claremore 2/5/8. All notified
Feb 5 08	Case continued to Feb 6, 1908 by consent
Feb 6 08	Case called all to be present evidence taken. Defendant to present affidavit with a certified copy of an order of Judge Parker rendered about two years ago in case of James Bell vs C.A. Schmar who was a tenant of Mitchell, awarding land to defendant which decision Department of Interior refused to recognize. This was a matter between two citizens and Mr. W.W.B. requested both sides to file briefs in 20 days which was agreed to. *(Last sentence illegible.)*
Apr 16 08	Judgment in favor of plaintiff copy sent both parties and deft given 10 days
May 9 08	Plaintiff requested to advise if in possession
5-18 08	Instructions issued to Capt West to place pltf in possession
5-23 08	Capt West reports placing pltf in possession & case is
5-26 08	Certs ret'd. Dismissed
Oct 13 08	Defdt advised in re status of case.

Cherokee Intruder Cases 1901 - 1909

	INTRUDER CASE. 1134	
	Cherokee NATION	
Plaintiff	Peggie McClemore nee Gritts Tahlequah Atty. IT	
	Versus	
Defendant	Dr J. A. Upton Welling Atty. IT	*(Name Illegible)* Tahlequah Okla

Complaint filed Sept 23 1907 Commissioner Reports   Oct 11/07   No Contest. Notice Sent   Oct 14 1907

Oct 12 1907	Com^r asked to report
" 16 07	Proof of service returned dated Oct 14, 1907
Jan 14 08	Case set for hearing Muskogee 1/30/08 All parties notified
Jan 27 08	Plf requests dismissal of case and encloses lease contract stating she did not file complaint nor authorize anyone to do so for her
Jan 30 08	Case called Dr J. A Upton present and he stated same as letter *(remainder illegible)*
Jan 29 08	Plaintiff encloses request for dismissal. <u>Dismissed</u>.
4/21 08	Set for hearing at Muskogee 4/22/08 see letter of 4/21/08
4/21 08	*(Entry illegible)*
4/27 08	*(Entry illegible)*
5/1 08	Com^r asked for report as to degree of blood of pltf.
4/29 08	*(Entry illegible)*
May 2 08	*(Entry illegible)*
5-8 08	*(Entry illegible)*
5-7 08	*(Entry illegible)*
5-13 08	Brief filed by defdt's Atty
6-4 08	Judgement[sic] rendered in favor of pltf & defdt given ten days
6-15 08	*(Entry illegible)*
8-3 08	Dept affirms judgement[sic] of this office
8-4 08	Instructions issued to Policeman Roach
8-7 08	Capt West reports that dept and pltf in possession
8-8 08	W^m *(Illegible)* requested to not interfere with pltf.
8-19 08	Capt West reports placed pltf in possession *(illegible)*
Sept 2 08	*(Entry illegible)*

	INTRUDER CASE. 1135	
	Cherokee NATION	
Plaintiff	Moses Middleslecker *(Illegible)* Atty. I.T.	

Cherokee Intruder Cases 1901 - 1909

		Versus		
Defendant		Bryant Wood *(Illegible)* Ark	Atty.	

Complaint filed Oct 3 1907 **Commissioner Reports** Oct 19 07 **No Contest. Notice Sent** Oct 14 1907

Oct 3 07	Allotment Homestead No. *(remainder illegible)*
" 24 07	Proof of service returned dated Oct 18 1907
" 30 07	Answer filed by defendant
Nov 16 07	Plaintiff asks possession and advised case will be set for hearing in near future and action taken accordingly.
Dec 9 07	Plff sets case for hear'g at this office Dec 19/7 at 9:00 a.m.
Dec 14 07	Plff advised to arrange with deft to be present on Dec 19/7
Jan 15 08	Case set for hearing Muskogee 1/30/8 all notified
Jan 30 08	Case called no appearance
Mch 24 08	Case <u>Dismissed</u> as pltf states he has possession
	Dismissed
Mch 27 08	Allotment certificates ret'd to Pltf.

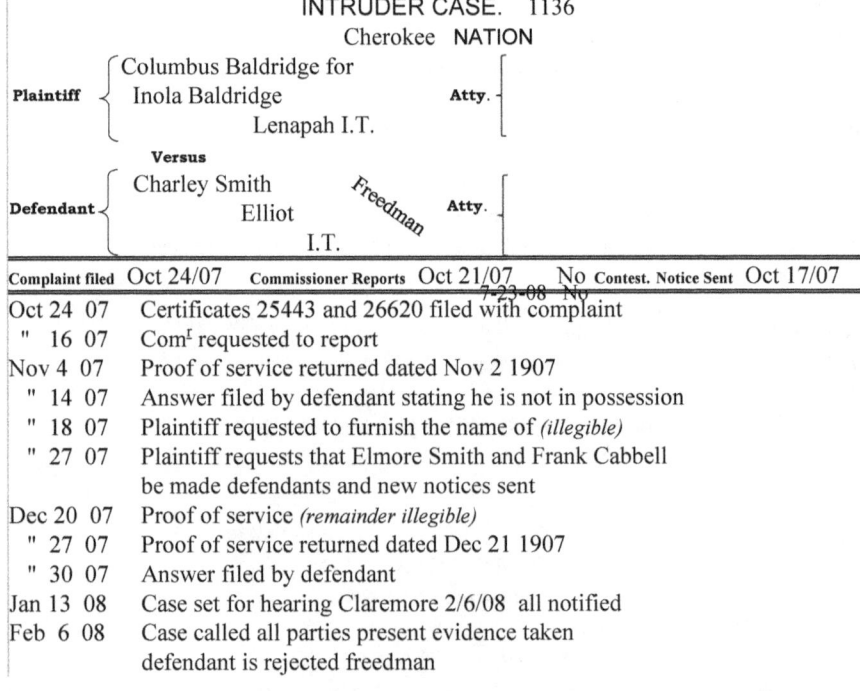

INTRUDER CASE. 1136
Cherokee **NATION**

Plaintiff		Columbus Baldridge for Inola Baldridge Lenapah I.T.	Atty.	
		Versus		
Defendant		Charley Smith Elliot I.T.	*Freedman* Atty.	

Complaint filed Oct 24/07 **Commissioner Reports** Oct 21/07 **No Contest. Notice Sent** Oct 17/07
                                                                           7-23-08 No

Oct 24 07	Certificates 25443 and 26620 filed with complaint
" 16 07	Com^r requested to report
Nov 4 07	Proof of service returned dated Nov 2 1907
" 14 07	Answer filed by defendant stating he is not in possession
" 18 07	Plaintiff requested to furnish the name of *(illegible)*
" 27 07	Plaintiff requests that Elmore Smith and Frank Cabbell be made defendants and new notices sent
Dec 20 07	Proof of service *(remainder illegible)*
" 27 07	Proof of service returned dated Dec 21 1907
" 30 07	Answer filed by defendant
Jan 13 08	Case set for hearing Claremore 2/6/08 all notified
Feb 6 08	Case called all parties present evidence taken defendant is rejected freedman

Cherokee Intruder Cases 1901 - 1909

Mch 14 08	Plaintiff advised in re stats of case
Oct 10 08	Pltf again *(remainder illegible)*
3/26 1912	Form 330 to allottee

INTRUDER CASE. 1137
Cherokee NATION

Plaintiff: Mrs Dara Dickson, Vian   **Atty.**

Versus

Defendant: Geo Stovall   **Atty.**

Complaint filed Oct 2 1907   Commissioner Reports Oct 14/7   No Contest. Notice Sent Oct 17 1907

Oct 31 07	Proof of Service returned dated October 28 1907
Nov 4 07	Plaintiff advised status of case
" 4 07	Answer filed by defendant
Jan 14 08	Case set for hearing Muskogee 1/30/8 all notified
" 14 08	Case called. Plaintiff appeared and evidence taken no appearance by defendant
April 8 08	Judgment rendered in favor of Pltf & defdt given ten days
May 9 08	Plaintiff requested to advise if in possession of land
6-27 08	Case dismissed as it is presumed pltf has possession

                                                                              Dismissed

INTRUDER CASE. 1138
Cherokee NATION

Plaintiff: Nancy Beamer, Moody, Ind. Ter.   **Atty.**

Versus

Defendant: James Johnson   **Atty.**

Complaint filed Oct 11 1907   Commissioner Reports Oct 22/07   No Contest. Notice Sent Oct 17/07

Oct 11 07	Allotment cert # 12765 filed with complaint
" 28 07	Proof of service returned dated Oct 23, 1907.
Jan 14 08	Case set for hearing Muskogee 1/30/08 All parties notified
Jan 18 08	Nancy Beamer by <u>Lewis Beamer</u> states case has been compromised

Cherokee Intruder Cases 1901 - 1909

Jan 23 08	Plaintiff asked to advise if she knows of settlement with deft.	
Jan 30 08	Case called no appearance by either party	
Mch 9 08	Case dismissed by request of pltf & certificates returned	Dismissed
Mch 18 08	Pltf advised in re status of case	

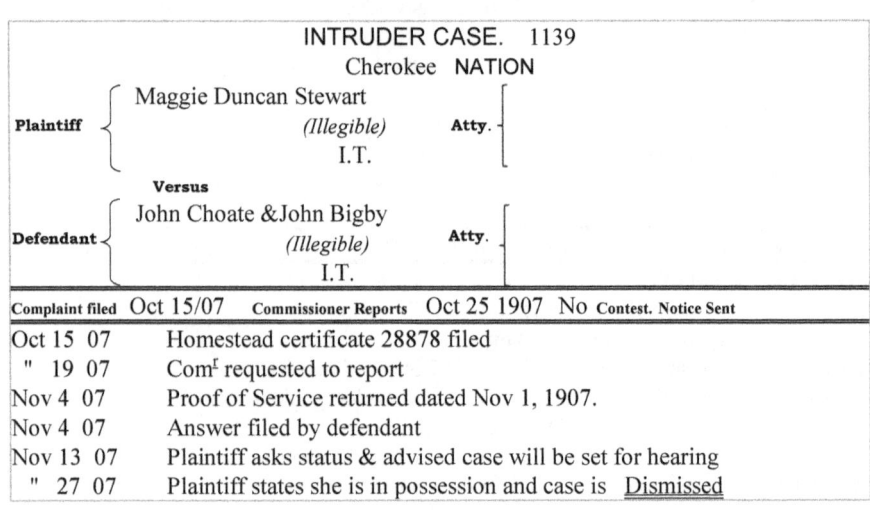

INTRUDER CASE. 1139
Cherokee NATION

Plaintiff: Maggie Duncan Stewart / (Illegible) / I.T.   Atty.

Versus

Defendant: John Choate & John Bigby / (Illegible) / I.T.   Atty.

Complaint filed Oct 15/07   Commissioner Reports Oct 25 1907   No Contest. Notice Sent

Oct 15 07	Homestead certificate 28878 filed
" 19 07	Com^r requested to report
Nov 4 07	Proof of Service returned dated Nov 1, 1907.
Nov 4 07	Answer filed by defendant
Nov 13 07	Plaintiff asks status & advised case will be set for hearing
" 27 07	Plaintiff states she is in possession and case is Dismissed

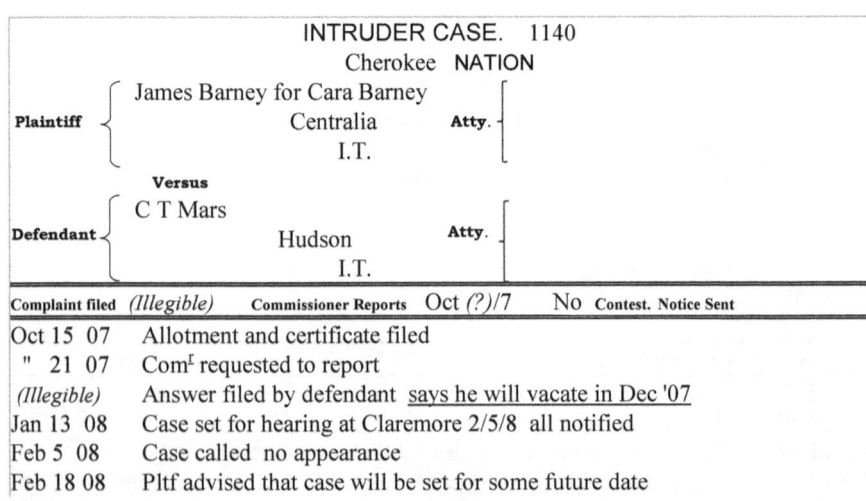

INTRUDER CASE. 1140
Cherokee NATION

Plaintiff: James Barney for Cara Barney / Centralia / I.T.   Atty.

Versus

Defendant: C T Mars / Hudson / I.T.   Atty.

Complaint filed (Illegible)   Commissioner Reports Oct (?)/7   No Contest. Notice Sent

Oct 15 07	Allotment and certificate filed
" 21 07	Com^r requested to report
(Illegible)	Answer filed by defendant says he will vacate in Dec '07
Jan 13 08	Case set for hearing at Claremore 2/5/8 all notified
Feb 5 08	Case called no appearance
Feb 18 08	Pltf advised that case will be set for some future date

236

Cherokee Intruder Cases 1901 - 1909

(Illegible)	Set for hearing at Claremore *(remainder illegible)*	
(Illegible)	No appearance by either party	
8-26 08	No response being made it is presumed *(remainder illegible)*.	
		Case Dismissed

INTRUDER CASE. 1141
Cherokee NATION

Plaintiff: Lewis H Budding, Eucha
Atty.: Fogle & Parks, Vinita IT

Versus

Defendant: Rosa Vann, Lynch I.T. *Freedman*
Atty.: A S McRea, Muskogee Okla

Complaint filed Oct 18 1907 **Commissioner Reports** Oct 30/07 **No Contest.** **Notice Sent** Oct 21 07

Oct 18 07	Allotment certificates 35589, 35590 Homestead certificate 24892 and Letters of guardianship filed.
Oct 21 07	Com.ʳ requested to report.
Nov 8 07	Answer filed by defendant
" 13 07	Proof of service returned dated Oct 28 1907.
Jan 13 08	Case set for hearing Claremore 2/5/8 All notified
Feb 5 08	Case called. Plaintiff's Attorney appeared and stated evidence was taken in 865 and no action was taken as defendant's application for citizenship no appearance by defendants, defendants rejected freedman
Feb 8 08	A.S. McRea called and asked to be permitted to file same motion as he filed on his *(illegible)* cases which was granted. Stenographer to write same and file with case.
3-26 1912	Form 330 to Allottee's[sic] son
4-3 -12	Bertha Starr Fallingpot, mother of allottee[sic] advises that gdn dead Letter # 1097521 J

INTRUDER CASE. 1142
Cherokee NATION

Plaintiff: Eliza Long, Dewey I.T.
Atty.:

Versus

Defendant: Morris F, Henry and Joe Knight
Atty.: Wᵐ P Thompson, Vinita Okla

Complaint filed	Commissioner Reports	Contest. Notice Sent
	(This entire entry is illegible.)	

INTRUDER CASE NO. 1143
Cherokee NATION

Plaintiff Alexander Coats guardian of *(Names Illegible)* Muskogee I.T. **Atty.**

Versus

Defendant Jesse & John Hill Oglesby I.T. **Atty.**

Complaint filed Oct 11 07 **Commissioner Reports** Oct 26, 07 No **Contest. Notice Sent** Oct 23 1907

Nov 7 07	Proof of service returned dated Oct 30, 1907
" 12 07	Defendant requested to advise why they are in possession
Dec 6 07	Case set for hearing at Muskogee Dec 14 1907 all parties notified
Dec 14 07	Case called. Plff appeared and his testimony taken. No appearance by deft.
Dec 20 07	Letters of gdnship certified copy, filed by plff today
Jan 3 08	Judgment for plaintiff all persons notified and instructions issued to John C West to place plaintiff
Jan 5 08	John C West reports he placed plaintiff in possession Case dismissed.
(Illegible)	Certs ret'd to plff in person

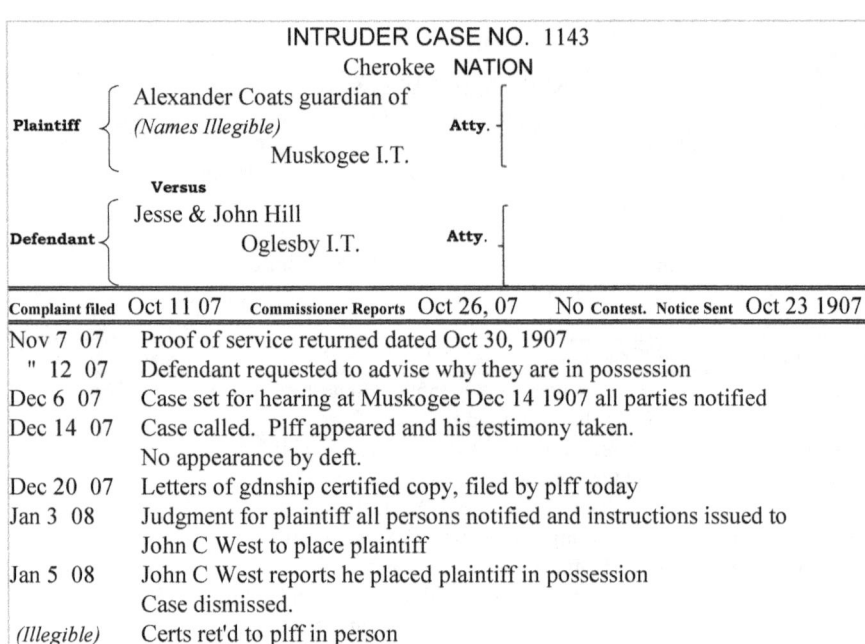

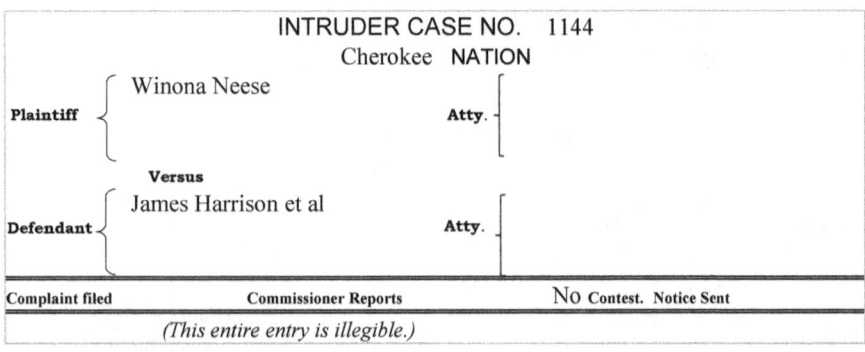

INTRUDER CASE NO. 1144
Cherokee NATION

Plaintiff Winona Neese **Atty.**

Versus

Defendant James Harrison et al **Atty.**

Complaint filed	Commissioner Reports	No Contest. Notice Sent
	(This entire entry is illegible.)	

Cherokee Intruder Cases 1901 - 1909

INTRUDER CASE. 1145
Cherokee NATION

Plaintiff: Susie Fox *(Illegible)* Ind. Ter.   Atty.

Versus

Defendant: John Bentley   Inola   I.T.   Atty.

Complaint filed Oct 24 1907 Commissioner Reports Oct 30/7   No Contest. Notice Sent Oct 24/07

Oct 24 07	Lease contract certificate allot #1705 and Homestead #5525 filed
" 24 07	Com^r requested to report
" 29 07	Proof of service returned dated Oct 28, 1907
" 30 07	Answer filed by defendant
Nov 7 07	Plff advised that defendant called in person and exhibited contract and case dismissed
Nov 9 07	Case re-opened and set for hearing at Muskogee IT Nov 20
Nov 13 07	Defendant requested case be continued and advised that he cannot make arrangements with plaintiff
Nov 18 07	Stipulation for dismissal filed by defendant
Nov 18 07	Case dismissed per above all parties notified. Dismissed

INTRUDER CASE NO. 1146
Cherokee NATION

Plaintiff: Polly Smith   Peggs   Ind Ter   Atty.

Versus

Defendant: Boone Hart   Peggs   Ind Ter   Atty.

Complaint filed Oct 25 1907 Commissioner Reports Oct 31/7   No Contest. Notice Sent Oct 25/07

Oct 25 07	Allotment certificate No 57463 filed with complaint
" 25 07	Com^r requested to report
" 31 07	Proof of service returned dated Oct 29 1907
Nov 12 07	Pltf requests action and advised status and plaintiff requested to render evidence or file *(illegible)*
(Illegible)	Defendant asks until Jan 15/08 to vacate and advised he must make satisfactory settlement with plaintiff
Nov 19 07	Plaintiff states that defendant *(remainder illegible)*

239

Cherokee Intruder Cases 1901 - 1909

(Illegible)	Defendant requested to vacate
Dec 21 07	Pltf advised that case will set for hearing in near future
" 26 07	Pltf asks for possession
Jan 14 08	Case set for hearing Muskogee 1/31/08 all notified
Jan 20 08	Plff advises that Deft has removed from her land
Jan 25 08	Cert 57463 returned to plff and <u>Case Dismissed</u>
	Notice of hearing to defdt returned unclaimed

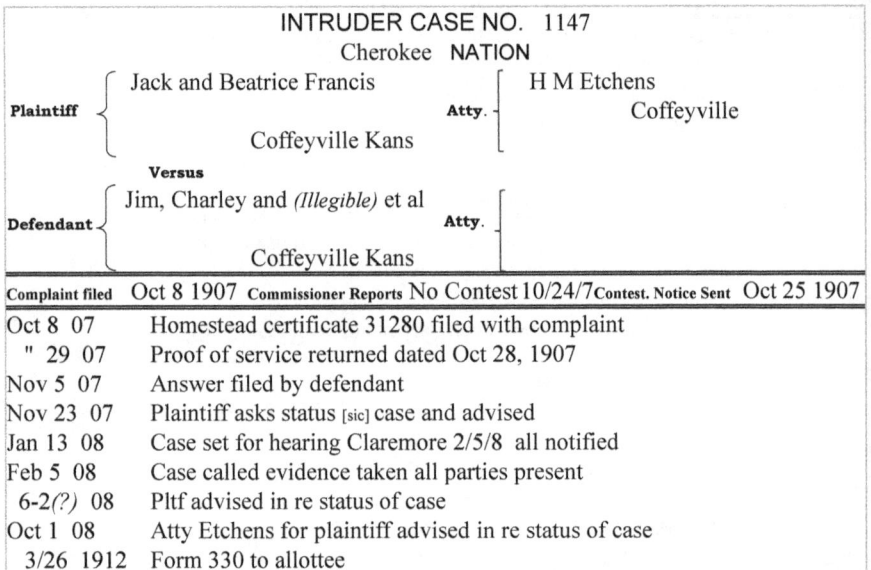

INTRUDER CASE NO. 1147
Cherokee NATION

Plaintiff: Jack and Beatrice Francis, Coffeyville Kans
Atty: H M Etchens, Coffeyville
Versus
Defendant: Jim, Charley and *(Illegible)* et al, Coffeyville Kans
Atty:

Complaint filed Oct 8 1907 **Commissioner Reports** No Contest 10/24/7 **Contest. Notice Sent** Oct 25 1907

Oct 8 07	Homestead certificate 31280 filed with complaint
" 29 07	Proof of service returned dated Oct 28, 1907
Nov 5 07	Answer filed by defendant
Nov 23 07	Plaintiff asks status [sic] case and advised
Jan 13 08	Case set for hearing Claremore 2/5/8 all notified
Feb 5 08	Case called evidence taken all parties present
6-2*(?)* 08	Pltf advised in re status of case
Oct 1 08	Atty Etchens for plaintiff advised in re status of case
3/26 1912	Form 330 to allottee

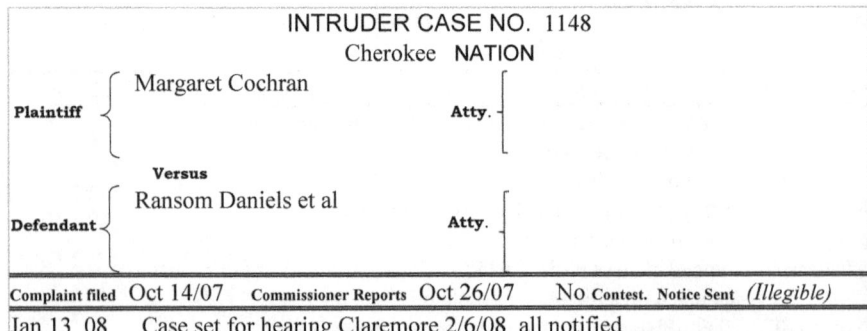

INTRUDER CASE NO. 1148
Cherokee NATION

Plaintiff: Margaret Cochran
Atty:
Versus
Defendant: Ransom Daniels et al
Atty:

Complaint filed Oct 14/07 **Commissioner Reports** Oct 26/07 **No Contest. Notice Sent** *(Illegible)*

Jan 13 08	Case set for hearing Claremore 2/6/08 all notified

Cherokee Intruder Cases 1901 - 1909

Jan 10 08   Proof of service returned dated *(illegible)*
Feb 6 08   Case called all parties present and evidence taken
Feb 20 08   Pltf advised in re status of case
3/26 1912   Form 330 to allottee

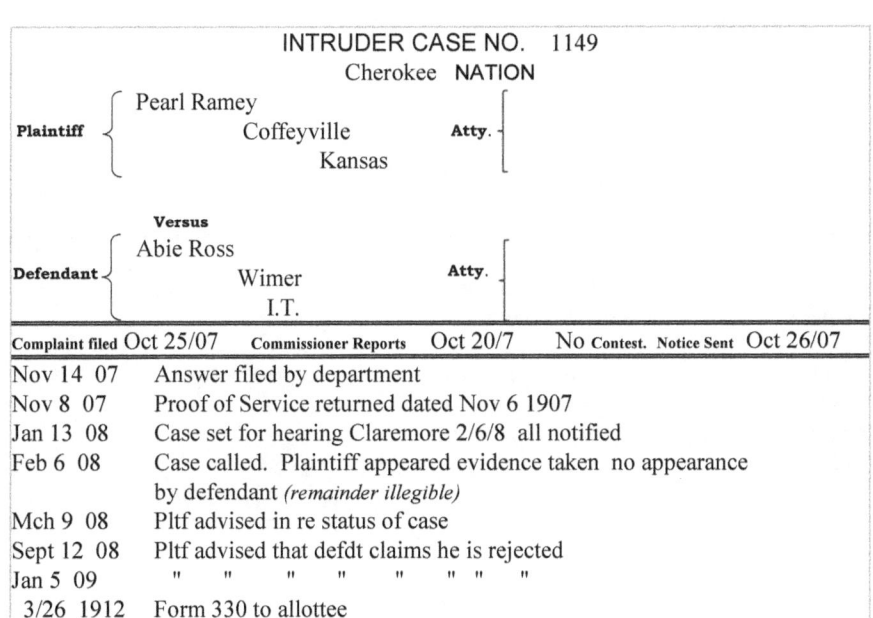

INTRUDER CASE NO. 1149
Cherokee NATION

Plaintiff: Pearl Ramey, Coffeyville, Kansas   Atty.

Versus

Defendant: Abie Ross, Wimer, I.T.   Atty.

Complaint filed Oct 25/07   Commissioner Reports Oct 20/7   No Contest. Notice Sent Oct 26/07

Nov 14 07	Answer filed by department
Nov 8 07	Proof of Service returned dated Nov 6 1907
Jan 13 08	Case set for hearing Claremore 2/6/8 all notified
Feb 6 08	Case called. Plaintiff appeared evidence taken no appearance by defendant *(remainder illegible)*
Mch 9 08	Pltf advised in re status of case
Sept 12 08	Pltf advised that defdt claims he is rejected
Jan 5 09	" " " " " " " "
3/26 1912	Form 330 to allottee

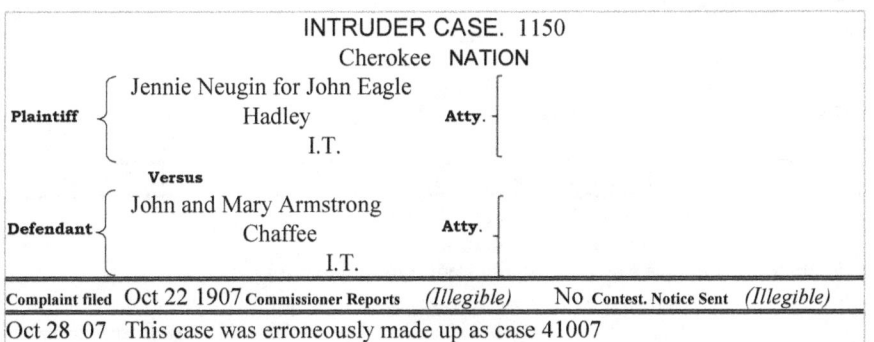

INTRUDER CASE. 1150
Cherokee NATION

Plaintiff: Jennie Neugin for John Eagle, Hadley, I.T.   Atty.

Versus

Defendant: John and Mary Armstrong, Chaffee, I.T.   Atty.

Complaint filed Oct 22 1907 Commissioner Reports *(Illegible)*   No Contest. Notice Sent *(Illegible)*

Oct 28 07   This case was erroneously made up as case 41007 was same parties and same land. Plaintiff was advised on Oct 28 that former case was dismissed as evidence showed John Eagle is dead and

Cherokee Intruder Cases 1901 - 1909

advised she must have heirs determined and then file new complaint
See carbon copy of Oct 28/07 in case #1606   Dismissed.

INTRUDER CASE NO. 1151
Cherokee NATION

Plaintiff: Andrew Bark, Chapel, Ind Ter   Atty.

Versus

Defendant: J M Riley, Pryor Creek, I.T.   Atty.

Complaint filed Oct 31 1907 Commissioner Reports Nov 7/7   No Contest. Notice Sent Oct 31 1907

Oct 31 07	Allotment certificates 26746, 26747 & 26748
" 31 07	Com^r requested to report
Nov 14 07	Proof of service returned dated Nov 11/07
Jan 13 08	Case set for hearing Claremore 2/6/8 All notified
Feb 6 08	Case called no appearance by either party
May 4 08	Plaintiff requested to advise if in possession or settlement had
6-27 08	Case dismissed as it is presumed pltf has possession

Dismissed

INTRUDER CASE NO. 1152
Cherokee NATION

Plaintiff: Scott Welch for Nat Gdn of Johnson Welch, Dragger I.T.   Atty.

Versus

Defendant: Lum Moore, Dragger, I.T.   Atty.

Complaint filed Oct 30 1907 Commissioner Reports Oct 14/07   No Contest. Notice Sent Nov *(illegible)*

Nov 11 07	Proof of service returned dated Nov 9 1907
" 19 07	Defendant advised of status of cate, etc
" 20 07	Plaintiff states intruder has not removed and is advised case will be set for hearing in near future
Nov 18 07	Kornegay files answer but *(illegible)* copy of comp & *(remainder illegible)*
Jan 13 08	Case set for hearing Claremore 2/6/8 all notified
Jan 19 08	Plff advises that deft has given him possession

Cherokee Intruder Cases 1901 - 1909

Jan 25 08	In accordance with advice of plff Case Dismissed
Feb 6 08	Case called no appearance by either party

INTRUDER CASE NO. 1153
Cherokee NATION

Plaintiff Victoria Berks for herself
 (Remainder illegible)   **Atty.**
 Vinita I.T.

Versus

Defendant Jess Richardson and NE Thompson   **Atty.** W H Kornegay
 Welch   Vinita
 I.T.   Okla

Complaint filed Oct 4 1907 **Commissioner Reports** Nov 4/7   **No Contest. Notice Sent** Nov 5 1907

Oct 4 07	Allotment cert *(illegible)* Homestead 739, 740 & 741 filed
Nov 11 07	Proof of service returned dated Nov 8 1907
" 19 07	Answer filed by defendant
" 24 07	Plaintiff advised status of case
Dec 18 07	Kornegay files answer, copy of comp & Demurrer & decision in USC in case of Mrs Summers vs this plaintiff to have allotment cancelled
Jan 13 08	Case set for hearing Claremore 2/6/8 All notified
Feb 6 08	Case called all parties present evidence taken. *(Remainder illegible)*
2/13 08	Letter to defdt returned
2/13 08	Letter rec'd from H. B Lindsey of Bluejacket
April 1 08	*(Entry illegible)*
Apr 14 08	Judgment in favor of plff and copy sent each party. Defendant given ten days to vacate & plff requested to advise if he does so
5-9 08	Instructions issued to Capt West to place pltf in possession
5-19 08	Capt J West reports placing pltf in possession & case is
1-7 09	Atty for pltf asks status: advised Dismissed
1-27 09	Letter of Jan 19 09 from Thompson answered & advised letters of Gdnshp not here if same filed with new complaint case to be given consideration
May 10 09	New case made as to minor Cherokee 1284; this case stands Dismissed

INTRUDER CASE NO. 1154
Cherokee NATION

Plaintiff Mary C Sane
 Vinita   **Atty.**
 I.T.

Cherokee Intruder Cases 1901 - 1909

Defendant	Versus Nathan Meigs	**Atty.**	A.S. McRea Muskogee Okla	

Complaint filed June 27 1907 **Commissioner Reports** Nov 4/7	**No Contest. Notice Sent** Nov 5 1907
Dec 10 07	Proof of service made
Dec 10 07	Deft writes that he is a claimant to citizenship
Dec 14 07	Deft advised to make answer
" 28 07	Answer filed by defendant
Jan 10 08	Com^r requested to report if defendant is a rejected freedman
Jan 13 08	Case set for hearing Claremore 2/6/8 all parties notified
Jan (??) 08	Com^r reports Meigs has been finally denied & no motion pend.
Feb 6 08	Case called plaintiff present evidence taken. Defendant is not present and attorney *(remainder illegible)*
3/26 1912	Form 330 to Allottee[sic].

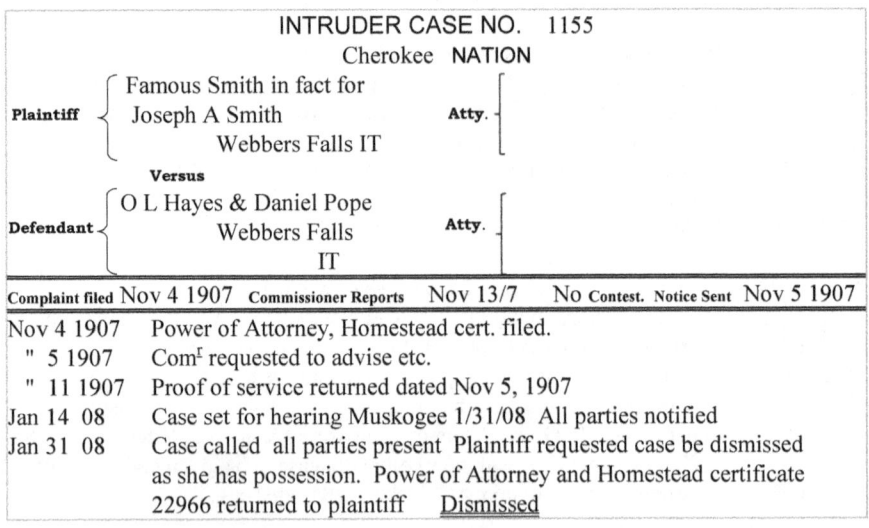

INTRUDER CASE NO. 1155
Cherokee NATION

Plaintiff	Famous Smith in fact for Joseph A Smith Webbers Falls IT	**Atty.**		
Defendant	Versus O L Hayes & Daniel Pope Webbers Falls IT	**Atty.**		

Complaint filed Nov 4 1907 **Commissioner Reports** Nov 13/7	**No Contest. Notice Sent** Nov 5 1907
Nov 4 1907	Power of Attorney, Homestead cert. filed.
" 5 1907	Com^r requested to advise etc.
" 11 1907	Proof of service returned dated Nov 5, 1907
Jan 14 08	Case set for hearing Muskogee 1/31/08 All parties notified
Jan 31 08	Case called all parties present Plaintiff requested case be dismissed as she has possession. Power of Attorney and Homestead certificate 22966 returned to plaintiff <u>Dismissed</u>

INTRUDER CASE NO. 1156
Cherokee NATION

Plaintiff	Dick Lowe for Lydia Lowe Chaffee I.T.	**Atty.**	

Cherokee Intruder Cases 1901 - 1909

	Versus		
Defendant	Fannie G Perry Salina I.T.	Atty.	

Complaint filed Nov 4 1907	Commissioner Reports Nov 4/7	No Contest. Notice Sent Nov 5 1907
Jan 13 08	Case set for hearing Claremore 2/6/8 All parties notified	
Feb 6 08	Case called no appearance by either party	
Jan 31 08	Proof of service filed today	
May 9 08	Pltf requested to advise if in possession or satisfactory settlement had	
(Illegible)	Case dismissed as it is presumed pltf has possession	
		Dismissed

INTRUDER CASE NO. 1157
Cherokee NATION

Plaintiff	Alden Rathbun	Atty.	
	Versus		
Defendant	Andrew Wales Hudson Okla	Atty.	

Complaint filed	Commissioner Reports Nov 21/07	No Contest. Notice Sent Dec 4/07
(Illegible)	(Entry illegible)	
(Illegible)	(Entry illegible)	
Jan 13 08	Case set for hearing Claremore 2/6/8 All notified	
Feb 6 08	Case called no appearance by either party	
May 9 08	Pltf requested to advise if in possession or sat. settlement had	
5-15 08	Starr & Patton advised in re status of case	
3/26 1912	Form 330 to Allottee	

INTRUDER CASE NO. 1158
Cherokee NATION

Plaintiff	Sallie Bigfeather Stilwell Oklahoma	Atty.	
	Versus		
Defendant	Charles McClellan	Atty.	Joe Lahay Claremore Okla

Cherokee Intruder Cases 1901 - 1909

Complaint filed Nov 16 1907	Commissioner Reports Nov 28/07	No Contest. Notice Sent Dec 4/07

Dec 16 07	Return of service dated Dec 11/07 incorrectly made enclosed to plff for delivery of copy to deft
Jan 13 08	Case set for hearing Claremore 2/6/8 all notified
Feb 6 08	Case called no appearance by either party
May 8 08	Plaintiff requested to advise if in possession / settlement made
6-4 08	Deft requested to show cause within ten days
6-10 08	*(Entry illegible)*
7-29 08	*(Entry illegible)*
7-31 08	*(Entry illegible)*
Aug 27 08	Defdt's Atty requested to advise if client wants to take further action
Dec *(??)* 1908	Referred to R. R. Bennett for investigation
Jan 14 09	R. R Bennett reports
Jan 15 09	Pltf requested to go to her allotment and take poss. <u>Case Dismissed</u>

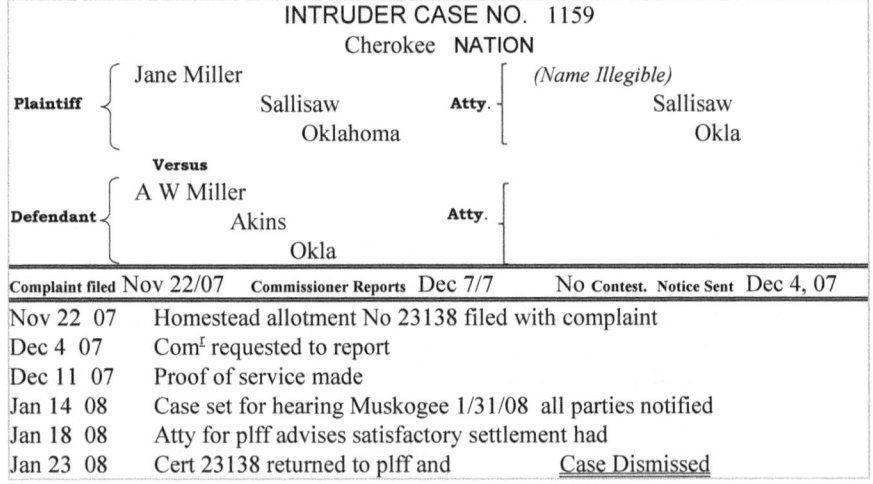

INTRUDER CASE NO. 1159
Cherokee NATION

Plaintiff: Jane Miller, Sallisaw, Oklahoma
Atty: *(Name Illegible)*, Sallisaw, Okla

Versus

Defendant: A W Miller, Akins, Okla
Atty:

Complaint filed Nov 22/07	Commissioner Reports Dec 7/7	No Contest. Notice Sent Dec 4, 07

Nov 22 07	Homestead allotment No 23138 filed with complaint
Dec 4 07	Com^r requested to report
Dec 11 07	Proof of service made
Jan 14 08	Case set for hearing Muskogee 1/31/08 all parties notified
Jan 18 08	Atty for plff advises satisfactory settlement had
Jan 23 08	Cert 23138 returned to plff and <u>Case Dismissed</u>

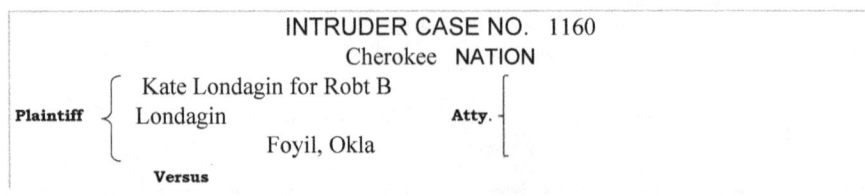

INTRUDER CASE NO. 1160
Cherokee NATION

Plaintiff: Kate Londagin for Robt B Londagin, Foyil, Okla
Atty:

Versus

Cherokee Intruder Cases 1901 - 1909

Defendant	John J R *(Illegible)* and Sarah E Downing	Atty.	
Complaint filed Nov 8/7	**Commissioner Reports** Dec 7/7		**Contest. Notice Sent**
Dec 4 07	Complaint sent Com^r to be checked etc		
Dec 7 07	Com^r Five C.T. reports Robt B Londagen is minor enrolled under provisions Act of Apr 26/6 therefore no certs have been issued		
Dec 20 07	Case dismissed at allottee[sic] enrolled under Act Apr 26/6		

INTRUDER CASE NO. 1161
Cherokee NATION

Plaintiff	John Martin	Atty.	D. G. Elliott Chelsea Okla
	Versus		
Defendant	W.C. Dillon	Atty.	

Complaint filed Nov 15/07	**Commissioner Reports** Dec 7/7	**No Contest. Notice Sent** 12/19/07
Nov 15 07	Letter of guardianship and allotment certificates filed	
Dec *(?)* 07	Com^r requested to report	
Dec 10 07	Proof of service made	
Dec 23 07	*(Entry illegible)*	
Jan 6 08	Pltf advised status case	
Jan 13 08	Case set for hearing Claremore 2/6/8 all parties notified	
Feb 6 08	Case called Plaintiff present evidence taken *(remainder illegible)*	
Mch 9 08	Pltf's Atty advised in re status of case	
(Illegible)	Judgment in favor of plff, copy sent each party; deft given 10 days and plff requested to advise if poss is given him in 10 days	
May 8 08	Plaintiff requested to advise if possession has been given	
5-14 08	Plff's Atty states deft has vacated and case is <u>Dismissed</u> and *(remainder illegible)*	

INTRUDER CASE NO. 1162
Cherokee NATION

Plaintiff	Minnie R Taylor for Stacy B. Taylor Coffeyville Kans	Atty.	
	Versus		

Cherokee Intruder Cases 1901 - 1909

Defendant	Della Hess and husband	Atty.	
Complaint filed	**Commissioner Reports**		No Contest. Notice Sent

(The entire entry is illegible.)

INTRUDER CASE NO. 1163
Cherokee NATION

Plaintiff	Nara Butler Claremore	Atty.	H. Jennings Claremore

Versus

Defendant	P E Wilkerson	Atty.	
Complaint filed	**Commissioner Reports**		No Contest. Notice Sent

(The entire entry is illegible.)

INTRUDER CASE NO. 1164
Cherokee NATION

Plaintiff	Mrs Amilio B. Henry for Agnes B. Henry Pryor Creek Okla	Atty.	

Versus

Defendant	S C Thompson Dewey Okla	Atty.	Fred B. Woodard Dewey Okla

Complaint filed Dec 17 07 **Commissioner Reports** Dec 27 07 No Contest. Notice Sent Dec 21 07

(The entire entry is illegible.)

INTRUDER CASE NO. 1165
Cherokee NATION

Plaintiff	Rose Marsh guardian of Clarence Marsh Muskogee Okla	Atty.	Masterson Peyton Muskogee Okla

Versus

Cherokee Intruder Cases 1901 - 1909

| Defendant | Alonzo Reynolds | Atty. | |

Complaint filed Dec 31 1907 **Commissioner Reports** Jan 8/8   **No Contest. Notice Sent** Dec 31 1907

January 2/08	Com^r requested to report
Jan 15 08	Case set for hearing Muskogee 1/31/08 all parties notified
Jan 15 08	Proof of service returned dated Jan 1, 1908
Jan 31 08	Case called No appearance by either party
May 8 08	Plaintiff requested to advise if in possession or if settlement has been made
6-27 08	Case dismissed as it is presumed pltf has possession
	<u>Dismissed</u>

INTRUDER CASE NO. 1166
Cherokee NATION

| Plaintiff | Rathbone Alden Gdn of Joseph Vinita, Okla | Atty. | Starr and Patton Vinita |

Versus

| Defendant | A R Green, et al | Atty. | |

Complaint filed Dec 7 1907 **Commissioner Reports** Dec 21/07   **No Contest. Notice Sent** Jan 3 1907

Dec 7 1907	Letters of guardianship filed by plaintiff
Jan 13 08	Case set for hearing Claremore 2/7/8 all parties notified
Jan 13 08	Proof of service returned dated Jan 8 1908
Jan 27 08	Plaintiff encloses an affidavit
Feb 7 08	Case called No appearance by plaintiff evidence of defendant taken. Lease filed by defendant. Defendant notified that if plaintiff appears later, case will again be set for hearing defendant notified. Defendant advised he will not be removed until a further hearing
April 1 08	*(Entry illegible)*
April 5 08	*(Entry illegible)*
4/21/08	*(Entry illegible)*
5-25 08	*(Entry illegible)*
6-6 08	*(Entry illegible)*
7-7 08	*(Entry illegible)* Dismissed.

Cherokee Intruder Cases 1901 - 1909

INTRUDER CASE NO. 1167
Cherokee NATION

Plaintiff: Stephens for Betsy, Cynthia B, *(Illegible)* & Lee M Stephens Claremore Okla

Atty.

Versus

Defendant: Jos McKebban Nowata Okla

Atty.

Complaint filed Dec 7 1907 **Commissioner Reports** Dec 21/7 **No Contest. Notice Sent** Jan 3 1908

Jan 13 08	Case set for hearing Claremore 2/7/8 All parties notified
Feb 7 08	Case called No appearance by either party
May 8 08	Pltf requested to advise if in possession or satisfactory settlement made
6-27 08	*(Entry illegible)*

Dismissed

INTRUDER CASE. 1168
Cherokee NATION

Plaintiff: Lewis Tyner for Myrtle Irene *(illegible)* and Lafayette & Mattie *(Illegible)* Campbell Okla

Atty. J. T. *(Illegible)* Muskogee Okla

Versus

Defendant: Geo Blackwell Albia Oklahoma

Atty. A S McRea Muskogee Okla

Complaint filed Dec 4 1907 **Commissioner Reports** Dec 30/7 **Contest. Notice Sent** Jan *(illegible)*

Dec 30 08[sic]	Com^r reports no contest on any of pltf's land except on Myrtle Irene Tyner and she is a 1/8 blood *(illegible)*
Jan 9 08	Proof of service returned dated Jan *(illegible)*
Jan 13 08	Case set for hearing Claremore 2/7/8 all parties notified
Feb 7 08	Case called All parties present *(remainder illegible)*
Mch 30 08	Plff writes asking for possession and is advised as to action

INTRUDER CASE NO. 1169
Cherokee NATION

Plaintiff: Edward Taylor Chelsea Okla

Atty. D. G. Elliott Chelsea Okla

Versus

Cherokee Intruder Cases 1901 - 1909

Defendant	J Camp and C M Melton	Atty.	

Complaint filed Dec 13 1908[sic] **Commissioner Reports** Dec 31/7   No **Contest. Notice Sent** Jan 5 1908

Dec 13 08[sic]	Case contract filed with complaint
" 28 08[sic]	Pltf requests status of case
Jan 13 08	Case set for hearing Claremore 2/7/8 all parties notified
Jan 20 08	DG Elliott returns all correspondence and papers in case and states that case has been settled
Jan 23 08	Agreeable to letter of Mr Elliott. <u>Case Dismissed</u>

INTRUDER CASE NO. 1170
Cherokee NATION

Plaintiff	Cull and Julia Thorne Tahlequah Okla	Atty.	

Versus

Defendant	Mr & Mrs Geo Hughes Tahlequah Okla	Atty.	Geo Hughes Tahlequah Okla

Complaint filed Dec 21 1907 **Commissioner Reports** Jan 10/8   No **Contest. Notice Sent** Jan *(illegible)*

Dec 21 07	Homestead certificates 2407 & 240*(8)* filed
Jan 4 08	Com^r requested to report
Jan 13 08	Proof of service returned dated Jan 11 1908
Jan 16 08	Case set for hearing Muskogee for Jan 27/8 all parties notified
Jan 18 08	Answer filed by defendant
Jan 27 08	Case called defendant Geo Hughes appearing and his testimony taken LB stenog
Jan 27 08	Plff advises *(remainder illegible)*
Feb 21 08	Pltfs requested to give evidence
Mch 21 08	Instructions issued to T. P. Roach
Mch 25 08	Report of Policeman Roach filed today & case <u>Dismissed</u> *(entry illegible)*
Mch 27 08	Certificates ret'd to pltf & *(remainder illegible)* Dismissed.

Cherokee Intruder Cases 1901 - 1909

	INTRUDER CASE NO. 1171 Cherokee NATION		
Plaintiff	Charley Tiblow Adm estate of (Name Illegible) deceased Muskogee Okla	Atty.	Thomas & Foreman Muskogee Okla
	Versus		
Defendant	One Fenwick Skiatook Okla	Atty.	

Complaint filed Dec 10 1907   Commissioner Reports Dec 21/7   No Contest. Notice Sent Jan 3 1908

Jan 13 08	Case set for hearing Claremore 2/7/8 all parties notified
Feb 7 08	Case called. Plaintiff appeared evidence taken. No appearance by defendant. Letters of administration filed by plaintiff
Apr 14 08	Judgment in favor of plff; copy sent each party; deft given 10 days plff requested to advise if poss is given in 10 days.
May 8 08	Plaintiff requested to advise if in possession at once
6-27 08	Case dismissed as it is presumed pltf has possession
	Dismissed

	INTRUDER CASE NO. 1172 Cherokee NATION		
Plaintiff	Moses Riley Muskogee Okla	Atty.	
	Versus		
Defendant	Miss Maud Manley Hayden Okla	Atty.	Preston Davis Sapulpa Okla

Complaint filed Jan 7 1908   Commissioner Reports Jan 10/8   No Contest. Notice Sent Jan 8 1908

Jan 8 1908	Certificate of Homestead 38682 and allotment cert 65288 filed
Jan 8 1908	Com^r requested to report
Jan 18 08	Proof of service made
Jan 27 08	Answer filed by defendant
Feb 14 08	Set for hearing at Muskogee on Feb 27-08
Feb 27 08	Case continued until Mch 13-08 at request of Defdts Atty
Mch 13 08	Case called all parties present evidence taken
4/24 08	Judgment rendered in favor of pltf.
5-5 08	Instructions issued to Capt West
5-4 08	Petition for appeal filed by defdt's Atty
5-13 08	Capt West reports that he placed pltf in possession & case is
	Dismissed

Cherokee Intruder Cases 1901 - 1909

12-28 08	Land in Jacket checked with certs 38682-65288 and same returned to Moses Riley in person

INTRUDER CASE NO. 1173
Cherokee NATION

Plaintiff	Mrs JJ Sevier for Leo E Sevier Webbers Falls Okla	Atty.	C. T. Walrond[sic] H. L. Sanders Muskogee Webbers Falls Okla
	Versus		
Defendant	Famous and Eliza Smith	Atty.	Cravens and Cravens Muskogee Okla

Complaint filed Jan 11 1908   **Commissioner Reports** Jan 28/8   **No Contest. Notice Sent** Jan 16/08

Jan 11 08	Cert of allotment filed No 23358
Jan 16 08	Com^r requested to report
Jan 22 08	Proof of service made and information requested
Jan 20 08	Com^r reports land allotted[sic] to Leo E Sevier & no contest
Feb 11 08	Ans filed by defdt's Attys
Feb 12 08	Registry return receipt filed by pltf today
	Set for hearing at Muskogee on Mch 21-08
Mch 21 08	Case called all parties present evidence taken
4/24 08	*(Entry illegible)*
4/27 08	Judgment rendered in favor of pltf & defdts given ten days
5-27 08	Instructions issued to Capt West
6-9 08	Capt West reports that he placed pltf in possession & case is <u>Dismissed</u>

INTRUDER CASE. 1174
Cherokee NATION

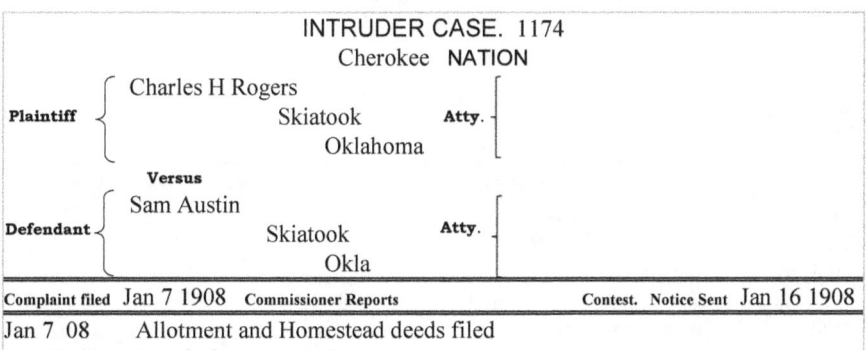

Plaintiff	Charles H Rogers Skiatook Oklahoma	Atty.	
	Versus		
Defendant	Sam Austin Skiatook Okla	Atty.	

Complaint filed Jan 7 1908   **Commissioner Reports**   **Contest. Notice Sent** Jan 16 1908

| Jan 7 08 | Allotment and Homestead deeds filed |
| Jan 18 08 | Proof of service made |

Cherokee Intruder Cases 1901 - 1909

Jan 28 08	Plaintiff advised to *(remainder illegible)*
Feb 12 08	Deeds returned to plaintiff
May 8 08	Pltf requested to advise if in possession or if further action is *(illegible)*
6-27 08	Case dismissed as it is presumed pltf has possession
	Dismissed

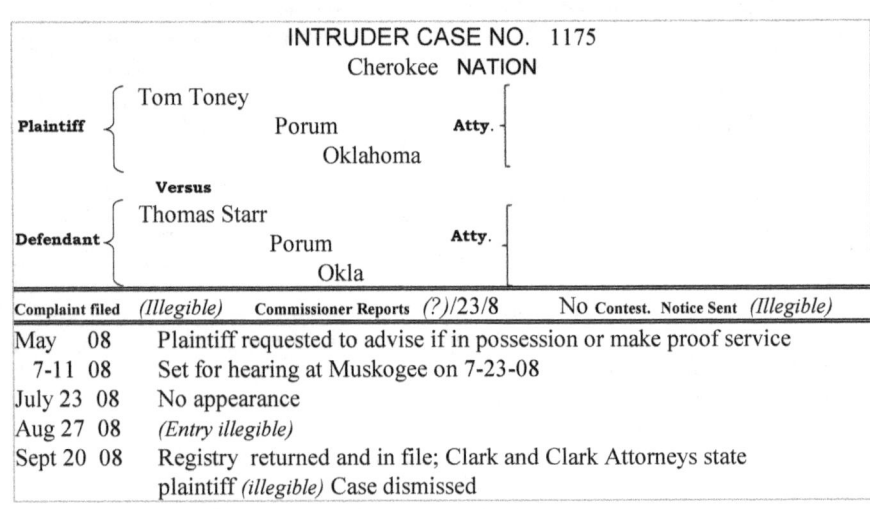

INTRUDER CASE NO. 1175
Cherokee NATION

Plaintiff: Tom Toney, Porum, Oklahoma Atty.

Versus

Defendant: Thomas Starr, Porum, Okla Atty.

Complaint filed *(Illegible)*   Commissioner Reports *(?)*/23/8   No Contest. Notice Sent *(Illegible)*

May 08	Plaintiff requested to advise if in possession or make proof service
7-11 08	Set for hearing at Muskogee on 7-23-08
July 23 08	No appearance
Aug 27 08	*(Entry illegible)*
Sept 20 08	Registry returned and in file; Clark and Clark Attorneys state plaintiff *(illegible)* Case dismissed

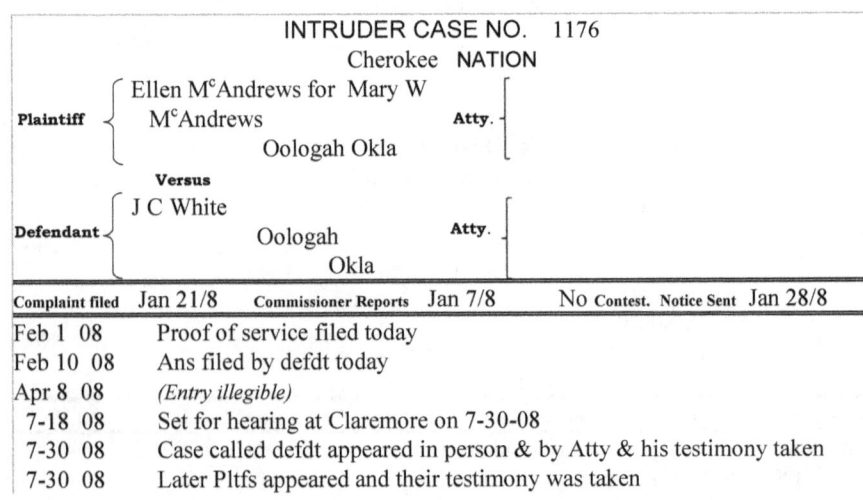

INTRUDER CASE NO. 1176
Cherokee NATION

Plaintiff: Ellen McAndrews for Mary W McAndrews, Oologah Okla Atty.

Versus

Defendant: J C White, Oologah Okla Atty.

Complaint filed Jan 21/8   Commissioner Reports Jan 7/8   No Contest. Notice Sent Jan 28/8

Feb 1 08	Proof of service filed today
Feb 10 08	Ans filed by defdt today
Apr 8 08	*(Entry illegible)*
7-18 08	Set for hearing at Claremore on 7-30-08
7-30 08	Case called defdt appeared in person & by Atty & his testimony taken
7-30 08	Later Pltfs appeared and their testimony was taken

Cherokee Intruder Cases 1901 - 1909

> Testimony shows pltf (minor) is N.B. Cherokee case pending in Court of Claims & Deft simply claims value of his impts

INTRUDER CASE NO. 1177
Cherokee NATION

Plaintiff: Sittingbull Tatum, Vian, Okla **Atty.**

Versus

Defendant: John E and Rachel Stevenson, Campbell, Okla **Atty.**

Complaint filed Jan 15/8	Commissioner Reports 1/23/8 — No Contest. Notice Sent Jan 28/8
Feb 3 08	Proof of service filed today
Feb 8 08	Ans filed today
Mch 25 08	Set for hearing at Muskogee on Apr 2nd/08
4/2 08	Case Dismissed as pltf is a minor

INTRUDER CASE. 1178
Cherokee NATION

Plaintiff: Joseph T Johnson guardian of *(Illegible)* and *(Illegible)* Johnson, Vinita Okla **Atty.**

Versus

Defendant: Arthur W. Anderson, Delaware, Okla **Atty.**

Complaint filed *(Illegible)*	Commissioner Reports *(Illegible)* — Contest. Notice Sent Jan 27/8
	Letters of gdnship dated June 7/7 *(illegible)* filed with complaint
Jan 31 08	Proof of service filed today
Feb 12 08	Ans filed by defdt
Feb 18 08	Pltf advised that defdt has ack. service
Feb 25 08	Pltf furnished lease & advised as to status of case
7-12 08	Set for hearing at Claremore on 7-30-08
7-27 08	*(Entry illegible)*
(Illegible)	Case dismissed *(remainder illegible)*

Dismissed

Cherokee Intruder Cases 1901 - 1909

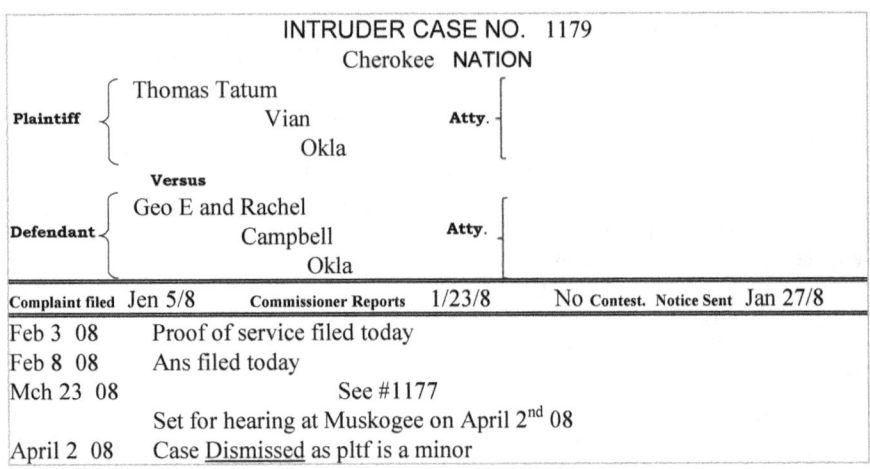

	INTRUDER CASE NO. 1179			
	Cherokee NATION			
Plaintiff	Thomas Tatum Vian Okla	Atty.		
	Versus			
Defendant	Geo E and Rachel Campbell Okla	Atty.		
Complaint filed Jen 5/8	Commissioner Reports 1/23/8		No Contest. Notice Sent Jan 27/8	
Feb 3 08	Proof of service filed today			
Feb 8 08	Ans filed today			
Mch 23 08	See #1177			
	Set for hearing at Muskogee on April 2nd 08			
April 2 08	Case Dismissed as pltf is a minor			

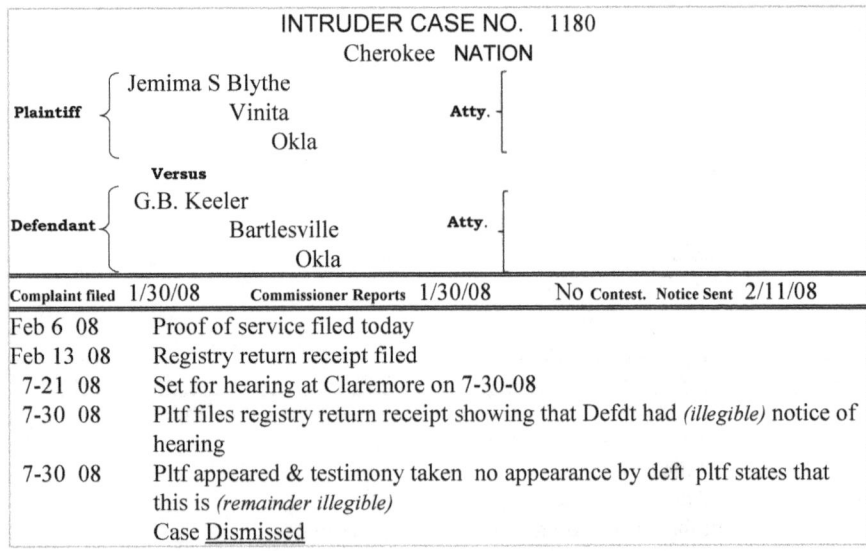

	INTRUDER CASE NO. 1180		
	Cherokee NATION		
Plaintiff	Jemima S Blythe Vinita Okla	Atty.	
	Versus		
Defendant	G.B. Keeler Bartlesville Okla	Atty.	
Complaint filed 1/30/08	Commissioner Reports 1/30/08		No Contest. Notice Sent 2/11/08
Feb 6 08	Proof of service filed today		
Feb 13 08	Registry return receipt filed		
7-21 08	Set for hearing at Claremore on 7-30-08		
7-30 08	Pltf files registry return receipt showing that Defdt had *(illegible)* notice of hearing		
7-30 08	Pltf appeared & testimony taken no appearance by deft pltf states that this is *(remainder illegible)* Case Dismissed		

Cherokee Intruder Cases 1901 - 1909

INTRUDER CASE NO. 1181
Cherokee NATION

Plaintiff	Aaron Webber for *(Illegible)* Webber, Cedar Okla	**Atty.**	
	Versus		
Defendant	John & Cora Dennumber, Ruby Okla	**Atty.**	Thomas & Foreman, Muskogee Okla

Complaint filed 2/6/08 **Commissioner Reports** 2/6/08 **No Contest. Notice Sent** 2/12/08

Mch 2 08	Proof of service filed today
7-12 08	Set for hearing at Claremore on 7-30-08
7-25 08	*(Entry illegible)*
Aug 27 08	*(Entry illegible)*
Sept 26 08	No response is being made to above Case <u>dismissed</u>

INTRUDER CASE NO. 1182
Cherokee NATION

Plaintiff	Lora J Sellers nee Allison, Sageeyah Okla	**Atty.**	A.F. Wood, Claremore Okla
	Versus		
Defendant	K & A V R.R., Sageeyah Okla	**Atty.**	Lorick P. Miles, Ft Smith Okla

Complaint filed 2/3/08 **Commissioner Reports** 2/17/08 **No Contest. Notice Sent** 2/12/08

	Certificates in file
Feb 17 08	Com reports Pltf is 1/32 blood Cherokee
Feb 17 08	Proof of service filed today
Feb 21 08	Defdt's Atty requests that hearing in this case be postponed for <u>some time</u>
April 2 08	Pltf's & defdt's Atty advised in re status of case
Apr 14 08	Lorick P Miles advises he will go into matter *(illegible)* and plff so advised
7-14 08	Set for hearing at Claremore on 7-30-08 - <u>Testimony taken</u>
Aug 18 08	Allotment certs ret'd to pltf
May 8 09	Requested to advise if settlement made
May 20 09	Pltf states no settlement
" " "	R R Co requested to make showing in re right of way
June 6 09	R R Co states will advise at an early date
June 26 09	" " requested to vacate or make arrangements with allottee[sic] to occupy land & pltf requested to advise if same is done

Cherokee Intruder Cases 1901 - 1909

INTRUDER CASE NO. 1183
Cherokee **NATION**

Plaintiff: W. M. Clines, Sallisaw, Okla   Atty.

Versus

Defendant: Sam Elk, Sallisaw   Atty.

Complaint filed	2/8/08	Commissioner Reports	2/18/08	No Contest. Notice Sent	2/18/08

	Certificates in file
Feb 18 08	Proof of service filed today
5-8 08	(Entry illegible)
5-22 08	(Entry illegible)
6-22 08	Pltf requested to advise if he has possession
7-11 08	Set for hearing at Muskogee 7-22-08
Dec 21 1908	Referred to R R Bennett for investigation
Jan 14 09	R R Bennett reports that settlement has been made
	<div align="right">Case Dismissed</div>

INTRUDER CASE NO. 1184
Cherokee **NATION**

Plaintiff: Simon Lynch, Spavinaw, Okla   Atty.   A.S. McRae, Muskogee, Okla

Versus

Defendant: T.T. Wimer, Vinita, Okla; G.S. White " "; G.W. McGeorge, Vinita Okla   Atty.   W.P. Thompson, Vinita, Okla

Complaint filed	Feb 18-08	Commissioner Reports	Feb 18-08	No Contest. Notice Sent	Feb 20-08

Mch 2 08	Proof of service filed today
Mch 5 08	Ans filed by Defdt's Atty
Mch 13 08	Defdt McGeorge advised in re status of case
Mch 16 08	Set for hearing at Muskogee on Mch 26-08
	Pltf will not be *(illegible)*
Mch 24 08	*(Name Illegible)* advised in re status of case
Mch 26 08	All parties present & statements made & in file
4/28 08	Case dismissed by order of W W B as defdt does not claim possession Dismissed

Cherokee Intruder Cases 1901 - 1909

INTRUDER CASE NO. 1185
Cherokee NATION

Plaintiff: Elsie May / Bluejacket
Bluejacket
Okla

Atty:

Versus

Defendant: M. K. & T. Ry. Co

Atty: C L Jackson
Muskogee
Okla

| Complaint filed | Feb 18-08 | Commissioner Reports | Feb 21-08 | No Contest. Notice Sent | Feb 26-08 |

	Allotment certificate in file
Mch 3 08	Proof of service filed today
Mch 11 08	Ans filed by defdt's Atty
Mch 27 08	Defdt *(illegible)* certain information
(Illegible)	*(Entry illegible)*

INTRUDER CASE NO. 1186
Cherokee NATION

Plaintiff: John W Graham for
Robert L Graham
Inola Okla

Atty: *(Illegible)* G. Davis
Muskogee
Okla

Versus

Defendant: Robt Haggerman
Hollow
Okla

Atty:

| Complaint filed | Feb 29-08 | Commissioner Reports | Mch 6-08 | No Contest. Notice Sent | Mch 12-08 |

Mch 6 08	Proof of service filed today
	Allotment certificate in file
Mch 24 08	Ans filed by defdt today
(Illegible)	Set for hearing at Muskogee *(remainder illegible)*
(Illegible)	Case called all parties present evidence taken and case continued until 5-21-08 by agreement
5-21 08	All parties present evidence taken
7-22 08	Judgment rendered in favor of pltf
Sept 2 08	Pltf requests possession
" 4 08	Instructions issued to Capt West
Oct 3 08	Capt West reports placed pltf in possession
	<u>Case Dismissed</u>

Cherokee Intruder Cases 1901 - 1909

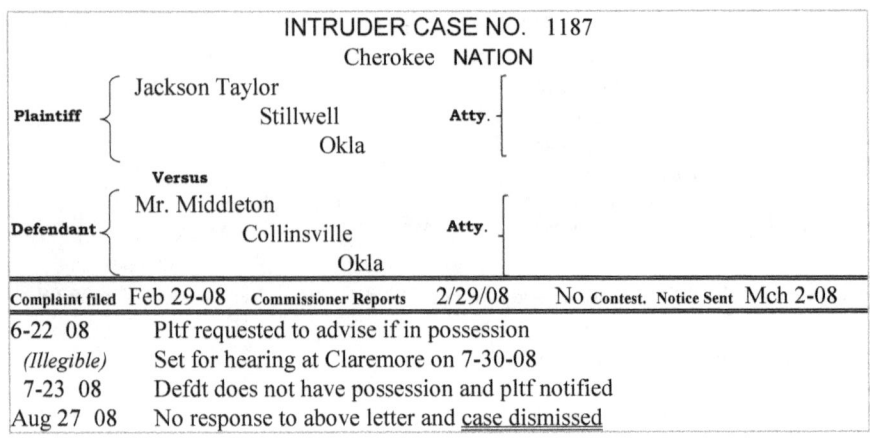

	INTRUDER CASE NO. 1187 Cherokee NATION		
Plaintiff	Jackson Taylor Stillwell Okla	**Atty.**	
	Versus		
Defendant	Mr. Middleton Collinsville Okla	**Atty.**	
Complaint filed Feb 29-08	**Commissioner Reports** 2/29/08	**No Contest. Notice Sent** Mch 2-08	
6-22 08	Pltf requested to advise if in possession		
(Illegible)	Set for hearing at Claremore on 7-30-08		
7-23 08	Defdt does not have possession and pltf notified		
Aug 27 08	No response to above letter and <u>case dismissed</u>		

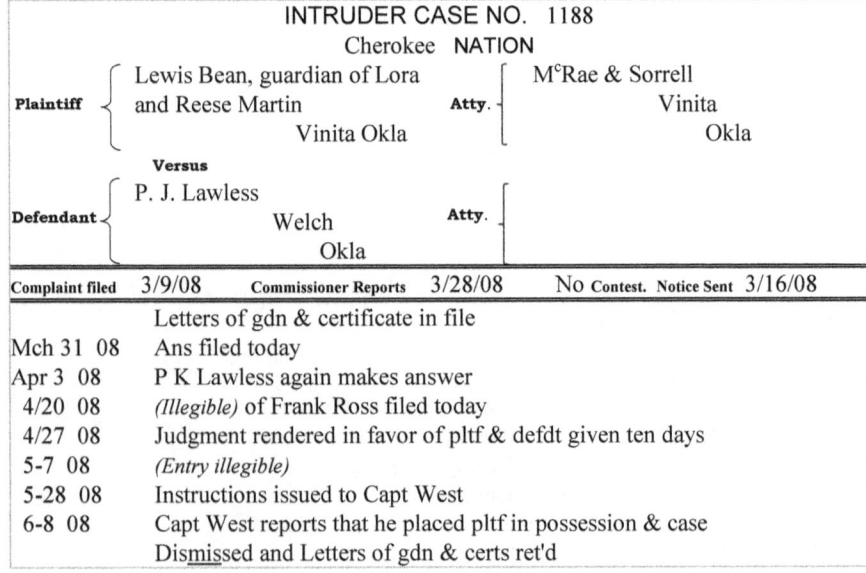

	INTRUDER CASE NO. 1188 Cherokee NATION		
Plaintiff	Lewis Bean, guardian of Lora and Reese Martin Vinita Okla	**Atty.**	McRae & Sorrell Vinita Okla
	Versus		
Defendant	P. J. Lawless Welch Okla	**Atty.**	
Complaint filed 3/9/08	**Commissioner Reports** 3/28/08	**No Contest. Notice Sent** 3/16/08	
	Letters of gdn & certificate in file		
Mch 31 08	Ans filed today		
Apr 3 08	P K Lawless again makes answer		
4/20 08	*(Illegible)* of Frank Ross filed today		
4/27 08	Judgment rendered in favor of pltf & defdt given ten days		
5-7 08	*(Entry illegible)*		
5-28 08	Instructions issued to Capt West		
6-8 08	Capt West reports that he placed pltf in possession & case <u>Dismissed</u> and Letters of gdn & certs ret'd		

260

Cherokee Intruder Cases 1901 - 1909

INTRUDER CASE NO. 1189
Cherokee NATION

Plaintiff: Sarah Sixkiller, Sole and only heir of Katie Downing, dec'd.
Tahlequah Okla
Atty.

Versus

Defendant: John F. McClellan
Claremore
Okla
Atty. Joe Lahay
Claremore
Okla

| Complaint filed | 3/12/08 | Commissioner Reports | Mch 27-08 | No Contest. | Notice Sent | 3/21/08 |

Mch 26 08	Report of Frank Robbin filed / Return of service made
4/2 08	Set for hearing at Muskogee 5/7/08
5-7 08	Case called Pltf appeared evidence taken no appearance by defdt
5-7 08	Letter from defdt stating that his Atty is sick & unable to attend asks for continuance for *(illegible)*
5-9 08	Defdt notified to appear *(remainder illegible)*
7-10 08	Judgment rendered in favor of pltf & defdt given ten days
(Illegible)	(Entry illegible)
12-22 08	Letter to defdt thru Atty asking for certified copy of <u>perfected</u> appeal
1-2 08[sic]	Receipt acknowledged of Deft's Atty's letter in re appeal and judgment *(remainder illegible)*
(Illegible)	(Entry illegible)
(Illegible)	Judgment rendered in favor of pltf and defdt given 10 days
July 4 09	Police ordered to place pltf in possession
" 7 09	" reports he placed pltf in possession
" 8 09	Petition for injunction served on Agent
July 31 09	Com^r advised that injunction was dissolved and <u>case dismissed</u>

INTRUDER CASE. 1190
Cherokee NATION

Plaintiff: Pearl Murphy
Sallisaw
Okla
Atty.

Versus

Defendant: Charles Avery
Maple
Okla
Atty.

Cherokee Intruder Cases 1901 - 1909

Complaint filed	3/20/08	Commissioner Reports		Contest. Notice Sent	3/27/08
	Allotment Patents in file				
(Illegible)	Proof of service filed today				
(Illegible)	*(Entry illegible)*				
(Illegible)	*(Entry illegible)*				
(Illegible)	*(Entry illegible)*				
(Illegible)	*(Entry illegible)*			Dismissed	

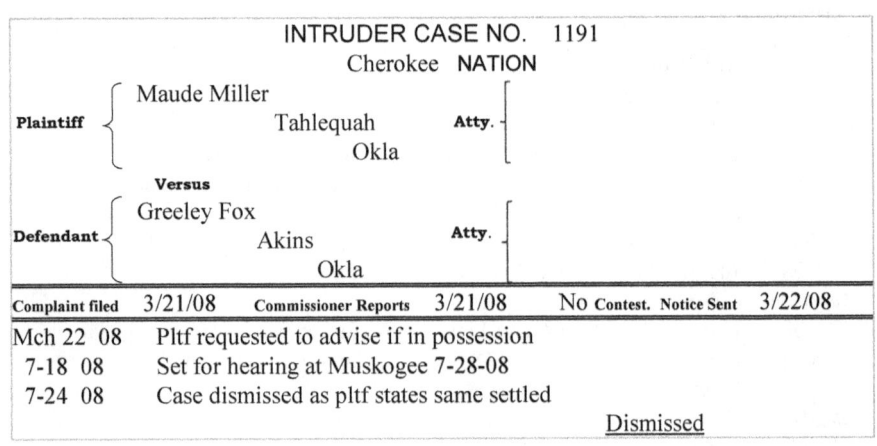

INTRUDER CASE NO. 1191
Cherokee NATION

Plaintiff: Maude Miller, Tahlequah, Okla   **Atty.**

Versus

Defendant: Greeley Fox, Akins, Okla   **Atty.**

Complaint filed	3/21/08	Commissioner Reports	3/21/08	No Contest. Notice Sent	3/22/08
Mch 22 08	Pltf requested to advise if in possession				
7-18 08	Set for hearing at Muskogee 7-28-08				
7-24 08	Case dismissed as pltf states same settled				
				Dismissed	

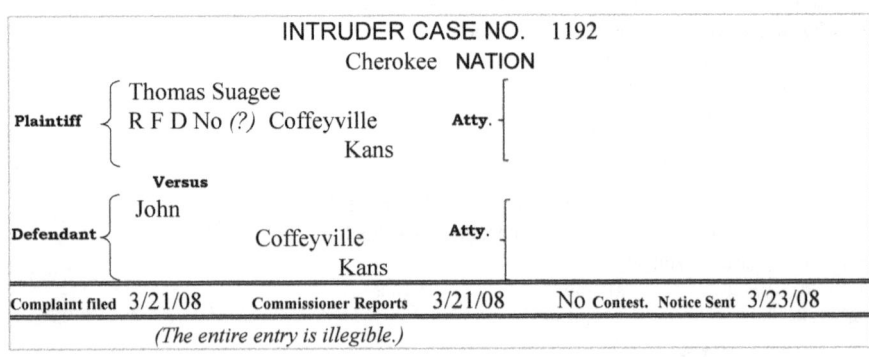

INTRUDER CASE NO. 1192
Cherokee NATION

Plaintiff: Thomas Suagee, R F D No *(?)* Coffeyville, Kans   **Atty.**

Versus

Defendant: John, Coffeyville, Kans   **Atty.**

Complaint filed	3/21/08	Commissioner Reports	3/21/08	No Contest. Notice Sent	3/23/08
(The entire entry is illegible.)					

Cherokee Intruder Cases 1901 - 1909

INTRUDER CASE NO. 1193
Cherokee NATION

Plaintiff: Bettie Clark, Stigler, Okla — Atty.

Versus

Defendant: Frank McGinnis, Collinsville, Okla — Atty.

Complaint filed 3/18/08   Commissioner Reports 3/27/08   No Contest. Notice Sent 3/23/08

	Allotment certificates in file
(Illegible)	Proof of service filed today
(Illegible)	Allotment certs returned to pltf
(Illegible)	Set for hearing at Muskogee (illegible)
5-20 08	Ans filed
5-22 08	No appearance
5-25 08	Pltf requested advise in re status of case
6-22 08	" " " " " " "
7-11 08	Set for hearing at Muskogee 7-22-08
7-21 08	Case Dismissed as pltf states she has possession (illegible) settled
	<u>Dismissed</u>

INTRUDER CASE NO. 1194
Cherokee NATION

Plaintiff: Josef S Heard for Bessie Heard, White Oak, Okla — Atty.

Versus

Defendant: S G Mills, White Oak, Okla — Atty.

Complaint filed 3/17/08   Commissioner Reports 3/28/08 (illegible) Contest.   Notice Sent 3/27/08

	Allotment certificates in file
Mch 28 08	Return of service made
(Illegible)	Proof of service filed today
Mch 31 08	Ans filed today
4/23 08	(Entry illegible)
	and case <u>Dismissed</u>

Cherokee Intruder Cases 1901 - 1909

INTRUDER CASE NO. 1195
Cherokee NATION

Plaintiff: Fannie Richardson, Claremore, Okla   Atty.

Versus

Defendant: Charley Holley *(illegible)*, Catoosa, Okla   Atty.

| Complaint filed 3/22/08 | Commissioner Reports 3/23/08 | No Contest. Notice Sent 3/24/08 |

3-22 08	Pltf requested to advise *(illegible)*
7-2 08	Set for hearing at Claremore on 7-30-08
7-30 08	Case called pltf & defdt Holley appeared testimony taken
7-30 08	*(Entry illegible)*
Aug 7 08	Defdt filed two affidavits
Aug 8 08	Pltf requested to advise if letter executed *(remainder illegible)*
Dec 24 08	Referred to R.R. Bennett for investigation
1-8 09	R.R.B. reports land sold since July 27-08 & she being 1/16 blood Case is dismissed.

INTRUDER CASE NO. 1196
Cherokee NATION

Plaintiff: Malinda Parker for Ola Parker, Vian Okla   Atty.

Versus

Defendant: Joshua Drew, Vian, Okla   Atty.

| Complaint filed Mch 20-08 | Commissioner Reports *(Illegible)* | No Contest. Notice Sent April 1-08 |

	Allotment certificates in file
April 8 08	Proof of service filed today
April 23 08	Set for hearing at Muskogee May 4th -08
5/4 08	Case called all parties present evidence taken defdt has been *(remainder illegible)*
5/4 08	Allotment certificates ret'd *(remainder illegible)* Dismissed

Cherokee Intruder Cases 1901 - 1909

INTRUDER CASE NO. 1197
Cherokee NATION

Plaintiff: Julia Nivens guardian of Andrew J. Griffin, Muskogee Okla
Atty: Owen, Stone & *(Illegible)*, Muskogee Okla

Versus

Defendant: Bettie *(Illegible)*, Muskogee Okla
Atty: Mr *(Illegible)* Payton, ~~Thos H Owen~~ ~~Muskogee Okla~~

Complaint filed Mch 28-08 **Commissioner Reports** in file **Contest. Notice Sent** April 1-08

	Letters of gdn in file
April 8 08	Set for hearing at Muskogee on April 26-08
Apr 10 08	Proof of service made
5-9 08	Ans filed today by Defdt's Atty
5-9 08	All parties appeared & case was continued by stipulation until 5-23-08
5-23 08	Case again called pltf appeared in person & by Atty defdt by Atty only Pltf's evidence taken Continued until Monday 5-25-08 at $2^{\underline{00}}$ P.M.
5-25 08	Case again called & testimony taken
Aug 15 1909	Owen & Stone requested to advise if desire further action
" 17 09	" " " " immediate action
" 22 09	*(Name Illegible)* requested to vacate
" 22 09	" " states she has surrendered land
" 25 09	Owen & Stone advised of above and requested to advise as to disposition of case

INTRUDER CASE NO. 1198
Cherokee NATION

Plaintiff: John Coats for Lillie M Coats, Choteau Okla
Atty: Geo E M$^{\underline{c}}$Culloch, Vinita Okla

Versus

Defendant: Jim Estes and Mattie L Choate, Choteau Okla
Atty:

Complaint filed Mch 25-08 **Commissioner Reports** Mch 25-08 No **Contest. Notice Sent** Apr 15/8

	This is a N.B. allottee[sic] and M.L. Choate owns improvements but case is made up & to be investigated under order of Com$^{\underline{r}}$ *(Illegible)*
4/20 08	Proof of service as to both defdts filed
4/23 08	Ans filed by Mattie Choate

Cherokee Intruder Cases 1901 - 1909

4/28 08	Set for hearing at Muskogee 5/11/08
5/4 08	*(Entry illegible)*
5/1 08	Ans filed by defdt Choate
5-8 08	Pltf advised in re status of case
5-11 08	Case called defdt appeared & her evidence taken no appearance by pltf defdt agreed to surrender land to pltf if he would *(illegible)* *(illegible)* of improvements
5-12 08	Pltf requested to advise *(remainder illegible)*
5-16 08	Set for hearing at Muskogee 5-28-08
5-28 08	Continued by agreement until 6-10-08 at 10 AM
6-8 08	Case Dis<u>miss</u>ed as allottee[sic] is N.B. & certs have not been issued Dismissed

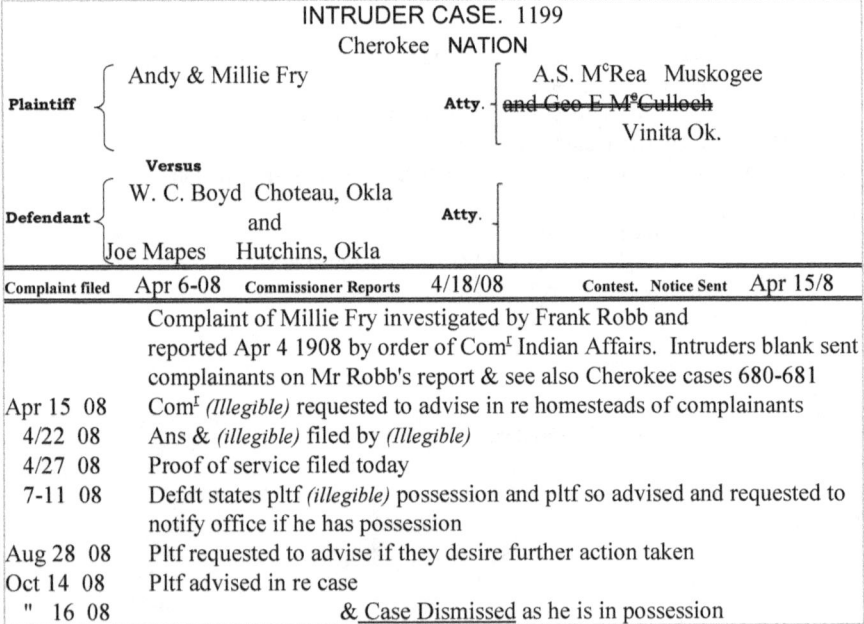

INTRUDER CASE. 1199
Cherokee NATION

Plaintiff: Andy & Millie Fry
Atty.: A.S. McRea Muskogee ~~and Geo F McCulloch~~ Vinita Ok.

Versus

Defendant: W. C. Boyd Choteau, Okla and Joe Mapes Hutchins, Okla
Atty.:

| Complaint filed | Apr 6-08 | Commissioner Reports | 4/18/08 | Contest. Notice Sent | Apr 15/8 |

	Complaint of Millie Fry investigated by Frank Robb and reported Apr 4 1908 by order of Com^r Indian Affairs. Intruders blank sent complainants on Mr Robb's report & see also Cherokee cases 680-681
Apr 15 08	Com^r *(Illegible)* requested to advise in re homesteads of complainants
4/22 08	Ans & *(illegible)* filed by *(Illegible)*
4/27 08	Proof of service filed today
7-11 08	Defdt states pltf *(illegible)* possession and pltf so advised and requested to notify office if he has possession
Aug 28 08	Pltf requested to advise if they desire further action taken
Oct 14 08	Pltf advised in re case
" 16 08	& Case Dismissed as he is in possession

INTRUDER CASE NO. 1200
Cherokee NATION

Plaintiff: Mary Terrell Eureka Okla
Atty.:

Cherokee Intruder Cases 1901 - 1909

Defendant	Versus Alonzo Ward Dawson or Tulsa Okla	Atty.

Complaint filed Mch 27 08	Commissioner Reports 4/8/08	No Contest. Notice Sent Apr 15 1908
Apr 15 08	Com^r requested to report Certs 23846 17502 having been filed *(illegible)*	
(Illegible)	Proof of service filed today	
(Illegible)	Set for hearing at *(remainder illegible)*	
5-28 08	Case dismissed as pltf now has possession and certs returned	
		Dismissed

INTRUDER CASE NO. 1201
Cherokee NATION

Plaintiff	Kittie J Shoemaker Nowata Okla	Atty.
Defendant	Versus O J Smith White Oak Okla	Atty.

Complaint filed Mch 21 1908	Commissioner Reports Apr 7-08	No Contest. Notice Sent Apr 15 1908
3-22 08	Pltf requested to advise in re possession	
7-(??) 08	Set for hearing at Claremore on 7-31-08	
7-31 08	O J Smith appeared & stated that he was in possession of land in testimony and exhibited a letter rec'd by him from pltf stating was sick and unable to appear *(illegible)* he might *(illegible)* on land with debt of $250^{00} which she owed him for improvements was cancelled	
7-31 08	Proof of service filed	
Dec 21 08	Referred to R.R. Bennett for investigation	
1-9 09	Reports transmitting signed statement from pltf & Case Dismissed	

INTRUDER CASE NO. 1202
Cherokee NATION

Plaintiff	Nancy Bird Long Okla	Atty.
Defendant	Versus Geo Waters Long Okla	Atty.

Cherokee Intruder Cases 1901 - 1909

Complaint filed Mch 19 1907	Commissioner Reports Apr 7-08	No Contest. Notice Sent Apr 15 1908
5-15 08	Proof of service filed today	
6-22 08	Pltf requested to advise in re possession	
(?)-13 08	Set for hearing at Muskogee *(illegible)*	
July 24 08	Case called Plaintiff did not appear Deft present testimony taken LB stenog.	
Aug 28 08	Pltf requested to advise if in possession	
(?)-28 08	Referred to R R Bennett for investigation	
(?)-25 08	*(Entry illegible)*	Case Dismissed

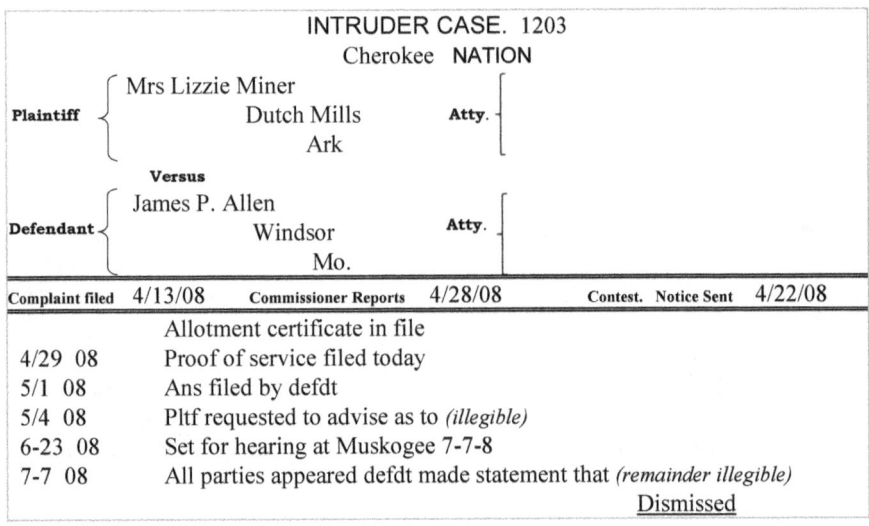

INTRUDER CASE. 1203
Cherokee NATION

Plaintiff: Mrs Lizzie Miner, Dutch Mills, Ark   Atty.

Versus

Defendant: James P. Allen, Windsor, Mo.   Atty.

Complaint filed 4/13/08	Commissioner Reports 4/28/08	Contest. Notice Sent 4/22/08
	Allotment certificate in file	
4/29 08	Proof of service filed today	
5/1 08	Ans filed by defdt	
5/4 08	Pltf requested to advise as to *(illegible)*	
6-23 08	Set for hearing at Muskogee 7-7-8	
7-7 08	All parties appeared defdt made statement that *(remainder illegible)*	Dismissed

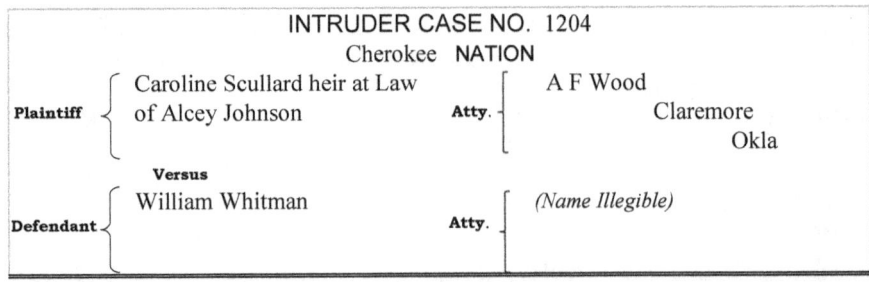

INTRUDER CASE NO. 1204
Cherokee NATION

Plaintiff: Caroline Scullard heir at Law of Alcey Johnson   Atty.   A F Wood, Claremore, Okla

Versus

Defendant: William Whitman   Atty.   *(Name Illegible)*

Cherokee Intruder Cases 1901 - 1909

Complaint filed	*(Illegible)*	Commissioner Reports	*(Illegible)*	No Contest. Notice Sent	*(Illegible)*
5-5 08	Proof of service filed today				
5-18 08	Ans filed by defdt's Atty				
7-13 08	Set for hearing at Claremore *(illegible)*				
7-31 08	Pltf's Atty filed reply to defdts *(illegible...)* each & every material *(illegible)*				
7-31 08	Case called Pltf appeared in person & by Atty Defdt by Atty only Pltf testimony taken and *(remainder illegible)*				
9-14 08	*(Entry illegible)*				

INTRUDER CASE NO. 1205
Cherokee NATION

Plaintiff: Wash England Guardian of Pigeon, Betsy, Andrew and John England Atty.
Dodge Okla

Versus

Defendant: Frank Gaines Atty.
Fairland
Okla

Complaint filed 4/17/08	Commissioner Reports 2/25	No Contest. Notice Sent 4/22/08
	Allotment certificates and letter of gdn in file	
5-5 08	Proof of service filed	
5-5 08	Power of Atty filed by G.R. McLaughlin	
5-9 08	Ans filed today also lease contract	
6-9 08	G R McLaughlin advised in re status of case	
7-14 08	Set for hearing at Claremore on 7-31-08	
7-31 08	G R McLaughlin appeared & filed two affidavits and Power of Atty & stated that Pltf was sick & unable to appear	
Aug 19 08	G R McLaughlin request early action	
" 24 08	*(Illegible)* of case will be taken up at early date	
Oct 21 08	Judgment in favor of pltf	
Dec 28 08	Pltf given 10 days to advise if in poss Registered *(illegible)*	
1-27 09	*(Illegible)* to letter of Jan 19-09 instructions issued to Capt West to place allottee[sic] in possession.	
2-4 09	Capt West reports defts have been removed, turned over to *(Illegible)* Breedlove a Cherokee to hold for Wash England who lived some 20 miles from the allotment	
2-25 09	In view of above Case Dismissed	
3-29 09	Cusey (D.E.) requested to assist in making new lease	

Cherokee Intruder Cases 1901 - 1909

INTRUDER CASE. 1206
Cherokee NATION

Plaintiff: Martin and Alice Miller, Eureka, Okla   Atty.

Versus

Defendant: Joe Alberty and Joe Thompson, *Freedmen*, Fort Gibson, Okla   Atty.

Complaint filed	4/(?)/08	Commissioner Reports	4/(?)/08	Contest. Notice Sent	(Illegible)
(Illegible)	Pltf advised in re status of case				
5-5 08	Proof of service filed today				
5-8 08	Ans filed by defdt Alberty				
5-14 08	Set for hearing at Muskogee *(illegible)*				
5-26 08	Pltf & Defdt appeared defdt is a claimant				
3/26 1912	Form 330 to allottee				

INTRUDER CASE NO. 1207
Cherokee NATION

Plaintiff: Violet Randler, Choteau, Okla   Atty.

Versus

Defendant: Jack McConnell   Atty.

Complaint filed	(?)/27-08	Commissioner Reports	(Illegible)	Contest. Notice Sent	(Illegible)
(Illegible)	Set for hearing at Muskogee on 7-24-08				
(Illegible)	*(Entry illegible)*				
Dec 19 08	*(Illegible...)* case is <u>dismissed</u>				

INTRUDER CASE NO. 1208
Cherokee NATION

Plaintiff: Emma White, White Oak, Okla   Atty.

Versus

Cherokee Intruder Cases 1901 - 1909

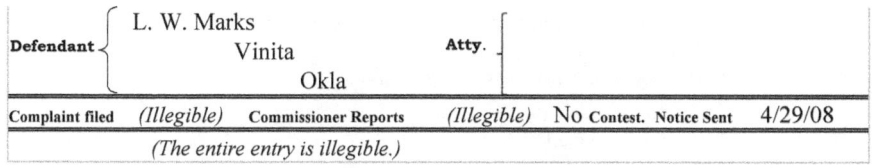

Defendant	L. W. Marks Vinita Okla		Atty.		
Complaint filed	*(Illegible)*	Commissioner Reports	*(Illegible)*	No Contest. Notice Sent	4/29/08
	(The entire entry is illegible.)				

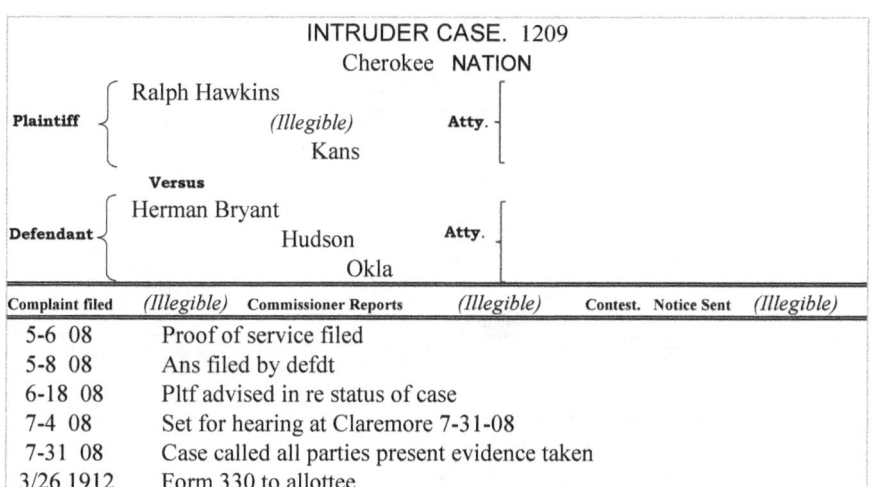

INTRUDER CASE. 1209
Cherokee NATION

Plaintiff	Ralph Hawkins *(Illegible)* Kans		Atty.		
	Versus				
Defendant	Herman Bryant Hudson Okla		Atty.		
Complaint filed	*(Illegible)*	Commissioner Reports	*(Illegible)*	Contest. Notice Sent	*(Illegible)*

5-6 08	Proof of service filed
5-8 08	Ans filed by defdt
6-18 08	Pltf advised in re status of case
7-4 08	Set for hearing at Claremore 7-31-08
7-31 08	Case called all parties present evidence taken
3/26 1912	Form 330 to allottee

INTRUDER CASE NO. 1210
Cherokee NATION

Plaintiff	Jennie Hare nee Littlejohn Halbert Okla		Atty.	J D Cox Tahlequah	
	Versus				
Defendant	Tom Ford Rhoda Ford (Reg Fr) Melvin Okla		Atty.		
Complaint filed	4-28-08	Commissioner Reports	7-23-08	No Contest. Notice Sent	*(Illegible)*

	Allotment and Deeds in file
5-8 08	Proof of service filed today
5-12 08	Ans filed by Rhoda Ford
5-16 08	Set for hearing at Muskogee 5-29-08
5-29 08	Case called Pltf's husband & defdt appeared Defdt's evidence taken

Cherokee Intruder Cases 1901 - 1909

	& *(illegible...)* for pltfs evidence as she was sick and unable to appear
6-6 08	Deeds ret'd to pltf
10-13 08	Letter from Deft referred by *(illegible)*
10-17 08	" answered & pltf advised
2-6 08[sic]	Pltfs again advised
Oct 23 09	*(Entry illegible)*
3/26 1912	Form 330 to allottee

INTRUDER CASE. 1211
Cherokee NATION

Plaintiff	Ollie T. Barker Bartlesville Okla	Atty.	*(Name Illegible)* *(Illegible)* Okla
	Versus		
Defendant	Bartlesville *(Illegible)* Buck Co Bartlesville Okla	Atty.	*(Illegible)* and Rowland Bartlesville Okla

Complaint filed	4-21-08	Commissioner Reports	4-26-08 7-23-08 No	Contest. Notice Sent	5-4-08
5-1 08	Ans filed				
5-15 08	~~Ans~~ Proof of service filed				
5-22 08	Set for hearing at Muskogee on 6-*(?)*-08				
5-27 08	Pltf and defdt advised in re status of case				
6-3 08	Pltf's Atty asks that dept take no further action				
6-10 08	Defdt *(illegible)*				
(?)-21 08	*(Entry illegible)*				
(Illegible) 09	*(Entry illegible)*				
June 20 1910	W W Bennett instructed to proceed to Bartlesville and place allottee[sic] in poss. *(Remainder illegible)*				
June 21 10	Affidavit of *(Illegible)* filed & service of notice to vacate ~~on~~ made				
June 22 10	Report of WW B filed				

INTRUDER CASE NO. 1212
Cherokee NATION

Plaintiff	*(Name Illegible)* killer Proctor Okla	Atty.	
	Versus		
Defendant	William P. M{c}Clellan Claremore Okla	Atty.	

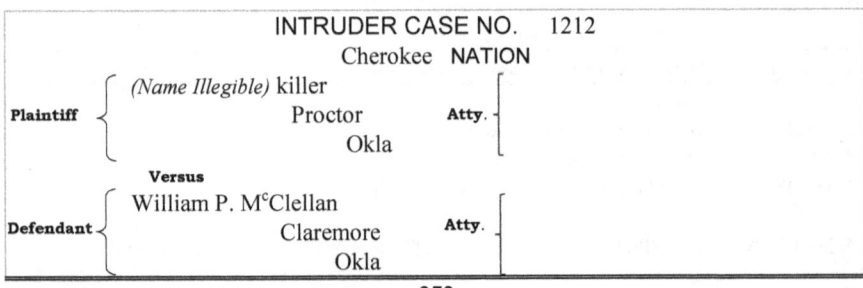

Cherokee Intruder Cases 1901 - 1909

Complaint filed	Commissioner Reports	No Contest. Notice Sent
	(The entire entry is illegible.)	Dismissed

INTRUDER CASE NO. 1213
Cherokee NATION

Plaintiff *(Name Illegible)* Atty.

Versus

Defendant *(Name Illegible)* Atty.

Complaint filed	Commissioner Reports	Contest. Notice Sent
	(The entire entry is illegible.)	Dismissed

INTRUDER CASE NO. 1214
Cherokee NATION

Plaintiff C.P. Clark guardian of Herman Clark, Webbers Falls Okla   Atty.

Versus

Defendant R.P. and F.J. Vann   Atty.

Complaint filed	5-5-08	Commissioner Reports		No Contest. Notice Sent 5-13-08

	Commissioner Reports
	Letters of gdn & Plat in file
(Illegible)	Proof of service filed today. 5-(?)-08 Ans filed
5-23 08	Defdt Vann called in person today and stated that he did not think they were in possession of pltf's land and pltf so notified & requested to have lines located, defdts stated that they would vacate if shown to be in possession of pltf's land.
(Illegible)	*(Entry illegible)*
May 11 09	Pltf requested to advise if defdt & himself have entered into agreement or if satisfactory settlement made
(?)-20 09	Pltf advises that lines not been located
" " "	Com^r to the 5 requested to send out a gov't surveyor

Cherokee Intruder Cases 1901 - 1909

INTRUDER CASE NO. 1215
Cherokee NATION

Plaintiff: Houston Downing gdn of Mary and Hill Downing Grove Okla   Atty.

Versus

Defendant: J.A. Frasier and J.L. Link Southwest City Mo   Atty.

Complaint filed 5-19-08   **Commissioner Reports** 5-29-08   No **Contest. Notice Sent** 5-22-08

	Certificates & Letters of gdn and two contracts in file
6-6 08	Ans filed by both defdts
6-2(?)-08	Proof of service filed
7-12 08	Set for hearing at Claremore on 7-29-08
7-29 08	Pltf appeared & testimony taken no appearance by defdt
Aug 24 08	(Entry illegible)
Sept 8 08	Advised action will be taken as soon as possible
" 7 08	Judge. rendered in favor of pltf & deft given 10 days to vacate
" 18 08	G. R. McLaughlin also notified of above
Oct 1 08	Instructions to Capt West and pltf advised
Oct 21 08	Capt West reports he placed pltf in possession and allotment cert # 34976-57245-57243-34974, letters of gdnship and 2 let lease contract returned

<u>Case dismissed</u>

INTRUDER CASE NO. 1216
Cherokee NATION

Plaintiff: Helen Whitmire Smith   Atty.

Versus

Defendant: Joe Pettit   Atty.

Complaint filed 5-9-08   **Commissioner Reports** 5-20-08   No **Contest. Notice Sent** 5-23-08

6-6 08	Ans filed by defdt
6-10-08	Proof of service
7-13 08	Set for hearing at Claremore on 7-29-08
7-23 08	(Entry illegible)
7-29 08	Pltf appeared no appearance by defdt pltf states land in controversy is her surplus allotment & that she has possession of her homestead

Cherokee Intruder Cases 1901 - 1909

Pltf is a Cherokee Freedman and case is therefore Dismissed

INTRUDER CASE NO. 1217
Cherokee NATION

Plaintiff: Fannie Gilbert, Cookson Okla   Atty.

Versus

Defendant: Andy Cookson, Cookson Okla   Atty.

Complaint filed	5-12-08	Commissioner Reports	5-29-08	No Contest. Notice Sent	5-(?)-08

	Allotment certificates in file
6-(?) 08	Ans & *(remainder illegible)*
6-(?) 08	Proof of service filed
6-18 08	Set for hearing at Muskogee on 6-25-08
6-25 08	Case called defdt appeared & gave evidence no appearance by pltf
6-26 08	Pltf advised that she can not be present at hearing on 6-25-08
7-25 08	Pltf states allotment & certs ret'd & case Dismissed

INTRUDER CASE. 1218
Cherokee NATION

Plaintiff: John Sanders, Catoosa Okla   Atty.

Versus

Defendant: Jack Gan   Atty.

Complaint filed	5-29-08	Commissioner Reports	5-29-08	Contest. Notice Sent	6-1-08

6-17 08	Proof of service filed
6-24 08	Ans filed by defdt
6-24 08	Set for hearing at Claremore 7-31-08
7-31 08	Pltf appeared & his testimony taken no appearance by defdt
July (?) 08	*(Entry illegible)*
Aug 25 08	Defdt appeared and testimony taken by L.B. (not written)
Sept 12 08	Judgment in favor of pltf & defdt given 10 days
(Illegible)	*(Entry illegible)*
Oct 22 08	Instructions issued to Capt West

Cherokee Intruder Cases 1901 - 1909

Nov 9 08   Capt West reports he placed pltf in poss.
Nov 10 08   Pltf advised case dismissed
                                                                    Dismissed

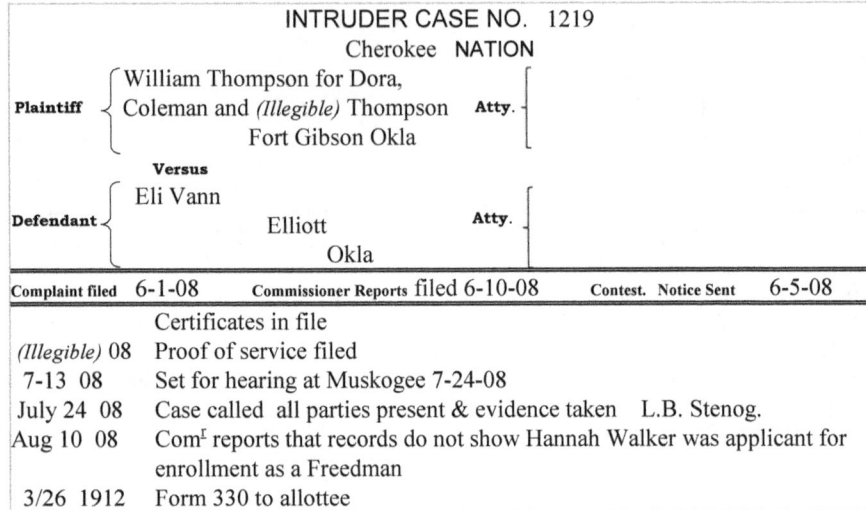

INTRUDER CASE NO. 1219
Cherokee NATION

Plaintiff: William Thompson for Dora, Coleman and *(Illegible)* Thompson   Atty.
Fort Gibson Okla

Versus

Defendant: Eli Vann   Atty.
Elliott
Okla

| Complaint filed 6-1-08 | Commissioner Reports filed 6-10-08 | Contest. Notice Sent 6-5-08 |

Certificates in file
(Illegible) 08   Proof of service filed
7-13 08   Set for hearing at Muskogee 7-24-08
July 24 08   Case called all parties present & evidence taken   L.B. Stenog.
Aug 10 08   Com^r reports that records do not show Hannah Walker was applicant for enrollment as a Freedman
3/26 1912   Form 330 to allottee

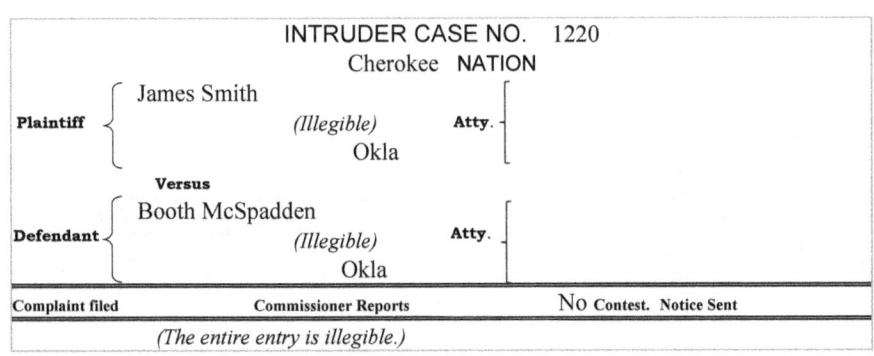

INTRUDER CASE NO. 1220
Cherokee NATION

Plaintiff: James Smith   Atty.
(Illegible)
Okla

Versus

Defendant: Booth McSpadden   Atty.
(Illegible)
Okla

| Complaint filed | Commissioner Reports | No Contest. Notice Sent |

(The entire entry is illegible.)

Cherokee Intruder Cases 1901 - 1909

INTRUDER CASE NO. 1221
Cherokee NATION

Plaintiff: Stephen Ross, Ft Gibson Okla
Atty: (Name Illegible), Muskogee Okla

Versus

Defendant: Jodie and Jane Moore, Ft Gibson Okla
Atty: (Name Illegible), Muskogee Okla

Complaint filed 5-25-08 **Commissioner Reports** 6-6-08 **No Contest. Notice Sent** *(Illegible)*

6-20 08	Ans filed by defdt's Atty
6-20 08	Set for hearing at Muskogee 7-(?)-08
6-22 08	Proof of service filed
7-7 08	Set for hearing at Muskogee on 7-23-08
7-23 08	Case *(remainder illegible)*
Oct 7 08	Upon request of Attys case set for Oct 19-08
Oct 19 08	Testimony taken in this case by L.B. Stenog.
Nov 25 08	Pltf's Atty files surveyors plat showing improvements
Nov 30 08	Judgment for pltf, defdt given 10 days
Dec 18 08	Certs # 16768 & 22627 returned to Stephen Ross in person
" 23 08	Capt West instructed to remove intruder
Jan 18 09	Capt West reports

<u>Case dismissed</u>

INTRUDER CASE. 1222
Cherokee NATION

Plaintiff: Charley Jones, Ft Gibson Okla **Atty.**

Versus

Defendant: W<u>m</u> Farrie, Elliott Okla **Atty.**

Complaint filed 6-15-08 **Commissioner Reports** **Contest. Notice Sent** 6-17-08

	Deed in file
6-27 08	Proof of service filed
6-30 08	Ans filed
7-11 08	Set for hearing at Muskogee 7-24-08
July 24 08	Case called. Plaintiff appeared No appearance by defdt Testimony taken LB Stenog
9-19 08	Pltf advised no action can be taken at this time

Cherokee Intruder Cases 1901 - 1909

Sept 28 08	Com^r reports
Dec 14 1909	Deeds Nos 20127-77/A & 20127-80/A returned
3/26 1912	Form 330 to Allottee

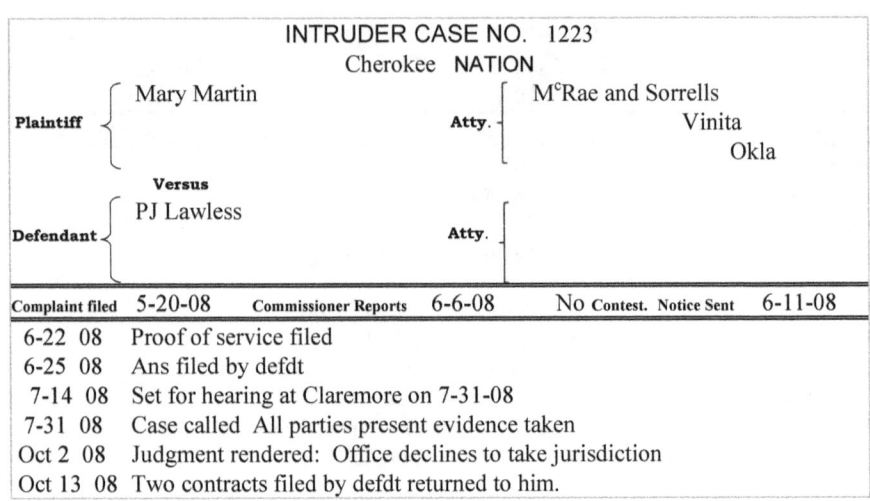

INTRUDER CASE NO. 1223
Cherokee NATION

Plaintiff	Mary Martin	Atty.	McRae and Sorrells Vinita Okla
	Versus		
Defendant	PJ Lawless	Atty.	

Complaint filed	5-20-08	Commissioner Reports	6-6-08	No Contest. Notice Sent	6-11-08

6-22 08	Proof of service filed
6-25 08	Ans filed by defdt
7-14 08	Set for hearing at Claremore on 7-31-08
7-31 08	Case called All parties present evidence taken
Oct 2 08	Judgment rendered: Office declines to take jurisdiction
Oct 13 08	Two contracts filed by defdt returned to him.

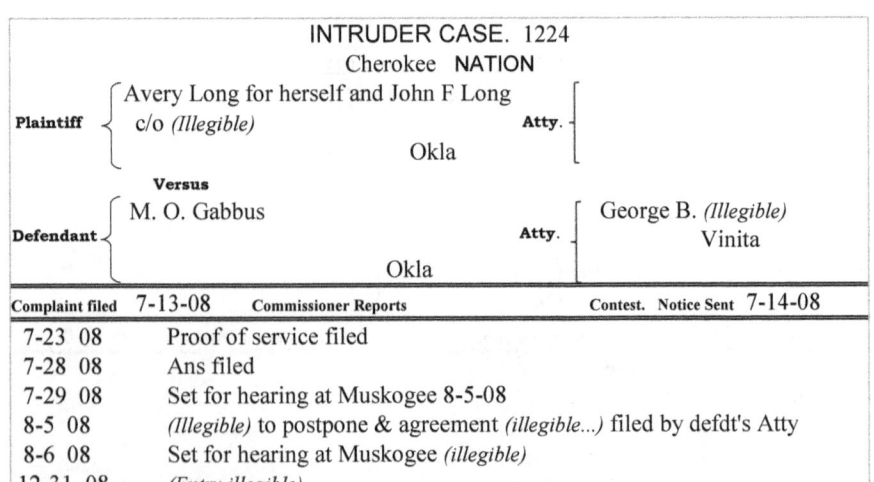

INTRUDER CASE. 1224
Cherokee NATION

Plaintiff	Avery Long for herself and John F Long c/o *(Illegible)* Okla	Atty.	
	Versus		
Defendant	M. O. Gabbus Okla	Atty.	George B. *(Illegible)* Vinita

Complaint filed	7-13-08	Commissioner Reports		Contest. Notice Sent	7-14-08

7-23 08	Proof of service filed
7-28 08	Ans filed
7-29 08	Set for hearing at Muskogee 8-5-08
8-5 08	*(Illegible)* to postpone & agreement *(illegible....)* filed by defdt's Atty
8-6 08	Set for hearing at Muskogee *(illegible)*
12-31 08	*(Entry illegible)*

Cherokee Intruder Cases 1901 - 1909

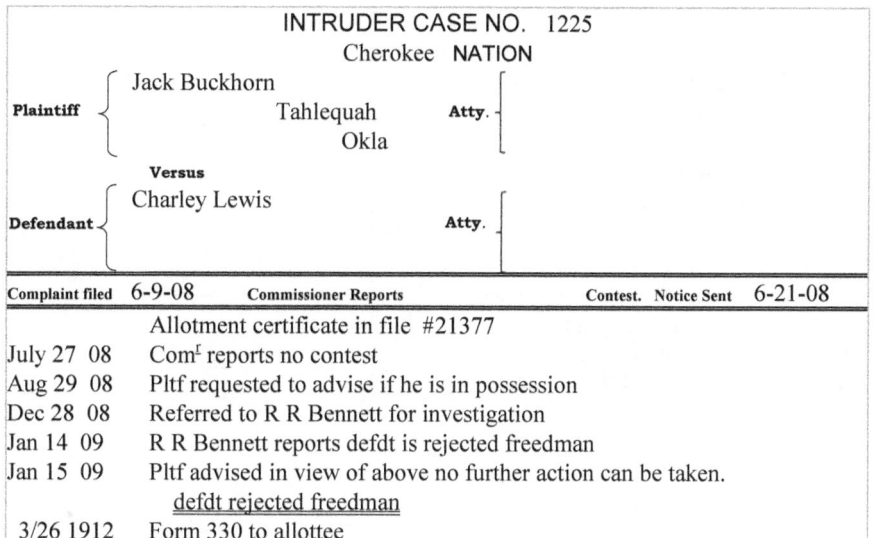

	INTRUDER CASE NO. 1225 Cherokee NATION			
Plaintiff	Jack Buckhorn Tahlequah Okla		Atty.	
	Versus			
Defendant	Charley Lewis		Atty.	
Complaint filed 6-9-08	Commissioner Reports		Contest. Notice Sent	6-21-08

	Allotment certificate in file #21377
July 27 08	Com^r reports no contest
Aug 29 08	Pltf requested to advise if he is in possession
Dec 28 08	Referred to R R Bennett for investigation
Jan 14 09	R R Bennett reports defdt is rejected freedman
Jan 15 09	Pltf advised in view of above no further action can be taken. <u>defdt rejected freedman</u>
3/26 1912	Form 330 to allottee

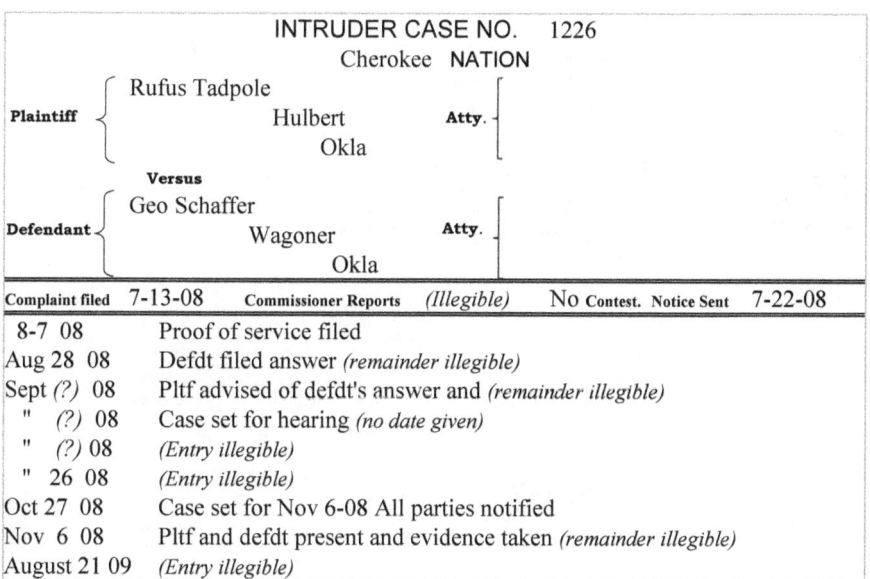

	INTRUDER CASE NO. 1226 Cherokee NATION			
Plaintiff	Rufus Tadpole Hulbert Okla		Atty.	
	Versus			
Defendant	Geo Schaffer Wagoner Okla		Atty.	
Complaint filed 7-13-08	Commissioner Reports	*(Illegible)*	No Contest. Notice Sent	7-22-08

8-7 08	Proof of service filed
Aug 28 08	Defdt filed answer *(remainder illegible)*
Sept *(?)* 08	Pltf advised of defdt's answer and *(remainder illegible)*
" *(?)* 08	Case set for hearing *(no date given)*
" *(?)* 08	*(Entry illegible)*
" 26 08	*(Entry illegible)*
Oct 27 08	Case set for Nov 6-08 All parties notified
Nov 6 08	Pltf and defdt present and evidence taken *(remainder illegible)*
August 21 09	*(Entry illegible)*

Cherokee Intruder Cases 1901 - 1909

INTRUDER CASE. 1227
Cherokee NATION

Plaintiff: Arch Spears gdn of Clarence W *(Illegible)*
Atty: Geo W Hughes, Tahlequah, Okla

Versus

Defendant: C. C. Greenlees
Atty:

Complaint filed 7-25-08 Commissioner Reports Contest. Notice Sent 7-27-08 / 8-4-08

	Letters of gdn in file
Aug 10 08	Proof of service filed
Aug 11 08	Ans filed by *(illegible)*
Aug 15 08	Proof of service filed
Aug 4 08	Ans filed by D G Elliott
Aug 22 08	Set for hearing at Muskogee 8/31/08
Aug 28 08	Proof of service *(remainder illegible)*
(Illegible)	*(Entry illegible)*
Sept 3 08	*(Entry illegible)*
Oct 30 08	formal judgment sent parties showing position of office
2-8 09	Judgment vacated & parties advised
2-15 09	*(Illegible)* advised
2-15 09	Judgment rendered favor pltf; parties advised defts given 10 days to vacate
2-27 09	Atty for pltf advises deft has not vacated
3-15 09	Instructions issued to Capt West & defts advised
3-24 09	Capt West reports pltf placed in possession & Case Dismissed
May 26 09	*(Illegible)* returned to Hughes Atty in person

INTRUDER CASE NO. 1228
Cherokee NATION

Plaintiff: Minnie Mackey, Muskogee, Okla
Atty:

Versus

Defendant: W M Starr, Checotah, Okla
Atty:

Cherokee Intruder Cases 1901 - 1909

Complaint filed 7-24-08	Commissioner Reports	Contest. Notice Sent 7-28-08
	Patent in file	
Aug 15 08	Proof of service filed	
Aug 29 08	Set for hearing *(illegible)* All parties notified	
Sept *(?)* 08	Answer filed	
Sept 10 08	*(Entry illegible)*	
Oct *(?)* 08	*(Entry illegible)*	
1-2 09	Case Dismissed *(remainder illegible)*	

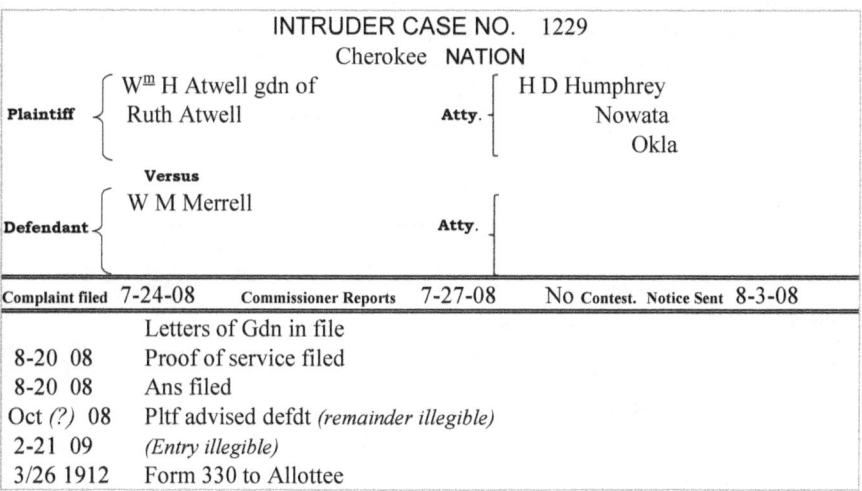

INTRUDER CASE NO. 1229
Cherokee NATION

Plaintiff: Wᵐ H Atwell gdn of Ruth Atwell
Atty.: H D Humphrey, Nowata Okla

Versus

Defendant: W M Merrell
Atty.:

Complaint filed 7-24-08	Commissioner Reports 7-27-08	No Contest. Notice Sent 8-3-08
	Letters of Gdn in file	
8-20 08	Proof of service filed	
8-20 08	Ans filed	
Oct *(?)* 08	Pltf advised defdt *(remainder illegible)*	
2-21 09	*(Entry illegible)*	
3/26 1912	Form 330 to Allottee	

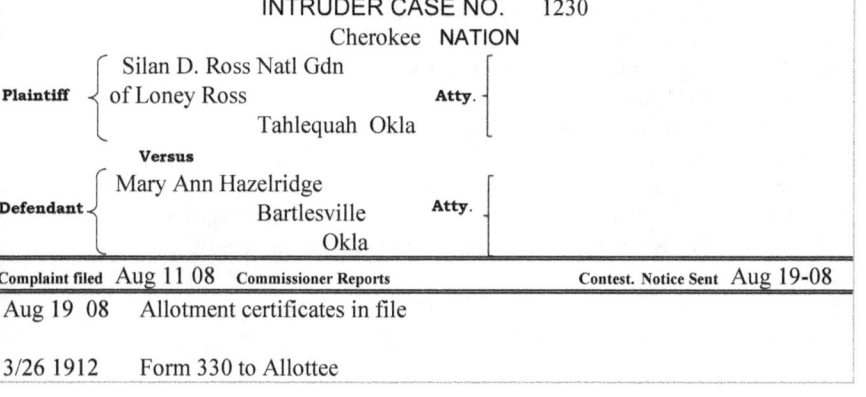

INTRUDER CASE NO. 1230
Cherokee NATION

Plaintiff: Silan D. Ross Natl Gdn of Loney Ross, Tahlequah Okla
Atty.:

Versus

Defendant: Mary Ann Hazelridge, Bartlesville Okla
Atty.:

Complaint filed Aug 11 08	Commissioner Reports	Contest. Notice Sent Aug 19-08
Aug 19 08	Allotment certificates in file	
3/26 1912	Form 330 to Allottee	

281

Cherokee Intruder Cases 1901 - 1909

INTRUDER CASE NO. 1231
Cherokee NATION

Plaintiff: Johnson Spade, Proctor, Okla — Atty.

Versus

Defendant: C. King and A.P. Ragan, Lenapah, Okla — Atty.

Complaint filed July 27 08   **Commissioner Reports**   **Contest. Notice Sent** Aug 19-08

Aug 19 08	Allotment certificates & contract in file
1-5 09	Letter from Kemp (DA) with *(illegible)* to serving notices
1-20 09	Proof of service acknowledged
	(Illegible) answer filed in 1264; same deft
1-29 09	Case dismissed & (DA) Kemp requested to render assistance

INTRUDER CASE NO. 1232
Cherokee NATION

Plaintiff: Mrs Foster Baltz nee Stone, Oologah, Okla — Atty.

Versus

Defendant: E. P. Mitchell, Oologah, Okla — Atty.

Complaint filed Aug 10-08   **Commissioner Reports**   **Contest. Notice Sent** Aug 19-08

Aug 19 08	Allotment certificates in file
Aug 25 08	Defdt files answer dated Aug 22-08
Aug 26 08	Proof of service dated Aug 21-08
Aug 22 08	Com^r advised no contest
Sept 17 08	Case set for hearing Sept 28-08
Sept 28 08	Evidence taken
Oct 17 08	Copy of evidence furnished Jas E Bell
Jan 9 09	Jas E Bell requests possession
Jan 9 09	Judgment rendered in favor of pltf 10 days given
1-29 09	J.E. Bell advised police will be sent if *(remainder illegible)*
2-6 09	Inst issued Capt West as Bell furnished Power of Atty
2-26 09	J E Bell advised
3-6 09	Capt West advises Bell placed in possession
3-9 09	In view of above, Case Dismissed

Cherokee Intruder Cases 1901 - 1909

INTRUDER CASE NO. 1233
Cherokee NATION

Plaintiff: William Duval, Vian Okla   **Atty.**

Versus

Defendant: J P Allen Muskogee Okla, E R Myers & H *(Illegible)*   **Atty.**

Complaint filed 9-17-08   **Commissioner Reports** 9-26-08   **Contest. Notice Sent** 9-17-08

	Copy of Rental contract & certs filed
9-23 08	Patents returned
" " "	Case set for Oct 2-08 - Muskogee
" 26 "	Proof of service acknowledged
" " "	Answer of defdt " & filed
Oct 2 08	Plaintiff appeared and evidence taken LB Beard appeared for Allen and requested *(illegible)* for 15 days *(illegible)*
Oct 17 08	Defdt *(illegible)* to appear at the expiration of 15 days
" 21 08	Judgment in favor of pltf; defdt given 10 days
" 28 08	*(Illegible)* to R R Bennett for investigation
Jan 4 09	R R Bennett reports satisfactory had been made
Jan 18 09	Pltf adv. case dismissed
	Dismissed

INTRUDER CASE NO. 1234
Cherokee NATION

Plaintiff: Sarah E Tell, Choteau   **Atty.**

Versus

Defendant: Chas Ketcher, Jr.   **Atty.**

Complaint filed 9-15-08   **Commissioner Reports**   **Contest. Notice Sent** 9-29-08

9-29 08	*(Entry illegible)*
	Certificates & letters filed
Oct 2 08	Com^r advises no contest
Oct 3 08	Proof of service
Jan 2 "[sic]	Case set for Jan 20 08[sic] at Musk
" 20 09	Case set for 10 days later
3-5 09	Case set at Vinita March 19 09 Case Dismissed

Cherokee Intruder Cases 1901 - 1909

INTRUDER CASE NO. 1235
Cherokee NATION

Plaintiff: Josie Brady nee *(Illegible)* Hulbert, Okla **Atty.**

Versus

Defendant: W M Thurman Eureka, OK **Atty.** Bruce L Keenan Atty Tahlequah

Complaint filed July 7-08	Commissioner Reports	Contest. Notice Sent 9-29-08
9-29 08	Referred to Com^r for report Certif filed	
Oct 1 08	*(Entry illegible)*	
Oct 5 08	Proof of service filed	
(Illegible)	Answer by defdt's Atty	
(Illegible)	Case set for hearing at Muskogee October 21 1908	
Oct 21 08	Plaintiff appeared no appearance by defdt	
Oct 22 08	*(Entry illegible)*	
May 12 09	Judgment rendered refusing to take jurisdiction All parties advised and case <u>dismissed</u>	
Febr 8 1910	Warranty deed above referred to, returned to Defdt's Atty.	

INTRUDER CASE NO. 1236
Cherokee NATION

Plaintiff: Ida Dix SW City Mo **Atty.**

Versus

Defendant: E. S. Scoggins Bartlesville **Atty.**

Complaint filed 9-26-08	Commissioner Reports 9-26-08	No Contest. Notice Sent 9-29-08
9-29-08	Proof of service filed	
Oct 10 08	Pltf advised that defdt does not claim her land and requested to go and take possession of same, see letter	<u>Case Dismissed</u>

Cherokee Intruder Cases 1901 - 1909

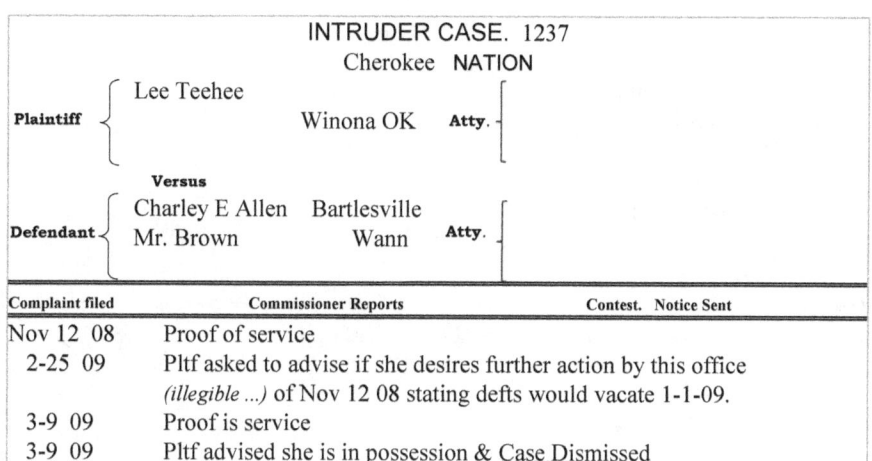

	INTRUDER CASE. 1237 Cherokee NATION	
Plaintiff	Lee Teehee Winona OK **Atty.**	
	Versus	
Defendant	Charley E Allen Bartlesville Mr. Brown Wann **Atty.**	
Complaint filed	**Commissioner Reports**	**Contest. Notice Sent**
Nov 12 08	Proof of service	
2-25 09	Pltf asked to advise if she desires further action by this office *(illegible ...)* of Nov 12 08 stating defts would vacate 1-1-09.	
3-9 09	Proof is service	
3-9 09	Pltf advised she is in possession & Case Dismissed	

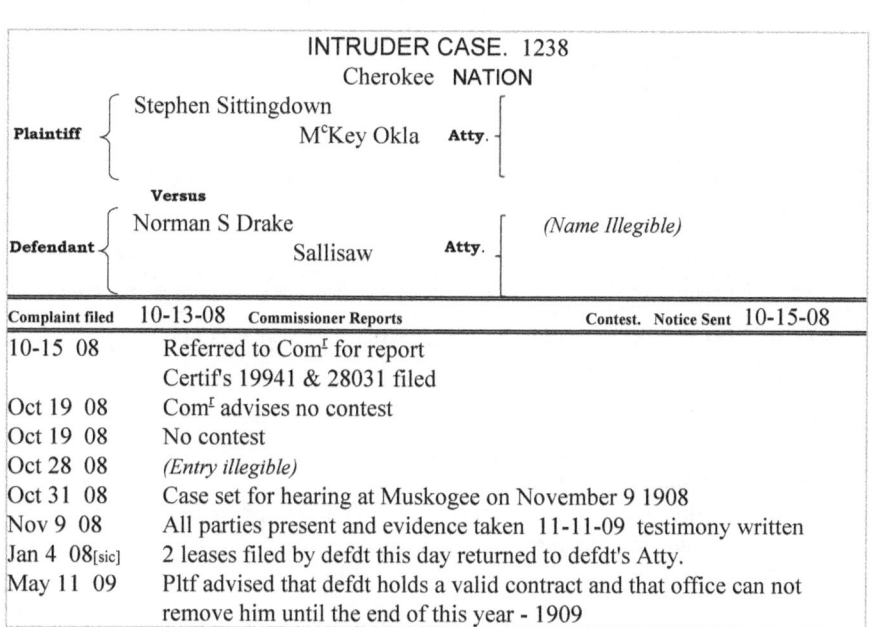

	INTRUDER CASE. 1238 Cherokee NATION	
Plaintiff	Stephen Sittingdown McKey Okla **Atty.**	
	Versus	
Defendant	Norman S Drake Sallisaw **Atty.**	*(Name Illegible)*
Complaint filed 10-13-08	**Commissioner Reports**	**Contest. Notice Sent** 10-15-08
10-15 08	Referred to Com^r for report Certif's 19941 & 28031 filed	
Oct 19 08	Com^r advises no contest	
Oct 19 08	No contest	
Oct 28 08	*(Entry illegible)*	
Oct 31 08	Case set for hearing at Muskogee on November 9 1908	
Nov 9 08	All parties present and evidence taken 11-11-09 testimony written	
Jan 4 08[sic]	2 leases filed by defdt this day returned to defdt's Atty.	
May 11 09	Pltf advised that defdt holds a valid contract and that office can not remove him until the end of this year - 1909	

Cherokee Intruder Cases 1901 - 1909

INTRUDER CASE. 1239
Cherokee NATION

Plaintiff: Sarah E Tell Nat. Gdn
Frankie M Adair   Minor
Choteau   **Atty.**

Versus

Defendant: Chas Ketcher Sr & Jr.
Choteau   **Atty.**

Complaint filed 9-29-08   **Commissioner Reports** 10-5-08   **No Contest. Notice Sent** 10-15-08

Jan 2 08[sic]	Case set for hearing Jan 22 09 at Muskogee
Jan 18 "	Letter from Deft asking for continuance Set for 10 das later
3-5 09	Case set for Vinita 3-18-09 See notice in 1234
3-5 09	*(Entry illegible)* " "

INTRUDER CASE. 1240
Cherokee NATION

Plaintiff: Emma Howard nee Keener   **Atty.**   J L *(Illegible)*   Atty Musk.

Versus

Defendant: Sam Howard   **Atty.**   Jas Watkins Atty

Complaint filed 10-3-08   **Commissioner Reports** 10-3-08   **No Contest. Notice Sent** 10-18-08

10-3 08	Rental contract filed
Nov 12 08	Case set for hearing December 1 1908 All parties notified
Nov 23 08	Answer filed by defdt's Atty
1-7 09	Pltf & Atty for deft advised
Dec 1 08	Case called for hearing, Atty for defdt & plaintiff in person present & evidence taken
Jan 13 09	Judgment for pltf, defdt given 10 days
Jan 23 09	Pltf advised office in person that she is in possession and requested that case be dismissed

INTRUDER CASE NO. 1241
Cherokee NATION

Plaintiff: Esther Young
Vian   **Atty.**

Cherokee Intruder Cases 1901 - 1909

Defendant	Versus Martin Bolin Vian Atty.	
Complaint filed	10-3-08 Commissioner Reports	No Contest. Notice Sent
	Patent filed	
Oct 21 08	Proof of service	
Jan 4 09	Referred to R R Bennett	
2-26 09	Pltf requested to advise if in possession	
3-19 09	Case referred to *(Illegible)* (D.A.)	
Oct 25 09	Deed #12928 returned	

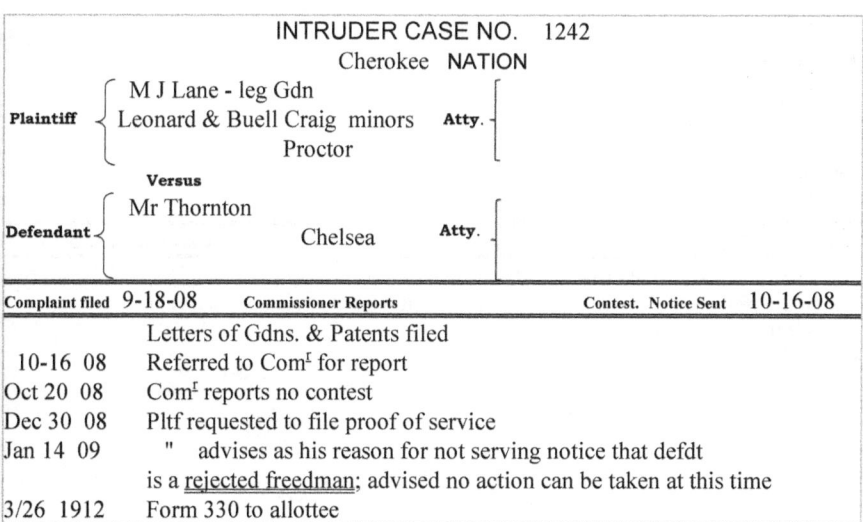

INTRUDER CASE NO. 1242
Cherokee NATION

Plaintiff — M J Lane - leg Gdn
Leonard & Buell Craig minors Atty. Proctor

Versus
Defendant — Mr Thornton
Chelsea Atty.

Complaint filed 9-18-08 Commissioner Reports	Contest. Notice Sent 10-16-08
10-16 08	Letters of Gdns. & Patents filed
	Referred to Com^r for report
Oct 20 08	Com^r reports no contest
Dec 30 08	Pltf requested to file proof of service
Jan 14 09	" advises as his reason for not serving notice that defdt is a <u>rejected freedman</u>; advised no action can be taken at this time
3/26 1912	Form 330 to allottee

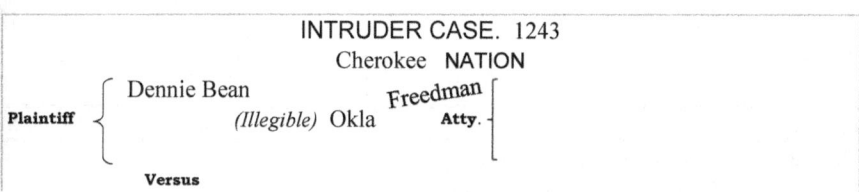

INTRUDER CASE. 1243
Cherokee NATION

Plaintiff — Dennie Bean Freedman
(Illegible) Okla Atty.

Versus

Cherokee Intruder Cases 1901 - 1909

Defendant	D W Adams *(Illegible)* Okla	Atty.

Complaint filed Oct 12 1908 **Commissioner Reports** Oct 21-08 No **Contest. Notice Sent** Nov 5-1908

Nov 21 08	Proof of service
Dec 2 08	Answer filed by defdt
Dec 30 "	Dismissed - controversy over boundary lines: Can be renewed if *(illegible)* showing by surveyor furnished
1-7 09	Pltf again advised
Jan 15 09	*(Illegible)* of pltf referred from Com^r of I.A; pltf again adv.

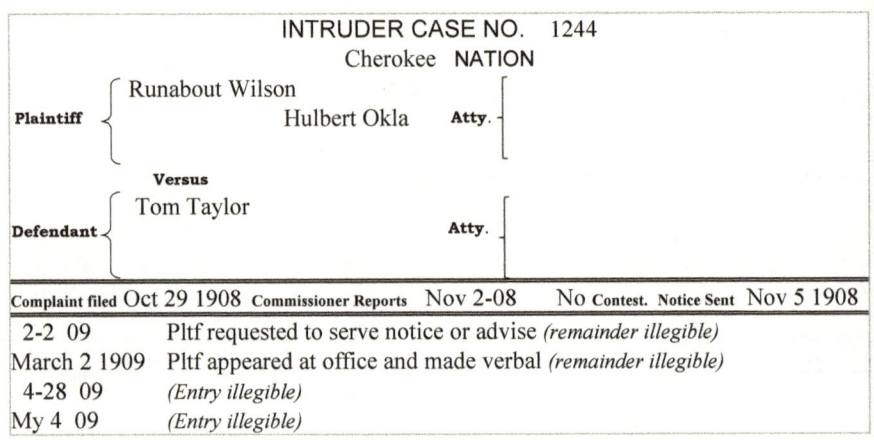

INTRUDER CASE NO. 1244
Cherokee NATION

Plaintiff	Runabout Wilson Hulbert Okla	Atty.

Versus

Defendant	Tom Taylor	Atty.

Complaint filed Oct 29 1908 **Commissioner Reports** Nov 2-08 No **Contest. Notice Sent** Nov 5 1908

2-2 09	Pltf requested to serve notice or advise *(remainder illegible)*
March 2 1909	Pltf appeared at office and made verbal *(remainder illegible)*
4-28 09	*(Entry illegible)*
My 4 09	*(Entry illegible)*

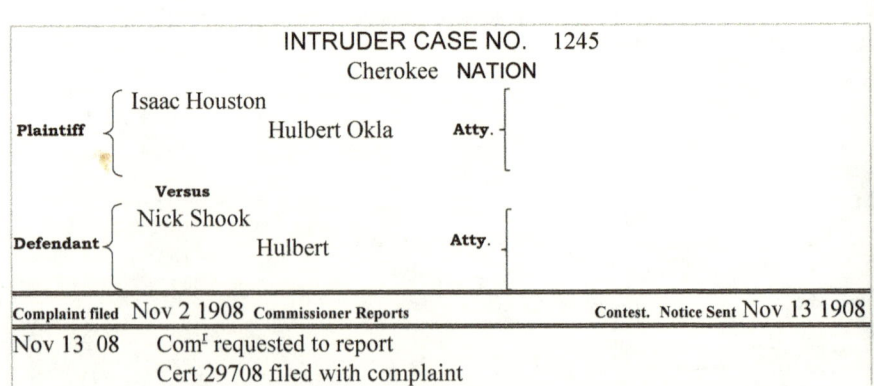

INTRUDER CASE NO. 1245
Cherokee NATION

Plaintiff	Isaac Houston Hulbert Okla	Atty.

Versus

Defendant	Nick Shook Hulbert	Atty.

Complaint filed Nov 2 1908 **Commissioner Reports**   **Contest. Notice Sent** Nov 13 1908

Nov 13 08	Com^r requested to report Cert 29708 filed with complaint

Cherokee Intruder Cases 1901 - 1909

Nov 18 08	Proof of service
Nov 24 08	Set for hearing December 8-1908
Nov 25 08	Com^r reports
Dec 8 08	Both parties appeared and an agreement entered into
	<u>Case Dismissed</u>

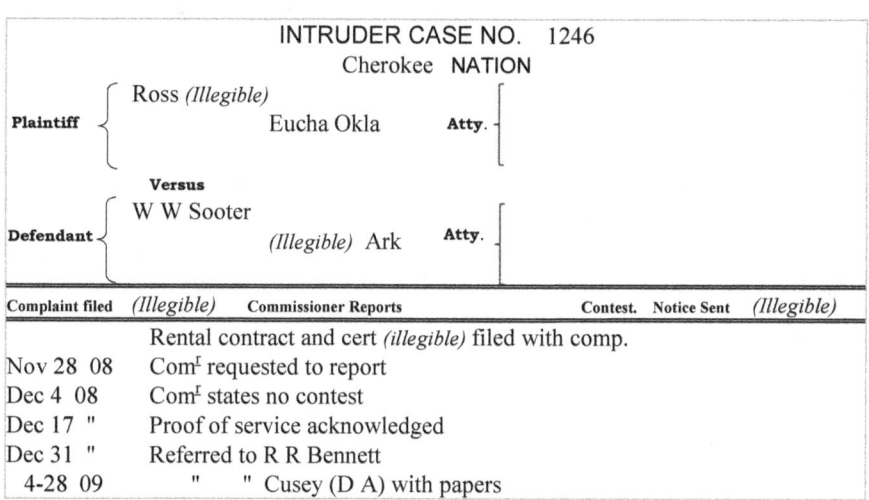

INTRUDER CASE NO. 1246
Cherokee NATION

Plaintiff: Ross *(Illegible)* — Eucha Okla — **Atty.**

Versus

Defendant: W W Sooter — *(Illegible)* Ark — **Atty.**

Complaint filed	*(Illegible)*	Commissioner Reports		Contest.	Notice Sent	*(Illegible)*
	Rental contract and cert *(illegible)* filed with comp.					
Nov 28 08	Com^r requested to report					
Dec 4 08	Com^r states no contest					
Dec 17 "	Proof of service acknowledged					
Dec 31 "	Referred to R R Bennett					
4-28 09	" " Cusey (D A) with papers					

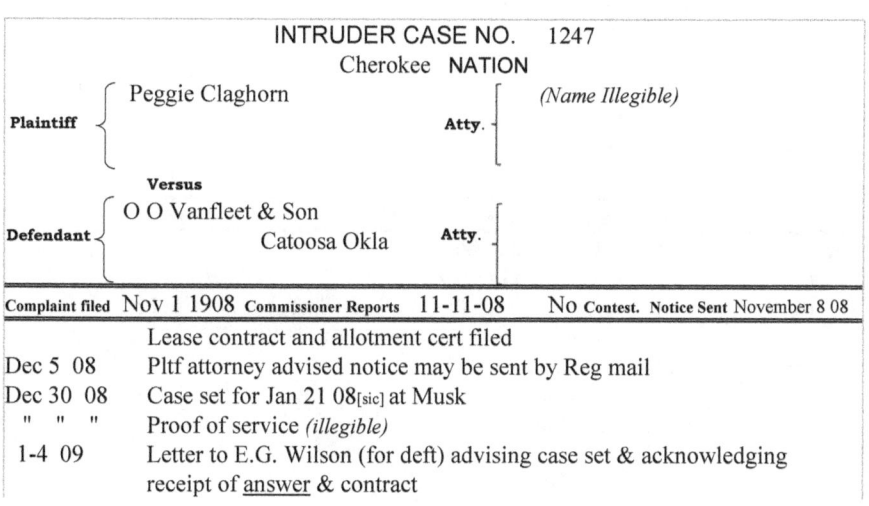

INTRUDER CASE NO. 1247
Cherokee NATION

Plaintiff: Peggie Claghorn — **Atty.** *(Name Illegible)*

Versus

Defendant: O O Vanfleet & Son — Catoosa Okla — **Atty.**

Complaint filed	Nov 1 1908	Commissioner Reports	11-11-08	No Contest.	Notice Sent	November 8 08
	Lease contract and allotment cert filed					
Dec 5 08	Pltf attorney advised notice may be sent by Reg mail					
Dec 30 08	Case set for Jan 21 08[sic] at Musk					
" " "	Proof of service *(illegible)*					
1-4 09	Letter to E.G. Wilson (for deft) advising case set & acknowledging receipt of <u>answer</u> & contract					

Cherokee Intruder Cases 1901 - 1909

Jan 18 09	*(Entry illegible)*
Jan 21 09	Both parties appeared & testified: test. transcribed
3-8 09	*(Entry illegible)*
Dec 4 09	Lease contract returned to pltf.

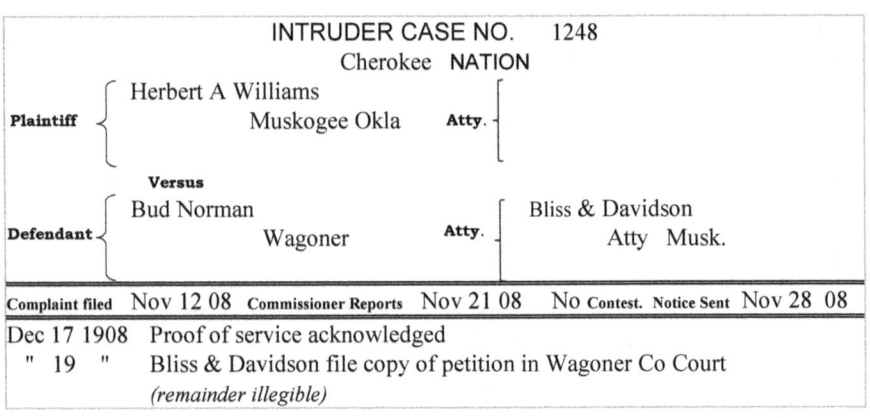

INTRUDER CASE NO. 1248
Cherokee NATION

Plaintiff: Herbert A Williams, Muskogee Okla **Atty.**

Versus

Defendant: Bud Norman, Wagoner **Atty.**   Bliss & Davidson Atty Musk.

Complaint filed Nov 12 08 **Commissioner Reports** Nov 21 08 **No Contest. Notice Sent** Nov 28 08

Dec 17 1908	Proof of service acknowledged
" 19 "	Bliss & Davidson file copy of petition in Wagoner Co Court *(remainder illegible)*

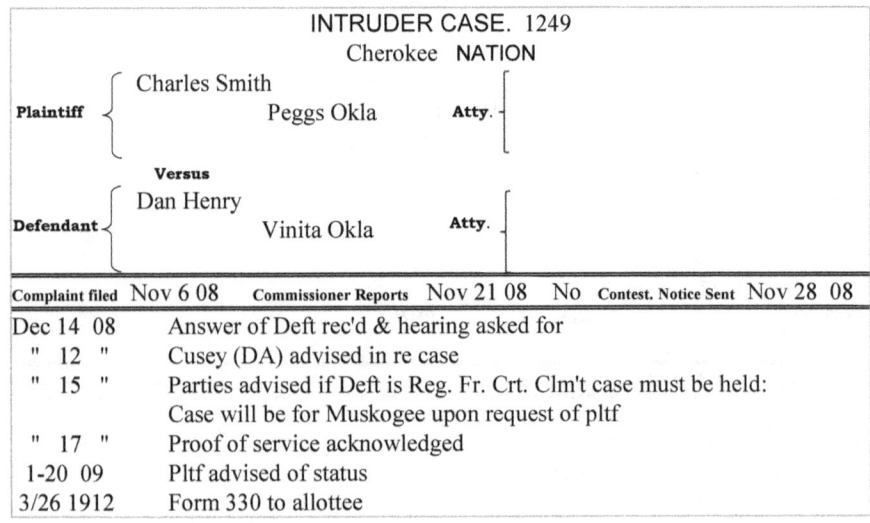

INTRUDER CASE. 1249
Cherokee NATION

Plaintiff: Charles Smith, Peggs Okla **Atty.**

Versus

Defendant: Dan Henry, Vinita Okla **Atty.**

Complaint filed Nov 6 08 **Commissioner Reports** Nov 21 08 **No Contest. Notice Sent** Nov 28 08

Dec 14 08	Answer of Deft rec'd & hearing asked for
" 12 "	Cusey (DA) advised in re case
" 15 "	Parties advised if Deft is Reg. Fr. Crt. Clm't case must be held: Case will be for Muskogee upon request of pltf
" 17 "	Proof of service acknowledged
1-20 09	Pltf advised of status
3/26 1912	Form 330 to allottee

290

Cherokee Intruder Cases 1901 - 1909

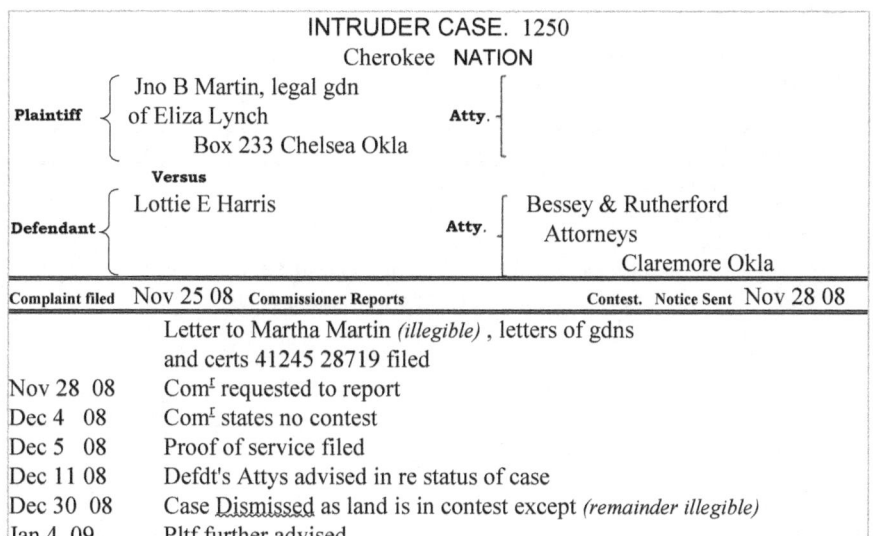

INTRUDER CASE. 1250
Cherokee NATION

Plaintiff: Jno B Martin, legal gdn of Eliza Lynch, Box 233 Chelsea Okla

Versus

Defendant: Lottie E Harris
Atty: Bessey & Rutherford Attorneys, Claremore Okla

Complaint filed Nov 25 08   **Contest. Notice Sent** Nov 28 08

Commissioner Reports

	Letter to Martha Martin *(illegible)*, letters of gdns and certs 41245 28719 filed
Nov 28 08	Com^r requested to report
Dec 4 08	Com^r states no contest
Dec 5 08	Proof of service filed
Dec 11 08	Defdt's Attys advised in re status of case
Dec 30 08	Case Dismissed as land is in contest except *(remainder illegible)*
Jan 4 09	Pltf further advised

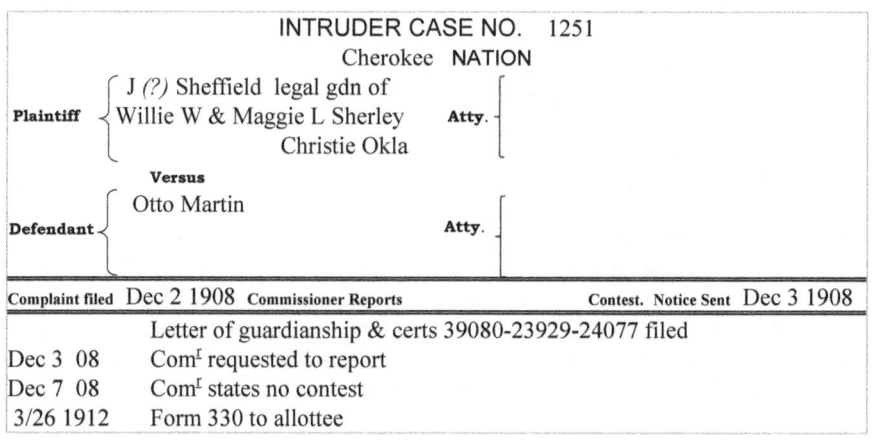

INTRUDER CASE NO. 1251
Cherokee NATION

Plaintiff: J (?) Sheffield legal gdn of Willie W & Maggie L Sherley, Christie Okla

Versus

Defendant: Otto Martin

Complaint filed Dec 2 1908   **Contest. Notice Sent** Dec 3 1908

Commissioner Reports

	Letter of guardianship & certs 39080-23929-24077 filed
Dec 3 08	Com^r requested to report
Dec 7 08	Com^r states no contest
3/26 1912	Form 330 to allottee

INTRUDER CASE NO. 1252
Cherokee NATION

Plaintiff: Geo Ketcher, Baptist Okla

Cherokee Intruder Cases 1901 - 1909

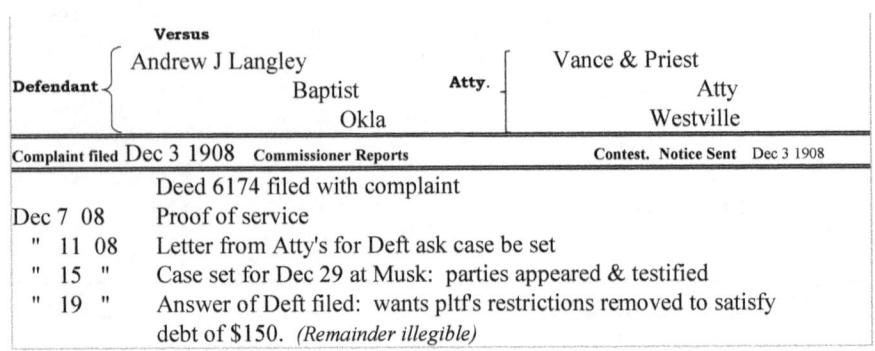

Defendant	Versus Andrew J Langley Baptist Okla	Atty.	Vance & Priest Atty Westville

Complaint filed Dec 3 1908 Commissioner Reports		Contest. Notice Sent Dec 3 1908
	Deed 6174 filed with complaint	
Dec 7 08	Proof of service	
" 11 08	Letter from Atty's for Deft ask case be set	
" 15 "	Case set for Dec 29 at Musk: parties appeared & testified	
" 19 "	Answer of Deft filed: wants pltf's restrictions removed to satisfy debt of $150. *(Remainder illegible)*	

INTRUDER CASE NO. 1253
Cherokee NATION

Plaintiff	Mrs Lena Mathews Coffeyville Kas.	Atty.	
Defendant	Versus A S *(Illegible)* Coffeyville Kansas	Atty.	

Complaint filed Dec 1 1908 Commissioner Reports		Contest. Notice Sent Dec 3 1908
	Receipt & certs 12327 filed	
Dec 3 08	Com^r asked to report	
Dec 11 08	Answer filed by defdt	
Dec 11 08	Proof of service	
Dec 7 08	Com^r states no contest	
Jan 09	Case set for Jan 23-08 at Musk.	
1-7 09	Deft's son asked to represent deft: granted	
1-20 09	Letter from Deft asking that case be set for 1 P.M. answered - yes	
Jan 23 09	Both parties present and evidence taken & transcribed	
1-26 09	Judgment rendered in favor of Deft & Case <u>Dismissed</u>	
2-16 09	Cert # 12327 ret'd pltf.	

INTRUDER CASE NO. 1254
Cherokee NATION

Plaintiff	Jettie Vann Lenapah Okla	Atty.	

Cherokee Intruder Cases 1901 - 1909

	Versus	
Defendant	O B Clevenger Bartlesville Okla	Atty.

Complaint filed Nov 21 1908	Commissioner Reports Nov 5th 08	No Contest. Notice Sent Dec 5th 08
1-26 09	Pltf advises she has <u>not</u> served the notice sent asks about collection of rent	
2-5 09	Advised	

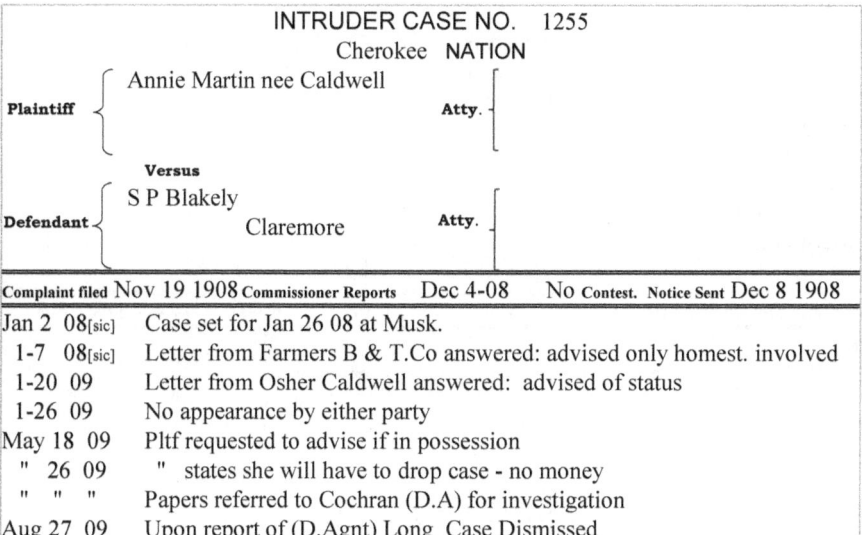

INTRUDER CASE NO. 1255
Cherokee NATION

Plaintiff	Annie Martin nee Caldwell	Atty.

	Versus	
Defendant	S P Blakely Claremore	Atty.

Complaint filed Nov 19 1908	Commissioner Reports Dec 4-08	No Contest. Notice Sent Dec 8 1908
Jan 2 08[sic]	Case set for Jan 26 08 at Musk.	
1-7 08[sic]	Letter from Farmers B & T.Co answered: advised only homest. involved	
1-20 09	Letter from Osher Caldwell answered: advised of status	
1-26 09	No appearance by either party	
May 18 09	Pltf requested to advise if in possession	
" 26 09	" states she will have to drop case - no money	
" " "	Papers referred to Cochran (D.A) for investigation	
Aug 27 09	Upon report of (D.Agnt) Long Case <u>Dismissed</u>	

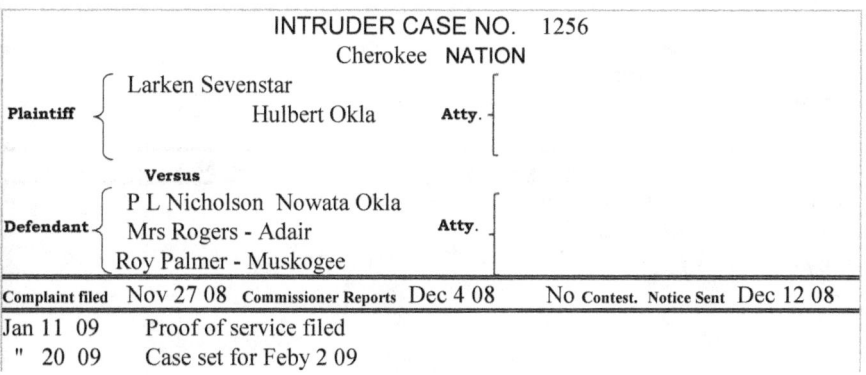

INTRUDER CASE NO. 1256
Cherokee NATION

Plaintiff	Larken Sevenstar Hulbert Okla	Atty.

	Versus	
Defendant	P L Nicholson Nowata Okla Mrs Rogers - Adair Roy Palmer - Muskogee	Atty.

Complaint filed Nov 27 08	Commissioner Reports Dec 4 08	No Contest. Notice Sent Dec 12 08
Jan 11 09	Proof of service filed	
" 20 09	Case set for Feby 2 09	

Cherokee Intruder Cases 1901 - 1909

Febr 2 09	All parties appeared & testified Mrs Rogers & Roy Palmer declared *(illegible)*
1-3 09	Notices sent to Nancy Rogers & Roy Palmer
2-12 09	Proof of service
2-17 09	Letter from Mrs Rogers calling attention to former case #775 in which judgment was rendered in her favor against deft also she has told her renter to vacate
2-20 09	In view of said judg. in 775 *(remainder illegible)* Case Dismissed

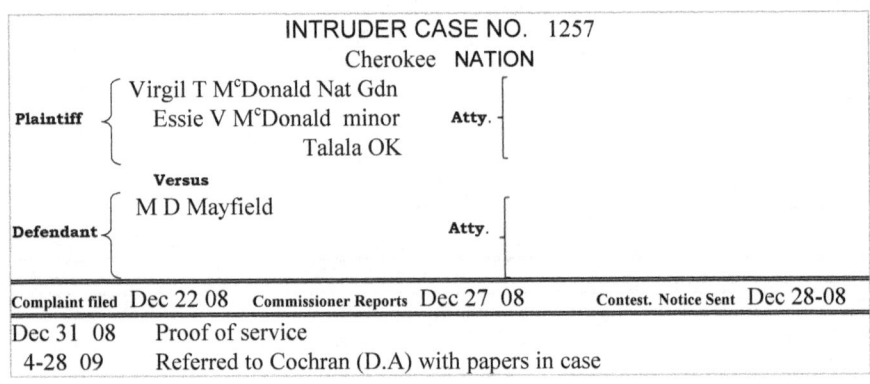

INTRUDER CASE NO. 1257
Cherokee NATION

Plaintiff: Virgil T McDonald Nat Gdn
Essie V McDonald minor
Talala OK   **Atty.**

Versus

Defendant: M D Mayfield   **Atty.**

Complaint filed Dec 22 08	Commissioner Reports Dec 27 08 Contest. Notice Sent Dec 28-08
Dec 31 08	Proof of service
4-28 09	Referred to Cochran (D.A) with papers in case

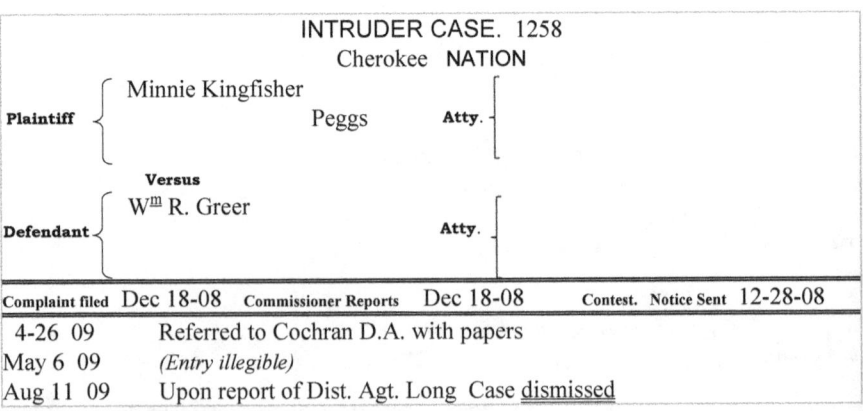

INTRUDER CASE. 1258
Cherokee NATION

Plaintiff: Minnie Kingfisher
Peggs   **Atty.**

Versus

Defendant: Wm R. Greer   **Atty.**

Complaint filed Dec 18-08	Commissioner Reports Dec 18-08 Contest. Notice Sent 12-28-08
4-26 09	Referred to Cochran D.A. with papers
May 6 09	*(Entry illegible)*
Aug 11 09	Upon report of Dist. Agt. Long Case dismissed

Cherokee Intruder Cases 1901 - 1909

INTRUDER CASE. 1259
Cherokee NATION

Plaintiff: Chas W. Poole Leg Gdn of Walton C & Carlisle Poole minors Chelsea Atty.

Versus

Defendant: Mr. Goss & Geo. H Wetzel Atty.

Complaint filed Dec 20 08   Commissioner Reports   Contest. Notice Sent 1-5-09

Dec 15 08	Deeds *(illegible)* & Gdns. papers filed Pltf advised
1-20 09	Pltf files proof of service & says Wetzel is dead & Goss promises to vacate in 5 days - will notify office then.
2-25 09	Pltf requested to advise if in possession
3-20 09	" advised deft has vacated & Case Dismissed

INTRUDER CASE NO. 1260
Cherokee NATION

Plaintiff: William Smith Moodys[sic] Atty.

Versus

Defendant: W.A. Kinsey Moodys Atty.

Complaint filed Dec 31 08   Commissioner Reports Dec 31 08   No Contest. Notice Sent 1-5-09

Jan 12 09	Proof of service
Jan 15 09	Defdt appeared at office in person and made verbal answer; also filed lease contract
Jan 15 09	Case set for hearing on January 27-1909 Parties appeared & test taken
2-11 09	Judgment favor pltf & Deft given 10 days to vacate
May 4 09	Pltf requested to advise if in possession
May 24 09	*(Entry illegible)*
" 29 09	*(Entry illegible)* Case Dismissed

Cherokee Intruder Cases 1901 - 1909

INTRUDER CASE NO. 1261
Cherokee NATION

Plaintiff: James Foreman, Marbelle[sic] **Atty.**

Versus

Defendant: J M Mayo, Sallisaw **Atty.**

Complaint filed 1-2-09 **Commissioner Reports** **Contest. Notice Sent** 1-5-09

	Certificate #16949 filed
Jan 5 09	Com^r requested to report
Jan 9 09	Com^r reports no contest
1-20 09	Proof of service acknowledged
1-29 09	Deft's answer & lease contract filed
2-2 09	Pltf states in possession & case is <u>dismissed</u>: signed statement

INTRUDER CASE NO. 1262
Cherokee NATION

Plaintiff: Ezekiel Tucker *(Illegible)* **Atty.**

Versus

Defendant: Buck Lasley *(Illegible)* **Atty.**

Complaint filed Dec 31 1908 **Commissioner Reports** Jan 7-09 **No Contest. Notice Sent** Jan 11 1909

4-26 09	*(Entry illegible)*
July 23 1909	Upon report of Cochran <u>case dismissed</u>

INTRUDER CASE NO. 1263
Cherokee NATION

Plaintiff: Diana Vann Holt **Atty.**

Versus

Defendant: D B Plecker, Jno *(Illegible)* **Atty.**

296

Cherokee Intruder Cases 1901 - 1909

Complaint filed Dec 31-08	Commissioner Reports Jan 7-09	No Contest. Notice Sent Jan 11 1909
(Illegible)	To Cochran (DA) with papers	
May 9 09	Cochran reports as to Records	
" " "	Referred to Kemp for further report	
June 1 09	*(Entry illegible)*	
" 15 09	Case again referred to Cochran (D.A.)	
Aug 7 09	Long (DA) advised in re case	

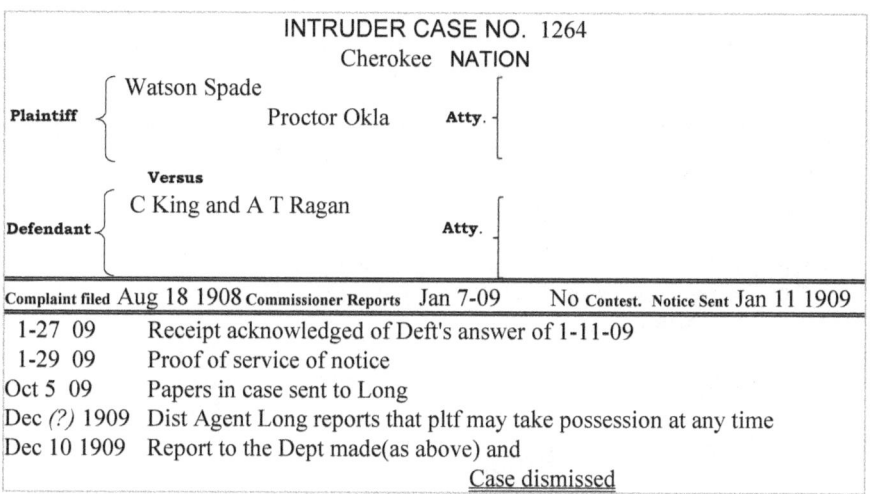

INTRUDER CASE NO. 1264
Cherokee NATION

Plaintiff: Watson Spade, Proctor Okla   Atty.

Versus

Defendant: C King and A T Ragan   Atty.

Complaint filed Aug 18 1908	Commissioner Reports Jan 7-09	No Contest. Notice Sent Jan 11 1909
1-27 09	Receipt acknowledged of Deft's answer of 1-11-09	
1-29 09	Proof of service of notice	
Oct 5 09	Papers in case sent to Long	
Dec (?) 1909	Dist Agent Long reports that pltf may take possession at any time	
Dec 10 1909	Report to the Dept made (as above) and	
	<u>Case dismissed</u>	

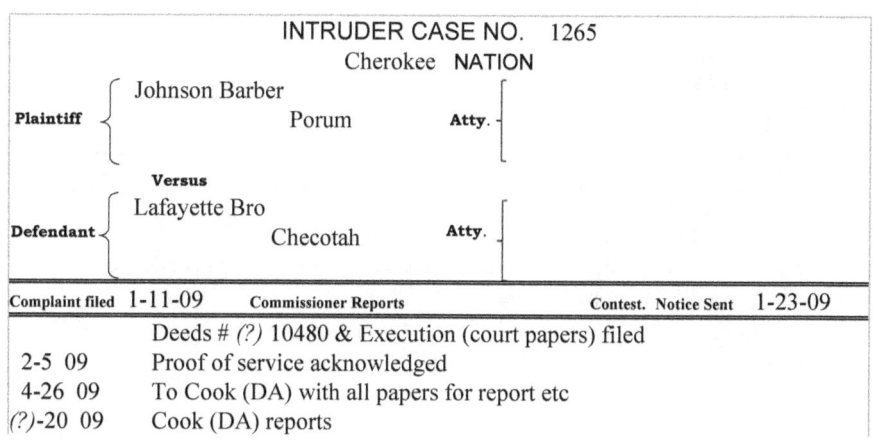

INTRUDER CASE NO. 1265
Cherokee NATION

Plaintiff: Johnson Barber, Porum   Atty.

Versus

Defendant: Lafayette Bro, Checotah   Atty.

Complaint filed 1-11-09	Commissioner Reports	Contest. Notice Sent 1-23-09
	Deeds # (?) 10480 & Execution (court papers) filed	
2-5 09	Proof of service acknowledged	
4-26 09	To Cook (DA) with all papers for report etc	
(?)-20 09	Cook (DA) reports	

Cherokee Intruder Cases 1901 - 1909

(?)-22 09	*(Entry illegible)*
(?)-26 09	Pltf states he is not in pos. & Cook so advised

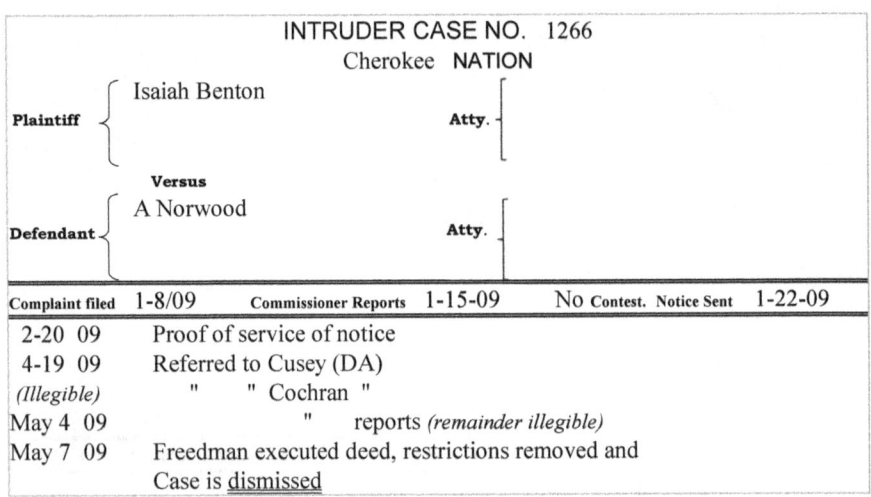

INTRUDER CASE NO. 1266
Cherokee NATION

Plaintiff: Isaiah Benton **Atty.**

Versus

Defendant: A Norwood **Atty.**

Complaint filed	1-8/09	Commissioner Reports	1-15-09	No Contest. Notice Sent	1-22-09

2-20 09	Proof of service of notice
4-19 09	Referred to Cusey (DA)
(Illegible)	" " Cochran "
May 4 09	" reports *(remainder illegible)*
May 7 09	Freedman executed deed, restrictions removed and Case is <u>dismissed</u>

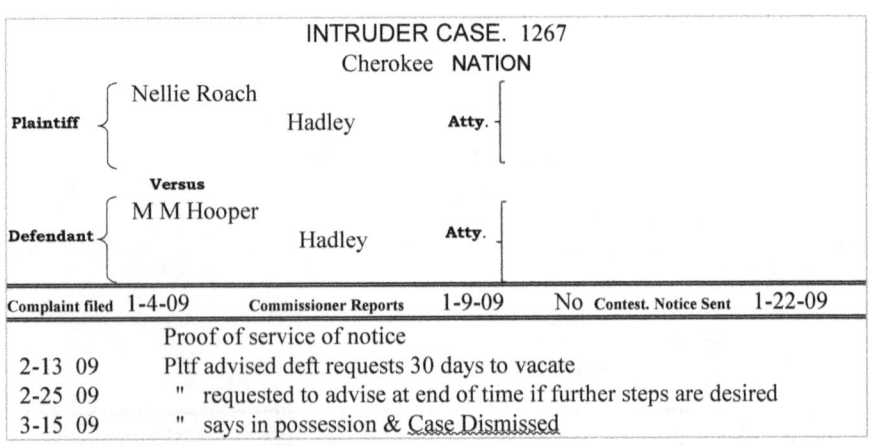

INTRUDER CASE. 1267
Cherokee NATION

Plaintiff: Nellie Roach Hadley **Atty.**

Versus

Defendant: M M Hooper Hadley **Atty.**

Complaint filed	1-4-09	Commissioner Reports	1-9-09	No Contest. Notice Sent	1-22-09

	Proof of service of notice
2-13 09	Pltf advised deft requests 30 days to vacate
2-25 09	" requested to advise at end of time if further steps are desired
3-15 09	" says in possession & <u>Case Dismissed</u>

Cherokee Intruder Cases 1901 - 1909

INTRUDER CASE NO. 1268
Cherokee NATION

Plaintiff John Reese Atty.

Versus

Defendant Proctor Merc. Co.
Proctor Okla Atty.

Complaint filed	Commissioner Reports	Contest. Notice Sent Jan *(?)* 09
Feb *(?)* 09	*(Entry illegible)*	
2-5 09	Acknowledged proof of service of notice sent	
2-25 09	*(Entry illegible)*	
3-*(?)* 09	*(Entry illegible)*	
(Illegible)	*(Entry illegible)*	
May 5 09	*(Entry illegible)*	
(Illegible)	*(Entry illegible)*	

INTRUDER CASE NO. 1269
Cherokee NATION

Plaintiff Charles M McClellan
Claremore Okla Atty.

Versus

Defendant D. S. Warren Atty.

Complaint filed Jan 8-09	Commissioner Reports 2-20-09	No Contest. Notice Sent Feb 5-09
	Allotment certificate in file - (ret'd 4-14-09)	
2-8 09	Acknowledged proof of service of notice	
2-17 09	Proof of service Answer of deft filed	
3-30 09	Set for hearing at Vinita April 9 & Cusey (DA) & parties advised	
4-14 09	Cusey advised written relinquishment of deft & Case Dismissed.	

INTRUDER CASE NO. 1270
Cherokee NATION

Plaintiff Ida B Allison
Muskogee Okla Atty.

Cherokee Intruder Cases 1901 - 1909

	Versus		
Defendant	Huck Rogers gdn of Clare Huckleberry Rogers	Atty.	

| Complaint filed | *(Illegible)* | Commissioner Reports | Jan 29-09 | No Contest. Notice Sent | Feb 2-09 |

| May 11 09 | Papers in case referred to Cochran (DA) |
| Aug 16 09 | Upon report of Dist. Agt Long case <u>dismissed</u> |

INTRUDER CASE. 1271
Cherokee NATION

Plaintiff	Daky Earbob *(Illegible)* Okla	Atty.	
	Versus		
Defendant	Clum Hayden *(Illegible)* Okla	Atty.	

| Complaint filed | | Commissioner Reports | | Contest. Notice Sent | Feb 5-09 |

	Allotment deed in file
2-28 09	Proof of service acknowledged.
3-3 09	Receipt acknowledged of deft's answer
3-3 09	Referred to Cusey D.A. for investigation
4-5 09	<u>Case Dismissed</u> DA reporting valid lease there on till Dec 19-09 memo of *(remainder illegible)*
Aug 17 09	Deed returned to pltf
	<u>Dismissed</u>

INTRUDER CASE NO. 1272
Cherokee NATION

Plaintiff	Jennie Barber Porum Okla	Atty.	
	Versus		
Defendant	Lafayette and Bros Checotah Okla	Atty.	

| Complaint filed | Feb 1-09 | Commissioner Reports | | Contest. Notice Sent | Feb 5-09 |

| | Allotment deed in file |
| 2-5 09 | Ack. proof of service |

300

Cherokee Intruder Cases 1901 - 1909

4-19 09	Referred to Cook (D.A.)
May 20 09	Cook (D.A.) reports
" 22 09	Papers returned to Cook for further report
" 26 09	Pltf advises she is not in pos. and Cook is advised

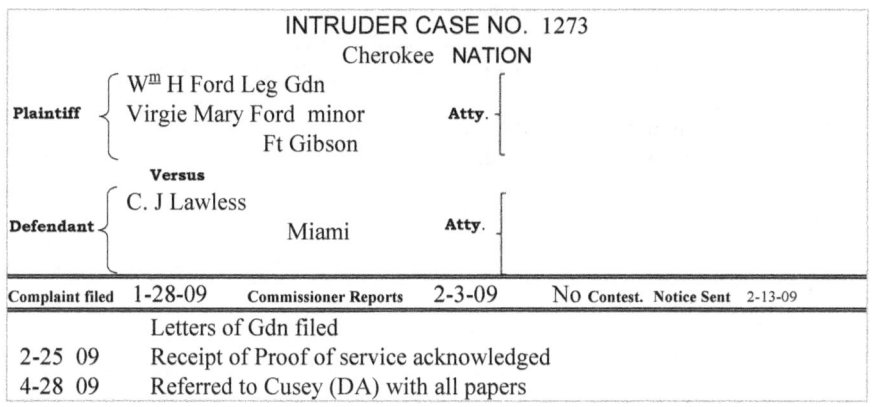

INTRUDER CASE NO. 1273
Cherokee NATION

Plaintiff: W^m H Ford Leg Gdn
Virgie Mary Ford minor   Atty.
Ft Gibson

Versus

Defendant: C. J Lawless
Miami   Atty.

Complaint filed 1-28-09   Commissioner Reports 2-3-09   No Contest. Notice Sent 2-13-09

Letters of Gdn filed
2-25 09   Receipt of Proof of service acknowledged
4-28 09   Referred to Cusey (DA) with all papers

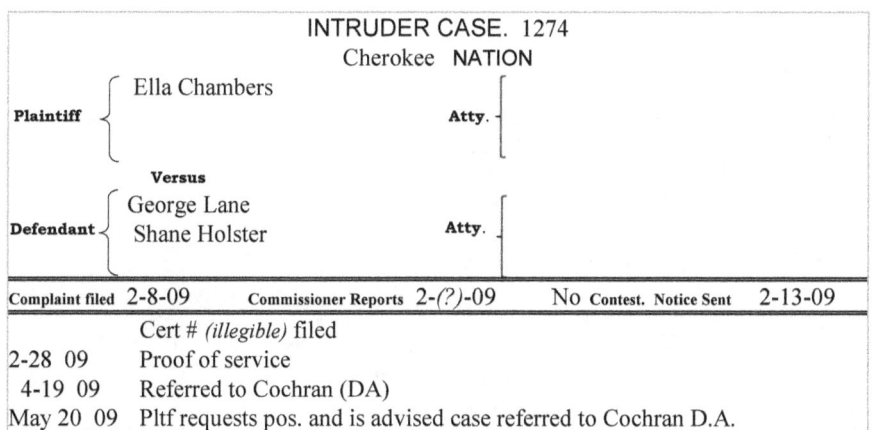

INTRUDER CASE. 1274
Cherokee NATION

Plaintiff: Ella Chambers   Atty.

Versus

Defendant: George Lane
Shane Holster   Atty.

Complaint filed 2-8-09   Commissioner Reports 2-(?)-09   No Contest. Notice Sent 2-13-09

Cert # *(illegible)* filed
2-28 09   Proof of service
4-19 09   Referred to Cochran (DA)
May 20 09 Pltf requests pos. and is advised case referred to Cochran D.A.

Cherokee Intruder Cases 1901 - 1909

INTRUDER CASE NO. 1275
Cherokee NATION

Plaintiff: Lula C Christie
Christie OK
Atty.

Versus

Defendant: Martin Bradford
Mrs. Tracey
Westville
Atty.

Complaint filed 2-8-09   Commissioner Reports 2-19-09   No Contest. Notice Sent 2-13-09

	Cert # 873
2-20 09	Acknowledged *(illegible)* proof of service
2-27 09	Cert # 873 ret'd to husband James
2-27 09	*(Entry illegible)*
2-27 09	Pltfs request Case Dismissed

INTRUDER CASE. 1276
Cherokee NATION

Plaintiff: James Christie
Christie
Atty.

Versus

Defendant: Martin Bradford
Mrs. Tracey
Joe Deldine
Atty.

Complaint filed 1-7-09   Commissioner Reports 2-19-09   No Contest. Notice Sent 1-3-09

	Certs # *(illegible)* & rental contract filed
	Referred to Com^r for report
2-20 09	Proof of service
2-27 09	Pltfs request Case Dismissed

INTRUDER CASE NO. 1277
Cherokee NATION

Plaintiff: Samuel and Amanda Perry
Ramona
Atty.

Versus

Defendant: George L Barlow
Ramona
Atty.

302

Cherokee Intruder Cases 1901 - 1909

Complaint filed	2-2-09	Commissioner Reports	2-6-09	No Contest. Notice Sent	1-13-09
2-20 09	Proof of service				
2-20 09	Answer by deft & records here showing deed since rest. removed				
	Case Dismissed				
4-1 09	Record furnished Dept in accordance with request *(remainder illegible)*				
May 13 09	Defts attention invited to answer in this case in reply to their request for report in re land of Amanda Perry: see letter				

INTRUDER CASE. 1278
Cherokee NATION

Plaintiff: Eliza Beavers, Bartlesville
Atty: John H Kane

Versus

Defendant: Noah Holland & family
Atty: Veasey & Rowland

Complaint filed	2-24-09	Commissioner Reports	2-25-09	Contest. Notice Sent	2-26-09
2-26 09	Case set for *(illegible)* at Vinita				
3-6 09	Proof of service acknowledged				
3-6 09	Defts answer				
3-9 09	Atty for pltf advised				
3-9 09	*(Illegible)* report of Com^r rec'd				
3-19 09	Defts fully advised & given 5 days to vacate				
3-30 09	Attys for pltf reports defts still on land				
3-30 09	Instructions issued to *(remainder illegible)*				
4-(?)-09	Police reporting Case Dismissed				

INTRUDER CASE NO. 1279
Cherokee NATION

Plaintiff: Carrie Burgess by Earl H Ortman, Ft Gibson
Atty: Atty

Versus

Defendant: Chas & Frank Ogan, Fort Gibson Okla
Atty:

Cherokee Intruder Cases 1901 - 1909

Complaint filed 2-12-09	Commissioner Reports 2-18-09	No Contest. Notice Sent 2-27-09
March 9 09	Chas Ogan appeared in person and stated he locked the land under a contract	
3-9 09	Proof of service	
3-18 09	Case set for 3-25-09 at Muskogee: testimony of both taken	
(Illegible)	Pltf requested to advise if in possession	
4-28 09	" says no & judgment rendered his favor: deft given 10 days	
May 9 09	Contract returned to Chas Ogan in pesson[sic]	

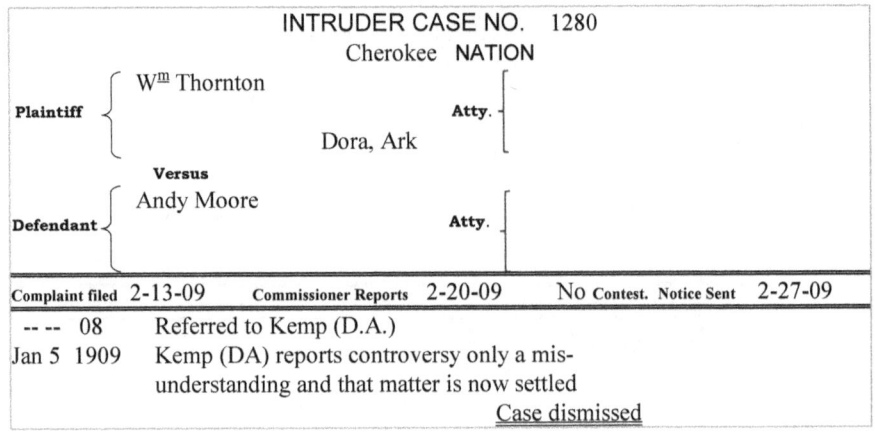

INTRUDER CASE NO. 1280
Cherokee NATION

Plaintiff: Wᵐ Thornton, Dora, Ark — Atty.

Versus

Defendant: Andy Moore — Atty.

Complaint filed 2-13-09	Commissioner Reports 2-20-09	No Contest. Notice Sent 2-27-09
-- -- 08	Referred to Kemp (D.A.)	
Jan 5 1909	Kemp (DA) reports controversy only a misunderstanding and that matter is now settled	
		Case dismissed

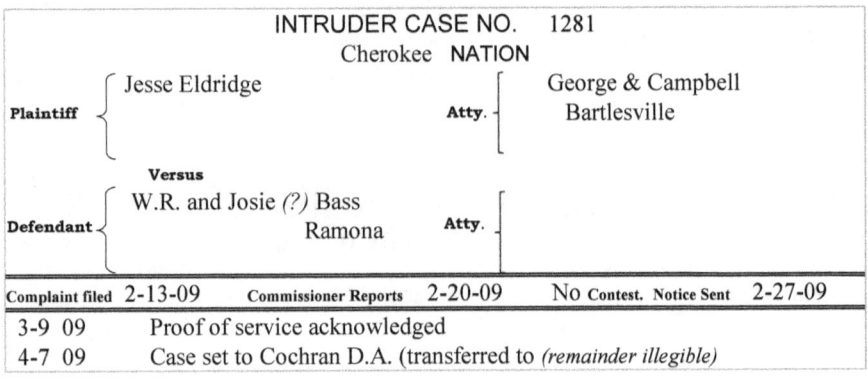

INTRUDER CASE NO. 1281
Cherokee NATION

Plaintiff: Jesse Eldridge — Atty. George & Campbell, Bartlesville

Versus

Defendant: W.R. and Josie (?) Bass, Ramona — Atty.

Complaint filed 2-13-09	Commissioner Reports 2-20-09	No Contest. Notice Sent 2-27-09
3-9 09	Proof of service acknowledged	
4-7 09	Case set to Cochran D.A. (transferred to *(remainder illegible)*	

Cherokee Intruder Cases 1901 - 1909

INTRUDER CASE NO. 1282
Cherokee NATION

Plaintiff: Joshua Drew — Vian — Atty.

Versus

Defendant: Wm Wilson — Atty.

| Complaint filed | 2-11-09 | Commissioner Reports | *(Illegible)* | No Contest. Notice Sent | 2-29-09 |

March 8 1909	Defdt made answer in person stating that he has *(remainder illegible)*
3-(?) 09	Pltf advised *(remainder illegible)*
3-13 09	Josh writes
3-17 09	Referred to Kemp (DA) *(remainder illegible)*

INTRUDER CASE NO. 1283
Cherokee NATION

Plaintiff: Sarah A Brown — Narcissa — Atty.

Versus

Defendant: Mr McQuarter — Afton — Atty. — H. O. Bland

| Complaint filed | 2-(?)-09 | Commissioner Reports | 2-25-09 | No Contest. Notice Sent | 3-1-09 |

3-6 09	Proof of service
3-15 09	*(Entry illegible)*
" 29 09	*(Entry illegible)*

INTRUDER CASE NO. 1284
Cherokee NATION

Plaintiff: John E Barks Leg Gdn / Willie H " minor / Welch — Atty. — W.P. Thompson, Vinita

Versus

Defendant: Henry B Lindsey & tenants — Atty.

Cherokee Intruder Cases 1901 - 1909

Complaint filed	2-29-09	Commissioner Reports	Contest. Notice Sent	3-6-09
		Deeds filed		
		Proof of service filed		
3-8 09		Proof of service		
3-13 09		Defts answer filed		
4-4 09		Com^r requested to advise in re *(remainder illegible)*		
Apr 30 09		Referred to Cusey D.A. with papers		
Apr 30 09		Atty Thompson advised that case is referred		

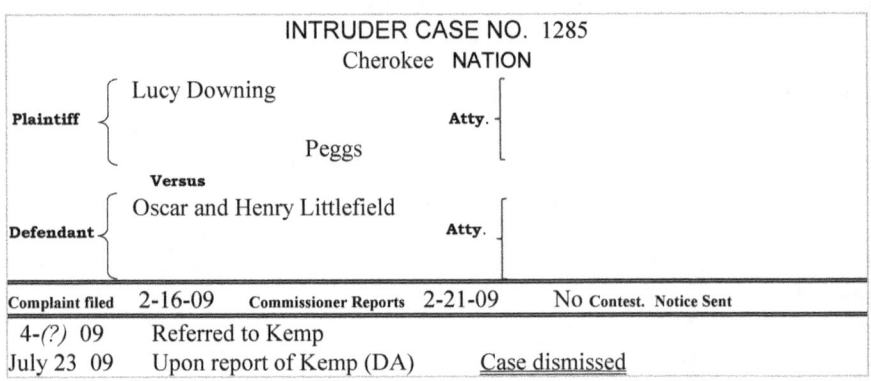

INTRUDER CASE NO. 1285
Cherokee NATION

Plaintiff: Lucy Downing / Peggs   Atty.

Versus

Defendant: Oscar and Henry Littlefield   Atty.

Complaint filed	2-16-09	Commissioner Reports	2-21-09	No Contest. Notice Sent
4-(?) 09		Referred to Kemp		
July 23 09		Upon report of Kemp (DA)		Case dismissed

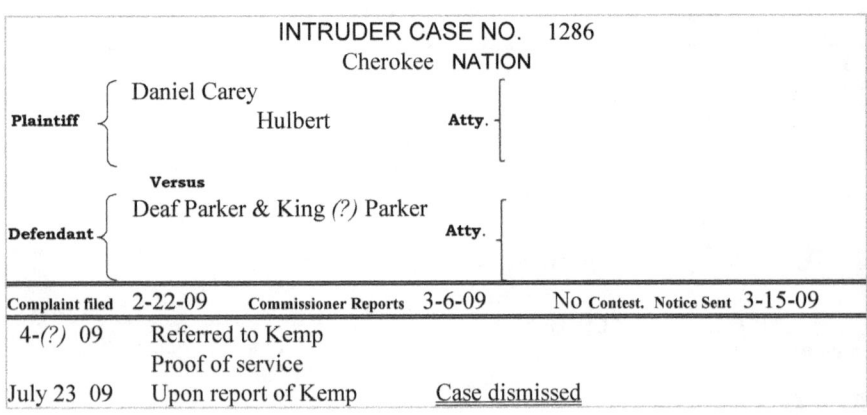

INTRUDER CASE NO. 1286
Cherokee NATION

Plaintiff: Daniel Carey / Hulbert   Atty.

Versus

Defendant: Deaf Parker & King *(?)* Parker   Atty.

Complaint filed	2-22-09	Commissioner Reports	3-6-09	No Contest. Notice Sent	3-15-09
4-(?) 09		Referred to Kemp			
		Proof of service			
July 23 09		Upon report of Kemp	Case dismissed		

Cherokee Intruder Cases 1901 - 1909

INTRUDER CASE NO. 1287
Cherokee NATION

Plaintiff: James Welch, Miami **Atty.**

Versus

Defendant: W.T. Kissire, SW City, Mo **Atty.**

| Complaint filed | 3-11-09 | Commissioner Reports | 3-8-09 | Contest. Notice Sent | 3-15-09 |

	Cert #12911 filed
3-15 09	Com^r asked for report
3-24 09	Proof of service filed
3-29 09	Answer filed by deft
4-2 09	Referred to Cusey (DA)
4-26 09	*(Illegible)* letter from pltf.

INTRUDER CASE NO. 1288
Cherokee NATION

Plaintiff: Nancy Lacey nee Toney, Porum **Atty.**

Versus

Defendant: J N Moore, *(Illegible)* **Atty.** *(Name Illegible)*, Porum

| Complaint filed | 3-3-09 | Commissioner Reports | *(Illegible)* | No Contest. Notice Sent | 3-15-09 |

(Illegible)	Proof of service
(Illegible)	Deft's answer *(illegible)*
May *(?)* 09	Papers in case sent to Cook D.A. for investigation
" 28 09	Cook (DA) reports
June 15 09	Pltf advised of Cook's report and case <u>is dismissed</u>

INTRUDER CASE. 1289
Cherokee NATION

Plaintiff: Bertha H Baker, Afton **Atty.**

Cherokee Intruder Cases 1901 - 1909

Defendant	Versus Henry Gaines Narcissa	**Atty.**			
Complaint filed 3-8-09	**Commissioner Reports** 3-18-09		**Contest. Notice Sent** 3-29-09		
(The entire entry is illegible.)					

INTRUDER CASE NO. 1290
Cherokee NATION

Plaintiff	*(Illegible)* Buzzard Afton	**Atty.**
Defendant	Versus Adam *(Illegible)*	**Atty.**
Complaint filed *(Illegible)*	**Commissioner Reports** *(Illegible)*	**Contest. Notice Sent** *(Illegible)*
(The entire entry is illegible.)		

INTRUDER CASE. 1291
Cherokee NATION

Plaintiff	F. B. Brown Leg Gdn Jesse C & *(Illegible)* Brown Minors Afton	**Atty.**
Defendant	Versus Eddie Danforth	**Atty.**
Complaint filed 3-17-09	**Commissioner Reports**	**Contest. Notice Sent** 3-30-09
	Deeds & Gdnshp papers filed These returned to Gdn in person 4/1/12-J	
4-(?) 09	Referred to *(Illegible)*	
4-(?) 09	Notice returned unclaimed	

INTRUDER CASE NO. 1292
Cherokee NATION

Plaintiff	Mrs Bettie Mitchell - Nat Gdn *(Name Illegible)*	**Atty.**

Cherokee Intruder Cases 1901 - 1909

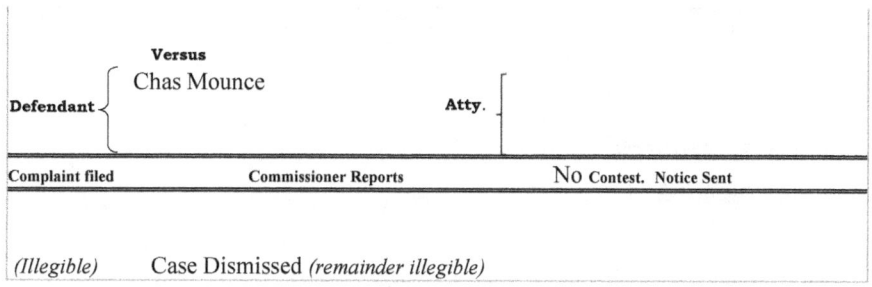

Defendant	Versus Chas Mounce	Atty.	
Complaint filed	Commissioner Reports		No Contest. Notice Sent
(Illegible)	Case Dismissed *(remainder illegible)*		

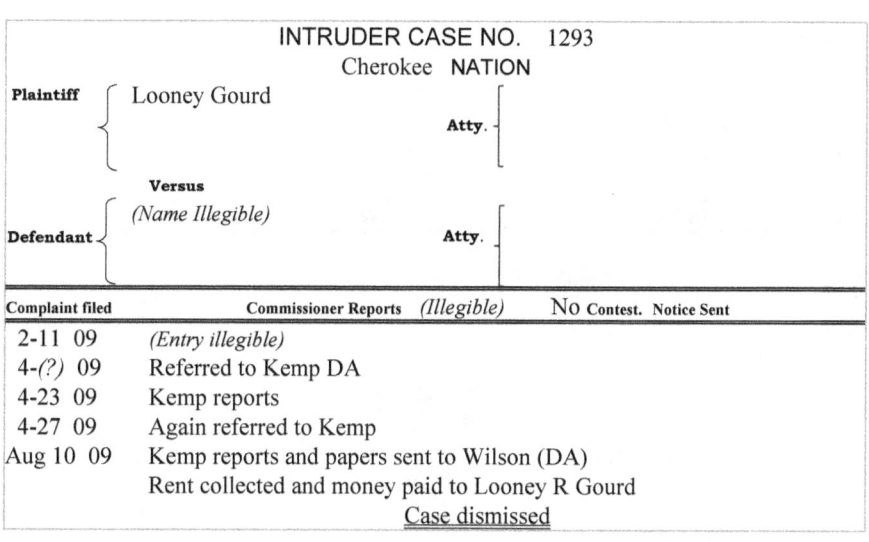

INTRUDER CASE NO. 1293
Cherokee NATION

Plaintiff	Looney Gourd	Atty.	
Defendant	Versus *(Name Illegible)*	Atty.	
Complaint filed	Commissioner Reports	*(Illegible)*	No Contest. Notice Sent
2-11 09	*(Entry illegible)*		
4-(?) 09	Referred to Kemp DA		
4-23 09	Kemp reports		
4-27 09	Again referred to Kemp		
Aug 10 09	Kemp reports and papers sent to Wilson (DA)		
	Rent collected and money paid to Looney R Gourd		
	<u>Case dismissed</u>		

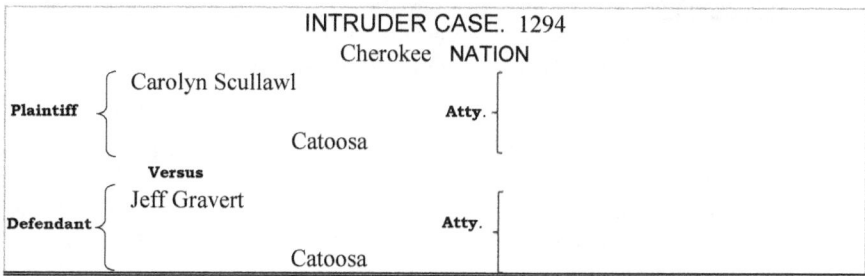

INTRUDER CASE. 1294
Cherokee NATION

Plaintiff	Carolyn Scullawl Catoosa	Atty.	
Defendant	Versus Jeff Gravert Catoosa	Atty.	

Cherokee Intruder Cases 1901 - 1909

Complaint filed	(?)-3-09	Commissioner Reports	4-27-09	Contest. Notice Sent	4-28-09
	Cert #14686 filed				
Apr 28 09	Proof of service				
May (?) 09	Papers and case referred to Cochran D.A.				
Sept 10 09	Papers returned by Long (DA) and case, upon request of pltf dismissed				

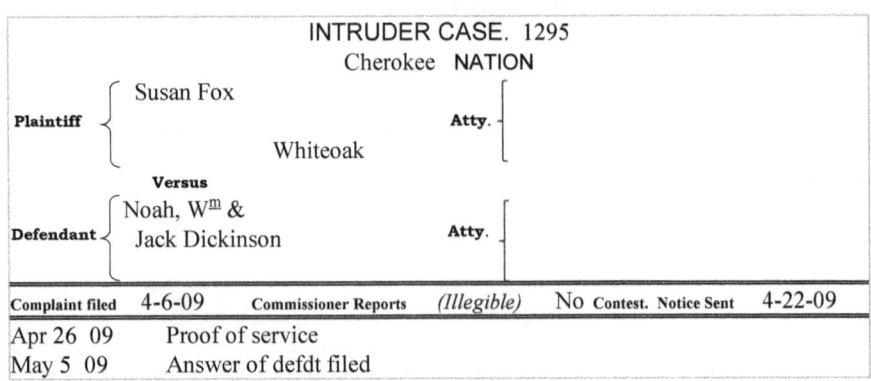

INTRUDER CASE. 1295
Cherokee NATION

Plaintiff: Susan Fox / Whiteoak   Atty.

Versus

Defendant: Noah, W^m & Jack Dickinson   Atty.

Complaint filed	4-6-09	Commissioner Reports	(Illegible)	No Contest. Notice Sent	4-22-09
Apr 26 09	Proof of service				
May 5 09	Answer of defdt filed				

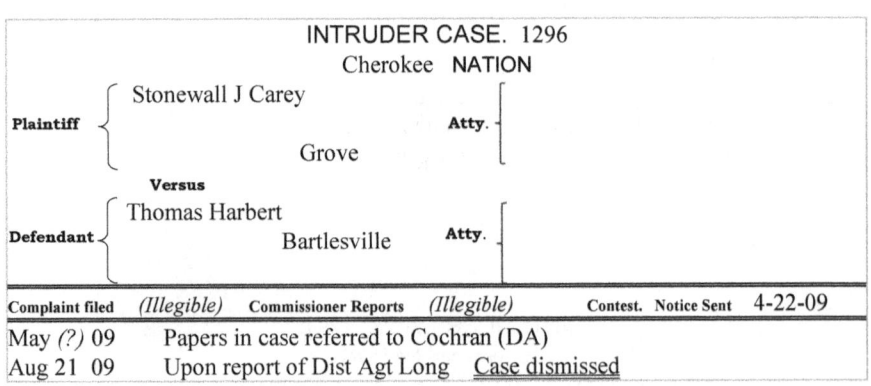

INTRUDER CASE. 1296
Cherokee NATION

Plaintiff: Stonewall J Carey / Grove   Atty.

Versus

Defendant: Thomas Harbert / Bartlesville   Atty.

Complaint filed	(Illegible)	Commissioner Reports	(Illegible)	Contest. Notice Sent	4-22-09
May (?) 09	Papers in case referred to Cochran (DA)				
Aug 21 09	Upon report of Dist Agt Long Case dismissed				

INTRUDER CASE. 1297
Cherokee NATION

Plaintiff: Blue Hothouse / (Illegible) Okla   Atty.

310

Cherokee Intruder Cases 1901 - 1909

Defendant	Versus (Joe Hoovey)	Atty.
Complaint filed	**Commissioner Reports**	**Contest. Notice Sent**
	(The entire entry is illegible.)	

INTRUDER CASE. 1298
Cherokee NATION

Plaintiff	Maggie Johnson Moodys[sic] Okla	Atty.
Defendant	Versus Commonwealth Trust Co Muskogee	Atty.
Complaint filed	**Commissioner Reports**	**Contest. Notice Sent**

Lease found of record executed by pltf.
(Illegible...) to the defdt for a term of 5 years from February 8-07.
Case dismissed

INTRUDER CASE. 1299
Cherokee NATION

Plaintiff	Ned Olila Wilson	Atty.
Defendant	Versus James P. Allen	Atty.
Complaint filed	**Commissioner Reports**	**Contest. Notice Sent**

Long (DA) requested to get data

INTRUDER CASE. 1300
Cherokee NATION

Plaintiff	(Rosie Streeter)	Atty.

Cherokee Intruder Cases 1901 - 1909

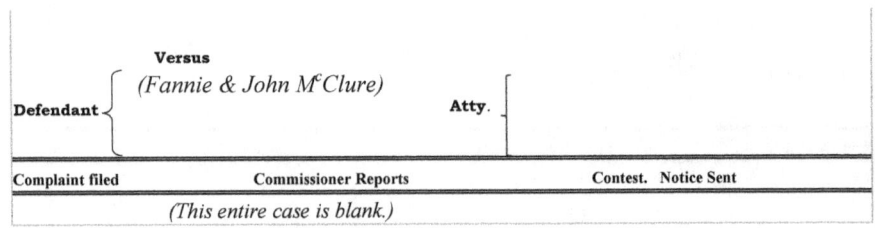

Defendant	Versus (Fannie & John McClure)	Atty.	
Complaint filed	Commissioner Reports		Contest. Notice Sent

(This entire case is blank.)

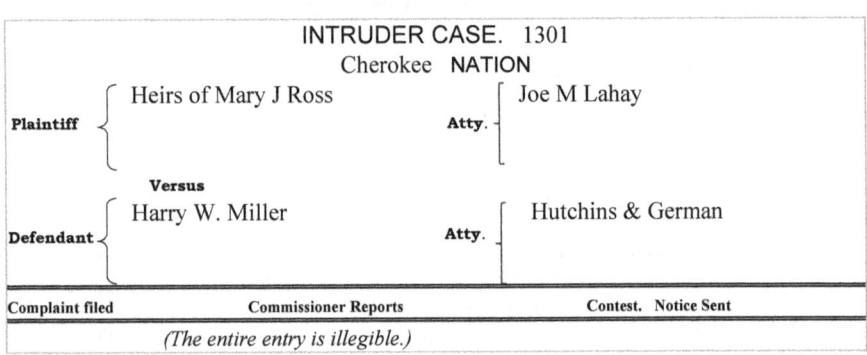

INTRUDER CASE. 1301
Cherokee NATION

Plaintiff	Heirs of Mary J Ross	Atty.	Joe M Lahay
Defendant	Versus Harry W. Miller	Atty.	Hutchins & German
Complaint filed	Commissioner Reports		Contest. Notice Sent

(The entire entry is illegible.)

INTRUDER CASE. 1302
Cherokee NATION

Plaintiff	Ada M Thompson minor by W C Thompson Natural Gdn	Atty.	
Defendant	Versus George Bell Hayden I.T.	Atty.	C.T. Atkinson Arkansas City KS.
Complaint filed	6-17-12 $^{\#}34880$ Commissioner Reports 6-17-12		Contest. Notice Sent 6-19-12

7-10-1912	Proof of Service recieved[sic]
7-2-1912	Defts answer recieved[sic] $^{\#}$38578
7-9-1912	" (by Atty) notified that he has right to possession as freedman claimant
" "	& should vacate premises immediately
7-15-1912	Thos P. Roach Chief of Police & John L Brown Private instructor to
"	despass[sic] anyone on land and place allottee[sic] in possession through her
"	natural gdn. Dist. agent H.C. Cusey having reported that Intruder has shown
"	disposition to gain possession of small grain, to be threshed in few days, by
"	force if nec.

Cherokee Intruder Cases 1901 - 1909

7-20-12   Thos P Roach Chief of Police reports allottee[sic] placed in possession

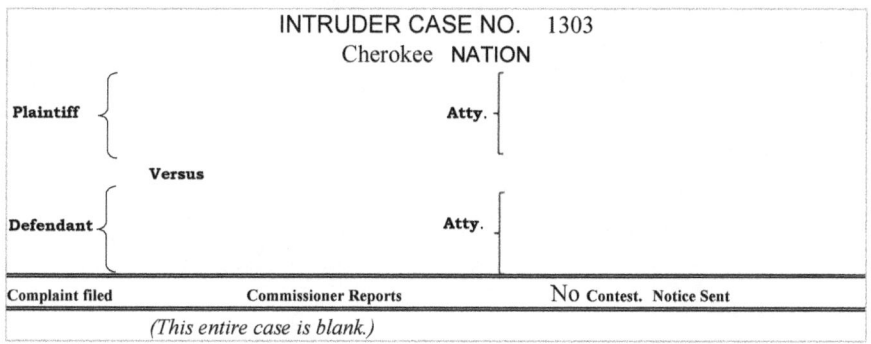

INTRUDER CASE NO. 1303
Cherokee NATION

Plaintiff   Atty.

Versus

Defendant   Atty.

Complaint filed   Commissioner Reports   No Contest. Notice Sent

(This entire case is blank.)

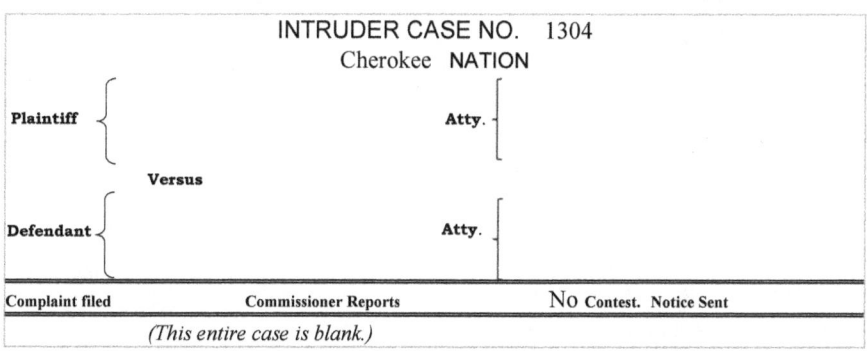

INTRUDER CASE NO. 1304
Cherokee NATION

Plaintiff   Atty.

Versus

Defendant   Atty.

Complaint filed   Commissioner Reports   No Contest. Notice Sent

(This entire case is blank.)

Index

(ILLEGIBLE) & ROWLAND............. 272
ACORN
   Annie... 46
   John B... 46
   Lizzie... 46
ADAIR
   Frankie M 286
   Goldie... 151
   Hugh M 136
   Mollie E... 111
   Policeman 78
   Robert.. 61
   T W.. 78
   Tandy W 34,35,39,78
   William... 61
ADAMS
   D W 288
   Dock... 158
   Jno 107
   John O 133
   Mr J O... 133
   Richard C... 56
ADKISON
   Ella M 81
   Ora B 81
AKIN, Strange W 213
AKINS
   Don 213
   F R 29
   Frank R 29
   R L.. 29
   Robt L... 29
ALBERT, Jerry............................. 134,135
ALBERTA
   Cora 54
   Daisy... 54
ALBERTY
   Cora 49,54
   Daisy.. 49,54
   Daisy Reed 49
   Joe 270
   Silas 107
ALDEN
   Joseph 249
   Rathbone... 249
ALDRICH
   William.. 151

Wm... 151
ALEXANDER, Pleasant 203
ALLEN
   Charley E... 285
   J P 283
   James P 268,311
   Mrs Aletha B 5
ALLISON
   Ida B 299
   Lora J.. 257
ALLSUP, Sussanna............................... 5
ALRID, Wm... 151
ALRIDGE, Wm................................... 151
ALWELL
   Emma 161
   Ruth.. 161
ANDERSON
   Albert... 18
   Arthur W 255
   Charles.. 163
   Frank M 125
   Harry... 200
   Louisa... 18
   Thomas... 200
ANDERSON & ERTEL..................... 226
ANIBLE, Caldonie E........................... 32
ARMSTRONG
   Houston 108
   James 108
   John 157,241
   Mary 241
   Oldman... 108
ATKINSON, C T.................................. 312
ATWELL
   Ruth.. 281
   Wm H 281
AUSTIN, Sam 253
AVERY, Charles 261
BAILEY
   De Roos 83
   De Ross 16
   DeRoss 16
BAKER
   Bertha H 307
   Tom 93
BALDRIDGE....................................... 222
   Columbus.. 234

Index

Inola 234
Maze 221
BALLARD
   Bill 67
   William 67
BALTZ, Mrs Foster 282
BARBEE
   Jno 63
   John 117
   Policeman 117
BARBER
   Jennie 300
   Jno 43
   Johnson 297
BARD
   Thomas D 213
   Thos D 213
BARK, Andrew 242
BARKER, Ollie T 272
BARKS
   John E 305
   Willie H 305
BARLOW, George L 302
BARNES, John 46,118
BARNEY
   Cara 236
   Charles 98
   James 236
BARNSDALE, Ned 148
BARRICK, David A 39
BARRY
   Stella 87
   William 87
BARTLESVILLE *(ILLEGIBLE)* BUCK CO . 272
BARTLETT, Lon 193
BARTON, Frank 48
BASS
   Josie *(?)* 304
   W R 304
BAT
   Akie 46
   Ellie 46
   Ellis 45
BATES, H H 138
BATTENFIELD, A L 138
BAUGH, Joel L 166
BEAGLES, Mary B 201

BEAM
   Louisa 6
   Murphy 6
BEAMER
   Lewis 235
   Nancy 235
BEAN
   Dennie 287
   Lewis 260
BEAR
   Johnson 139
   Oscar 139
   Polly 139
   Simon 139
BEARD
   Bill 169
   L B 283
   M B 169
BEATTY, J L 131
BEAVERS, Eliza 303
BEBONT
   G N 182
   Gaylord N 181
BECK
   Amy 32,33
   Ary 19
   Bell 88
   Carrie 88
   Charles 88
   Dora 32,33
   Halin 20
   Harlin B 19
   Homer 19
   Jesse 19
   Joseph 19
   Leona 88
   Mary 209
   Rutherford 20
   Stella 19
BELL
   Geo 149
   George 149,312
   James 232
   James E 206,232
   James E, Jr 206
   Jas E 206,282
   Jas E, Jr 206

Index

July 149
Mark 206
Mark R 206
Martin A 232
BENGE, Cornelia C 77
BENNETT 7
  Henry 59
  Mr 28
  R R 24,88,93,100,106,114,122,
  139,143,246,258,264,267,268,279,283
  ,287,289
  Robert R 56
  Robt E 133
  Robt R 2,20,23,24,28,29,32,38,
  39,42,50,57,59,60,69,70,85,86,88,90,
  93,95,102,106,107,108,110,111,113,
  114,121,123,124,125,126,127,128,130
  ,144,149,167,168,170
  Robt T 1
  W W 16,48,117,148,272
BENTLEY, John 239
BENTON, Isaiah 298
BERKS, Victoria 243
BESSEY & RUTHERFORD 291
BIGBY
  Fannie 141
  John 236
  Walter 141
BIGFEATHER, Sallie 245
BILLINGS, Starr 93
BIRD
  L88
  Lewis 88
  Nancy 267
BIXBY, Comr 60
BLACK, Will 90
BLACKWELL
  Frank 122
  Geo 250
  Katie 141
  Lucinda 123
BLAKELY, S P 293
BLAKEMAN
  G W 144
  Walter 144
  William 144
BLAND

H O 12,305
Harry O 11,12
BLEAKMORE, W N 5
BLEVINS
  A 55
  Minnie Lee 54
  Nellie May 55
BLISS 130
  Hattie 96,97
BLISS & DAVIDSON 290
BLUEJACKET
  Elsie 259
  Mike 222
BLYTHE, Jemima S 256
BOB, Mrs Emeline Lembles 80
BOLAND, Bill 67
BOLIN, Martin 287
BOOTH, F M 48
BOSTON
  Chas 48
  Frank 48
BOUDINOT, Frank J 79
BOWELS
  Betsy 47
  Jennette 47
BOYD, W C 266
BRACKETT
  Voil 163
  W B 163
BRADFORD, Martin 302
BRADLEY, Cris M 41
BRADY, Josie 284
BRAINERD, Ezra 220
BRANNAN, W I 103
BRANNON, N A 66
BREAD, Jennie 4
BREEDLOVE 269
  James W 118
  Jas W 46
BREWER 160
  B 87
  Sallie 165
  Sally 165
BREWSTER
  A C 10,11,19,29,135,138
  Mr A C 29
BRIDGE

Index

Nellie 224
Runaway 224
BRIDGES, J W 226
BRIGGS
  J L 44
  Lewis 3
  Louis 3
BRISTOW, Dr J E 224
BROWN
  A 151
  Clyde 185
  Dock 210
  E M 32
  F B 308
  F L 120,152
  Henry 59,230
  Henry T 119
  I B 125
  Ida B 126
  Isabel 190
  Isabella 191
  J T 89
  James A 91
  Jane 230
  Jesse C 308
  John 125
  John L 312
  Josie 147
  Louis T 49,54,71
  Luther 185
  Mr 285
  R 147,158
  Sallie 116,203,204
  Sarah 185
  Sarah A 305
  T L 61,96,133
  Thomas 223
  Wylie 207
BRUCE, L C 179
BRUTEN, W O 114
BRYANT, Herman 271
BUCHER, Carroll S 7
BUCKHORN, Jack 279
BUCKNER, Mary 23
BUDDER, Lewis 184
BUDDING
  Lewis 74

Lewis H 237
BUELL
  Garfield 7,8
BUFFINGTON
  Alex 53
  William E 103
BULLETTA, John 85
BUNCH
  Eli 76
  Garland 113
BURGESS
  Carrie 303
  J B 159
  Mrs 159
BURKE, D H 83
BURLINGAME, P L 204
BURNEY
  James 231
  Willie 231
BURR
  Alexander 24,25
  Geo W 24
BUSHYHEAD, Maggie 114
BUTLER
  Chas 85
  Lone 72
  Nara 248
BUTTE 130
  Geo C 129,130,153
BUTTLER, Emeline 142
BUTTS, R L 223
BUTZ, R B 2
BUZZARD 308
BYRD
  Alfred 86
  Louis J 86
  Maud M 86
  Minnie L 86
  Nina 86
  William T 86
CABBELL, Frank 234
CALDWELL
  Annie 293
  Osher 293
CALLIES, Katie 190
CAMERON, D 72
CAMP, J 251

Index

CAMPBELL
  Atty 56
  Geo E 256
  Jane Philip 21
  Ned 2,36
  Nev 56,110,111,136
  Oma 79
  Rachel 256
  Wm 21
CARBEN
  Lee 164
  Malzy 165
CARBIN
  Aleck 164
  James 164
  Lee 164,165,204
  Malzy 164,165
  Sanford 164
CAREY
  Daniel 306
  Stonewall J 310
CARPENTER, Sam 66
CARRIGER, William D 146
CASNER
  C W 51
  F W 51,81
CASNOR, F W 50
CATES, Emma C 91
CAYWOOD
  Lizzie 222
  Thomas P 222
CCROGGINS, Georgia A 90
CHAMBERLIN, Dollie E 33
CHAMBERS
  Ella 301
  Henry 141
  Joseph W 198
  Nellie Jane 154
  Turie 198
  W E 198
CHAMP, M 143
CHANEY
  Alfred H 125
  Florence E 126
  Florence Ellen 125
CHARLES, Lizzie Bell 87
CHASE, W A 1,144,216,217

CHAVOSE, Mr W Norman 53
CHILDERS
  J H 66,131,199,229
  Mr 42,43
  Mr J H 42
CHOATE 266
  John 236
  Joshua 171
  M L 265
  Martha 171
  Mattie 265
  Mattie L 265
CHOTEAU, Addie 22
CHRISMAN, Agnes 146
CHRISTIE
  Hester 189
  James 302
  Lula C 302
  Pleasant 157
  Rachel 28
  Wm 189
CHUCKLUCK, Tyler 144
CLAGHORN, Peggie 289
CLAPMAN 86
CLAPPER
  Arthur H 168
  Arthur M 168
  Carl E 168
  Elouise M 168
CLARK
  Andrew 185
  Bettie 263
  C P 273
  Herman 273
CLARK & CLARK 254
CLAYTON, W H H 220
CLEVENGER, O B 293
CLINES, W M 258
CLYNE, Zeke 83
COATS
  Alexander 238
  John 265
  Lillie M 265
COBB 104
COBBS, Mr 182
COCHRAN 293,294,296,297,298,
300,301,304,310

Index

Dora 185
Josie 185
Margaret 240
Rufus 185
COKER
    Bunk 169
    Mrs M 169
COLBERT 178
    James 177,178
    Jas 177
COLLINS
    Agusta B 11
    Albert H, Jr 11
    Eli H 11
    A H 11,12
    Mary F 12
    Mrs Annie 12
COMMONWEALTH TRUST CO 311
CONSEEN, Lillie M 202
COODY, Joe 205
COOK 297,298,301,307
    George 166
    Joanna 166
COOKSON, Andy 275
COON, M F 90
COOPER
    One 187
    William A 81
COPPEDGE, Ad V 220
CORBEN
    Felix 164
    Melzy 164
CORDRAY, Mary B 201
COUNSEL
    Andy 131
    Mr 228
COUNSELER, Andy 130
COUNSELOR, Andy 130
COURTNEY, J L 220
COX, J D 155,197,271
CRAIG
    Buell 287
    J H 177
    Leonard 287
CRAVENS & CRAVENS 223,253
CRITTENDEN, John 21
CROMMELL, Frank 95

CROMWELL, Frank 95
CROSS, Jennie 209
CROSSLAND, Eliza 43
CRUMP
    W J 66
    Walter 94
CRUNNY, Mr 228
CRUTCHFIELD
    A 136
    J K 41,212
    Mrs 198
CULLISON, I B 7
CULVER
    Ed 69
    Maggie 52
CUMMINGS, Wm A 180
CUPP, D M 170
CURRAY, Sonny 167
CURRY
    G W 40
    Miss Florence 40
    Sonny 166
CURTAIN, Sam 10
CURTIS, Mr 39,41,194
CUSEY 22,74,269,298,299,300,301, 306,307
    H C 168,312
CUSTER, Clarence 184
DAMILS, Joe 200
DANFORTH, Eddie 308
DANIELS
    Burrell 208
    Ransom 240
    Wiley 123
DANNENBERG
    Daniel E 207
    J C 207
    Jno C 207
    John C 207
DAUGHERTY
    Belle C 113
    Thos J 156
DAVENPORT
    Atty 31
    J S 51,221
    James S 178,194
    James Sa 179

Index

Jas 50,51
Jas S 221
DAVIDSON, W H 132
DAVIS
   (Illegible) G 259
   Carl 63
   Charles 108
   Chas 63
   Ella 162
   Joe 63
   Lucy 153
   Preston 252
DAVIS & MASON 49
DAVIS, MASON & BLAND 139
DAWES, Thomas 195
DEAL, Charlie 143
DECOOUE, Jacob 45
DECOU, Jacob 45
DEERMAN, Jesse 111
DEGRAFFENREID, R P 68
DEHART, Lige 113
DELDINE, Joe 302
DENBO, Laura A 156
DENISON, G B 50
DENISON WICHITA & MEMPHIS RY CO ... 50,51
DENNING, Leger 119
DENNUMBER
   Cora 257
   John 257
DENNY
   Lewis 47
   Noble 47
DENTON, J C 125
DEPRIEST, P F 9
DEPUY, John M 204
DERRICK, John 200
DICK, J Henry 4
DICKINSON
   Jack 310
   Noah 310
   Wm 310
DICKSON
   Mr 6
   Mrs Dara 235
DILLON, W C 247
DIMMONS, James W 39

DIRTEATER
   Annie 186
   Charles 186
   Chas 186
   Joe 197
DIX, Ida 284
DODGE, V 231
DODSON
   Jas 160
   W J 17
DOE, John 229
DOGGET, Dr E E 50
DOGGETT
   Dr E E 51
   E E 51,81
DOTTS, Dan 64
DOWELL, Frank 121
DOWNING
   Eli 149
   Hill 274
   Houston 274
   Jack 142
   Jackson 178
   Katie 36,261
   Lucy 306
   Mary 274
   Sarah E 247
   Tom 153
DOYLE, John 187
DRAKE, Norman S 285
DREW
   James 170
   Joshua 264,305
DUNCAN
   Cleo D 102
   Fred B 181
   Inola Josephine 181
   James 117
DUNN
   James L 137
   Luther A 128
DURALL
   Ada 150
   B H 151
   Geo Marvin 151
   George Marvin 150
   Hugh Allen 150

Index

DUVAL, William 283
EAGLE
   Annie 112,187
   Jno 158
   John 157,241
EARBOB, Daky 300
EATON
   Ada G 44
   Johann 96
   John E 44
   Nina 96
   Phil 96
   Thomas 96
EDINGTON
   Bettie 131
   J R 131
EDMONSON, Florence 138
EDWARDS, Silas 30
EIFFERT 79
ELAM, J T 42
ELDRIDGE, Jesse 304
ELK, Sam 258
ELLIOT, L G 10
ELLIOTT
   D G 62,170,247,250,251,280
   Mr 251
   Mr D G 62
ELLIS
   J 175
   Lizzie 132
EMERSON, J S 199
ENGLAND
   Andrew 269
   Betsy 269
   James 73
   John 269
   Pigeon 269
   R L 73
   Sarah 226
   Wash 269
ERTEL, Frank 60
ERWIN, R M 98
ESTES, Jim 265
ETCHEN, A M 87
ETCHENS
   Atty 240
   H M 240

EVANS, Robert H 122
FAIR, Rena 146
FALLINGPOT
   Bertha Starr 237
   Maudie 74
FARKS, Atty 68
FARRIE, Wm 277
FAULKNER, Charley 110
FENWICK
   Harve 38
   One 252
FERGUSON
   J W 24
   Waller 155
   Walter 155,156
FIELDS
   Bush 9
   Howard 35,176
   W H 35
   William 176
   William E 176
   Wm E 35
FILLMORE, George 66
FINDLAY, W W 70
FITE
   Dr 189,219
   Dr F B 56,188,219
FLESHER, W H 174
FLINT
   Essie 200
   Eva 200
   James E 200
   M G 200
FLIPPENS, Mr 173
FLYING, Crawford D 57
FOGG
   Jno 36
   John 36
FOGLE
   G P 72
   Mr 16
FOGLE & PARKS 67,117,237
FONTLEROY
   Joshua 190
   Mose 190
FORD
   G S 91

Index

John 6	**FRENCH**
Rhoda 271	Charlotte 198
Tom 271	Policeman 33,172
Virgie Mary 301	Tom B 32
Wm H 301	**FRY**
FOREMAN	Andy 266
Bessie J 172	Millie 266
Cherokee 111	**FRYE, E M** 175
Jacob 27	**FUGATE, S D** 110
James 296	**FULLERTON, S C** 134
Jane 164	**GABBUS, M O** 278
John 94	**GAINES**
Richard D 7	Frank 114,269
Robby 27	Henry 308
W W 172	**GAN, Jack** 275
William B 193	**GANN, George** 118
William W 172	**GANNON, Wm** 26
FOSTER	**GARVIN**
Clem 107	Ernest 64
Edward 107	Henrietta 64
Quinnie 107	**GEORGE, Tom** 157
FOX	**GEORGE & CAMPBELL** 304
Greeley 262	**GERMAN, Mr** 70,73
Susan 310	**GHORMLEY, Don Carlos T** 145
Susie 239	**GIDNEY, Samuel E** 70,71
FRANCIS	**GILBERT, Fannie** 275
Beatrice 240	**GILL, Joseph A** 140
Jack 240	**GILLILAND, Jeff** 107
FRASIER, J Q 274	**GILLISPIE, W P** 13
FRAZIER	**GILLMAN**
Benjeman 41	Henrietta 207
Famous 41	Mary A 207
N F, Jr 46	**GILSTRAP**
Virgin 41	Albert L 144
Wm T 41	Artelia 144
FREAR, Theo D B 63	Nora E 144
FREE	**GLASCOW, M R** 180
J E 227	**GLASS & WEAVER** 127
Ruth C 227	**GLEASON, John W** 187
FREEMAN	**GODARD, W P** 44
C R 75	**GODDARD** 44
Charles R 75	James W 112
Chas R 89	**GOEGLE,** *(Illegible)* 74
Jno 58	**GOINGS, Taylor** 162
O U 213	**GOODEN, Lula** 115
Oce 213	**GOODRIDGE, Walter** 115
Osa 213	**GOODWIN, J O** 82

Index

GORMLY, C W 160
GOSS, Mr 295
GOTTLULP, Ed J 71
GOURD
    Alice 82
    Eliza 82
    Looney 309
    Looney R 309
    Mariah 82
    Mariah R 83
    Sarah 82
    Thomas R 82
    William 82
    Wm R 82
GRAHAM
    John W 259
    Robert L 259
GRAVERT, Jeff 309
GRAVES
    Alex 145
    A S 159
GREEN
    Emeline 21
    A R 249
GREENLEES, C C 280
GREER, Wm R 294
GRIFFIN, Andrew J 265
GRINER, John 89
GRITTS
    Peggie 233
    A W 163
GROOM
    Leeot 205
    Robert 205
GROOMER
    Della 83
    Willia 83
GRUBBS, Nelson 196
GUNTHER, George W 109
GUTHRIE
    Grace 181
    James 181
    Jas 181
    William 181
HACKLEMAN, John 181
HADLEY
    Mr 66

W W 24,25
HAGGERMAN, Robt 259
HAIR, Bird 228
HALL 159
    Geo 205
    Jenny 205
    Josephine 205
    Julia 124
    Thos 1
    Tom 1
HAMLIN, Emma H 7
HANNAH
    C E 80
    H E 80
HARBERT, Thomas 310
HARDRICK
    Eliza J 176
    Moses 170
    Mrs Eluja 35
    Silas 178
HARDY
    E B 1
    Earl 69
HARE
    Andy 84
    Jennie 271
HARELE, Frank 128
HARLAN
    Sol 155
    Walter 155
HARLIN
    Ellis C 23
    Jim 182
HARRINGTON
    Elizabeth 207
    L H 207
HARRIS
    Charles 152
    Charlotte E 62
    John F 62
    Lottie E 291
    Malinda 89
    Philo H 30
HARRISON
    Hannah E 199
    James 238
HART, Boone 239

Index

HARTER, Charles 227
HARTFIELD, J D 53
HARTNESS
   David 109
   Katie 108
HASTINGS, E L 133
HATFIELD, Winnie D 106
HAWKINS
   Charles 56
   Mr 188
   Ralph 271
HAWLEY, Susan B Chaney 56
HAYDEN
   Clum 300
   Henry 128
HAYES
   Hugh M 193
   O L 94,244
   Oscar L 94
HAYS, James 176
HAZELRIDGE, Mary Ann 281
HEADDY, J B 87
HEADY
   Bud 169
   J P 88
HEALTON, Todd 19
HEARD
   Bessie 263
   Josef S 263
HEFFERFINGER, Pace 103
HENEGAR, Leona E 174
HENRY
   Agnes B 248
   Dan 290
   Morris F 237
   Mrs Amilio B 248
HENSLEY, J A 130
HESS
   Della 248
   Maud 91
HIATT, E A 82
HIBBS
   David A 219
   Emma 188
   Emma M 188
   James A 58
   Sarah I 58

HICKORY, John 226
HICKS, Austin 225
HILDEBRAND, Betsy 22
HILDERBRAND
   Brice 37
   Mary 37
HILL
   Jesse 238
   John 238
   Sallie 43
HILLS, H A 215
HINES, R W 36
HIX, Frank 171
HOGAN
   John C 19,202
   W D 12,13
HOGG
   John 85
   Oliver 85
HOLDERMAN
   C C 58
   C E 24,57,120,139,145,203,205
   M 57,145
HOLLAND
   A E 31
   Georgia A 90
   Noah 303
HOLLEY
   Charley 264
   Dora M 50
HOLLINGER, Will H 164
HOLLINGSMITH, O M 215
HOLLOWAY, D D 71
HOLSTER, Shane 301
HOLT, Diana Vann 296
HOOPER, M M 298
HOOVEY, Joe 311
HOPKINS
   Emma M 26
   Philip B 187
HOPPER, Martin 216
HORTON
   Lucinda 49,54
   Robert 49
   Robt 54
HOSLEY, R W I 128
HOTHOUSE, Blue 310

Index

HOUSEBURG, Lidy 163
HOUSTON
    Annie 4
    Isaac... 288
HOWARD
    Bessie Byrne................................... 178
    Emma 84,286
    Sam.. 286
HUCKLEBERRY
    J H 218
    James... 173
HUDDLESTON, Horace..................... 40
HUGHES
    Charley 145
    Charley, Jr 184
    David... 215
    Emmett 184
    Geo 251
    Geo W 280
    Hiram.. 19
    Mr & Mrs Geo 251
    Mrs Martha 184
HUMAN, Harvey 68
HUMES, Chas L................................... 78
HUMPHREY, H D.............................. 281
HUNNICUTT, J E............................... 131
HUNT, W T.. 96
HURLEY, P J 100
HUTCHING, MURPHY & GERMAN 73
HUTCHINGS & MURPHY 37
HUTCHINGS, MURPHY & GERMAN70
HUTCHINS & GERMAN.................. 312
HYATT, Mr Ed 82
INGLE, G G 159
INGRAM
    Emma L 221
    A T 62,199
INLOW
    Nancy 31
    William.. 31
    Wm.. 31
ISRAEL
    John 176
    Phillip 176
ISREAL, William 21
J BLAIR SHOENFELT & SONS 90
JACKSON

C C 222
C L 259
Hannah E 199
Jack 10
Mrs Lizzie.. 44
Osie... 44
JARBO, B A 228
JARBOE, B A 64
JENNINGS
    H..60,88,222,248
    Mr 60
    Mr H 89
JILES
    Mrs Mary A 3,4
    Wm... 3
JOHNSON
    Alcey 268
    Bessie 149
    Bud 32
    Chas... 32
    George 86
    James... 235
    John 85,216
    Joseph T 255
    L R 32,149
    Leander... 42
    Leonidas R 32
    Loss 135
    Maggie.. 311
    Redbird 85
    Redeland... 176
    William R 35
JONES
    Charley 277
    E R 204
    Emma P 126
    Frank... 126
    Haywood 77
JORDAN
    Thos J 67
    Vannie 166
JORDON, Tom...................................... 72
JOYCE, Mr.. 99
JULIAN, Chas C 209
K & A V R R 257
KEEFER, Louis 90
KEELER

Index

G B 256
   George B 179
KEENAN, Bruce L 284
KEENER, Emma 84,286
KELLY, Lige 187
KEMP 282,297,304,305,306,309
KENDRIX, L N 29
KERNEL, Katie 160
KETCHER
   Chas, Jr 283,286
   Chas, Sr 286
   Geo 291
   John 4
   Key 4
KETCHUM, Watson 126
KIEFER, Henry 220
KING
   Arthur 210
   C 282,297
   Geo W 210
   Pauline M 210
KINGFISHER, Minnie 294
KINNERMAN, Sam 106
KINSEY, W A 295
KIRBY, Charles 115
KIRCUM, Andy 170
KIRK
   Mrs Ruth 95
   Samuel 80
KIRKLAND
   W M 77
   William 77
KIRKSEY, R J, MD 99
KISSIRE, W T 307
KLASE, Flora 89
KLASSE, Flora 89
KLAUSE, Flora 89
KNIGHT
   Benjamin 225
   Joe 237
KNISELY, Geo 207
KNOTT, Penny 180
KORNEGAY 242
   W H 232,243
KRIGBAUM
   James A 183
   James E 183

KRONGA, W H 206
LACEY
   Charlotte C 72
   James 9
   Nancy 307
   Rufus V 72
LACIE
   J A 15
   Jennie A 15
LAFAYETTE & BROS 300
LAFAYETTE BRO 297
LAHAY
   Joe 245,261
   Joe M 174,312
LAHAY & SHAW 174
LANDRUM
   Arkansas 220
   Hiram W 220
   James K 220
LANE
   Geo 185
   George 301
   John H 303
   M J 287
   Mrs L 174
LANGLEY
   Andrew J 292
   Sallie 48
LASLEY, Buck 296
LATTY, Luvina 83
LAWLESS
   C J 301
   P J 20,260,278
LAWRENCE
   Jno F 130
   Judge 101
   M E 231
   Milo E 204
   Wm R 117
LAWSON, E B 17
LEADER
   David 26
   Lucinda 26
LEARNARD, Oscar E, Jr 141
LEE
   Arthur 99
   Harry 85

Index

Lafelia 196
   Mrs Maggie 99
LEEBER, John G 45
LEEDS, Mr. 98
LEEDS & MARTINDALE 7,98,129
LEIBER
   John 187
   John G 187
LEON, E 102
LETCHER, Fred 153
LEWIS
   Charles 121
   Charley 279
   E E 59
   Estella 59
   Joseph 2
   S R 97
LINDSEY
   H B 243
   Henry B 305
LINK, J L 274
LITTLE
   Mrs Aggie 100
   Squire 77
LITTLEFIELD
   H L 69
   Henry 306
   Oscar 306
LITTLEJOHN, Jennie 271
LOGAN
   G D 64
   Levi L 64
LONDAGEN, Robt B 247
LONDAGIN
   Kate 246
   Robt B 246
LONG 293,294,297,300,310,311
   Avery 278
   Eliza 237
   Ida 164,183
   John F 278
LOONEY
   Al 2
   Geo 167,172
   George 167,172
   Jake 191
   Jane 172

Jordan 166
Josie 1,2,129
   Messers 1
   Tobe 2
LOW, Eldon 9
LOWE
   Dick 244
   Eldon 1,3,4,5,6,9,10,11,13,14,
   15,16,17,22,25,26,27,69
   Lydia 244
LOWREY
   James 95
   James Fite 95
LUCAS, J B 90
LUSTER, A J 137
LYNCH
   Chas J 22
   Eliza 291
   Elzira 63
   Simon 258
M K & T RAILWAY CO 222
M K & T RY 222
M K & T RY CO 259
MABRY, Sallie 62
MCAFFREY
   Andrew 158
   Cleora 158
   William Hugh 158
MCANDREWS
   Ellen 254
   Mary W 254
MCCLELLAN
   C M 193
   Charles 245
   Charles M 299
   Charlie 219
   J F 193
   John F 36,261
   William P 272
MCCLURE
   Charles 101
   Chas 199
   Fannie 312
   John 312
MCCOMBS, W T 116
MCCONNELL
   Felix 140

Jack 270
MCCOY
   Ida 163
   J D 163
   Jeff 163
   Mayes 163
   Sincy 143
MCCRAFACKEN, Andrew 156
MCCRARY, Louisa 7
MCCREARY, Harry 174
MCCULLOCH
   Chas 5
   Geo E 265
MCCULLOCH & PROBASCO 142
MCCULLOUGH, Mr 20
MCCURRY, Alick 60
MCCURTAIN
   Sam 160
   Samuel 161
MCD, Mrs J T 131
MCDANIEL, Joseph T 130
MCDANIELS, Lana M 208
MCDONALD
   Essie V 294
   Jno 18
   John 18,19,28
   Virgil T 294
MCDOUGAL
   Carrol 97
   Walker 97
MCELHNEY, C F 216
MCELMEELE, Elizabeth 68
MCGEE
   C C 159
   S B 52
MCGEORGE, G W 258
MCGHEE
   Miss Esther L 113
   Thomas J 51
MCGINNIS, Frank 263
MCINTOSH
   Lennie 117
   Policeman 117
MCKEBBAN, Jos 250
MACKEY, Minnie 280
MCKINNEY
   John 96

Johnson P 114
   Mary 43
MCKINZEY, Simon 56
MCLAIN
   George 66
   J A 112
MCLANE, Ellen C 75
MCLAUGHLIN, G R 269,274
MCLEMORE
   Peggie 233
   William 169
MCNARE, Rosa 141
MCNEER, Rosa 141
MCNIER, Rosie 141
MCQUARTER, Mr 305
MCRAE, A S 177,194,258
MCRAE & SORRELL 260
MCRAE & SORRELLS 278
MCRAY 214
MCREA
   Atty 100
   A S 23,26,33,91,92,97,116,119,
   140,147,198,208,209,210,237,244,250
   ,266
MCRHEA
   Atty 140
   A S 27,34,139
MCSPADDEN, Booth 276
MCWATERS, Hannah 14
MAJORS, J M 133
MALONE, Annie P 180
MALVERN, Peggie 70,72
MANLEY, Miss Maud 252
MANNING, Lucy 153
MAPES, Joe 266
MARAY 205
MARCH, Role 186
MARKS, L W 271
MARRS
   Amanda O 23
   Amanda Olivia 116
   Barney 23,116
   D M 23
   David M, Jr 23,116
   L M 116
   William C 116
   Wm C 23

MARS, C T 236
MARSH
   Clarence 248
   Rose 248
MARTIN
   Annie 45,293
   Austin 229
   Charles 102
   Chas 102
   Eathie 112
   Edward 229
   Fred 62
   Gertie 105
   Gurtie 175
   Harrey 190
   Harve 145,184
   Harvey 104,105,175
   Jerry 45
   Jno B 291
   John 247
   Lora 260
   Martha 291
   Mary 278
   Miller 192
   Otto 291
   Reese 260
   Tobe 112
MARTINDALE, D M 7
MASON, Mr 50
MATHES
   J L 42
   Leander 43
MATHEWS
   J A 67
   Leander 42
   Mrs Lena 292
MATTHEWS
   Florence 170
   Sammie M 170
MAY, Elsie 259
MAYBERRY, Ellen 129
MAYES
   Charles T 136
   Cherrie W 136
   Geo W 188
   Mary L 208
   Robert 14

   Robt 14
   W L 208
   Wat 2,3
   Watt 17,36,110
   Wm P 9
MAYFIELD, M D 294
MAYO, J M 296
MEASLES, Chlora 185
MEEKER, Geo 37
MEIGS, Nathan 244
MELTON
   C M 251
   Wyly 50
MERRELL, W M 281
MERRIFIELD, G C 41
MERRILL, Will 162
MERRITT, Hope E 138
MIDDLESLECKER, Moses 233
MIDDLETON, Mr 260
MILENDER, O M 106
MILES
   Lorick P 257
   O L 39
   Oscar L 39
   Robt J 188
MILLENDER, O M 106
MILLER
   Alice 270
   C B 133
   Harry W 312
   Jane 246
   John W 131
   Joseph S 91,92
   Martin 270
   Maude 262
   Nannie 57,58,106
   Nicholas Landrum 185
   Rufus 58
   Urban 137
   Ute B 91,92
   A W 246
MILLETTE WEST & JONES 231
MILLS
   O L 39
   S G 263
MINER, Mrs Lizzie 268
MITCHELL

Index

Bruce 232
E P 282
F P 206
Mrs Bettie 308
MIZER
   Geo W 183
   Jane 183
MONTGOMERY
   B H 78
   Bud 56,57
   W H 56
MOOD, A F 104
MOORE
   Andy 304
   J N 307
   Jane 277
   Jodie 277
   Katie 108
   Lum 242
   M A 192
   Maud 203
   Melton A 225
   Robert 71,72
MORGAN
   Cynthia 207
   Jno 207
MORMAN
   Albert 16
   Mrs Martha J 16
MORRIS, Elija 37
MORRISON
   Sussanna 5
   Wm E 5
MORTON
   C C 227
   Mr A D 144
   Mrs Millie 192
MOSS 222
   Millard 221
MOUNCE, Chas 309
MOUSE, Price 199
MULLEN, Wayne 155
MULLER, Wayne 104
MULLSLOGLE, A S 47
MUMBLES, Patsy J 112
MUNDIS
   Arrell 201

Nellie 201
Sarah 201
MURPHY
   Nelson 203
   Pearl 261
MUSKOGEE DEVELOPEMENT CO. 73
MUSKOGEE DEVELOPMENT CO ... 70
MYERS, E R 283
NANCE
   R Y 193
   Winfield S 139
NARROW GUAGE RY 81
NASH, W H 80
NAVE, Cornelius 154
NEAL & LONDON 6,77
NEESE, Winona 238
NELSON
   Eddie 211
   Jennie 211
NEUGIN
   Jennie 241
   Mrs Jennie 157
   Rachel 93
NICHODEMUS, James 136
NICHOLSON, P L 293
NIELSON, Rev N L 21
NIVENS
   Alex 181
   Julia 265
NORMAN
   Bud 290
   Mrs 16
NORTON
   Ashley 11
   Geo E 38
   Jennie 38
NORWOOD
   A 298
   Chas 31
NOURSE, J A 223
OAKS, Mrs Harriet 136
O'FIELDS
   Nora 228
   Robert 228
OGAN
   Chas 303,304
   Frank 303

Index

ONEAL, Lieu A 110
ORTMAN, Earl H 303
OSAGE, Mary E 97
OSBORN
    Roy T 87,215
    S J 15
    W J 15,72
    W L 15
OSBORN & OSBORN 2,86
OSBORNE 177
    Roy T 216
OSBORNE & ORSBORNE 129
OSBORNE & OSBORNE 177
OWEN
    Arthur 75
    E T 75
    Mr E T 75
    R L 28,107
    Robt L 28
    Thos H 94
OWEN & STONE 265
OWEN STONE & *(ILLEGIBLE)* 265
OWENS
    Arthur 75
    Charles 152
    Laina E 179
PADEN, M L 168
PAGE, Estella 128
PALMER
    R D 17
    Roy 293,294
    Roy D 17
PALMOUR
    D S 109
    Mary M 109
PANN, Susan 108
PARDA, James 105
PARDU, Jas 105
PARKER
    Deaf 306
    Judge L T 207
    King *(?)* 306
    Malinda 264
    Mary A F 152
    Myrtle 53
    Ola 264
PARKS
    Atty 118
    Geo B 161
    Howell 198
    Margarette 161
    Mr 15
    S F 19,72,73
PARRIS, S E 15
PATRICK
    Fannie 188
    George W 188
PATTON
    Atty 40
    Chas H 10
    M V 74
    Mr 164
    S H 74
PAXTON, John 24,25
PAYTON, Mr *(Illegible)* 265
PERDUE, James 105
PERRY
    Amanda 8,302,303
    C S 226
    Ernest G 64
    Ezekiel 7
    Fannie G 245
    Mrs Val 55
    Mrs Vall 55
    N M 55
    Nathan M 55
    Samuel 8,302
PETTIT
    Joe 274
    Rufus R 195,196
PEYTON, Masterson 248
PHILLIPS
    Hattie 96
    Henry C 226
PIGEON
    Joseph 81
    Sanders 81
PIPPIN, N M 159
PLECKER, D B 296
PLUMLEY, Henry M 80
POINDEXTER, Maggie 65
POLECAT
    Isaac 13
    Lucy 13

Index

Walter 13
POLTSON, John 127
POOLE
  Carlisle 295
  Chas W 295
  Walton C 295
POPE, Daniel 244
PORTER
  Maud 71
  Willie 70
POTTS, Lucy 93
POWE, Thomas 137
POWELL
  Charles 92
  Charley 91
PRATER, Mrs Jane 137
PRICE, Skid 146
PRICHARD, George 75
PROCTOR MERC CO 299
PROVINCE
  Maggie 105
  Maggie E 104
PUMPKIN, Mary 145
QUINN
  Edwin 174
  Thomas L 174
RAGAN
  A P 282
  A T 297
RAGSDALE, Johnsanna 98
RAMEY, Pearl 241
RANDLER, Violet 270
RANSTEAD, C C 47
RATHBUN, Alden 245
RATLEY, Wallace 107
RATLIFF
  Eliza 177
  Ella 177
RAWLS
  Minzy 106
  Winnie D 106
REED
  Anna 102
  Aurthor 14
  Cora 49,54
REESE
  Annie 121

John 299
Richard 121
REEVES, John R 10
REID
  Arthur 14,220
  Clarence A 89
REYNOLDS
  Alonzo 249
  Bill 201
  C R 156
  Cinderella 216
RICE, Mantie 173
RICHARDSON
  Fannie 264
  Jess 243
RICHMOND, Alexander 129
RICHMOND & SULLIVAN 129
RIDDLE
  Seymour 20
  Seymour G 86,87
RIDER
  Augustus 194
  Austin W 194
  J W 194
  Jennie May 210
  O L 33,92,97,148
  Thos N 194
  Tip P 194
  Wm P 210
RIDGE
  Alla 167
  Ana 214
RILEY
  Ed 161
  J M 242
  Moses 252,253
RINEHART, W A 157
ROACH
  Frank 180
  Nellie 298
  Policeman 102,233,251
  T P 251
  Thomas P 13,47,162,186,212
  Thos 4
  Thos P 60,87,102,126,194,212, 312,313
  Tom 162

Index

ROBB
- Frank 143
- Mr 266

ROBBIN, Frank 261
ROBERTS, Edith Wickett 69
ROBERTSON
- Dan 220,221
- G C 223
- Jess 209
- Wm H 209

ROBERTSON, KING & KEAN 32
ROBINSON
- Jack 133
- Mrs 133

ROBISON & MCKINNEY 8
RODD, Lee 50
ROGERS
- Beulah E 77
- C B 8,184
- Charles H 253
- Chas B 8
- Clare Huckleberry 300
- H L 77,78
- Huck 300
- Lizzie 1
- Malt Lee 215
- Mamie E 1,215
- Matt L 1
- Mrs 293,294
- Mrs Lizzie 215
- Nancy 294
- Nancy E 17
- Reuben 140
- Samuel 63
- Sylvester A 1,215
- T L 215

ROSS
- Loney 281
- Silan D 281

ROLAND, Benjamin F 151
ROSE, John 194
ROSS
- Abie 241
- Albert 12
- Charles M 28
- Charley G 142
- Chas M 18
- Elnora 198
- Frank 260
- Geo 61,97
- George 61,96,120
- J B 143
- John Henry 103
- Mariah 139,140
- Martin 34
- Mary J 312
- Mose 140,205
- Moses 119
- Mosses 119
- Nelson 197
- Nelson Grubbs 197
- Polly 123
- Stephen 277
- Susie E 18
- Walter F 142
- Will 92,205
- William W, Jr 74
- Willie 91

ROWLAND, Robt F 151
RUNABOUT, Charlotte 204
RUSH
- Mrs Bell 191
- Mrs Belle 173

RUSSELL, Ed 138
SALTER, J R 49
SAMPLE, R E 205
SANDERS
- H L 253
- Jack 23,116
- John 23,116,275
- Mary 24
- Mrs Minnie 173
- Rebecca A 37

SANE, Mary C 243
SAUCO, Nat 154
SAUNDERS
- L S 24
- Lee 155,156
- Mary 24

SAWYER
- H G 218
- W T 219

SCALES, Mrs Sarah 222
SCANTHUG, W J 217

Index

SCARBOROUGH, Narcissus............ 134
SCHAFFER, Geo 279
SCHMAR, C A................................... 232
SCHNOY, A C 206
SCOGGINS, E S 284
SCOTT
   David Orvial.................................. 109
   John 138,217
SCULLARD, Caroline 268
SCULLAWL
   Caroline.. 17
   Carolyn 309
   Wm.. 17
SELLERS, Lora J 257
SEQUOYAH, Daniel.......................... 127
SEVENSTAR
   Larken.. 293
   Larkin 17
SEVIER
   Leo E 253
   Mrs J J 253
SHAFER, Henry L 86
SHASTEEL, A J.................................... 89
SHEFFIELD, J *(?)*............................. 291
SHERLEY
   Maggie L 291
   Willie W 291
SHEVOSE, Norman 53
SHIPMAN, James 11,12
SHOEMAKER, Kittie J...................... 267
SHOOK, Nick 288
SHORT, R 214
SHULTZ, P W...................................... 86
SIMERSON, John 49
SIMMONS
   Charley 223
   Dochie 223
SIMON, M.. 8
SITTINGDOWN, Stephen 285
SIX, John 51
SIXKILLER, Sarah 261
SKIDMORE, O S 142
SLAGLE
   Mrs Minnie H 134
   Won Samuel 134
SLAPE, Laura 158
SLATE, J W 103
SLAUGHTER
   Josie 27
   Josie A 26,33,34
SLEEPER, G D 65,127
SMITH
   Ada G 44,45
   C C 217
   Calley 22
   Charles... 290
   Charles C 216
   Charley 234
   Chas... 217
   Chas C 217
   Chs... 160
   Eliza... 253
   Elmira.. 148
   Elmore 234
   F M 53
   Famous 244,253
   Helen Whitmire 274
   J 153
   J J... 151
   James 133,276
   Jane.. 217
   Joseph A 244
   Melinda.. 154
   Mr O A 55
   Mrs Ada G 4
   Nancy 201
   O J 267
   Pearl... 122
   Polly 239
   Robert.. 38
   Robt... 38
   Samuel L 148
   William.. 295
   Wyly 48
SMOKER, Nancy 227
SNARR, L J.....................4,186,196,202
SNELL, Eli 40
SNOW, Daniel.................................... 121
SOOTER, W W 289
SOPER, HUCKLEBERRY & OWEN ....
50,51,160,173,193
SOPER, HUCKLEBERRY & OWENS...........
33,51
SOURJOHN, Isaac 196
SPADE

Johnson	282
Watson	297

SPEARS
Arch	280
Polly Ballard	122

SPIGHT
Delilah	135
Rachel	135

SQUIRREL, Jack 117
ST LOUIS & IRON MOUNTAIN RR CA .. 39
STALA, Sever 105
STALLINGS, J T 223
STANDFIELD, Wade S 207

STANFIELD
W S	207
Wade S	207

STANTON, Lucy 42
STANTSON, Lucy 42
STARBUCK, Goldie 218
STARK, W J 71

STARR
F C	76
Fannie	76
Fannie C	154
J C	34,49,53,54,67,78
Jack	168
Monie	168
Monnie	168
Mr	49
Pearl M Miller	20
Thomas	254
W M	280

STARR & PATTON 22,23,26,27,
30,31,33,34,35,40,62,63,74,104,143,164,
183,204,211,245,249

STEPHENS
Betsy	250
Bill	93
Cynthia B	250
Emery	93
John	93
Lee M	250

STEVENSON
John E	255
Rachel	255

STEWART, Maggie Duncan 236
STEWART & STEWART 230

STILL
James	200
John	225

STONE 282

STOP
Flora	135
Gilbert	135

STOPP, John 93
STOVALL, Geo 235
STRANK, W J 160

STRANKS
Emily J	160
W J	160

STREETER, Rosie 311
STRUBLE, Geo L 212
STUBLER, Henry 83
SUAGEE, Thomas 262
SULLIVAN, W J 79,122,151
SULT, Iola M 100
SUMMERS, Mrs 243

SUNDAY
James	153
Kelly	76
Kittie	76
Policeman	72,130
Tom	76
William M	72
Wm M	10

SWAKE
Jim	88
Liza	88

SWAN
Geo	34
William R	124

SWARTZ, J W 162

SWEETWATER
Golda	67
Jno	67,68
Viola	67
Wm	67

SWIFT, G S 159
SWIMMER, Lizzie 30
TACKETT, L H 10

TADPOLE
Grover	48
Rufus	48,279

TALALA, Johnson 139

Index

TALLY
  Andrew 75
  Maggie 75
TANNER, T B 226
TATUM
  Jay 124
  Lula 124
  Sittingbull 255
  Thomas 256
TAYLOR
  A A 45
  Alfred 10
  Carl 10
  Edward 250
  J A 53
  Jackson 260
  Joanna 6
  John 203
  Minnie R 247
  Stacy B 247
  Tom 288
  William 116,203
  Wm 203
TEEHEE, Lee 285
TEEKAHNEYESKEE, Jim 120
TELL, Sarah E 283,286
TEMBERLAKE, John 160
TENNEY, Sarah 13
TERRELL
  Mary 266
  A P 24,30
TEVEBAUGH, Minnie Lee 54,55
THOMAS
  A G 65,127
  George H 148
  Ira 205
  James H 148
  Jno R 154
THOMAS & FOREMAN 154,252,257
THOMPSON
  Ada M 312
  Alonzo J 227
  Annie 190
  Atty 306
  Coleman 276
  Dora 276
  George 229

  Joe 270
  Lucinda 123
  Mary 161
  N E 243
  S C 248
  Sanday 211
  Sandy 211
  Sarah 190
  Scott 126
  T J P 29
  W [.... 305
  W C 312
  W P 83,117,258
  William 276
  Wm P 237
THORN, Luella 99
THORNE
  Cull 251
  Julia 251
THORNTON
  Henry Joseph 128
  Johnson 219
  Mr 287
  Mrs Peggie 188
  Wm 304
THURMAN
  William J 87
  Wm 284
TIBLOW, Charley 252
TIPTON
  Jno L 59
  Lonie 59
TOMSON, Arch 105
TONEY
  Nancy 307
  Tom 254
TRACEY, Mrs 302
TRAMMELL
  Lizzie W 212
  Miss Rossie I 41
TREASUERER, Nancy 86
TRIPLETT, Ella 162
TROTT, William L 199
TUCKER
  Albert 132
  Ezekiel 296
TURNER, Harry 211

Index

TWEEDLE, Florence M 32
TWINE, W H 100
TYNER
    Cordelia 38
    Daniel W 38
    Lewis 250
    Myrtle Irene 250
ULREY, A J 151
UMMARTESKEE, Runabout 69
UNDERWOOD, Margaret 9
UPTON, Dr J A 233
VAN HOY, W C 45,46
VAN LEWAN, Bert 218
VANCE & PRIEST 292
VANDERFORD
    Albert 171
    Lottie 171
VANDIVER, J M 57
VANFLEET, O O 289
VANN
    Ed 74
    Eli 276
    F J 273
    Frank 15
    Geo 229,230
    George 230
    Jess 30
    Jesse 15,31
    Jettie 292
    Joe 219
    Lucy 229,230
    Lula 49,54,74
    Lydi 219
    Nicey 167
    Nicy 214
    R P 273
    Rachel 113,187
    Rosa 74,237
    Rose 74
    Willie 54
VEASEY & ROWLAND 303
VEITS, John 11,12,18
VENNETT, Robt R 21
VIETES, John 6
VIETS, John 6,7,8,11,12,17,18,19,20, 21,22,28,29,30
VINSON, Yancy 35

WADE, James 111
WALES, Andrew 245
WALKER 142
    Atty 98,104
    Chas 210
    Daisy 95
    Estella 128
    Hannah 276
    J L 60,64,82,101,140,167
    James L 101,186
    Jas 2
    Jas L 186
    Mr 82
    Mrs Emeline 142
    Policeman 64,82,101,140,141,167
    Sam 100
WALKINGSTICK
    Ethel 192
    James M 192
WALL, Frank 205
WALLACE, Mrs Emma 60
WALROND, C T 253
WALTERS, Mrs Sarah 49
WARD
    Aletha B 5
    Alonzo 267
    Willard 129
    William 130
WARREN
    D S 299
    Mary 161
WASHINGTON
    Clifford 181
    George 181
WASSON, Mrs 44
WATERKILLER, Ellis 165
WATERS
    Annie 30
    Chas 30
    Geo 267
    Jennie 30
    Mary 220
    Mrs Annie 231
    Wm 30
WATKINS
    Jas 286
    Lillie C 99

Index

Ollie 217
  Sarah J 217
WATKINS & BURLINGAME 131
WATSON, Tom 178
WATT, John 95
WATTS
  Jess W 195
  Lizzie Terrell 47
  Mr 43
  Thomas J 43
  Thos J 6,43
WATTS & CURTIS 12,13,18,30,36, 39,41,85,87,88,171,194,212
WEALY, Joe 189
WEAVER, C I 126
WEBBER
  Aaron 81,257
  Katie 129
WELCH
  Alexander 125
  George T 66
  James 307
  Johnson 242
  Mary 175
  Maud 91
  Scott 242
WELLS
  Emma 27
  I T 17
  Lee 115
WEST
  C D 74
  C P 165
  Capt .... 69,97,120,140,151,166,168, 175,191,206,217,221,232,233,252,253 ,259,260,269,274,275,276,280,282
  Capt J 243
  Capt J C 120,221
  Capt Jno C 33,43,45,61,92,101, 105,118,120,140,148,153,154,160,187
  Capt John C ... 26,119,149,158,172,212
  Dave 148
  Frank 177
  George W 204
  J B 214
  J C 177
  James B 167

  Jno C 68,191
  John 200
  John C 68,118,123,176,190, 191,200,238
  Nannie 79
  Richard F 19,20
  T C 101
WEST & MELLETTE 204
WETZEL, Geo H 295
WHITE
  Amos 218
  Annie E 104
  Emma 270
  G S 258
  J C 254
  Joe 182
  L Nora 217,218
  Mary J 93
  Thomas J 192
  W H 139
  William H 139
  Wm H 139
WHITEWATER, Famous 176
WHITMAN, William 268
WHITNEY, Mack W 96
WICKETT
  Edith 69
  Lottie 1
  Webster 1
WIGGINS, Peggy 15
WILKERSON, P E 248
WILKINS
  Josephine 211
  Ruby E 211
WILLACE, Willie 179
WILLIAM & NELSON 68
WILLIAMS
  Benjamin W 223
  Clem 2
  E E 26
  Herbert A 16,290
  Kettie 2
  Leonord W 2
  R E 79
  Riley 52
  Robt B 16
  Robt L 223

Index

Tom 52,177,178
Tuxie 2,3,110
Viola 2
W J 223
Wallie G 223
Will 231
WILLIAMS, WILLIAMS & NASLEE 193
WILLIAMSON
  Mr E N 147
  Mrs Nellie 147
  Nellie 147
  Nettie 147
  William 148
  William F 147
WILLIS
  M A 37
  Maggie 215,216
WILLY, Dave 38
WILSON 309
  D 40
  Dee 40
  E G 51,289
  Emma 78
  Hope E 138
  Lula 115
  Ned Olila 311
  Oliver 165,180
  Robert 180
  Runabout 288
  Sarah 165
  Winnie 78
  Wm 305
WILY, R Lee 19
WIMER, T T 258
WISE, Geo W 174
WITFIELD, Luke 115
WOLF
  Ben 13
  William 13
  Wm M 51
WOLFE, E P 199
WOOD
  Bryant 234
  A F 257,268
  John 164,183
  Marion F 150
WOODARD, Fred B 248

WOODEN
  John 150
  Lizzie 150
WOODS
  A H 60
  Hannah 13
WRIGHT
  Ella W 202
  J G 215
  J George 25
WYATT, Webb 199
WYLY
  Policeman 84
  R Lee 84
XOLEY, Wm 40
YANCY, Mr 219
YATES, Ellen 18
YMMARTESKEE, Runabout 69
YOUNG
  Esther 286
  Monroe 76
  Rosa 71
  Samuel L 129
  Tom 76
YOUNGBLOOD
  Oakley 6
  Reedy 6
ZEVERLY, GIVENS & SMITH 82
ZIEGLER
  Charlotte 73
  Henry W 73
  Jeremiah 73
  Nancy 73
  Samuel 73

www.ingramcontent.com/pod-product-compliance
Lightning Source LLC
Chambersburg PA
CBHW020240030426
42336CB00010B/555